REDS AND THE GREEN

REDS AND THE GREEN
IRELAND, RUSSIA AND THE
COMMUNIST INTERNATIONALS
1919–43

Emmet O'Connor

Published by the
UNIVERSITY COLLEGE DUBLIN PRESS
PREAS CHOLÁISTE OLLSCOILE BHAILE ÁTHA CLIATH

2004

First published 2004 by
University College Dublin Press
Newman House
86 St Stephen's Green
Dublin 2
Ireland

www.ucdpress.ie

ISBN 1 904558 19 4 hb
1 904558 20 8 pb

CIP data available from the British Library

*The right of Emmet O'Connor to be identified as
the author of this work has been asserted by him.*

Typeset in Ireland in Adobe Caslon and Bodoni Oldstyle
by Elaine Shiels, Bantry, County Cork
Text design by Lyn Davies
Printed in England on acid-free paper
by MPG Books Ltd, Bodmin, Cornwall

Contents

Illustrations

Abbreviations and acronyms

CI   Communist International
CPGB   Communist Party of Great Britain
CPI   Communist Party of Ireland
CPUSA   Communist Party of the United States of America
ECCI   Executive Committee of the Communist International
GHQ   General Head Quarters
ICWPA   International Class War Prisoners' Aid, also known as
         International Red Aid, or Mezhdnarodnaia Organizatsiia
         Pomoshchi Revoliutsoneram (MOPR)
ILPTUC   Irish Labour Party and Trade Union Congress
ITGWU   Irish Transport and General Workers' Union
INUM   Irish National Unemployed Movement, also known as the
         Irish Unemployed Workers' Movement and other variations
         on that name
IRA   Irish Republican Army
IRB   Irish Republican Brotherhood
ITUC   Irish Trade Union Congress
ITGWU   Irish Transport and General Workers' Union
IWL   Irish Worker League
KPD   Kommunistische Partei Deutschlands (Communist Party of
         Germany)
MP   Member of Parliament
NILP   Northern Ireland Labour Party
Narkomindel Narodny Kommissariat Inostrannykh Del (People's
         Commissariat of Foreign Affairs)
O/C   Officer Commanding
OMS   Otdel Mezhdunarodnoi Sviazi (Department of International
         Liaison)
POUM   Partido Obrero de Unificación Marxista (Worker's Party of
         Marxist Unification)
RILU   Red International of Labour Unions
ROP   Russian Oil Products
RUC   Royal Ulster Constabulary
RWG   Revolutionary Workers' Groups

SLP   Socialist Labour Party
SPI   Socialist Party of Ireland
TD   Teachta Dála
USA   United States of America
USSR   Union of Soviet Socialist Republics
VKP(b)   Vsesoyuznaya Kommunisticheskaya Partiya (bolshevikov) All-
         Union Communist Party (Bolsheviks)
WEB   Western European Bureau
WIR   Workers' International Relief, also known as Mezhdunarodnaia
         Rabochiia Pomoshch (Mezhrabpom), or Secours Ouvrier
         International, or Internationale Arbeiterhilfe (IAH)
Wobbly   A member of the American syndicalist labour union, the
         Industrial Workers of the World
WUI   Workers' Union of Ireland

ARCHIVES AND PRIMARY SOURCES

BPP   British Parliamentary Papers
DJ   Department of Justice files
DT   Department of the Taoiseach files
FBI   Federal Bureau of Investigation
NA   National Archives, Dublin
NLI   National Library of Ireland
PROL   Public Record Office, London
PRONI   Public Record Office of Northern Ireland
RGASPI   Rossiiskii Gosudartsvennyi Arkhiv Sotsial'no-Politischeskoi
         Istorii (Russian State Archive for Social and Political History)
UCDA   University College Dublin, Archives Department

Note

In the Russian archival system every page of every document has a call number, but not every document has a title or rubric. Where documents have no titles, the footnotes give the rubric, and where there is no rubric, a short identification is provided, based on the principals as cited in the document. This may involve inconsistency in referencing, with, for example, one document addressed to the political secretariat and another to the politsecretariat.

Acknowledgements

In the early 1990s I was advised by Dr Barry McLoughlin of papers of Irish relevance in the former Comintern archive in Moscow. We both excavated the bulk of these papers in 1994–5, and my own part in the process was very secondary to Barry's expertise in navigating his way through the vast quantity of records. The objective was to write a book of documents and commentaries. That project has yet to see the light of day, and hopefully this volume will generate some interest in its publication.

Though it sounds odd in retrospect, the Comintern papers seemed less enticing than a biography of Brigadier General Thomas Francis Meagher until 1997, when Tom Crean requested a talk on Jim Larkin and communism for the Labour History Society. Since then, the material has been a consuming interest, and finishing this book is like saying goodbye to an old friend. Inevitably, countless debts have been accumulated. Barry McLoughlin has never tired of interrupting his own work on Irish and Austrian connections with Soviet Russia to handle endless queries on matters beyond the anglocentric world of Irish history. I am obliged to University College Dublin Press for commissioning this book, and in particular to Barbara Mennell: her confidence and enthusiasm have been inspirational. Others in Dublin generously offered advice on research, notably the late John Joe O'Dowd, Nóirín Greene, Brian Hanley, Jim Monaghan, Theresa Moriarty, D. R. O'Connor Lysaght, Eunan O'Halpin and Manus O'Riordan. Andrew Boyd, in lively and observant correspondence, shared his recollections of Belfast and other contemporaries, and Anne Boran offered an unexpected memory of her father, Nixie. Thanks are due also to Tom and Teena Casey for sleuthing in Waterford between Munster finals; Máirtín Ó Catháin for discussions on Derry and Glasgow connections; Janette Martin, Alan Campbell and Charlie McGuire, for advice on British sources; Helga Woggon for assistance with questions on German archives; Virginia Hyvarinen and Emmet Larkin for details on Jack Carney; and Tim O'Neil for research in the United States.

I am indebted to the ever cheerful Janice McQuilkan and the staffs of Magee College Library, Derry Central Library, the university libraries at Coleraine, Belfast, and Jordanstown, the Gilbert Library, the Labour History Archives, the Military Archives, the National Archives, the National Library, University College Dublin Archives Department, Waterford Municipal Library and Waterford City Archives, the Public Record Office, London, the British Library, the British Newspaper Library, the Marx Memorial Library, the State Archive of the Russian Federation, and the United States Federal Bureau of Investigation. The British Academy provided financial assistance for research in Moscow, and the University of Ulster granted sabbatical leave to expedite the writing and paid for translation, photocopying, microfilming and off-printing. The Russian State Archives for Social and Political History was, of course, the key resource, and I am indebted for the co-operation of Director Kyril Anderson and his staff, especially Ludmilla Karlova, Svetlana Rozental and Irina Novichenko. It was a pleasure most recently to meet Dr Sergei Zhuravlev, who renewed my acquaintance with Moscow and its wonderful archives.

The British academic life is not the happiest station these days, and in trying times one is all the more appreciative of the students at Magee College for their humanity, idealism and common sense, and of the freedom to call on that great bank of experts in the university, particularly Gerry Devine, Frank Cassidy, Gillian Coward and Michael Doherty for technical assistance; John McCann, Monika McCurdy and Ray Pearson for translation to and from Russian; and Catherine Russell, Julie Conway and Patricia Doherty for secretarial help. And a personal thank you is due to Mena Ward for logistical support in Peterborough, and to Colette, Deaglán, and Laura.

All errors that follow are my own.

Thomas Francis Meagher must wait, and this book is dedicated to the memory of another great Waterford soldier, Johnny Power, twice wounded at Brunete, thrice cited for bravery, commissar and captain in the Comintern's army in Spain. I measc laochra na nDéiseach go raibh a ainm.

EMMET O'CONNOR
Magee College
Derry,
April 2004

INTRODUCTION

—

In August 1922, at the height of the Civil War, when the Communist Party of Ireland (CPI) could count on barely 50 activists, two British communist leaders held a secret meeting in a Dublin suburb with two senior Irish Republican Army (IRA) commandants. The four signed an agreement providing for the transformation of Sinn Féin into a new republican party with a socialist programme. In return the Communist International, or Comintern, was to assist with the supply of weapons to the IRA. The incident illustrates what made the Comintern a beacon of hope to beleaguered revolutionaries or an object of sometimes hysterical suspicion. It is also an example of the hidden way in which communism shaped Irish politics. Shortly after the meeting Ernie O'Malley, the IRA's second in command, asked Liam Mellows for advice on strategy. Mellows replied with his 'Notes from Mountjoy', a seminal document in the evolution of socialist republicanism during the Free State era. Over the next 12 years, communists, in Dublin or Moscow, would be integral to the politics of the republican left, prompting its development at almost every step.

With the exception of the Spanish Civil War, in which all are heroes of the good fight, historians have not been kind to Ireland's communists. General histories measure their parties – there have been several, sequentially, under different titles – by their numerical strength, and dismiss them summarily. All eight references to 'communism' in Lee's acclaimed *Ireland: 1912–1985* actually deal with anti-communism.[1] Certainly, the fear of communism exerted the greater effect on Irish minds after 1930. It was a factor in the rise of the Blueshirts, led to riots in Dublin in 1933 and contributed to rioting in Belfast in 1935, provided an excuse for splitting the Labour Party in 1944, and terrorised the public at the height of the Cold War in the 1950s. From 1920 to 1948 the more substantial publications on communism came from red scaremongers rather than reds.[2] Recent research is redressing the balance. Communists

1   J. J. Lee, *Ireland, 1912–1985: Politics and Society* (Cambridge, 1989).

2   Richard Dawson, *Red Terror and Green* (London, 1920); British Parliamentary Papers (BPP), *Intercourse Between Bolshevism and Sinn Féin*, Cmd 1326 (1921); James Hogan, *Could Ireland Become Communist?* (Dublin, 1935); National Labour Party, *Communist Bid to Control Irish Labour* (Dublin, 1944); S. P. McEoin, *Communism and Ireland* (Dublin, 1948).

acquired a visibility in Irish history in seven fields, and are acknowledged to varying degrees in studies related to the Civil War;[3] Larkinism;[4] unemployed workers' protests in the 1920s and 1930s;[5] socialist republicanism;[6] the Spanish Civil War;[7] trade unionism in Northern Ireland;[8] and the Northern Ireland Civil Rights Association.[9] Communists also made a major contribution to historiography through T. A. Jackson and C. Desmond Greaves, the twin pillars of the Connolly school of history, which in turn hegemonised Irish radical historiography up to the 1970s.[10] History, it has been said, is the Irish ideology, and it is remarkable that so marginalised a group should have been so influential in this respect.

The Irish connection with Soviet communism was broader than the communists themselves; less of a thin red thread than a pyramid, with a wide base tapering in three steps to the pinnacle of insignificance. The Bolsheviks were very popular in Ireland in the immediate aftermath of the October revolution, more perhaps for their opposition to the First World War and support for national self-determination than anything else. During the War of Independence, representatives of the Republic in the United States of America (USA) discussed a recognition treaty with agents of the Soviet Russian government, and Éamon de Valera despatched an emissary to Moscow to secure recognition and weapons. One of the first international initiatives of the pro-Treaty provisional government was to have an official meet the Soviet

---

3   C. Desmond Greaves, *Liam Mellows and the Irish Revolution* (London, 1971).

4   Emmet Larkin, *James Larkin: Irish Labour Leader, 1876–1947* (London, 1965); Séamus Cody, John O'Dowd, and Peter Rigney, *The Parliament of Labour: 100 Years of the Dublin Council of Trade Unions* (Dublin, 1986); Donal Nevin (ed.), *James Larkin: Lion of the Fold* (Dublin, 1998); Emmet O'Connor, *James Larkin* (Cork, 2002).

5   Paddy Devlin, *Yes We Have No Bananas: Outdoor Relief in Belfast, 1920–39* (Belfast, 1981).

6   Henry Patterson, *The Politics of Illusion: Republicanism and Socialism in Modern Ireland* (London, 1989); Richard English, *Radicals and the Republic: Socialist Republicanism in the Irish Free State, 1925–37* (Oxford, 1994); Brian Hanley, *The IRA, 1926–1936* (Dublin, 2002).

7   Michael O'Riordan, *Connolly Column: The Story of the Irishmen who Fought in the Ranks of the International Brigades in the National Revolutionary War of the Spanish People, 1936–39* (Dublin, 1979); Seán Cronin, *Frank Ryan: The Search for the Republic* (Dublin, 1980); Robert A. Stradling, *The Irish in the Spanish Civil War, 1936–1939: Crusades in Conflict* (Manchester, 1999); Fearghal McGarry, *Irish Politics and the Spanish Civil War* (Cork, 1999).

8   Terry Cradden, *Trade Unionism, Socialism, and Partition: The Labour Movement in Northern Ireland, 1939–53* (Belfast, 1993).

9   Bob Purdie, *Politics in the Streets: The Origins of the Civil Rights Movement in Northern Ireland* (Belfast, 1990).

10   See especially T. A. Jackson, *Ireland Her Own* (London, 1947), the first Marxist general history of Ireland, and C. Desmond Greaves, *The Life and Times of James Connolly* (London, 1961).

trade attaché in London. Not surprisingly, the Irish Trade Union Congress and Labour Party (ILPTUC), and especially the radical circle within it in the Socialist Party of Ireland (SPI), were more substantially pro-Bolshevik.[11] Support for Russia was central to Labour's foreign policy, a way of asserting its socialist credentials abroad, and legitimising its position on the independence struggle at home. The flirtation with revolutionism did not last long. As the political climate moved to the right, Labour distanced itself from the Comintern in 1920, and lost its enthusiasm for the Bolshevik regime in 1922.

After the War of Independence, Soviet and Comintern ties with Ireland became more intense and more confined, as communist parties – and some communist trade unions – were created, but contacts contracted to the labour left and republicans. The first CPI was launched in October 1921 after Roddy Connolly captured control of the SPI. Despite the IRA's intrigue with the Comintern in August 1922, the party made little progress. Following the return of Jim Larkin from the USA in 1923, it was dissolved to make way for Larkin's Irish Worker League (IWL). Larkin proved to be an even greater disappointment. The IWL never functioned as a communist party, and 'the big noise' had an extraordinarily troubled relationship with the Comintern. Moscow began to build an infrastructure of alternative networks in 1927, inviting promising young communists for training at the International Lenin School, the Comintern's 'cadre-forge', and encouraging republicans to develop a web of 'front' organisations. After Larkin cut his ties with Moscow in 1929, the Executive Committee of the Communist International (ECCI) directed a fresh offensive in Ireland, which would lead to the creation of the Revolutionary Workers' Groups (RWG) in 1930 and the second CPI in 1933. Excluding the ill-defined support of the IWL, the RWG's tally of some 340 in November 1932 represented the peak membership of the Comintern in Ireland.

If no longer sympathetic, the political climate of the 1920s was tolerant of communism. That would change dramatically from 1930, when the Catholic Church took a more forthright stand against all association with communism. In the next big contraction of support, the IRA dissociated itself from the CPI in 1933. There remained the fellow travellers of the republican and labour left, who would join the CPI in convening the Republican Congress in 1934. The disintegration of the Congress reduced the communist orbit to little more than the CPI. With only 20 activists, the CPI in Éire was dissolved in July 1941, to avoid confronting the state's near universally popular neutrality, and

11 The Irish Trade Union Congress added 'and Labour Party' to its title in 1914, and was known from 1918 to 1930 as the Irish Labour Party and Trade Union Congress. To minimise the alphabet soup, it will be referred to here, for the years between 1914 and 1930, as the ILPTUC, Congress, or the Labour Party, and otherwise as the ITUC or Congress. Between 1914 and 1930 the Labour Party was not distinct from Congress.

allow the party to pursue a vigorous pro-war policy in Northern Ireland, where it flourished for as long as it took the Red Army to turn the tide of war against the Wehrmacht.

Again excepting the Spanish Civil War, literature bearing directly on the communist parties is sparse, and often indifferent to the problems of communist history. The CPI's own *Outline History* is little more than a collection of commemorative sketches.[12] A rather didactic critique of the first CPI was featured in the *Irish Socialist Review* in 1983, based in part on Comintern files in Moscow, though from the text it would appear that the access was selective.[13] The only substantial party publication on its history is O'Riordan's eulogistic *Connolly Column*, the title being a blanket term for the Irish in the International Brigades. Communist auto/biography rarely takes us inside the party, and tends to portray communists as victims of political intolerance. Both Nevin and Larkin are summary, and overly sympathetic on Jim Larkin's disastrous leadership of Irish communism, while the bulk of writing on Larkin charitably ignores this inglorious chapter in his career. Jim Gralton, deported to the USA in 1933 for communist activities, has been the hero of pamphlets and articles, whose theme is primarily the injustice and singularity of the affair.[14] The Connolly Column is virtually the only source of communist auto/biography. A trickle of memoirs and biographies of veterans has appeared from the 1980s which say little on Ireland apart from anti-fascist activities, indulging a romance with the Connolly Column as liberal opponents of Catholic reaction at home and abroad, and forerunners of modern, secular Ireland.[15] Some insight into the neglected role of communists in trade unions is found in Morrissey's biography of Betty Sinclair and interviews with party members in *Saothar*.[16] Other monographs in the field are confined to Bowler's

---

12   CPI, *Communist Party of Ireland: Outline History* (Dublin, 1975).

13   Hazel Morrissey, 'The first Communist Party of Ireland, 1921–23', *Irish Socialist Review* (summer, 1983).

14   Pat Feeley, *The Gralton Affair* (Dublin, 1986); Des Guckian, *Deported: Jimmy Gralton, 1886–1945* (Carrick-on-Shannon, 1988); Luke Gibbons, 'Labour and local history: the case of Jim Gralton, 1886–1945', *Saothar* 14 (1989), pp. 85–94.

15   Joe Monks, *With the Reds in Andalusia* (London, 1985); Joseph O'Connor, *Even the Olives are Bleeding: The Life and Times of Charlie Donnelly* (Dublin, 1992); Peter O'Connor, *A Soldier of Liberty: Recollections of a Socialist and Anti-Fascist Fighter* (Dublin, 1996); Eoghan Ó Duinnín, *La Nina Bonita agus an Róisín Dubh: Cuimhní Cinn ar Chogadh Cathartha na Spáinne* (Dublin, 1986); H. Gustav Klaus (ed.), *Strong Words, Brave Deeds: The Poetry, Life and Times of Thomas O'Brien, Volunteer in the Spanish Civil War* (Dublin, 1994). See also Peadar O Donnell, *Salud! An Irishman in Spain* (London, 1937).

16   Hazel Morrissey, *Betty Sinclair: A Woman's Fight for Socialism* (Belfast, 1983); Betty Sinclair, 'A woman's fight for socialism, 1910–80', *Saothar* 9 (1983), pp. 121–32; Joe Deasy, 'The evolution of an Irish Marxist, 1941–50', *Saothar* 13 (1988), pp. 112–19; Andy Barr, 'An undiminished dream: Andy Barr, communist trade unionist', *Saothar* 16 (1991), pp. 95–111.

work on Seán Murray, CPI general secretary, 1933–41; Jackson's essay on the CPI paper the *Worker* and Spain in 1936–7; and McLoughlin's studies of the Irish in the Lenin School, the fruits of the first thorough research on documents of Irish relevance in the Comintern archives.[17]

Milotte's *Communism in Modern Ireland* is the sole general history of the topic; a partisan, Trotskyist critique, and relentlessly negative.[18] Understandably, given the sources available in 1984, Milotte understates the Moscow dimension, and decontextualises the communists from their global rationale, treating them as if they were essentially an indigenous force, hamstrung by a wilful, Stalinist, Moscow-centrism. Indeed, apart from the CPI publications and McLoughlin, the literature is uniformly negative on Comintern intervention, seeing it as insensitive of local circumstances, badly informed, and misguided.[19] The image of an isolated handful of radicals turning innocently for help to Russia, only to be handicapped by confounded orders from afar sounds plausible. What did the Irish understand of Bolshevism? What did the Comintern know of Ireland? How was it possible to run an Irish movement from Moscow?

THE INTERNATIONALS

The collapse of the Union of Soviet Socialist Republics (USSR) in 1991 led to the liberalisation of access to the Comintern files in the former Central Party Archive of the Communist Party of the Soviet Union in the Institute for Marxism–Leninism, now the Russian State Archive for Social and Political History (Rossiiskii Gosudartsvennyi Arkhiv Sotsial'no-Politischeskoi Istorii, RGASPI), in Moscow. Permission to consult the files was formerly restricted to approved communist party members, who were allowed to see material on their own party only. It is easy to understand why open access has revolutionised the study of communism internationally. The Comintern archive

17 Stephen Bowler, 'Stalinism in Ireland: the case of Seán Murray' (MSSc, Queen's University, Belfast, 1992); 'Seán Murray, 1898–1961, and the pursuit of Stalinism in one country', *Saothar* 18 (1993), pp. 41–53; Pete Jackson, '"A rather one sided fight": the *Worker* and the Spanish Civil War', *Saothar* 23 (1998), pp. 79–87; Barry McLoughlin, 'Proletarian academics or party functionaries? Irish communists at the International Lenin School, Moscow, 1927–37', *Saothar* 22 (1997), pp. 63–79, and 'Delegated to the "new world": Irish communists at Moscow's International Lenin School, 1927–1937', *History Ireland* (winter, 1999), pp. 37–9.
18 Mike Milotte, *Communism in Modern Ireland: The Pursuit of the Workers' Republic Since 1916* (Dublin, 1984).
19 Ibid., pp. 7–8; Bowler, 'Seán Murray', p. 44; W. K. Anderson, *James Connolly and the Irish left* (Dublin, 1994), p. 136; Jackson, 'A rather one sided fight', pp. 79–87.

houses some 55 million pages of documents, of which about 4,000 relate to Ireland.[20] When state papers – mostly police records – party newspapers and other publications are added to the pile, it is fair to say that no other political group in Ireland can boast of having had so much primary documentation generated by so few. For the Comintern years at least, the secretive communists are probably Ireland's best-documented political movement.

Internationals were a logical consequence of Karl Marx's contention that the proletariat had no motherland but socialism, and that the war of capital and labour knew no national boundaries. The first of the name, the International Working Men's Association, had been created, largely on the initiative of Marx himself, in 1864. It embraced individual as well as corporate affiliation, and undertook campaigns on issues of the day, notably the treatment of Fenian prisoners. Through the Fenian journalist, J. P. MacDonnell, it made a brief foray into Ireland in 1872, setting up a few branches, and organising coachmakers in Cork, before withering in the face of clerical induced opposition. The acronym of the cover name of the Dublin branch, the Hibernian Excelsior Labour League, would no doubt have confirmed clerical suspicions.[21] The International itself was crippled by internal disputes in 1872, and dissolved in 1876. A second international was convened in 1889. Much bigger than its forerunner, it took the form of a loose federation of, mainly, European socialist parties, and is remembered chiefly for doctrinal disputes at its congresses. While the International influenced Irish socialists, their only contact with it was the presence of delegates from the Irish Socialist Republican Party at the 1900 congress in Paris. The Second International regarded the prevention of another of the great powers' European wars as a defining objective, and its congresses repeatedly endorsed revolutionary action in the event of war. When most affiliates backed their national governments in August 1914, the International disintegrated in disgrace. A version of the Second International was revived at Berne in 1919. And in 1921 ten left-wing social democratic parties met in Vienna to form the International Working Union of Socialist Parties, nicknamed the 'two and a half International', as it stood between the Second and Third on the ideological spectrum. The Berne and Vienna conferences united in 1923 as the Labour and Socialist International, which survived until 1940.

Bitterly opposed to the re-establishment of the Second International, the Bolsheviks hastily founded the Third International in March 1919. The title was changed to Communist International in 1920. The Comintern would

20　See Barry McLoughlin and Emmet O'Connor, 'Sources on Ireland and the Communist International, 1920–43', *Saothar* 21 (1996), pp. 101–7.
21　See Seán Daly, *Ireland and the First International* (Cork, 1984).

become only one, if the most important, of a number of similar bodies, including KIM (Kommunisticheskii Internatsional Molodezhi, or Communist Youth International, 1919–43), the Profintern (Krasnyi Internatsional Professional'nykh Soyuzov, 1921–37, cited in some documents as the Red International of Labour Unions (RILU)), the Sportintern or Red Sport International (1921–37), and the Krestintern (Krestianskii Internatsional, or Peasants' International, 1923–33). To engage sympathisers or extend its reach, the Comintern also sponsored a series of 'fronts', such as Workers' International Relief (WIR, 1921–35), cited in some documents as Mezhdunarodnaia Rabochiia Pomoshch, or Mezhrabpom, or Secours Ouvrier International, or Internationale Arbeiterhilfe (IAH); International Class War Prisoners' Aid (ICWPA, 1922–41), also known as International Red Aid or Mezhdnarodnaia Organizatsiia Pomoshchi Revoliutsoneram (MOPR); and the League Against Imperialism (1927–35). With the exception of, alas, the Sportintern, all these organisations had a presence in Ireland.

V. I. Lenin was determined that the Comintern should not be a talking shop like the Second International, but the controlling body of all communist parties, and ideally 'a single communist party of the entire world'.[22] Sections, as they were called, were obliged to meet 21 conditions of membership, and a complex apparatus evolved to determine Comintern policy and ensure that it was applied. In theory at least, the supreme authority within the Comintern was the world congress. Initially it was envisaged that the congress would make a regular input into policy formulation, and five congresses were held between 1919 and 1924. As power within the Comintern became more centralised, only two further congresses were convened, in 1928 and 1935. The Executive Committee of the Communist International served as the highest organ between congresses. The congresses' method of choosing the ECCI varied over the years, from direct election, to the allocation of seats between parties, to the ratification of nominees selected by the presidium. The size of the ECCI increased unsteadily, from 35 in 1920, to 70 in 1924, and 78 in 1935. Real power lay with neither the congress nor the aggregate ECCI, and their rationale was to be as widely representative as possible. Meetings of what was called the enlarged plenum of the ECCI were initiated in 1922, and 13 such plenary sessions were held, the last in 1933. Between the plena, the ECCI's highest organ was the presidium (originally known as the little bureau). Each world congress or plenum would usually elect a new presidium. Membership grew over the years, from five in 1920 to 31 in 1935. The presidium restricted itself to general policy, and appointed an executive organ, the secretariat, with

22 Jane Degras (ed.), *The Communist International, 1919–1943, Documents, Vol. 1, 1919–1922* (London, 1971), p. 164.

five, six or seven members, to oversee policy application, and an organisational bureau, or orgbureau, to deal with organisational matters affecting the ECCI apparatus or national sections. A significant restructuring of the apparatus took place in 1926. The secretariat was restyled the political secretariat or politsecretariat, and its membership expanded to 14 in 1928, and 19 in 1931. The ECCI also established a minor or select commission to deal with clandestine activities, a standing commission to discuss matters deemed 'absolutely confidential', and, in 1929, a politcommission to handle administrative matters on behalf of the politsecretariat. More importantly from an Irish point of view, the ECCI created regional secretariats to supervise national sections. Ireland was placed initially under an Anglo-Dutch, and later under an Anglo-American secretariat. The last major revision of structures, in 1935, replaced the politsecretariat with a ten-man secretariat, abolished the regional secretariats, and allocated the supervision of national sections between each of the ten secretaries.[23] Ireland, and Britain, came under the secretariat of André Marty. Throughout the Comintern's history, at all levels, specific problems were frequently referred to ad hoc commissions.

This machinery, and the intention that the Comintern be a powerhouse of revolution in itself, entailed a sizeable bureaucracy. In 1926 the ECCI had a staff of 346 in 11 departments. By 1933, probably at the height of expansion, the numbers had grown to about 500 in 19 departments and eight regional secetariats, 12 of whom worked in the Anglo-American secretariat, supervising eight parties; another 300 or so were employed in Comintern related publishing projects, and in the Comintern's hotel, the Lux, in central Moscow. Aside from the structures cited above, and the International Lenin School – the Comintern's 'cadre-forge' – the only departments with which the Irish parties had some engagement with were Agitprop, the agitation and propaganda department, and the OMS (Otdel Mezhdunarodnoi Sviazi, or Department for International Liaison), which ran the Comintern's courier service. The Comintern also served as a model for the commandatura of affiliates, which were commonly governed by a central committee and a political bureau, corresponding respectively to the ECCI and the presidium.

It was hoped at the outset, to transfer the Comintern from Moscow to a western capital.[24] Had that happened, its history might well have been different. Instead, the Comintern remained in Moscow until its wartime evacuation in 1941, and was always controlled by the VKP(b) (All-Union

---

23   Peter Huber, 'Structure of the Moscow apparatus of the Comintern and decision-making', in Tim Rees and Andrew Thorpe (eds), *International Communism and the Communist International, 1919–43* (Manchester, 1998), pp. 42–52.

24   Degras, *The Communist International, Vol. 1*, p. 37.

Communist Party (Bolsheviks)) and by extension the Soviet Russian government.[25] The traffic was not entirely one way, and Comintern policy influenced debate within the VKP(b). The VKP(b) was of course by far the biggest cog in the wheel. In 1927 it contained 1.2 million of the Comintern's 1.7 million members. Of the other 46 affiliates, only the KPD (Kommunistische Partei Deutschlands, or Communist Party of Germany) and the Czech party had more than 100,000 members. In any evaluation of the standing of the Irish sections, it ought to be borne in mind that almost half of Comintern affiliates had fewer than 1,000 members.[26] There was nothing odd about the influence of the VKP(b) *per se*, and it was natural too that communists should prioritise the defence of the 'socialist sixth of the world'. What was a salient and unspoken anomaly was that the Comintern did not discuss the affairs of the VKP(b). It was never independent of the Soviet state, and the dominant men in the ECCI, if by no means invariably Russian, were all Soviet based, hired or fired by the regime, and ultimately at its mercy. Grigori Zinoviev chaired the ECCI up to November 1926, when he fell from grace and was succeeded by Nikolai Bukharin. After Bukharin too fell into disfavour, and was removed from office in April 1929, he was replaced with Vyacheslav Molotov. Molotov's appointment to a government post in December 1930 left the ECCI without an identifiable principal until 1935, when Georgi Dimitrov emerged as secretary-general and the last Comintern chief. In the early days there was some confusion as to the extent of ECCI authority over national sections, and as to how tensions between the interests of international communism and those of the Soviet state were to be reconciled. From 1924 the ECCI intensified efforts to discipline its affiliates under the rubric of Bolshevisation. As the Soviet state consolidated, the role of the Comintern became more circumscribed by raisons d'état, and as the regime more totalitarian, the Comintern was subordinated increasingly to Soviet foreign policy.

The ECCI was successful in achieving a relatively high degree of centralisation and conformity in policy application, and affiliates became famous, or infamous, for their discipline in acccepting changes in 'the line'. The strategic history of the Comintern may be divided into six phases. Up to the autumn of 1920, there were robust expectations that Bolshevism would triumph in

25 The Russian Social Democratic Labour Party was founded in 1898, and split into Bolshevik (majority) and Menshevik (minority) factions in 1903. The Bolsheviks became a separate party in 1912, changing their name to the Russian Social Democratic Labour Party (Bolsheviks) in 1917, the Russian Communist Party (Bolsheviks) in 1918, the All Union Communist Party (Bolsheviks) in 1925, and the Communist Party of the Soviet Union in 1952. For simplicity, the commonly used abbreviation VKP(b) will be employed here throughout.

26 Tim Rees and Andrew Thorpe, 'Introduction', in Rees and Thorpe, *International Communism*, p. 2.

western Europe through indigenous revolt or the westward march of the Red Army. A second phase evolved from 1921, conditioned by the retreat of the Red Army from Poland, the need for reconstruction in war-torn, famine-stricken Russia, and the failure of attempted revolutions, notably that in Germany in October 1923. At the third world congress in 1921, Lenin advised co-operation with reformists in certain circumstances. Capitalism, according to ECCI theory, had achieved a temporary stabilisation, and communists should join united fronts to stem the decline of working-class forces. In some countries this thesis was taken to mean united fronts 'from below', i.e. with members but not leaders of reformist organisations; in others, such as Britain, it was interpreted as united fronts 'from above', with reformist leaders. In 1926 Bukharin argued, with some prescience, that the capitalist world was now entering a third period, of more intense competition for markets, a profits squeeze, falling living standards, a new round of imperialist wars, and a threat of war against Soviet Russia. As social democrats ultimately sided with the bourgeoisie, they should be 'unmasked' as enemies. Bukharin did not antici-pate these developments unfolding rapidly, and Comintern policy adjusted incrementally. In Stalin's struggle for absolute power in 1927–8, Bukharin found his theses used against him, and his supporters branded as 'right wing deviationists' for being too moderate. Stalin's triumph and tighter direction of Comintern policy gave the ECCI an added incentive to adopt the theory of the third period, and it was endorsed by the ninth ECCI plenum in February 1928. Guided by the slogan 'class against class', communists were now to attack social democratic parties as 'social fascist', while trying to build united fronts from below with the rank and file of reformist organisations.[27] The continued advance of fascism, and especially the inability of the KPD to resist the Nazi government, prompted a revision in 1934, leading the seventh world congress to call for 'popular fronts'. Unlike the united front, the popular front was sup-posed to include bourgeois democrats and be directed primarily against fascism. This fourth phase formally ended with Soviet Russia's conclusion of a non-aggression pact with Germany in August 1939. The world war which followed was declared 'imperialist', and the communists switched their hostility from the fascists to the Anglo-French 'imperialists'. The final phase of Comintern policy was dictated by the Nazi invasion of Russia in June 1941. From then until its liquidation in 1943 – as a gesture to the western Allies – the Comintern urged maximum support for the war effort and the Allied governments.

27 See Kevin McDermott and Jeremy Agnew, *The Comintern: A History of International Communism from Lenin to Stalin* (London, 1996), pp. 68–80.

While affiliates were expected to uphold general policy, the ECCI was concerned with all aspects of the progress of its sections, and willing to take national circumstances into account and negotiate on tactics. Within certain parameters, there were therefore different policies for different countries, based on local requirements and determined through the interaction of centre and periphery. How was the Comintern's Irish policy made? Up to 1924, when primordial questions as to the leadership, organisation and policy of Irish communism had yet to be resolved to the ECCI's satisfaction, the world congresses were vital points of contact. Irish delegates attended the second, third, fourth and fifth congresses, at which the major issues of the day were resolved in private discussions with senior Soviet officials, including Lenin, Zinoviev and Bukharin. For policy development between congresses, the ECCI hoped to appoint an Irish commission. Irish affairs were discussed by the Anglo-American colonial group in 1922, an Irish commission was appointed during the fourth world congress in December 1922, and another in 1923. However, the ECCI found the absence of a permanent Irish representative in Moscow a source of frustration in this respect. Throughout the 1920s it believed that it lacked adequate intelligence on Ireland, and for political reasons too was reluctant to create commissions on Ireland without an Irish representative. From 1922 onwards, the Communist Party of Great Britain (CPGB) was availed of, when possible, to foster organisation in Ireland; a similar role was given to the KPD in Austria, and to the Australian party in New Zealand. It was much resented by the Irish in the 1920s. Connolly preferred to communicate with Moscow via Berlin and his contacts in the KPD. Larkin's happy collaboration with the British ended once they had done his bidding in pressing for the dissolution of the CPI. He then insisted that the ECCI deal directly with himself or his representatives.

Formally, there were three channels of policy making and transmission during Larkin's leadership of Irish communism: the ECCI plena, to which Larkin was invited; Jack Carney, who took up a residency as IWL permanent representative in Moscow in 1925; and Comintern agents working in Dublin. Unfortunately for the ECCI, these mechanisms were all dependent on the goodwill of Larkin himself, which was rarely forthcoming. The ECCI and the Anglo-American secretariat kept Ireland under review with the aid of intelligence from emissaries to Ireland, British comrades in Moscow, and, occasionally, Irish visitors to Moscow or Irish students in the Lenin School. The great difficulty lay in policy application. Moscow's liaison with sympathetic republicans through divers front organisations was no compensation for Larkin's obstruction, and not intended to be anything but preliminary to the building of a new party.

The groundwork for the refoundation of the CPI was begun in 1929 by an ECCI commission, made up of an Irish graduate of the Lenin School and two Scots; whether coincidental or deliberate, the use of Scots as advisors or agents was characteristic of Comintern management of Ireland. By 1930, the Irish leadership was entirely indigenous, and the key men were alumni of the Lenin School. The normal procedures of policy control could now be applied to Ireland for the first time. Primarily that meant that the Irish reported regularly to the Anglo-American secretariat, which enforced the Comintern's closest ever scrutiny of Irish affairs. Anything not considered routine, such as problems of policy, the despatch of agents, or requests for money, was handled by one of the higher ECCI organs, usually the politsecretariat or the standing commission. From time to time the Comintern also seconded agents from the CPGB or the Minority Movement, the British section of the Profintern, together with at least one 'instructor' from the Western European Bureau (WEB), the ECCI's Berlin office. Undoubtedly the CPGB had an informal watching brief on Ireland during these years, but its role was a subordinate one until the Republican Congress in 1934, when the ECCI lost confidence in Seán Murray.

From late 1934, the CPGB had a crucial influence over Irish policy. That status was consolidated by the abolition of the regional secretariats at the seventh world congress in 1935. The CPI did not have a permanent representative in André Marty's secretariat, whereas the British did. In any case, the restructuring was intended to allow national sections greater autonomy from the ECCI, and Marty was content to delegate the supervision of Ireland to London. The CPI's last direct contact with the ECCI was in 1938. After that, it was dependent on the CPGB to shape Irish policy in Moscow, and interpret it to Dublin.

The implications of Ireland's relations with Soviet Russia and the Comintern will be discussed in the conclusion. Suffice it to say here that the many publications on the Comintern and national sections which have appeared since 1991 all address similar themes: How subordinate were affiliates to the ECCI? How important was the Comintern in the culture of affiliates? Were Moscow's interventions and policy directives a hindrance or a help to local parties? And what does the national experience tell us of the Comintern itself?

ONE

HAIL RUSSIA!

LABOUR AND BOLSHEVISM, 1917–19

We acclaim the Russian revolution, and our hearts respond to the call of the Russian
people to join with the workers throughout war stricken Europe in dethroning
Imperialism and Capitalism in our respective countries.
THOMAS JOHNSON,
Voice of Labour, 23 February 1918

—

Labour's crush on the Bolsheviks reflected the extraordinary novelty and promise of its situation between 1917 and 1921. Since the foundation of the Irish Trade Union Congress (ITUC) in 1894, unions had not recruited more than ten per cent of the workforce. The surge of general unionism before the First World War had culminated in defeat in the 1913 lockout. Yet within three years the war economy and the wartime manpower shortage had transformed labour's bargaining power. Between 1917 and 1920, the number of trade unionists rose from under 100,000 to about 250,000, or 25 per cent of the workforce, with membership of the Irish Transport and General Workers' Union (ITGWU) soaring from 5,000 to 120,000.[1] Labour was also politicised. But whereas it had an ancient history of trade unionism, and a distant history of involvement with nationalist politics, its experience of socialism and socialist party politics was slight. The Labour Party, notionally created in 1912, had no structure separate from the ITUC, and would not contest a general election until 1922. The consequences were both liberating and confusing. In a social climate radicalised by revolution at home and abroad, at a time when it seemed as if the world was being reconstructed, and that post-war society would herald a new age of the people, the Labour leadership felt free to embrace the most radical influences.

The SPI, in particular, would champion an ambiguous Bolshevism until 1921. It was not that the party was Leninist. For the SPI, Bolshevism, as the premier version of revolutionism, and as a resolutely anti-imperialist ideology – in contrast with the more temporising politics of the social democrats – was the natural orientation of a party that claimed the mantle of James Connolly. The

---

1   For the wider context see Emmet O'Connor, *A Labour History of Ireland, 1824–1960* (Dublin, 1992), pp. 94–116.

importance of the SPI, and of the Russian revolution, to Labour, reflected the significance of international policy to a movement whose domestic politics were severely circumscribed by its reluctance to engage with the national revolution. Having baulked at contesting the 1918 general election, Labour hoped it might establish a political identity in international affairs. The SPI became a battleground over the question of relations with the socialist and communist Internationals, and the embryo of communism in Ireland.

UP BOLSHEVIKS!

Labour acknowledged the Bolshevik revolution a trifle belatedly. When Congress acquired the weekly *Irish Opinion*, later renamed the *Voice of Labour*, in November 1917, the first issue on 1 December made no mention of Russia, despite including over a page of 'International notes'. It would soon make make amends. An editorial in the third issue on 'The Bolsheviks', encapsulated the popular response to the revolution up to 1920 at least, in treating the Bolsheviks as synonymous with 'labour', and emphasising their anti-imperialism and their opposition to the world war.

> Labour in Russia was and is honest. In consequence it has given to the world a formula which was worth a Czar's throne to have given. 'No annexations, no indemnities, and the right of every nation to determine its own destiny' . . . [Kerensky] asked definitely for a revision of war aims and was, not very politely, turned down . . . The saviours of small nations preferred diplomatic procrastination to the honesty displayed by the Russian Soviet and so the Maximalists displaced Kerensky.[2]

Contact was made with the Bolsheviks in the new year. In January a joint Labour Party and SPI deputation, comprising William O'Brien, D. R. Campbell and Cathal O'Shannon, met Maxim Litvinov, the Soviet plenipotentiary in London, and appealed for Russian backing for their objectives at international conferences. O'Shannon's glowing account of the meeting characterised the SPI's style:

> It was a great pleasure for us to hear him speak of James Connolly, and as he spoke I thought how Connolly's heart would have rejoiced at the success of the Bolsheviks, and how he would have handled the new situation. In Russia, Litvinoff told us, they had heard of Connolly and his work years ago, even before 1913.[3]

2 *Irish Opinion*, 15 Dec. 1917.3   3 *Irish Opinion*, 9 Feb. 1918.

Of course the Bolsheviks' position on Ireland was more complex. V. I. Lenin had been exceptional among them in supporting the Easter Rising. Karl Radek, notoriously, dismissed it as a 'putsch', while Leon Trotsky saw it as a hopeless gesture, indicating that 'The basis for a national revolution has disappeared even in backward Ireland'. Irish anti-imperialism would not subside, Trotsky believed, but the next revolt against British rule would require a working-class basis.[4] As late as 1920, Nikolai Bukharin, deputy leader of the Comintern, contended that nationalist unrest in the colonies could have 'absolutely no direct relation to the developing proletarian revolution'.[5] But the SPI rarely probed deeper than the propaganda on Russia. For the most part, its 'Bolshevism' amounted to a simple identification with the fact of the October revolution, with the principles of revolution and of a workers' state. Russian Bolshevism was fitted into Irish conceptions and was to serve Irish Labour's requirements; not the other way round. It was in its own way a tribute to the self-confidence which the left had acquired from Connolly.

The initial flush of enthusiasm for Russia climaxed at a rally to hail the revolution in Dublin's Mansion House on 4 February 1918. The attendance of some 10,000 people 'far exceeded the too modest expectations of the promoters and the gathering overflowed from the Round Room into the anterooms and passages and out onto Dawson Street'. Thousands lingered late into the night in Dawson Street, savouring the atmosphere. The resolutions passed again focused on international relations:

> Whereas the All-Russian Bolshevik Revolution has proved to be the first people's authority in the world which has applied its professed principles of no annexations and self-determination of subject races and territories within its own boundaries.
>
> Whereas it has fearlessly challenged the British people to loosen its grip upon Ireland and other so-called dependencies as incompatible with the aforesaid principles.
>
> Whereas it has so successfully hastened the realisation of suffering mankind's hopes for a genuine peace on all fronts and the elimination of international chaos and national animosities.
>
> Therefore be it resolved that this mass meeting of Dublin citizens hails with delight the advent of the Russian Bolshevik Revolution . . .[6]

---

4   D. R. O'Connor Lysaght (ed.), *The Communists and the Irish Revolution: Part One, The Russian Revolutionaries on the Irish National Question, 1899–1924* (Dublin, 1993), pp. 53–65.

5   Stephen White, 'Soviet Russia and the Irish revolution', *Irish Slavonic Studies* 5 (1984), p. 50.

6   *Irish Opinion*, 9 Feb. 1918. The attendance figure is claimed in RGASPI, Report of the SPI to the Third International, 1920, 495/89/3–10.

THE SPI: FORMATION AND AIMS

The SPI was the third party to bear that title. The first of the name had been founded on 4 March 1904, following the departure of Connolly to America in 1903 and the decline of his Irish Socialist Republican Party. Like Connolly at this time, the SPI was heavily influenced by the syndicalist precepts of Daniel De Leon and the Socialist Labor Party of America. In line with the antipathy of syndicalists to 'labour fakirs', it resolved in 1905 that 'no official of a Trades Union . . . be eligible for membership'. The implacable party made derisory progress, and news of Connolly's doctrinal disputes with De Leon contributed to its dissolution on 4 June 1908. In January 1909, Connolly urged the Dublin left to regroup in a broad-based party, open to leftist nationalists and non-Marxists as well as revolutionaries. The outcome was the launch of another SPI on 13 June 1909.[7] The second SPI became indelibly associated with Connolly on his return from the USA in July 1910 to work as party organiser. Branches were formed in Belfast and Cork, and a new programme adopted. Though obviously impressed by American syndicalism, the manifesto confirmed Connolly's drift to the centre, and was broadly social democratic in philosophy and open on method and aims. By 1912 Connolly had become more anxious about reaching the masses. On Easter Monday 1912, shortly before he proposed to the Irish Trade Union Congress that it create a Labour Party, he formed the Independent Labour Party (of Ireland) to act as a ginger group within the Congress party.[8] The Independent Labour Party comprised the SPI, the Belfast branch of the British Socialist Party, and four of Belfast's five branches of the British Independent Labour Party, united around a minimum programme of class unity. Again reflecting American syndicalism, its aim was an 'industrial commonwealth', to be realised through elections, and through industrial unionism, or the organisation of workers in industrial, as distinct from craft, unions. The unity did not survive internal tensions inflamed by the Home Rule crisis and the outbreak of the world war. The Belfast branch disintegrated after August 1914. The Dublin branch reverted to the name 'SPI', but took a back seat to Connolly's work with the ITGWU and the Citizen Army.[9] To all intents and purposes, it was defunct before the Easter Rising.

Remarkably, the Citizen Army's links with the left withered to insignificance after the Rising. When 210 (out of a total of 340) Citizen Army men and women marched out on Easter Monday, they left the labour movement

7   Vincent Morely, 'Sóisialithe Átha Cliath agus teagasc Daniel De Leon, 1900–1909', *Saothar* 12 (1987), pp. 22–33.
8   O'Connor, *A Labour History of Ireland*, pp. 81–3.
9   Greaves, *The Life and Times of James Connolly*, pp. 224–5.

behind them. Even the ITGWU had come close to repudiating Connolly ten days previously for hoisting a green flag over Liberty Hall. Eleven members of the Army were killed in action. Connolly's most promising lieutenant, Michael Mallin, was executed on 8 May, and Connolly himself was shot on the 12th. The Rising threw Labour on the defensive. The British had shelled Liberty Hall, seized ITGWU and Congress files, and arrested trade union leaders. The Congress report for 1916, presented in August, denied government and employer allegations of Labour involvement in Easter Week, and dissociated the ITGWU from the Citizen Army. When challenged on the point the ITGWU president, Tom Foran, said his union 'was proud of the actions taken by the Irish Citizen Army', but did not seek to amend the report.[10] The Citizen Army council was reconstituted in February 1917 and James O'Neill elected commandant, a post he would hold until January 1922. A carpenter and small contractor who had served in the General Post Office in Easter Week, O'Neill opposed anything that would bring the Army under the influence of other bodies. Relations with the ITGWU deteriorated, and it was pressured to vacate Liberty Hall. The Army maintained a limited liaison with the Dublin brigade, IRA, and conducted some arms procurement operations, but O'Neill prevented offensive action pending 'the big day'.[11]

The SPI was revived on 29 January 1917, and William O'Brien was elected chairman.[12] The precise context is unclear, but it was almost certainly part of O'Brien's design to place himself at the heart of the resurgent ITGWU. O'Brien had worked for the ITGWU from its inception, though a member of the Amalgamated Society of Tailors. During his internment following the Easter Rising, he confided in Cathal O'Shannon his ambitions for the ITGWU.[13] On his release from prison in August 1916, he collaborated with Tom Foran in rebuilding the union from the wreckage. With Connolly dead, Jim Larkin, the union's titular general secretary, in the USA since 1914, and Foran reluctant to take on the secretary's job, O'Brien had a unique opportunity before him. On 30 December 1916 he applied for membership of the union. Rapid promotion followed. Admitted to the no. 1 branch on 6 January, he was elected vice chairman of the branch committee at the branch's annual meeting on 21 January.[14] The committee was, in effect, the union executive,

10   O'Connor, *A Labour History of Ireland*, p. 93.

11   R. M. Fox, *The History of the Irish Citizen Army* (Dublin, 1944), pp. 206–15; Frank Robbins, *Under the Starry Plough: Recollections of the Irish Citizen Army* (Dublin, 1977), pp. 200–10.

12   NLI, William O'Brien papers, 15674(1).

13   Thomas J. Morrissey, SJ, *A Man Called Hughes: The Life and Times of Séamus Hughes, 1881–1943* (Dublin, 1991), p. 87.

14   C. Desmond Greaves, *The Irish Transport and General Workers' Union: The Formative years, 1909–23* (Dublin, 1982), p. 178.

and Foran was happy for O'Brien to serve, de facto, as general secretary. While O'Brien lacked agitational skills and popular appeal – his forte was management and bargaining – he had the cachet of having been active in Dublin socialist groups since 1899, and a personal friend of Connolly; it was under his roof that Mrs Connolly and her children sheltered in the days after Easter Week.[15] The revival of Connolly's party was the first of many schemes on O'Brien's part to associate himself with labour's national martyr, and not without effect. 'I did not like him', Peadar O'Donnell recalled, 'but I respected him. We regarded him as the Lenin of the Labour Movement. The Petrograd Revolution had occurred: we admired it and looked to someone like O'Brien to lead the way.'[16]

After O'Brien, the most important man in the SPI was O'Shannon. Born near Randalstown, County Antrim in 1893, O'Shannon's childhood set his political values in stone.

> My father collecting a few shillings to keep railwaymen on strike, the centenary of the insurrection of 1798, and a few old men talking Irish to a Gaelic League organiser are among my earliest memories. These are the three threads that have run together in one piece in me all through my life.[17]

Active in labour, republican and literary circles in Belfast from 1908, O'Shannon was drawn to socialism by reading Connolly, joined the second SPI, and worked with Connolly in the ITGWU's Belfast office in 1913. On Easter Saturday 1916, he mobilised with about 100 volunteers at Coalisland and was interned after the Rising. From 1917 he resumed work for the ITGWU. But if O'Shannon was the SPI's chief propagandist, and more genuine than O'Brien, he was subordinate to O'Brien in the union, and ultimately that meant the subordination of the party to the union. Tom Johnson was also depicted on occasion as completing the triumvirate of the SPI's moderate wing. In reality Johnson was not so influential within the party, and his importance derived from his position as treasurer, later secretary, and ideologist of the ILPTUC, the last role a recognition in equal measure of his interest in political writing in a fraternity desperately short of theorists, and his pliant character. A Fabian

15   William O'Brien, *Forth the Banners Go: Reminiscences of William O'Brien as told to Edward MacLysaght, D.Litt* (Dublin, 1969), p. 4.

16   Uinseann MacEoin (ed.), *Survivors: The Story of Ireland's Struggle as Told Through Some of Her Outstanding Living People Recalling Events From the Days of Davitt, Through James Connolly, Brugha, Collins, De Valera, Liam Mellows, and Rory O'Connor to the Present Time* (Dublin, 1980), pp. 22–3. O'Donnell worked as an ITGWU official from 1918 to 1920.

17   For a biographical sketch see Emmet O'Connor, 'Labour lives: Cathal O'Shannon', *Saothar* 24 (1999), pp. 89–90.

at heart, Johnson invariably twisted with the prevailing wind. With its first office in room 3, Liberty Hall, the SPI drew its second echelon leaders from ITGWU officials initially. As the party expanded, it attracted a corps of more independent officers. In contrast to its forerunners, the SPI was not a fringe group. Not only would it become the best connected, best resourced Marxist party in Irish history, but it operated during a very propitious period, with ready access to the Labour press. O'Shannon was appointed editor of the *Voice of Labour* in March 1918; and after the *Voice* was suppressed in September 1919, he edited its successor, the *Watchword of Labour*.

The SPI advertised itself as founded by Connolly, and adopted the same Irish language title as its predecessor, Cumannacht na hÉireann, sometimes using the Irish title only. O'Shannon, of course, was a keen Gaeilgeor, and articles in Irish by Pádraic Ó Conaire and W. P. Ryan were published occasionally in *Irish Opinion*, the *Voice*, and *Watchword*.[18] Ó Conaire spoke on 'Cumannachas in Éirinn' in Liberty Hall in March 1919, the proceedings being entirely in Irish.[19] Theoretically, the SPI derived its ideas initially from Connolly's version of industrial unionism. Its object was: 'An Industrial Commonwealth based upon common ownership of the land and instruments of production, distribution, and exchange, with complete political and social equality between the sexes.'[20] By 1920 its constitution had replaced the syndicalist term 'industrial commonwealth', with 'workers' republic'.[21] Despite the early influence of syndicalism, the leading brand of revolutionary socialism of Connolly's day, party propaganda displayed a livelier interest in Bolshevism, the pre-eminent form of revolutionism after November 1917. O'Shannon, who delighted in describing himself as an 'Irish Bolshevik' and insisted that the SPI was Bolshevist, had no difficulty in reconciling syndicalism with Bolshevism, but in the process displayed a dubious grasp of Leninism. Speaking to a Sinn Féin meeting in Belfast on 'Connolly a Bolshevik' he declared:

It was important that the similarity of ideas between Connolly and Bolshevism be understood. This similarity was particularly striking in their conception of . . . representative institutions . . . in the Soviets the state desiderated by Connolly and the Socialists' government [was] not by territorial but by industrial representation.[22]

18 See for example *Irish Opinion*, 8 Dec. 1917, 28 Feb. 1918; *Watchword of Labour*, 29 Nov. 1919, 24 Jan. 1920.
19 *New Ireland*, 8 Mar. 1919.
20 *Irish Opinion*, 9 Feb. 1918.
21 RGASPI, application for affiliation to the Third International, 17 May 1920, 495/89/3–5.
22 *Irish Opinion*, 23 Feb. 1918.

This naïve view of the meaning of communist rule in Russia would be matched by a simple equation of revolution with democratic direct action, as from December 1917 the Labour weeklies gave favourable coverage to communism throughout Europe, in addition to welcoming soviets – or the seizure by workers of land, creameries, and factories – at home. In the *Communist*, organ of the CPGB, the *Watchword* advertised itself as 'Ireland's Revolutionary and Communist Organ'.[23]

A fatal lack of clarity hamstrung the role of the SPI. Like the Independent Labour Party (of Ireland), it was to be a party within a party; its principles were to be realised by industrial, political and educational means. Industrially it stood for industrial unionism.[24] But while the syndicalist impact on labour was very evident by 1918, in the ITGWU especially, and most ITGWU leaders were members of the SPI, the party was not perceived as a distinct influence. Politically, the SPI was committed to the organisation of labour 'to take political action on independent lines for securing the control of all public elective bodies, and for the mastery of all the public powers of the state'.[25] Yet it was reluctant to act independently of the ITGWU or the Labour Party. It found a role in propaganda and education, and its most celebrated initiatives came in foreign policy, on Soviet Russia and assertions of Ireland's right to self-determination. Arguably, the affirmation of national rights through internationalism was the hallmark of the party, and it is best known for its insistence on recognition of Ireland at international conferences.

UNLESS YE BECOME AS PROLETARIANS

The SPI held its inaugural public meetings in March 1917, and enjoyed a promising, if low key, infancy. O'Brien's diary of 25 March noted that a lecture on 'The national revival of Bulgaria' – not the most obvious of topics – attracted 22 recruits, raising membership to 100.[26] This mixture of nationalism and internationalism – so graphically captured, in Irish eyes, by the Bolshevik revolution – proved a popular cocktail.

After the Mansion House meeting in February 1918, an ebullient SPI embarked on a hectic lecture programme. On 9 March *Irish Opinion* gave notice of forthcoming commemorations of the Paris Commune, May Day, and the centenary of the birth of Karl Marx, a lecture in the Dublin Trades'

23 See for example the *Watchword of Labour*, 31 Jan., 9–16 Oct. 1920; *Communist*, 5 Aug., 7 Oct. 1920.
24 RGASPI, application for affiliation to the Third International, 17 May 1920, 495/89/3–5.
25 NLI, SPI papers, LOp107; Fr Thomas J. Morrissey, SJ, 'William O'Brien, the Socialist Party, and the Church, 1917–21', unpublished paper.
26 NLI, O'Brien papers, 15705 (10).

Hall on 'Ireland and the International', and a lecture to Cumann na mBan, in addition to its usual weekly business meetings. In October the SPI and Dublin trades' council formed a Russian revolution and republic committee to mark the first anniversary of the Bolshevik revolution. Although the British banned the proposed festivities, two illegal meetings were held, and the SPI published the pamphlet *The New Russia*.²⁷ The party also moved from Liberty Hall to more spacious accommodation at 42 North Great George's Street, and reported rising membership.²⁸ Rounding off the year, a mass rally was held on 1 December in the Dublin Trades' Hall to 'celebrate the downfall of imperialism in Central Europe, welcome the German and Austrian Republics, and make common cause with the Social Revolution'.²⁹ The SPI's participation in the international socialist conference in Berne in February 1919 marked the height of the party's self-confidence. O'Brien attended a number of SPI meetings in January and February 1919 on Berne and labour's relations with Sinn Féin, noting of one on 28 February: 'a good attendance . . . the future looks promising'.³⁰

Other SPI activities included running internal discussion groups, a choir, and a 'workers' library on Bolshevism', which introduced Peadar O'Donnell, among others, to Marxism.³¹ Its edition of *Labour, Nationality, and Religion* was intended to be the first in a series of Connolly's selected works. In October 1918 Walter Carpenter Sr undertook a lecture tour of Scotland for the party, addressing 16 meetings on the Irish question.³² Members enjoyed too a lively entertainment scene, featuring regular Saturday socials at 42 North Great George's Street. On 27 September 1919, the *Watchword of Labour* reported that 'The great event of the SPI programme [for the coming season] is the Ceilidh next Saturday in the Round Room of the Mansion House'. 'Several combinations of musicians' were promised.

The party's most ambitious undertaking was the James Connolly Labour College. The project originated in the Connolly Memorial Children's Treat, held at Christmas for the poor of Dublin in 1917 and 1918. When the sponsors of the 1918 treat were left with a surplus of £40, they donated the money to the

27 Edited by SPI member Semyon Aronson (alias Sidney Arnold), the pamphlet contained the constitution of the Soviet Republic together with various articles. *Voice of Labour*, 16 Nov. 1918.
28 NLI, O'Brien papers, 15705 (11).
29 *Irish Labour and its International Relations in the era of the Second International and the Bolshevik Revolution* (Cork Workers' Club, n.d.), p. 26.
30 NLI, O'Brien papers, 15705.
31 NLI, *James Connolly Birthday Celebrations* (Dublin, 1919) [programme], LOp71; *Connolly Souvenir* (Dublin, 1919); Dónal Ó Drisceoil, *Peadar O'Donnell* (Cork, 2001), p. 11.
32 *Voice of Labour*, 2 Nov. 1918. Carpenter was the doyen of Dublin Marxists and had been secretary of the SPI's Dublin branch in 1911.

SPI to set up the college.[33] The party started courses of lectures in economics
and industrial history in early 1919. On 5 June, Connolly's birthday, O'Brien
chaired a fund-raising concert for the college in the Mansion House. The
meeting was proscribed and police barred the entrance after about 100 people
had been admitted. Efforts by the police to move the crowd towards Grafton
Street led to scuffles and an attempt to arrest one of the Citizen Army
stewards. Two Citizen Army officers opened fire. Four policemen and two
civilians were wounded. The venue was promptly shifted to the Trades' Hall,
and survivors of the shooting sensation arrived in Capel Street astonished to
see the festivities in full swing.[34] The SPI made good the financial loss
through selling a handsome Connolly souvenir. Other subvention came
mainly from the ITGWU and rallies in Glasgow and Manchester, at which
Constance Markievicz and Hanna Sheehy Skeffington spoke.[35] The college
was founded at a conference of trade union, co-operative, and SPI delegates in
Banba Hall on 2 November 1919, and located in 42 North Great George's Street.
Two hundred and thirty students were enrolled, and lectures – on history,
economics, literature, public speaking and the social sciences – commenced
on 18 January 1920.[36] All of the administrative staff, and many of the teaching
staff, were SPI members. An appeal for lecturers in the *Watchword of Labour*
had advised that 'the working class outlook' was an essential requirement of
their curricula vitae, 'for unless ye become as proletarians ye cannot enter the
"Workers' Republic"'.[37] Tutors included Professor George O'Brien – who
presumably became an honorary proletarian – and whose *Labour Organization*
(1921) was the only book on labour written by an Irish academic before 1977.
Mrs George Bernard Shaw endowed the college library with 32 volumes of
literature. In February the Belfast SPI took steps to initiate a college in the
city. Courses were under way in Newbridge, County Kildare, and others were
being planned in Meath. Similar initiatives were later reported from Cork,
Solohead, Cobh, Bray and Dún Laoghaire, and in August the college held a
summer camp at Skerries.[38]

33 *Watchword of Labour*, 15 Nov. 1919. I am obliged to Tom Crean for this and other references to the
Connolly College.
34 Reports conflict on whether the civilians were hit by the Citizen Army or the police returning fire.
Robbins, *Under the Starry Plough*, pp. 210–12; *The Irish Times*, 6 June 1919; *Irish Independent*, 6 June 1919.
35 *Watchword of Labour*, 25 Oct., 6 Dec. 1919; *Socialist*, 15 Feb. 1920; NLI, Connolly Memorial
Labour College Fund, Grand Concert, 7 Oct. 1919 [St Andrew's Hall, Glasgow], Ir941p22.
36 *Watchword of Labour*, 15 Nov. 1919; Robbins, *Under the Starry Plough*, pp. 210–11. Staff included
Nora Connolly, president, Joseph M. M. MacDonnell, alias Reverend Malcolm McColl, director,
Charles Kenny, secretary, and Frank Robbins, registrar.
37 *Watchword of Labour*, 25 Oct. 1919.
38 *Watchword of Labour*, 24 Jan., 13–20 Mar., 10 July, 14 Aug., 2–23 Oct. 1920.

The SPI's enigmatic reluctance to construct a branch network further illustrates the tenuousness of its à la carte Bolshevism. *Irish Opinion* had reported on 2 February 1918 that the Dublin branch was 'preparing for a forward move in Socialist propaganda in the city and outside' and urged the creation of branches in the provinces. 'Scatter the seed to the "four winds of Éirinn" and build a branch now', ran an advertisement in the *Voice of Labour* on 10 August 1918. A Belfast section existed from 1918, when Seán MacEntee, later a hammer of the left as a minister in Fianna Fáil governments, led local SPI members in the anti-conscription campaign.[39] An 'informal' socialist conference was held in Drogheda in August 1919, during the ILPTUC annual congress, but the *Voice* could only cite meetings in Naas and Newbridge, County Kildare which resulted from it, and noted feebly that it 'would be gratified' to hear from other centres.[40] Peadar O'Donnell later claimed that his efforts to start branches in Monaghan and Derry in the summer of 1919 were frustrated by internal feuding in Dublin.[41] A Cork branch was reported in 1919, and others in Sligo and Newbridge in 1920.[42] It was a bewilderingly meagre performance for a party with the Labour press, the ITGWU's extensive infrastructure, and most of the sharpest organisers in the trade union movement at its disposal.

BOLSHEVISM AS FOREIGN POLICY

With members in the highest councils of the Labour Party, and links with the Easter Rising, the SPI was well placed to influence both Labour and Sinn Féin. Even as O'Brien was founding the SPI, he was canvassing for Count Plunkett in the Roscommon by-election. Subsequently he assisted Sinn Féin in the South Longford and East Clare by-elections of 1917. He was also a grey eminence behind the 'national assembly' summoned by Count Plunkett in April 1917, though Dublin trades' council recoiled from association with Sinn Féin at this time, and instructed him not to attend.[43] The conscription crisis in the spring of 1918 shifted Labour's position to one of enthusiastic involvement with consensus nationalism; the more so as the general strike against

39   Michael McInerney, 'Roddy Connolly: 60 years of political activity', *The Irish Times*, 27 Aug. 1976.

40   *Voice of Labour*, 30 Aug. 1919.

41   Peter Hegarty, *Peadar O'Donnell* (Cork, 1999), p. 59.

42   *Watchword of Labour*, 20 Dec. 1919, 7, 21 Feb. 1920; RGASPI, Report of the SPI to the Third International, 11 June 1920, 495/89/3–12.

43   Arthur Mitchell, *Labour in Irish Politics, 1890–1930: The Irish Labour Movement in an Age of Revolution* (Dublin, 1974), pp. 82–3.

conscription on 23 April contributed to a significant growth in trade union membership over the following weeks. In September Labour was sanguine enough to appoint O'Brien, Johnson and O'Shannon to write its manifesto for contesting the forthcoming general election on an independent, abstentionist platform. Subsequently, O'Brien, O'Shannon and Tom Farren held secret talks with Sinn Féin on an election pact.[44] The collapse of the national consensus on abstention from Westminster – precipitated by the approaching end of the world war and the conscription threat – left Labour timorous about a deal with Sinn Féin, while its lack of a political machine made it uneasy about standing independently. Although a high proportion of those who spoke against withdrawal from the election at Labour's special conference on 1 November were SPI men, other members, such as O'Brien and Johnson, argued in favour.[45] Over the next two years the pattern repeated itself; SPI leaders were at the heart of Labour's collusion with republicans, yet the party was redundant to Labour policy on nationalism.

The SPI retained a niche role in Labour's foreign policy. It was perceived as being more acceptable to continental parties than the ILPTUC, which did not adopt a socialist programme until November 1918, and more easily intelligible than Labour's syndicalist format which contained no specific political structures. The demise of the Second International on the outbreak of the First World War had closed one chapter in socialist internationalism. The first Russian revolution opened the prologue to another. While four inter-allied socialist meetings were held in London during the war, a universal conference was regarded as an essential symbol of a new beginning. In a prescient reading of the times, Dublin trades' council called in February 1917 for separate Irish representation at all international labour conferences.[46] When the Petrograd soviet and a Dutch–Scandinavian socialist committee called for an international labour conference to meet in Stockholm, the ILPTUC executive agreed to send a delegation, mandated to 'seek to establish the Irish Labour Party as a distinct unit in the international labour movement', and to support peace without annexations or indemnities, on the basis of national self-determination. The SPI too intended to send a representative, but the initiative came to nothing as the British government refused passports to the delegates.[47] O'Brien attended the conference at Leeds in June 1917, how-ever, convened by the British United Socialist Council to salute the Russian revolution, and he insisted on speaking as a fraternal emissary from the SPI, and not as a 'British' delegate. His speech pleaded for the release of Irish

44   Brian Farrell, *The Founding of Dáil Éireann: Parliament and Nation Building* (Dublin, 1971), pp. 29–44.

45   Mitchell, *Labour in Irish Politics*, pp. 99–100.

political prisoners, and Countess Markievicz in particular.[48] After meeting Litvinov in January 1918, the joint Labour Party–SPI deputation attending the British Labour Party conference at Nottingham, and held discussions with Camille Huysmans, secretary of the International Socialist Bureau. Another mission to England followed in April, and secured the opposition of the British labour movement to the application of conscription in Ireland.[49]

Labour's foreign policy took shape in late 1918. At its annual conference in August, the ILPTUC called for the re-establishment of the Second International. The motion enjoyed SPI approval, despite the Bolsheviks' hostility to the Second International, and a Congress–SPI committee was created as the 'Irish section of the International'. In November, an ILPTUC special conference endorsed a 'statement of international aims', proclaiming Labour's adherence to 'the Russian formula' of peace based on self-determination, no annexations, and no indemnities; demanding that the right of self-determination be extended to all subject peoples; and protesting at the 'capitalist outlawry' of Soviet Russia. The 'international committee' of the Labour Party also addressed an open letter to the workers of Britain, seeking their support for self-determination.[50]

Sinn Féin's landslide victory in the 1918 general election left Labour with misgivings about its pre-election timidity. Anxious to assert itself within the new order, it determined to make the most of the forthcoming conference in Berne on reviving the International. Congress appointed a four-man team for Berne on 28 December.[51] The SPI was unanimously in favour of participation. It later pleaded to Moscow that its aims were:

First: to cleanse the working class movement from the elements of social patriotism and coalition with capitalism which had characterised, in particular, the British, French, Belgian, and German constituents during the war.

Second: to bring before the world the subject condition of Ireland under a military terrorism fully endorsed by the British Labour Party.[52]

46 Ibid., p. 90.

47 J. Anthony Gaughan, *Thomas Johnson, 1872–1963: First Leader of the Labour Party in Dáil Éireann* (Dublin, 1980), p. 81.

48 O'Brien, *Forth the Banners Go*, pp. 116, 291. Mrs Despard also spoke. See *What Happened at Leeds?* (London, 1917), pp. 9, 12.

49 *Irish Labour and its International Relations*, pp. 21–2.

50 Ibid., pp. 22–5.

51 Ibid., pp. 27.

52 RGASPI, report of the SPI to the Third International, 11 June 1920, 495/89/3–10.

On 1 January O'Brien and Séamus Hughes, secretary to the ITGWU executive and an SPI activist, met Richard Mulcahy, TD, regarding Berne. Republicans too had an agenda for Berne, hoping to have their case aired internationally, and Éamon de Valera later acknowledged: 'When we wanted the help of Labour in Berne, Labour gave it to us'.[53] After TDs assembled on 14 January to prepare constitutional documents for the first Dáil, a Sinn Féin press release stated:

> A document drafted by the Irish Workers' Delegation of the International Conference was submitted to the members present, and it was decided that the statement of national claims set out were heartily approved. A committee was appointed to draw up the draft of a programme of constructive work on democratic lines in consultation with the Labour leaders.

The upshot of the quid pro quo was Dáil Éireann's Democratic Programme, drafted by Johnson and O'Shannon, though modified by Seán T. Ó Ceallaigh to make it more palatable to his party.[54] The programme served the twin functions of providing Dáil Éireann with a social manifesto, and Labour with something to offset its lack of parliamentary representation as it strode onto the world stage.

One objection to Labour's association with the Second International came from the ITGWU general secretary. Since October or November 1915 Larkin had devoted himself to freelance anti-war agitation, bankrolled secretly by the Germans.[55] Following the February revolution he spoke of going to Russia, and received $2,000 from Clan na Gael to attend the socialist peace conference in Stockholm that summer, but failed to get away, despite his excellent waterfront contacts. Shortly before the Bolsheviks came to power he helped the Germans recruit 'several men' in San Francisco for propaganda and sabotage in Vladivostok. In 1918, after the Germans had broken with him, he settled in New York, becoming active in the Socialist Party of America. Characteristically, he clashed with party policy and launched his own group, the New York James Connolly Socialist Club, on St Patrick's Day. In April he wrote to Tom Foran: 'You are aware that I have notified our comrades in Russia not to accept any delegations or agents pending advice from your side. My instructions will have reached Petrograd ere this.'[56] When John Reed

53 Mitchell, *Labour in Irish Politics*, p. 112.
54 Farrell, *The Founding of Dáil Éireann*, pp. 57–61.
55 On Larkin at this time see Emmet O'Connor, 'James Larkin in the United States, 1914–1923', *Journal of Contemporary History* 37, 2 (2002), pp. 183–96.
56 ITGWU, *The Attempt to Smash the Irish Transport and General Workers' Union* (Dublin, 1924), p. 167.

addressed the Connolly Club in May, Larkin was captivated. Recently back from Russia, the author of *Ten Days That Shook The World* was revitalising interest in the Bolsheviks. With Jack Carney and Éadhmonn MacAlpine, Larkin plunged his energies over the next 18 months into transforming the Socialist Party into a communist party.[57] The Connolly Club became the national hub of the communist project, housing the editorial offices of his Socialist Party faction's *Revolutionary Age* and Reed's *Voice of Labor*. Following Moscow's call for a communist International in January 1919, Larkin informed Foran: 'Our advice to you and those to be relied on is no conciliation with the Huysmans gang. We have opened up negotiations with Moscow officially.' On this, as on much else during his stay in America, Larkin's instructions to Dublin were ignored. In February Larkin helped to organise a left section of the party in New York, and in June topped the poll in elections to the Socialist Party's national left-wing council. He supported the majority view that the left should try to win control of the party at its national convention in August; a minority faction, dominated by the party's Russian language federation, favoured the immediate formation of a communist party and walked out in protest. The expulsion of the left from the Socialist Party's national convention led to the creation of two parties in September: the Communist Party of America, with some 50,000 members, and the Communist Labor Party, which had about 10,000 members, but more anglophones. Critical of the former's penchant for European style Marxist jargon, and convinced of the need for the party to be 'American', Larkin joined the latter.[58]

Meanwhile, only Johnson and O'Shannon travelled to Switzerland, accredited by the Labour Party and SPI respectively.[59] Both were received as a national delegation, and carried with them lengthy memoranda on Ireland's case for self-determination.[60] The conference passed two resolutions on Ireland, endorsing its right to self-determination and calling for peace talks. Prior to the votes, the Irish persuaded the British Labour Party delegation, led

57 MacAlpine was from Belfast. Carney was raised near Liverpool, and claimed to have been converted to socialism by Larkin in 1906. He worked for the ITGWU in Belfast in 1912, and went to the United States in 1916.

58 Larkin, *James Larkin*, pp. 219–34; Manus O'Riordan, 'Larkin in America: the road to Sing Sing', in Donal Nevin (ed.), *James Larkin: Lion of the Fold* (Dublin, 1998), pp. 67–9.

59 Gaughan, *Thomas Johnson*, p. 160.

60 Two 16-page documents were presented to the conference: *Mémoire sur l'Irlande présenté par la délégation du Parti Ouvrier et Congrés Syndical Irlandais á la Conférence Internationale Ouvrière et Socialiste de Berne*, and *Denkschrift uber irland. Dem Syndikalkongress und der Internationalen Arbeiter- und Sozialistenkonferenz in Bern 1919 von der Abordnung der Arbeiterpartei vorgelegt*. Labour also published the 52-page *Ireland at Berne: Being the Reports and Memoranda presented to the International Labour and Socialist Conference held at Berne, February 1919* (Dublin, 1919).

by Ramsay MacDonald, to replace home rule with self-determination as its position on Ireland. In return, the Irish agreed not to seek recognition of the republic at Berne. Johnson and O'Shannon were elected to the permanent commission of the conference, and drafted a memorandum on Ireland for the congress's delegation to the Paris peace conference. Returning via Paris, they also briefed the Dáil mission to the peace conference. On the main issue at Berne the Irish sided with the leftwing minority, voting against a motion favouring parliamentary democracy as it 'tended to condemn the Soviet system of government', and signing the Adler/Longuet resolution resolution calling for a 'dictatorship of the proletariat'.[61]

The Irish arrived home to acclamation in Sinn Féin circles. 'Thomas Johnson and Cathal O'Shannon have done a good day's work in a very short space of time', noted the republican weekly, *New Ireland*, which published a variety of features on Russia, Bolshevism, and soviets – not uniformly approving – in March and April.[62] In May Frank P. Walsh of the American Friends of Irish Freedom impressed on de Valera the value of a similar embassy to the American Federation of Labor. De Valera agreed, but Johnson thought it impracticable for the moment.[63] Labour too was pleased. When the Johnson and O'Shannon reported at a mass rally in the Mansion House on 7 April, O'Brien judged it 'a good type of meeting'.[64] Next day, de Valera urged the Sinn Féin árd fheis to support Labour's call for a one day strike on 1 May.[65] Declared as a gesture of international proletarian solidarity and for the self-determination of all peoples, the strike applied a recommendation of the Berne conference that May Day celebrations highlight its demand for a democratic league of free peoples, based upon national self-determination. Trumpeting a fanfare for 'the red flag times', 1 May was observed with parades throughout nationalist Ireland, headed in most instances by red flags and banners, despite police warnings that red emblems would be treated as Bolshevist and illegal. In many areas the festivities continued with a concert or an aeríocht.[66]

What was seen by Labour as a shift to the left looked otherwise to the Bolsheviks, in the SPI and in Moscow. The foundation of the Comintern presented the ITGWU leadership with the dilemma of continuing to associate the SPI with the Second International, and suffering the wrath of the left for discarding Bolshevism, or offering a hostage to fortune by committing the

---

61 Mitchell, *Labour in Irish Politics*, pp. 110–11.
62 *New Ireland*, 22 Feb., Mar. and Apr. 1919.
63 Gaughan, *Thomas Johnson*, pp. 160–3.
64 NLI, O'Brien papers, 15705 (12).
65 Gaughan, *Thomas Johnson*, p. 162.
66 Emmet O'Connor, *Syndicalism in Ireland, 1917–23* (Cork, 1988), p. 44.

SPI, and by extension the union, to revolutionism. The Comintern compelled a redefinition of what it meant to be pro-Bolshevik in Ireland, one that would alienate Labour and divide the SPI.

TWO

THE RACE FOR MOSCOW, 1919-21

The centre has sent its representatives to Berne, to the international conference of compromising socialists ...
It is absolutely essential to split the most revolutionary elements off from the 'centre';
this can be done only by the ruthless criticism and exposure of the 'centrist' leaders. The organisational break with the 'centre' is an absolute historical necessity.
Resolution of the first congress of the Third International on the Berne conference[1]

—

Between 1917 and 1920, Bolshevik internationalism was grounded on three convictions: that the October revolution was but one example of a world crisis presaging the death of capitalism; that revolution in the more industrially advanced states of western Europe was vital to the success of Soviet Russia; and that revolutionary struggle in all countries must be directed by the Bolsheviks, or it would succumb to the reformism of the social democrats. The failure to carry the revolution to the west, and the reluctant acceptance of 'socialism in one country' after 1924, merely reinforced belief in the third conviction. By 1918 communist parties had been formed in Germany and eastern Europe. Lenin's urgent requirement was to bring them into the fold. To rally opposition to the Berne congress and pre-empt a revival of the Second International, an invitation was published in *Pravda* on 24 January 1919 to 39 parties or tendencies to send representatives to the first congress of the Third International. One of the 39 was described as 'the revolutionary elements in the Irish workers' organisations'.[2] The congress was to have met on 15 February, but was postponed because of the prevalent problems of communications and travel. Without prior press coverage, and against the wishes of the KPD, the congress convened in the Kremlin on 2 March 1919. Just nine of the 51 delegates were based outside Russia. Swallowing apprehensions about the wisdom of splitting the socialist movement or Russian domination of the new departure, they bowed to Bolshevik pressure to found the Third International on 4 March.[3]

1 Degras, *The Communist International, Vol. 1*, p. 26.
2 Ibid., p. 4.
3 McDermott and Agnew, *The Comintern*, p. 12.

Despite the divisive impact of the Comintern on Ireland, the SPI shared none of the doubts of European revolutionaries. Affiliation to the Third International was seen as the hallmark of revolutionism, and three factions eventually jostled for recognition from the ECCI. Moscow's imprimatur was too of potential importance in acquiring resources. Within weeks of the October revolution, Narkomindel (Narodny Kommissariat Inostrannykh Del, or the Soviet People's Commissariat of Foreign Affairs) was given two million roubles to propagate revolution abroad. In March 1919 Grigori Zinoviev, soon to be president of the Comintern, announced that the VKP(b) would 'offer the workers of other countries great financial and material support'. On 13 April the VKP(b) transferred the funding of foreign communists from Narkomindel to the International.[4] It was not long before Irish communists started to look on the Comintern as a crock of gold.

TRUE BOLSHEVIKS?

From March 1919, policy towards the Third International became a litmus test of revolutionism in the eyes of SPI militants, particularly those in contact with the Glasgow-based Socialist Labour Party of Great Britain (SLP) and its organ the *Socialist*. The SLP felt a kinship with James Connolly and, more than cognate British groups, regarded Ireland as the 'Achilles heel of British capitalism'.[5] Connolly had done much to develop the party in Scotland in 1903, in his De Leonist days. The first issue of the *Socialist* was printed on the press of the Irish Socialist Republican Party, and when the *Irish Worker* was suppressed in 1914, the SLP had it produced in Glasgow and smuggled to Dublin.[6] After Connolly's death, certain ideological affinities continued. Like the SPI, the SLP blended syndicalism and Bolshevism, prioritised education and propaganda over electioneering, and could be risibly sectarian. In 1919 the *Socialist* went weekly, and started a regular column on Ireland, written by Kitty Coyle under the pseudonym Selma Sigerson. A peppery little lady who liked to dress in the syndicalist colours of red and black, Coyle repeatedly attacked the SPI and labour leadership, and stooped to cheap invective against Tom Johnson.[7] Yet she was not alone in Belfast in being impressed by the massive engineering

4   Ibid., pp. 10, 21–2.
5   Raymond Challinor, *The Origins of British Bolshevism* (London, 1977), pp. 266–8.
6   Walter Kendall, *The Revolutionary Movement in Britain, 1900–21: The Origins of British Communism* (London, 1969), p. 375.
7   *Socialist*, 27 Mar. 1919. See also Coyle's pamphlet in *Sinn Féin and Socialism* (Cork Workers' Club Historical Reprints no. 19, n.d.).

strike in the city in January and February, and correspondingly dismayed at the SPI's continuing inaction. At a party general meeting on 27 March, Johnson described her articles in the *Socialist* as 'insane', and Cathal O'Shannon her attack on Johnson as 'damnably rotten, low, and mean', while they in turn were assailed for their 'satisfaction' with Berne, despite its rejection of Bolshevism.[8] O'Shannon attended the next meeting of the Berne conference's permanent commission in Amsterdam on 26–29 April. Though it was to be the SPI's last contact with the Second Internationalists, the party suffered its first split on 7 May when Belfast members launched the Revolutionary SPI in response, it was said, to the SPI's betrayal of the Belfast engineering strike and the Limerick soviet. The party's aim was 'the establishment of socialism' by means of 'direct and revolutionary action upon the industrial and political field', and it made a vain approach to the Citizen Army. The authorities responded vigorously to its initial propaganda campaign, arresting Jack Hedley, alias John or Seán O'Hagan, national organiser, Charles O'Meagher, business manager, and Joseph Ferguson, chairman, together with Simon Greenspon, on charges of unlawful assembly. Ferguson was released with a fine, on account of his age and health. The others were sentenced to six months imprisonment, but released following a hunger and thirst strike.[9] The party failed to develop beyond Belfast, though it claimed the backing of seven ITGWU organisers. Hedley later became an ITGWU organiser himself and, with Seán Dowling, co-ordinated the seizure of 13 Limerick creameries in May 1920 during a strike in the Cleeve Company. The 'soviets', as they were called, were run by the employees until a wage settlement was reached.[10] Hedley's spectacular may have inspired the formation of a branch of the SLP in Belfast in June, but it survived no more than a few weeks.[11]

In Dublin the ITGWU's grip in the SPI faced a more serious challenge from the precocious Roddy Connolly and Seán McLoughlin. Though neither was yet 19 years old, both carried the mantle of Connolly – Roddy par excellence as the son of James – and were brash and impatient, with a wealth of experience under their belts. After the Easter Rising, in which he was aide-de-camp to his father and Patrick Pearse, and a short internment, Roddy had returned to school in Dublin and then in Belfast, where he joined the SPI and

8   *Socialist*, 3 Apr. 1919.

9   *Socialist*, 15 May, 5, 19 June, 3, 24–31 July 1919, 27 May 1920; Austen Morgan, *Labour and Partition: The Belfast Working Class, 1905–23* (London, 1991), pp. 235–6.

10 Greaves, *The Irish Transport and General Workers' Union*, pp. 234–5; O'Connor, *Syndicalism in Ireland*, pp. 51–2; D. R. O'Connor Lysaght, 'The Munster soviet creameries', *Saotharlann Staire Éireann* 1 (1981), pp. 41–2; obituary of Dowling, *Irish Democrat*, Feb. 1949.

11 *Socialist*, 10 June, 15 July 1920.

the Irish Volunteer's H company, led by Joe McKelvey. Later he moved to Dublin and devoted his energies to Fianna Éireann and the Volunteers. In the summer of 1918 he emigrated to Glasgow and worked as a 'dilutee' fitter at the Parkhead forge, a major engineering complex and a centre of Clydeside radicalism, and at Brown's shipyard. Glasgow's Marxists, the Scottish brigade of the Irish Volunteers, and a workers' defence force organised by Willie Gallacher, were currently consolidating a Clydeside connection with Irish revolutionaries that would last into the 1930s. Connolly kept his distance from Glasgow's politics, always pursuing his own line, but Seán McLoughlin was heavily influenced by the SLP. Renowned as the 'boy commandant' of Easter Week, having earned the promotion from James Connolly for leading the insurgents out of the burning General Post Office, McLoughlin had reorganised the Volunteers in Tipperary in 1917–18, and was acquiring a reputation as an outstanding orator.[12] Sharing a frustration with the absence of a socialist input into the independence struggle, and flushed with ambition, talent, and the conceited sectarianism of the hard left, the dynamic duo joined in determining to drive the SPI towards communism. Connolly published an article in the *Voice of Labour* on 10 May 1919 advocating a dictatorship of the proletariat. McLoughlin gave notice in the *Voice* of 21 June of a formal proposal to rename the SPI the Workers' Republican Party, with a programme rejecting 'the principle laid down by many in Ireland, that the functions of a Socialist Party are purely educational'.[13] In September they led a soi-disant Bolshevik faction to win control of SPI, elect McLoughlin as president, rescind ties with the Berne International, and pass a resolution for affiliation to the Comintern.[14]

The Bolshevik coup prompted a reaction from clergy and the press. An editorial in the *Irish Independent* deplored the anti-Christian doctrines 'championed by the Russian Soviets and by the late James Connolly, doctrines which the "Socialist Party of Ireland" distribute among the illiterate in Dublin from their headquarters in Liberty Hall'.[15] It has been suggested that the 'red scare' threw the left on the defensive, frightened the *Watchword of Labour* into publishing the front page article, 'A Catholic may be a socialist', on 19 October, and panicked the ITGWU into reining in the SPI; all of which is

---

12　NA, McLoughlin's submission to the Bureau of Military History, WS 290.

13　I am obliged to Charlie McGuire for details on Connolly and McLoughlin. See also Milotte, *Communism in Modern Ireland*, pp. 39–40; McInerney, 'Roddy Connolly: 60 years of political activity'.

14　Milotte, *Communism in Modern Ireland*, p. 39; Thomas Darragh [Roddy Connolly and Éadhmonn MacAlpine], 'Revolutionary Ireland and communism', *Communist International*, no. 11–12, June–July 1920; *Socialist*, 23 Oct. 1919.

15　*Irish Independent*, 3 Oct. 1919.

doubtful.[16] There was little fear of Russia or the Church in the contemporary labour movement. 'A Catholic may be a socialist' reviewed Fr J. E. Canavan's pamphlet *How Far May a Catholic Agree with Socialists?*, which the *Watchword* commended as a refutation of the 'childish effusion on Socialism in *Studies*' by Fr Peter Finlay, theological censor of the archdiocese of Dublin. Moreover, O'Brien, Johnson and O'Shannon, joined their SPI critics at a well attended celebration of the second anniversary of the October revolution in Dublin Trades' Hall on 8 November. After the speeches, the festivities continued with an 'all-night social and dance' at 42 North Great Georges' Street, interrupted by a midnight lecture on, inevitably, 'the Bolshevik revolution'. Other SPI commemorations were held in Cork's City Hall, and the Co-operative Hall, Queenstown, and O'Shannon devoted the next issue of the *Watchword* to Russia.[17]

The ITGWU's commitment to the SPI began to slacken in 1920 as O'Brien's attention turned to wars on other fronts. O'Brien and Dublin trades' council's secretary, P. T. Daly, were old antagonists. Daly was identified with Larkinite elements in the ITGWU, and it was no secret that O'Brien was hostile to Larkin and suspected that Larkinites would attempt to remove him from office on Big Jim's return. In October Éadhmonn MacAlpine, who would become a prominent Irish Bolshevik, addressed the council on Larkin's difficulties in obtaining a passport from the British to return to Ireland. The council's response was soon overtaken by events. With America gripped by major strikes and a 'red scare', bodies like the New York Senate's Lusk committee had been empowered to combat Bolshevism. On 8 November Larkin was one of 2,000 suspects detained by Lusk committee agents.[18] Two days later he was charged with 'criminal anarchy', i.e. advocating the violent overthrow of the government, for his part in publishing the Socialist Party of America's 'Left-wing manifesto' in *Revolutionary Age* on 5 July 1919.[19] On 3 May 1920 he was sentenced to five to ten years imprisonment. Meanwhile, O'Brien refused to co-operate with Dublin trades' council's Larkin defence committee, saying the union would look after its general secretary. The committee would become a centre of Larkinite opposition to

16 Michael Laffan, '"Labour must wait": Ireland's conservative revolution', in Patrick J. Corish (ed.), *Radicals, Rebels, and Establishments* (Belfast, 1985), p. 211. Roddy Connolly made similar claims in Darragh, 'Revolutionary Ireland and communism'.

17 *Watchword of Labour*, 15 Nov. 1919.

18 Benjamin Gitlow, *The Whole of Their Lives: Communism in America, A Personal History and Intimate Portrayal of its Leaders* (Belmont, Ma., 1965), p. 42; NLI, O'Brien papers, 15679 (15).

19 Larkin, *James Larkin*, p. 237.

O'Brien and complaints of ITGWU inaction.[20] In truth, the ITGWU did what it could. Tom Foran assured the New York Connolly Club of ITGWU support, and offered to pay Larkin's legal costs.[21] In December 1919 O'Brien objected to the trades' council's list of candidates for the forthcoming municipal elections, and the ITGWU disaffiliated. Now more influenced by Larkinites and less beholden to the interests of the Congress leadership, the trades' council moved to the left, voting in May 1920 for the ILPTUC to affiliate to the Third International, and earning for itself the soubriquet 'the all-red council'. Repeated attempts to heal the division proved fruitless and the ITGWU led the formation of a rival Workers' Council in 1921.[22]

Dublin labour's emerging civil war was more important to O'Brien than the SPI. He did not stand for an officership at the party's bi-annual general meeting on 2 January 1920, and to counter the trades' council's list in the municipal elections that month, the ITGWU fielded its own slate of six nominees – including two SPI comrades, O'Brien and Thomas Kennedy.[23] In its sole electoral intervention, the SPI was left to run a solitary candidate, Walter Carpenter Sr, secretary of the 700 strong International Tailors', Machinists', and Pressers' Trade Union, known colloquially as 'the Jewish union'. The SLP produced his election address, no Dublin printer being willing to risk invoking the wrath of the authorities. His polling card was printed locally, but the words 'workers' republic in Ireland' were omitted. Unlike the ITGWU men – who stood on a more ambiguous 'Workers' Republican' platform – Carpenter was not returned.[24]

The escalation of British counter-insurgency – with over 4,000 military raids in February 1920 alone – inevitably affected the increasingly republican labour movement, and managing the consequences of Labour's deepening entanglement with the national struggle presented a second distraction to the ITGWU. The practice of confiscating the *Watchword of Labour* each week, begun during the local elections, was continued over the coming months.

20 Greaves, *The Irish Transport and General Workers' Union*, pp. 284–5; C. Desmond Greaves, *Seán O'Casey: Politics and Art* (London, 1979), p. 99.

21 NLI, O'Brien papers, 15678 (1), 15676 (2); ITGWU, *The Attempt to Smash*, pp. 137–8.

22 Cody, O'Dowd, and Rigney, *The Parliament of Labour*, pp. 126–33.

23 *Watchword of Labour*, 10 Jan. 1920.

24 *Watchword of Labour*, 3–31 Jan. 1920; O'Brien, *Forth the Banners Go*, p. 170; *Socialist*, 15 Jan. 1920. The International Tailors', Machinists', and Pressers' Trade Union was founded in 1908 by Jewish immigrants from Russia. Carpenter became secretary in 1913, when membership stood at 35. After 1915 the union expanded and became predominantly Catholic. Terminal illness forced Carpenter's resignation as secretary in 1925. He died in 1926. Manus O'Riordan, 'Connolly socialism and the Jewish worker', *Saothar* 13 (1988), p. 127; Sarah Ward-Perkins (ed.), *Select Guide to Trade Union Records in Dublin: With Details of Unions Operating in Ireland to 1970* (Dublin, 1996), pp. 58–9.

More than a dozen ITGWU officials were arrested. Branch meetings were disrupted by soldiers, and union offices and Liberty Hall searched repeatedly.[25] O'Brien was arrested on 3 March, and imprisoned in Wormwood Scrubs, where he joined republicans on hunger strike. Irish sympathisers in Stockport, Cheshire, took advantage of a Westminster by-election in the constituency to lobby the British Labour Party on Ireland and on O'Brien's treatment. Receiving little satisfaction, O'Brien was nominated to stand on 16 March in protest at 'the apostasy of the [British] Labour Party on the question of Irish self-determination and against the inactivity in the face of military tyranny in Ireland'. O'Brien himself accused the party of retreating from the promises it had made at Berne to the British government policy of Home Rule. The ILPTUC and SPI invested heavily in the campaign. Under the pseudonym 'Conor Hayes', O'Shannon spoke at several meetings, and met his future wife, Margaret Doris Finn, at a rally in Manchester Free Trade Hall. O'Brien polled 2,336 votes, drawing the support of virtually the entire Stockport Irish community. He had earlier ended his hunger strike on being transferred to a nursing home and was released on 12 May.[26] O'Shannon, who was not in good health, was arrested at an international labour meeting in London on 11 April. He was eventually released from Mountjoy gaol on 5 May after an eight day hunger strike.[27] In the midst of this pressure, on 12 April, the ILPTUC enjoyed its finest hour, when it called an immediate, indefinite general strike – its third in three years – for the release of political prisoners on hunger strike. Co-ordinated by workers' councils, some of which assumed a 'soviet' style command of local government for the duration, the strike was a spectacular demonstration of Labour power. Dublin Castle released the prisoners after two days, leaving the ILPTUC simultaneously cock-a-hoop about its prospects and worried about how far it could go without provoking a ruinous reaction from the authorities.

Nonetheless there were elements in the ITGWU who remained interested in the SPI. O'Shannon was elected president in January, McLoughlin being absent in Scotland on a lecture tour.[28] Nor is it fair to say that O'Shannon's election swung the party to the right. The SPI sent repeated requests to Sylvia Pankhurst, secretary of the British Workers' Socialist Federation, and Albert

---

25 *Watchword of Labour*, 31 Jan. to 21 Feb., 13 Mar. 1920.

26 O'Connor, 'Labour lives: Cathal O'Shannon'; O'Brien, *Forth the Banners Go*, pp. 190–4; Greaves, *The Irish Transport and General Workers' Union*, pp. 263–4; Michael Herbert, *The Wearing of the Green: A Political History of the Irish in Manchester* (London, 2001), p. 99; *Manchester Guardian*, 12 Apr. 1920.

27 *Watchword of Labour*, 24 Apr. 1920; Greaves, *The Irish Transport and General Workers' Union*, pp. 264–5, 268.

28 *Watchword of Labour*, 10 Jan. 1920; *Socialist*, 10 June 1920.

Inkpin, secretary of the British Socialist Party, requesting them to pursue its affiliation to the Third International.[29] This meant nothing to their critics on the left, who responded to O'Shannon's election by convening their own factions, and cultivating contacts with the Comintern. Connolly, with Éadhmonn MacAlpine, created the Communist Groups, and liaised with Pankhurst and Inkpin.[30] McLoughlin formed the Workers' Communist Party, and forwarded a statement to the Comintern's Amsterdam sub-bureau. Describing the SPI as 'now nearly defunct', the document, astutely, pinned the blame on Berne: 'it never survived the blow when O'Shannon, Hughes [*sic*] and Johnson went to Berne . . . it is now practically in the hands of the Office staff of "Liberty Hall", who are anything but Socialists'. Amsterdam circulated the statement, and it was published in the *Socialist*.[31]

A patently peeved SPI sent two replies to the ECCI, both of which illustrated its misreading of Moscow's mind. A stiff rebuke deplored the Amsterdam bureau's 'un-comradely, indeed dastardly conduct', suggested the report was the work of a Dublin Castle spy, and affirmed the party as the only 'true' Bolsheviks in Ireland.[32] A more substantial and reasoned defence followed in June, citing its record in propaganda and education, and claiming to have maintained its 'Marxian character', and exerted a seminal influence in the development of the ITGWU's syndicalism and on the ILPTUC's direct action since 1917. Failure to make greater progress was attributed to British terrorism, 'approved and confirmed by the inaction of the British Labour Party', and 'the preoccupation of the people with the struggle against British Imperialism'. The latter excuse was at odds not merely with the facts, but with what the Comintern wanted to hear from Ireland. The SPI also underestimated the handicap of its association with Berne. While it now renounced the Second International, it blundered again in saying that one of its aims at Berne, 'to cleanse the working class movement from the elements of social

---

29 RGASPI, George Spain to Sylvia Pankhurst, 2 Mar. 1920, 495/89/3–3/4; George Spain to Albert Inkpin, 17 May 1920, 495/89/3–2; *Watchword of Labour*, 6 Mar. 1920.

30 *Socialist*, 18 Mar. 1920; RGASPI, report to Kobietsky for the ECCI, 10 Feb. 1921, 495/89/10–2/4a; report on the work of the Irish Communist Groups, 1921, 495/89/2–30/33; report of the CPI to the ECCI, Oct. 1921 to Oct. 1922, 495/89/16–44.

31 RGASPI, Communication of the Amsterdam sub-bureau of the IIIrd International: the political and working class organisation in Ireland, 495/89/104–150/152; *Socialist*, 27 May 1920. The Amsterdam bureau opened in Nov. 1919, to offset Moscow's peripherality, and was closed in 1920. Séamus Hughes had been delegated to Berne but withdrew to attend ITGWU business. Morrissey, *A Man called Hughes*, p. 102.

32 Anderson, *James Connolly and the Irish Left*, pp. 126, 142; Milotte, *Communism in Modern Ireland*, p. 40.

patriotism and coalition with capitalism . . . was defeated by the abstention of
the Communist elements'.[33]

McLoughlin had already slipped out of contention in the race for Moscow's
approbation. For the moment he had parted company with Connolly, and
knew nothing of his intrigues with the Comintern until September. In May
he had founded the Communist Labour Party, and written to Moscow for
financial assistance for a party paper.[34] June and July saw him in Scotland,
lecturing for the SLP, and working with Larkinites in Dublin for Big Jim's
release. In August he and Paddy Stephenson launched a weekly lecture
programme for the Communist Labour Party in Dublin Trades' Hall. The
trades' council denied them the hall in October, and the party in any case
never amounted to much more than McLoughlin and Stephenson.[35] Sometime
in mid 1920 McLoughlin was asked by Michael Collins and Cathal Brugha to
undertake agitational work with the British left, to generate support for
Ireland and establish networks of arms supply and sabotage. Although as
recently as 27 May he had argued that an Irish workers' republic would not
survive without a socialist Britain, he claimed subsequently – for reasons
maddeningly unspecified – that he was 'most hostile' to the proposal, and
agreed to go only because continual harrassment from the authorities in
Ireland gave him little alternative. Leaving Dublin for Sheffield three days
after 'Bloody Sunday', he spent the remainder of the War of Independence as
a roving orator for the SLP, 'The greatest propaganda speaker I have ever
heard', according to one party veteran.[36]

Still believing itself to be in good standing with Moscow, the SPI nominated two delegates, O'Shannon and Frank Robbins, to the second world
congress of the Comintern. In the event, neither attended, as the party was
unable to raise the required expenses at short notice. Whether it had received
a direct invitation or was responding to the 'call' of the congress is unclear.
What is known is that Connolly and Éadhmonn MacAlpine were already
Russia bound.[37] In Russia they would persuade the Comintern to endorse
their faction with an article in the *Communist International* attacking the SPI

33 RGASPI, report of the SPI to the Third International, 11 June 1920, 495/89/3–7/14.
34 RGASPI, report of the Irish Communist Labour Party to the Third International, 20 May 1920,
495/89/2–3/5.
35 *Socialist*, 8 July, 5 Aug., 16–23 Sept., 14–28 Oct. 1920.
36 NA, submission of Seán McLoughlin to the Bureau of Military History, WS 290; Challinor, *The
Origins of British Bolshevism*, pp. 266–8; *Socialist*, 27 May, 30 Dec. 1920, 14–21 Apr. 1921
37 Milotte, *Communism in Modern Ireland*, p. 41; *Watchword of Labour*, 3 July 1920; *Communist*, 8
Oct. 1921. See also Connolly's account of his journey in McInerney, 'Roddy Connolly: 60 years of
political activity'.

as 'a party numbering scarcely 150 members in Dublin, about 30 of whom may be considered effective members, and a few hundred throughout the country, badly organised and having no direct communication with each other or the Dublin headquarters'.[38] Connolly had won the race. He had the advantage of his pedigree and presence in Russia, but there were other factors involved. Getting the International up and running was the overriding concern at the first world congress. The second congress was intended to separate reliable from unreliable supporters. The SPI was compromised by its association with Berne and reformists, and McLoughlin by his ties with the SLP, which split over the unity talks on the formation of the CPGB, with a majority taking a hostile stance. Connolly on the other hand, was in cahoots with the right people, especially Inkpin, a co-founder of the CPGB, and Erkki Veltheim, the ECCI's emissary to Britain, who was instrumental in establishing communications with Russia.[39] Furthermore, whereas the SPI and McLoughlin had complained of the national struggle hindering the development of class politics, Connolly convinced his contacts that he had influence in the Citizen Army. This was more in line with what the Comintern wanted to hear.[40] In addition to credentials from the Communist Groups, he and MacAlpine carried to Russia 'a supplementary mandate' from the Citizen Army, along with a personal mandate from Jim Larkin. Evidently they hoodwinked the ECCI into thinking they enjoyed significant support in Ireland, as they were offered four decisive votes in the congress. With a rare touch of humility, they accepted only consultative votes.[41]

The SPI's tenuous relationship with communism continued. In August it announced that it was 'unable' to send an envoy to the foundation conference of the CPGB, but it posted fraternal greetings: 'no difference of principle or tactics divides us from the Communist international', stated the message, which pointedly went on: 'a Socialist Party which does not arise from the popular masses is no more than a Socialist sect'.[42] The ILPTUC's annual conference in August marked the end of Labour's flirtation with communism, signalled the beginning of a long isolation from labour internationalism, and further undermined the SPI's credibility. When the national executive's report cited

38   Darragh, 'Revolutionary Ireland and communism'.

39   Veltheim, a Finn, was also known as Andersen, Kendall, *The Revolutionary Movement in Britain*, pp. 246–55.

40   *Socialist*, 18 Mar. 1920; RGASPI, report to Kobietsky for the ECCI, 10 Feb. 1921, 495/89/10–2/4a; report on the work of the Irish Communist Groups, 1921, 495/89/2–30/33; report of the CPI to the ECCI, Oct. 1921 to Oct. 1922, 495/89/16–44.

41   *Socialist*, 6 Apr. 1922.

42   *Watchword of Labour*, 7 Aug. 1920; *Communist*, 5 Aug. 1920.

division and disorganisation among the socialist parties of the world as its reason for not affiliating to either International, Éamonn Rooney, an SPI rebel, tabled a resolution challenging Congress's specious neutrality. In the ensuing debate O'Shannon alone defended the SPI from disparagement from the right and denounced the Second International as 'a moribund body, dead and done with, having nobody supporting it except the pro-war Social Democrats in Germany and the pro-war Labour party in England'. Pointing out that the Comintern's decision to limit its membership to communist parties debarred the ILPTUC, he implied that the SPI would pursue an independent line from Congress, declaring 'the Socialist Party of Ireland is a Communist Party'. By contrast, O'Brien treated the debate with some amusement. When cited as one of the 'cranks who thought they were Socialists', he interjected 'Mr Chairman, I can produce documentary evidence that I am not a Socialist, and have never been a Socialist (laughter)', a reference to the Workers' Communist Party report. O'Shannon alone among the ITGWU delegates voted for Rooney's motion, which was rejected by 97–54 votes. Dublin trades' council then withdrew a motion calling on Congress to affiliate to the Comintern. The resolution is worth noting as an illustration of the tendency in Ireland to judge the Internationals in terms of their policy on international relations.

> Whereas the Second Internationale at a recent Conference in Lucerne passed a resolution embodying the principle of recognition of the right of Britain to send an Army of Occupation into Armenia; and whereas, in the opinion of this Congress, their attitude in regard to the Soviet Government of Russia is not above suspicion, this Congress hereby directs the National Executive to withdraw the affiliation of the Irish Labour Party and Trade Union Congress from the Second Internationale immediately; and, furthermore, directs its affiliation with the Third Internationale.[43]

O'Shannon persisted, publicising Moscow's call for the creation of the Profintern, and printing its manifesto – for the first time in western Europe – in the *Watchword of Labour* on 2 October.[44]

If O'Brien wanted an excuse to be rid of his nagging proto-communist colleagues, the British provided it. Aside from a summer recess, the Dublin SPI had sustained its usual weekly lectures up to November 1920, while greater activity was reported in the spring of the year from Belfast and Newbridge.[45]

---

43 Irish Labour History Archive, ILPTUC, *Annual Report* (1920), pp. 96–109. On Rooney see RGASPI, report on the work of the Irish Communist Groups, 1921, 495/89/2–30.

44 See also the *Watchword of Labour*, 4 Sept. 1920.

45 *Watchword of Labour*, 21 Feb., 6 Mar., 3, 24 Apr., 16 Oct. 1920.

In November the Auxiliary Division twice raided 42 North Great George's Street, confiscating SPI literature, records, regalia and furniture, causing extensive damage to its rooms and creating major financial liabilities. The Auxiliaries inflicted similar attention on the James Connolly Labour College, seizing its entire library and available lectures notes and records, and on Liberty Hall, arresting various officials, including O'Brien and George Spain, SPI secretary and an ITGWU clerk. The disruption compelled the suspension of the *Watchword* in December, which left Labour without a paper until October 1921. Despite efforts at holding classes in early 1921, the college never recovered.[46] The SPI remained inactive until the Anglo-Irish truce on 11 July 1921.

THE SECOND WORLD CONGRESS

Since March 1919 the Comintern had made a few favourable references to Ireland. At the inaugural congress, Iosef Fineberg, the sole British delegate, referred briefly to Sinn Féin as a 'purely national movement' and looked forward to the development of class struggle in Ireland. The congress's 'manifesto to the proletarians of the whole world' acknowledged 'enslaved' Ireland while affirming that the liberation of the colonies would only follow revolutions in Britain and France. Soviet propaganda was less circumspect. *Zhizn' natsional'nostei*, organ of the People's Commissariat of Nationalities, declared that the Irish revolution 'embraced the Irish masses totally', adding that Sinn Féin would find self-determination impossible under capitalism, and 'From this to Bolshevism is only one step'. In 1920 *Zhizn' natsional'nostei* observed that probably no threat to the stability of the British empire 'is so direct and serious as the Irish movement of Sinn Féiners'.[47] The Comintern's second world congress, held in Petrograd and Moscow between 19 July and 7 August 1920, marked the real beginning of communist policy on Ireland. Arguably it was also the real foundation of the Comintern. Over 200 delegates from 37 countries attended. The congress endorsed Lenin's belief that the Comintern should function as the general staff of a world party, directing national policies according to a global strategy, and adopted the controversial '21 conditions' stipulating for the first time the nature and tasks required of affiliates.[48]

46   *Watchword of Labour*, 27 Nov., 4 Dec. 1920; *Voice of Labour*, 22 Oct. 1921; ITGWU, *Fifty Years of Liberty Hall: The Golden Jubilee of the Irish Transport and General Workers' Union, 1909–59* (Dublin, n.d.), p. 77; *Socialist*, 17 Feb. 1921.

47   Stephen White, 'Ireland, Russia, communism, post-communism', *Irish Studies in International Affairs* 8 (1997), pp. 155–61.

48   McDermott and Agnew, *The Comintern*, pp. 17–18.

Getting to Russia was in itself an adventure, and a test of any cadre's mettle. Connolly and MacAlpine travelled with financial help from Captain Jack White, the former Citizen Army commander, and Veltheim, who sold Russian jewels to a Swede for the purpose.[49] Having stowed away from Hull to Bergen in a coal hold, they were passed through a network of Norwegian socialists to Vardo, from where they took the mailboat to Murmansk, surviving a storm which had the captain and crew incapacitated for a day, and Connolly resigned to a watery grave. There followed a three-day journey to Petrograd and an attack on their train by aircraft of the British intervention force. In Petrograd they were greeted by Zinoviev and John Reed. The credentials they received on 24 June made no reference to the SPI, Connolly being described as an Irish communist, and MacAlpine as 'presently with the American communist party'. In congress reports they were referred to as 'X' and 'Y'; the ECCI agreed to the anonymity on being told they were 'on the run'.[50] A third Irishman, Patrick Quinlan, who had worked with James Connolly and Larkin in the USA, vainly sought admission to the congress as an observer. Quinlan had travelled from America 'to deliver messages from Irish organisations' to the Soviet authorities, and said he wished to attend the congress on a fact-finding mission for William O'Brien and Tom Johnson, though he did not suggest that he had been sent on their behalf. If he was not affiliated to a communist party, neither, he added, were certain 'individuals who represent no one but themselves'.[51] As an activist in the Socialist Party of America, Quinlan was no doubt familiar with MacAlpine, and may have had Connolly in mind also.

The mood among those lucky enough to be admitted to the star-studded confluence of revolutionaries was euphoric. Aside from the prevailing expectation of the revolution being carried into western Europe as the Red Army advanced on Warsaw, they could gaze only in awe at the symbols of Bolshevism draping the old Tsarist capital. The congress met in the Tauride palace, former assembly house of the Duma, and now the Uritsky Theatre, after one of the Soviet leaders assassinated by counter-revolutionaries. As the grand opening parade set off from the Smolny Institute to the Uritsky, Reed escorted Connolly and MacAlpine to the head of the procession and introduced them

49 Kendall, *The Revolutionary Movement in Britain*, pp. 246–55.
50 Heather Laskey, 'Roddy Connolly revisits Moscow', *The Irish Times*, 22 Oct. 1974; RGASPI, Communist International, 24 June 1920, 489/1/30; *Socialist*, 6 Apr. 1922.
51 Quinlan's application was received through Tom Quelch, British Socialist Party. RGASPI, Quinlan to the committee, 1920, 495/89/4–21/23. It is possibly Quinlan who, writing as 'John P. Thomson', sent reports to Ireland from Stockholm and Petrograd, referred to in the *Watchword of Labour*, 29 May 1920.

to Lenin. Connolly thought he spoke English with a Rathmines accent, acquired from his tutor.[52] The Irish delegates had arrived with a report intended to secure backing for an Irish section of the International. Their paper opened with a short paragraph on Ireland's strategic position as a flashpoint adjacent to the heart of British imperialism and the homeland of a diaspora spread throughout the empire and the USA. In greater detail it anticipated a party engaging in various theatres of activity, such as trade unions and the co-operative movement, as well as with elements of the national struggle. Taking a purely tactical view of nationalism, it described the IRA as both 'potentially white guards' and fertile ground for red propaganda, and suggested that Ulster would be less complicated territory for communists as its anti-nationalist proletariat was more amenable to class politics. Implying that success in Ireland would be contingent on the British proletariat, the document looked forward to the closest co-operation with the CPGB, leading to a federated workers' republic of Britain and Ireland. All in all, the paper conformed to the thinking of the first world congress.[53]

Connolly was appointed to the commission on the national and colonial question, and the commission's theses caused the Irish to invert the emphasis in their analysis, and give priority to the national revolution and its geo-political significance instead of treating it as one factor in the matrix of party-building. It was already indicative of Comintern interests that items on Ireland in the congress news bulletins for delegates dealt entirely with the independence struggle, noting with implicit satisfaction that 'The revolutionary movement in Ireland continues unabated'.[54] Drafted and introduced by Lenin, the theses defined the international system in terms of oppressor and oppressed nations and the attitude of states to Soviet Russia, distinguished between oppressor and oppressed nationalisms, and decided that capitalism was not a prerequisite of revolution in backward countries. Critically, communists were enjoined to ally with liberation movements in the colonies. Opposition to truck with the bourgeoisie was surmounted with the adoption

---

52 Connolly also recalled meeting the ballerina Ekaterina Vasilyeona Geltzer, who complained to him of the state's neglect of the ballet. He relayed the complaints to Lenin, who addressed the problem. Impressed, Geltzer invited him to dinner and proposed marriage. Connolly declined, and thought the proposal was inspired by her desire to leave Russia. McInerney, 'Roddy Connolly: 60 years of political activity'.

53 RGASPI, report on the situation in Ireland, E. MacAlpine, Roderic J. Connolly, 7 July 1920, 5/3/581–1/8; a modified version of the report was published as Darragh, 'Revolutionary Ireland and communism'.

54 RGASPI, Bulletin for the delegates to the second congress of the Communist International, 5 July, 16 July 1920, 489/1/54–33/34.

of provisos that they should be 'national revolutionary', and not hostile to communist organisation of the masses.[55]

Connolly and MacAlpine quickly ditched their ambivalence on nationalism for something more akin to Lenin's worldview. Both addressed the congress on 28 July. 'Any force', said Connolly, 'that tends to hinder the free play of the imperialist states against the developing world revolution must be encouraged and actively supported by the Communist International'. He did not portray Irish republicans as socially radical. Rather would they pragmatically 'avail themselves of every weapon against British imperialism', and communists in Ireland could be empowered if the Comintern made them the vehicle of aid to the separatists.[56]

The Irish headed home with approval for a party and for their tactics, only to encounter setbacks in both respects. On 20 October Veltheim was arrested in London with a coded letter in his possession saying: 'Impossible to go successfully [to] Ireland to start party, etc., or negotiate Irish Republican mission without money. Present using £300 sent to Irish unions whilst awaiting news.'[57] In May Dublin dockers, and later railwaymen, had refused to handle or convey British munitions, emulating dockers who had blacked the *Jolly George* in London, as she awaited arms for Poland, then at war with the Red Army. Over 500 men were sacked before the struggle was called off on 14 December.[58] To add to Connolly's embarrassment, the *Russian Press Review* had already gazetted the donation of £300 to Irish railwaymen. Johnson, as secretary of the ILPTUC, denied receipt of any money from Russia, Moscow tendered no explanation, and Dr Pat McCartan, later the Irish Republic's envoy to Russia, informed the Dáil secretariat that Connolly and McAlpine had squandered the £300. More plausibly, McCartan concluded from his Russian sojourn that Connolly and MacAlpine had been promised £3,000 to activate the Citizen Army. Certainly they tried. The *Communist International* published Citizen Army resolutions of solidarity with the Red Army, adopted on the third anniversary of the Bolshevik revolution at a meeting with Connolly in the chair and MacAlpine as principal speaker. However, Connolly managed to stage this coup, its effect was

55   Degras, *The Communist International, Vol. I*, p. 139.

56   Pathfinder, *The Communist International in Lenin's Time, Vol. One: Workers' of the World and Oppressed Peoples Unite! Proceedings and Documents of the Second Congress, 1920* (New York, 1991), pp. 248–9.

57   Kendall, *The Revolutionary Movement in Britain*, p. 255.

58   Mitchell, *Labour in Irish Politics*, pp. 120–1; Charles Townshend, 'The Irish railway strike of 1920: industrial action and civil resistance in the struggle for independence', *Irish Historical Studies* XXI, 83 (1979), pp. 212–82.

ephemeral, and according to McCartan his failure to mobilise the Citizen Army led the Comintern to regard him as 'too lazy to be a Communist'.[59] In fairness to Connolly, the post Rising Citizen Army was more infamously lethargic under its procrastinating commandant.

If the Comintern endorsed the policy of channelling support to Ireland through Irish communists, Narkomindel had another agenda. Labour remained interested in developing trade with Russia, and in 1920 Johnson and O'Brien met Leonid Krassin and Lev Kamenev, then in London to secure an Anglo-Russian trade agreement and British backing for a Russo-Polish armistice. Johnson suggested, to no great effect, the political and economic advantages of a monopoly of Russian flax imports being granted to a Dublin-based co-operative. But Kamenev, a member of the ECCI and one of the ruling triumvirate on Lenin's death, was enthusiatic about a Labour dele-gation to Russia. Both sides promised to consider making arrangements.[60]

The Russians were no more discriminate towards republicans. In May 1917 the supreme council of the Irish Republican Brotherhood (IRB), deeming itself to be the government of the Republic, appointed McCartan as its envoy to Russia, where 'the representatives of the workmen, soldiers and sailors had referred to Ireland in a friendly resolution; and we believed they would soon be in power'.[61] McCartan was re-routed to the USA instead, when republicans decided that President Woodrow Wilson's talk of peace based on self-deter-mination sounded more promising. After the Bolshevik revolution, agents of the two pariah states opened contact in America. Harry Boland and de Valera had lengthy discussions with Russian representatives in Washington, DC in the spring of 1920. A mutual recognition treaty was negotiated in June, Dáil Éireann authorised a mission to Russia with a view to opening diplomatic relations, and in October the Republic loaned $20,000 to the Soviet govern-ment.[62] Connolly's hopes of exploiting this situation came to nothing. On 17 November he and MacAlpine advised the Dáil secretariat that they were the 'only accredited agents empowered to negotiate for the initiation of diplomatic negotiations' with Russia, and enclosed credentials. What may be a draft reads:

> In accordance with the instructions laid down by the Theses and resolutions on 'The National and Colonial Question' adopted by the Second Congress of the

59 Gaughan, *Thomas Johnson*, p. 153; RGASPI, Johnson to W. N. Ewer, 21 May 1921, 495/89/9–3; on McCartan in Russia see NLI, Patrick McCartan papers, reports on Russia from mission, Feb. to June 1921, as envoy of the Republic of Ireland, 17682; *Communist International* (1921), vol. 3, pp. 16–17 p. 120. I am obliged to Charlie McGuire for drawing my attention to the *Communist International*.

60 Gaughan, *Thomas Johnson*, pp. 196, 442–3.

61 Patrick McCartan, *With de Valera in America* (Dublin, 1932), pp. 2–3.

62 Mitchell, *Labour in Irish Politics*, pp. 189–92.

Third International, the Executive Committee of the Third International has decided to assist by all means in its power the National Revolutionary movement in Ireland. For this purpose it hereby invites a Commission composed of members of the presently constituted Republican Government to visit Russia for the purpose for the purpose of entering into direct negotiations as to how the Third International can exert its influence to actively assist the National Revolutionary movement in Ireland, and to allow the Commission to study, investigate and report on the structure and Constitution of and conditions of life in the Russian Socialist Federated Soviet Republic. The bearers of this document, RODERIC CONNOLLY and EADMONN MACALPINE, Irish Communists, are hereby appointed representatives of the Third International to negotiate for the acceptance of this invitation. The Commission must include a recognised member of the Communist Group of Ireland (Section of the Third International) . . . The Commission must not include any other except this one Communist . . . The first and essential condition of this invitation is the observance of the strictest secrecy in Ireland and elsewhere, regarding not only this invitation but all negotiations connected with it.[63]

The secretariat replied that it would deal with the Russian government alone and obliged the Comintern only in ordering the destruction of the credentials.[64]

While the Russians were keen on a treaty in 1920, de Valera hesitated, apprehensive about the impact on the bigger prize of winning recognition from the United States. He had to contend also with a British intelligence campaign to portray the independence struggle as increasingly Bolshevist. It was alleged in the House of Commons in November that the Soviets were sending four million roubles to Sinn Féin; an intelligence report later advised that Maxim Litvinov had arranged for the payment of £50,000. In March 1921 the British legation in Berne reported that a recent meeting of senior western European communists had decided that the CPGB 'should get in touch with the Sinn Feiners and arrange a programme of common action', and seek to replace certain Sinn Féin leaders with communist sympathisers. German communists were to acquire a printing plant for Sinn Féin propaganda. One month later the British secret service reported from Moscow that a British Labour Party representative had been asked to undertake Comintern work in Ireland. The British parliamentary paper, *Intercourse Between Bolshevism and Sinn Féin*, including the text of the proposed Ireland–Russia recognition

---

63   RGASPI, undated document, without a rubric, 1920, 495/89/3–24.
64   Arthur Mitchell, *Revolutionary Government in Ireland: Dáil Éireann, 1919–22* (Dublin, 1995), pp. 189–92; NA, Dáil Éireann papers, DE 2/119.

treaty, appeared in June 1921.[65] When de Valera finally decided to send McCartan to Moscow, the Soviets had gone cold on ties with the Republic, for fear of jeopardising trade negotiations with Britain. Johnson and O'Brien, drawing on their impressions of Krassin and Kamenev, said as much at a conference of the ILPTUC executive and Dáil ministers in January 1921.[66]

McCartan arrived in Moscow on 14 February to assess the value of a propaganda office in Russia and, he hoped, conclude trade and recognition treaties. Connolly met him off the train and escorted him to the Comintern's overcrowded Hotel Lux, grabbing the chance to move into McCartan's coveted single room.[67] McCartan suffered his compatriot, but protested when Connolly's bed was taken by a Welsh miner. McCartan appreciated the significance of being lodged in the Lux, rather than one of the Narkomindel hotels: the presence of an Irish diplomat embarrassed his hosts. Foreign commissar G. V. Chicherin received him promptly, and enquired after the Citizen Army, but refused to entertain the sale of rifles or ammunition to the IRA. Though assured by Santeri Nuorteva, his contact in Narkomindel, that Chicherin 'was not in a position to know' about arms sales, and that McCartan would be put in touch with 'the man who had charge of that department', Nuorteva was arrested within weeks as a British spy and executed. An Anglo-Russian trade agreement was signed on 17 March, providing, inter alia, for an end to Soviet propaganda against Britain. McCartan was still 'very optimistic' in May, but advised Dáil Éireann that Russian commitment to a treaty was affected by a belief that the Irish would compromise on their demand for independence. McCartan left empty handed in June, convinced that the Russians regarded the Irish struggle as absolutely nationalist and of little use to themselves.

In the wake of the raids on 42 North Great Georges' Street in November 1920, the SPI rebels had decided that it was not feasible to operate legally, and reformed the Communist Groups. Modelled on the conspiratorial IRB, the Communist Groups aimed to cultivate influence within the executives of the IRA, IRB, ITGWU and SPI. Of their 17 members, nine were trade union

65   White, 'Ireland, Russia, communism, post-communism', p. 157; White, 'Soviet Russia and the Irish revolution', p. 54; PROL, Theo Russell, Berne, 3 Mar. 1921 to London, FO 371/7142, and Report on Bolshevik propaganda no. 153, 15 Apr. 1921, FO 371/6844; BPP, *Intercourse Between Bolshevism and Sinn Féin*, Cmd 1326 (1921). Another example of contemporary British propaganda is Dawson, *Red Terror and Green*.

66   Gaughan, *Thomas Johnson*, pp. 440–3; McCartan said the same to de Valera. McCartan, *With de Valera in America*, p. 219.

67   See NLI, McCartan papers, reports on Russia from mission, Feb. to June 1921, as envoy of the Republic of Ireland, 17682.

officials, three were in the IRB, and two others had IRA connections. A few were indeed well placed for intrigue, notably Éamon Martin, a senior official in Na Fianna and close friend of Liam Mellows.[68] The Communist Groups were given a fillip when Séamus Robinson, the leftish commandant of the IRA's 3rd Tipperary Brigade, asked Connolly to help him procure weapons in Germany, Europe's illegal arms bazaar. Robinson had earlier approached Michael Collins's chief arms agent on the continent, Bob Briscoe, who declined to help. Munster units were currently with disgruntled not only with the arms supply methods of IRA General Head Quarters (GHQ), but with GHQ itself, feeling that they were doing most of the fighting while GHQ catered for the IRA in Dublin. On 3 December 1920 the IRA army council noted that the 3rd Tipperary Brigade had collected £3,000 and intended to seek its own supplies – in flagrant breach of IRA protocol. In tacit acknowledgement of its deficiencies, it felt obliged to let the 3rd Tipperary go ahead. The munitions supply problem would lead to further friction with GHQ and a more independent attitude among Munster IRA officers in 1921. Robinson envisaged seven brigades in Munster backing his initiative. Connolly duly embarked for Berlin with Billy Beaumont, a polo-playing ex-British army officer, whose brother Seán was prominent in the Communist Groups, the Irish language movement, and briefly a judge in the Sinn Féin courts. The adventure came unstuck in Germany and led to Connolly's suspension from the Groups. The Beaumonts joined a more successful IRA gun-run to Germany in the autumn.[69]

Shortly beforehand, Seán had travelled on to Moscow, where he tried to impress Mátyás Rakosi, the Comintern secretary and a future prime minister of Hungary, with claims that the 3rd Tipperary Brigade was unhappy with IRA policy, and that the Brigade adjutant with two members of the Communist Groups had made contact with an officer of the German general staff who offered to sell them 'three submarines, and a large quantity of minenwerfer and anti-tank guns'.[70] Beaumont alleged that since the truce Sinn Féin had been drifting towards compromise in the peace talks, and the implacables were ready to resume the war and were seeking fresh allies on the left. Soviet aid to the IRA would give the Communist Groups 'a tremendous

68   RGASPI, report to Kobietsky for the ECCI, 10 Feb. 1921, 495/89/10–2/4a; report on the work of the Irish Communist Groups, 1921, 495/89/2–30/33; report of the CPI to the ECCI, Oct. 1921 to Oct. 1922, 495/89/16–44.

69   Emmet O'Connor, 'Waterford and IRA gun-running, 1917–22', *Decies: Journal of the Waterford Archaeological & Historical Society*, no. 57 (2001), pp. 181–93; Éamon Ó Ciosáin, *An t-Éireannach, 1934–1937: Nuachtán Sóisialach Gaeltachta* (Dublin, 1993), pp. 67–70, 117.

70   The IRA had an established contact with Major Hassenhauer of the Orgesh, a secret right-wing organisation. Brian P. Murphy, *John Chartres: Mystery Man of the Treaty* (Dublin, 1995), pp. 48–9.

influence with the active revolutionary forces'. Beaumont also asked Rakosi to arrange urgent meetings with Lenin, Trotsky and Chicherin, no less. Rakosi declined to receive him.[71] Returning from Moscow through Hamburg, Beaumont rounded up a crew of communist sailors for Charlie McGuinness, an IRA agent who was preparing to skipper a leaky fishing trawler, the *Anita*, with an arms cache to Helvic, County Waterford. After embarrassing indiscretion and interception by the harbour police, the intrepid McGuinness eventually reached Waterford with two arms ships, the *Frieda* and the *Hanna*.[72]

Connolly meanwhile had attended the third Comintern congress, convened in Moscow between 22 June and 12 July 1921; travelling this time from Germany in a two-seater aeroplane with a wartime air-ace turned Bolshevik.[73] The congress devoted little attention to the colonial question, being preoccupied with Europe's retreat from revolution, and the possibility of great power rivalry culminating in war. However, Connolly managed to discuss Ireland with Lenin and presented him with a report, complete with maps of recent IRA actions. The report reiterated one of the few consistencies in Connolly's volatile mind: the leadership of the republican movement was bourgeois or narrowly nationalist, but the masses could be won to communism. The analysis lurched between fantasy and realism. Ireland had:

[a] great backward agricultural industry, which takes the form, not of peasant proprietorship, but of 'Kulacheatvo' [Kulaks], which has turned the vast mass of the agricultural population into proletarians; typically capitalistic conditions of industry in the large towns, which has produced a strong proletarian class consciousness . . . This is why the movement remains Sinn Féin on the outside: but only on the outside. It will be sufficient for a clear Communist core to be organised in every branch of the industrial movement – it is unlikely that this can happen in the near future without considerable extraneous assistance . . .'[74]

At the same time, he thought class revolution in Ireland unlikely before a collapse of British capitalism, and expected Sinn Féin to reach a deal with the British on dominion home rule, leaving Irish Labour isolated and the IRA in a hopeless military position. Despite the contradictions, he again received approval to form a party.

---

71 RGASPI, report on the work of the Irish Communist Groups, 495/89/2–30/33; Mac Neill [pseudonym of Beaumont] to Rakosi, 3 Sept. 1921, 495/89/8–2; F. E. Smith to Rakosi, 3 Dec. 1921, 495/89/8–40/41.

72 O'Connor, 'Waterford and IRA gun-running', pp. 187–92.

73 Milotte, *Communism in Modern Ireland*, pp. 45–6.

74 RGASPI, The conditions of Ireland, 1 July 1921, 5/3/582–2/8.

THE END OF THE SPI

The SPI had been revived after the truce. With about ten activists it was easy meat for a takeover. Connolly mustered support from a minority of the Communist Groups and Seán McLoughlin, who dissolved his Communist Labour Party on 1 September, which may have been the cause of his immediate expulsion from the SLP.[75] On 9 September, with the ITGWU faction largely absent, the rebels captured a majority of seats on the SPI executive.[76] Connolly was elected president, and would be the party's motor force for the next 17 months. For most of that period he would also edit the *Workers' Republic*. His sister, Nora, was elected treasurer, and Walter Carpenter Sr became secretary. The other members of the executive were Michael O'Leary, Séamus McGowan, Edward Mallon and Frank Robbins.[77] On 16 September Connolly rushed out the first issue of the *Workers' Republic*. Though it was not endorsed as the party organ until October, he presumptuously devoted it to one long article on the 'main points in a policy for the party'.[78] The third Comintern congress had further tightened ECCI control over the policy making of communist parties, and adopted detailed theses on organisation, stressing the importance of democratic centralism, and cells in factories and trade unions. It had also moved towards the approval of united front tactics with reformists, a position formally elaborated on by the ECCI in December.[79] Connolly reflected its thinking closely. In line with the congress slogan 'To the masses!', he concentrated on economic and trade union matters, and made no reference to the national struggle, envisaging the creation of nuclei in unions and factories, and only later in the Citizen Army and the IRA. The article claimed that the SPI's 20 or so activists were 'ample and sufficient to start with', but thought that until they had at least 300 members in Dublin and a branch in each main town they could not justify calling themselves a party. He also argued that the SPI be reorganised and expanded, in collaboration with reformists if necessary, before being turned into a communist party.[80]

---

75 *Socialist*, 15 Sept. 1921.

76 The Communist Labour Party claimed about 25 members on dissolution, and the Communist Groups had about ten members. RGASPI, CPI report, 495/89/8–6/7; report of the CPI to the ECCI, Oct. 1921 to Oct. 1922, 495/89/16–43/44.

77 *Communist*, 17 Sept. 1921. Robbins, an ITGWU official, was removed from the executive on 8 Oct. RGASPI, SPI to the ECCI, 8 Oct. 1921, 495/89/10–6/7.

78 RGASPI, report of the CPI to the Comintern, Oct. 1921 to Oct. 1922, 495/89/8–6/7, 495/89/16–44.

79 McDermott and Agnew, *The Comintern*, pp. 27–9, 31.

80 *Workers' Republic*, 16 Sept. 1921, and reprint, 21 Oct. 1922.

On the last point at least, the majority of members disagreed with him. On 8 October the SPI voted to apply for Comintern affiliation. Several members were expelled, including O'Brien and O'Shannon for 'reformism, consecutive non-attendance . . . and consistent attempts to render futile all efforts at building a Communist Party in Ireland': the removal of reformists and centrists from all responsible positions being one of the 21 conditions of admission to the Comintern.[81] In a further break with the old order, 20 members of the SPI were declared lapsed on 14 October. The final criteria of Comintern affiliation were met on 28 October when the SPI adopted a new constitution, committing it to struggle by political, economic and military means for the dictatorship of the proletariat. The constitution renamed the party as the Communist Party of Ireland (Section of the Communist International). On 9 November copies of a request for affiliation were forwarded to the Comintern via the CPGB and the KPD. An accompanying report appealed for £1,740 to fund two organisers and a press.[82] The party was formally recognised as an affiliate by the ECCI presidium on 13 January 1922.[83]

Who were the communists? The party claimed that membership had mushroomed from 22 on 9 September 1921 to 300 in October, but 'It was immediately apparent that most of this was useless material'.[84] The expulsions and the decision to join the Comintern trimmed the roll call to 120 by November, including 78 in Dublin, 28 in Cork, a small group in Mallow, and a scattering elsewhere. Most had had a connection with the SPI. Negotiations on a Belfast branch with the left wing of the local Independent Labour Party, which sold the CPGB's the *Communist*, never came to fruition.[85] The CPI was typical of kindred parties in that most of its members were young, and typical of counterparts in colonial countries in that most had been involved with the independence movement. The Connollys, Seán McLoughlin, Michael O'Leary, Séamus McGowan, Paddy Stephenson and Walter Carpenter Jr were Easter Week veterans, and Jim Phelan had been in the IRA. A second category of prominent recruits were émigrés and returned emigrants; notably George Pollock, alias McLay, who had come to Ireland from Scotland during the world war to avoid conscription; Liam O'Flaherty, Seán McIntyre and Paddy Read, who had been in the Wobblies;[86] a Russian intellectual named

81   RGASPI, SPI to the ECCI, 8 Oct. 1921, 495/89/10–6/7.
82   RGASPI, CPI to the ECCI, 9 Nov. 1921, 495/89/8–6/12.
83   RGASPI, Borodin to ECCI, interview with delegates from the Irish Party, 15 July 1922, 495/89/13–6.
84   RGASPI, report on the CPI to the ECCI, Oct. 1921 to Oct. 1922, 495/89/16–48/49.
85   RGASPI, CPI to the ECCI, 9 Nov. 1921, 495/89/8–6/12.
86   The American syndicalist labour union, the Industrial Workers of the World.

Peterson; and 15-year-old Pat Breslin, whose family had moved to Dublin
from London in early 1920, and who would form the Young Communist
League in 1922.

The ITGWU ignored the changes, though it may be more than
coincidental that the Dáil Department of Labour announced its intention to
occupy 42 North Great George's Street, and served the CPI with notice to
quit.[87] O'Shannon had a riposte in hand in the planned revival of the *Voice of
Labour* on 22 October and boasted it would sink the *Workers' Republic*. There
were rumours of a new SPI or an appeal to the ECCI.[88] Confident of Moscow's
favour, Connolly could not forbear to scoff at O'Brien, O'Shannon and Johnson
from the pages of the *Communist*, which had obliged him with a regular
column in September. The juvenilia antagonised the CPGB. On 15 October
the *Communist* noted 'a number of objections to some of the observations of
our Irish correspondent – particularly to his references to individuals'. The
paper apologised to the offended trio, and Connolly was replaced as Irish
correspondent. It was the beginning of a fraught relationship between the
British and Irish parties. In accordance with the 'fostering' role in Irish affairs
alloted the CPGB by the ECCI, T. A. Jackson and Willie Gallacher arrived
in Dublin on 21 November to assess the fractiousness, and interviewed leaders
of the ITGWU, the Citizen Army, the CPI and the Communist Groups.
While Connolly persuaded them to back the CPI's application to the
Comintern, relations between the CPI and CPGB remained tenuous and
irregular until July 1922.[89] The British could not flout Comintern principles by
siding openly with social democrats against communists, but their interest in
Ireland remained with the politics of mass anti-imperalism. In dealing with
Labour and republicans, they normally bypassed the CPI, leaving Connolly to
complain to Moscow that they had rendered his party no assistance. A typical
spat soon arose over the Communist Groups. On 4 October the Groups,
including MacAlpine and Nora Connolly, reaffirmed their commitment to
illegality and working to influence the IRA and IRB, and protested to Moscow
against Connolly's 'treachery' in seeking Comintern affiliation, contending
that legal activity in Ireland was futile.[90] The dissidents were suspended and
the Groups disintegrated in December, but, to the CPI's disgust, three of
them were admitted to the CPGB.[91]

87   RGASPI, CPI to the ECCI, 9 Nov. 1921, 495/89/8–6/12. Joseph McGrath, TD, assistant
     Minister of Labour since Oct. 1920, had formerly worked for the ITGWU's health insurance section
     and remained friendly with O'Brien.
88   *Communist*, 8 Oct. 1921; *Workers' Republic*, 10 Dec. 1921.
89   RGASPI, report of the CPI to the ECCI, Oct. 1921 to Oct. 1922, 495/89/16–71.
90   RGASPI, Communist Groups to the Comintern, 3 Dec. 1921, 495/89/8–40/41.
91   RGASPI, report of the CPI to the ECCI, Oct. 1921 to Oct. 1922, 495/89/16–40/80.

Impatient as ever, Connolly soon came to take a dim view of the CPI's potential and composition, abandoning his scheme for creating nuclei in unions and factories as too ambitious.[92] Finances were precarious. The *Workers' Republic* had been started 'on bluff', without a penny to its name, and early print runs were excessively optimistic. In November it was decided to limit the run to 2,000 copies, at a cost of £25 11*s.* but sales and advertisements would recoup no more than £14 17*s.*[93] Connolly admitted frankly that the party 'is not yet even in touch with the organizations of the masses in any definite manner'.[94] He had alienated the CPGB and appeals to the Citizen Army proved fruitless. In any case he deemed the membership too small to influence industrial unrest, something which did not stop him subjecting the party to two purges in its first year, reducing the Dublin branch to 100 members.[95] Part of his problem was that the third Comintern congress had acknowledged an abatement of revolutionism in Europe without specifying a response. On 26 November the *Workers' Republic* drew on Zinoviev's thesis at the third congress that the working class internationally was pausing between two revolutionary waves, to warn against expectations of membership growth: 'The masses are not in motion just now – they are apathetic'. The interpretation was clearly at odds with Irish facts. Nonetheless, Connolly decided the answer was a 'fierce internal struggle' for democratic centralism. When Peterson led resistance to the demand, his supporters were put on probation.[96] On 10 December the *Workers' Republic* slammed the 'so-called intellectuals' and 'petty bourgeois fops' who would not accept the 'acid test' of party discipline. The party was in danger of imploding.

The air of unreality reflected two weaknesses in Connolly's capacity for leadership: his reliance on ideas from Moscow, and his penchant for exogenous shocks that would catapult the party to power rather than the grind of organisation building. In any case, party strategy hinged on the outcome of the Anglo-Irish negotiations, and Connolly had shown some prescience on the talks in August:

> Strange as it might seem to some who imagined the present fighters as immovable extremists, the allegiance to the Throne on the part of Ireland will not be an insurmountable difficulty for the Republicans . . .

92 RGASPI, report of the CPI to the ECCI, Oct. 1921 to Oct. 1922, 495/89/16–55/56.
93 RGASPI, CPI to the ECCI, 9 Nov. 1921, 495/89/8–6/12.
94 Milotte, *Communism in Modern Ireland*, p. 50.
95 *Workers' Republic*, 12 Nov. 1921; RGASPI, report of the CPI to the ECCI, Oct. 1921 to Oct. 1922, 495/89/16–49/50.
96 Milotte, *Communism in Modern Ireland*, p. 50.

Not even the Ulster mock government will stand in the way. [Lloyd] George will be able to do a lot to get the Unionists of the North to throw over an attitude that renders agreement impossible . . . but those fanatical leaders of a desperately anxious capitalism will still claim some independence. Neither the English nor an Irish Government could use force to remedy this sore . . .

It is hardly likely that the extreme elements will rejoice in a settlement and a good lot of discontent will flow in various channels toward Communism. If this discontent is harnessed and applied the Communists might reasonably expect to enter the political field as a small Party at the first election of the Irish House of Assembly.[97]

Later, influenced by theses delivered at the third Comintern congress by Trotsky, Connolly became convinced of an approaching war for world domination between the superannuated British empire and its muscular young rival, the United States.[98] Trotsky's prognosis tranformed a dominion settlement from a benign to a malign scenario. If there was to be an international war, then it was vital to keep Ireland out of the British empire. That abiding objective would guide the CPI for the next 12 months. It did at least rescue the party from a slavish Moscow-centrism and give it an intense sense of mission.

97 *Workers' Republic*, 17 Dec. 1921. The article was submitted to the *Communist*, but not published because, Connolly believed, it contradicted the CPGB analysis.
98 *Workers' Republic*, 29 Oct. 1921.kj

THREE

CIVIL WAR COMMUNISM, 1921-2

*If we propound the solution of the right of self-determination for the colonies ... we
lose nothing by it ... The most outright nationalist movement ... is only water
for our mill, since it contributes to the destruction of English imperialism.*

NIKOLAI BUKHARIN

Eighth congress of the VKP (b), 1919[1]

—

In the autumn of 1921 a mood of expectancy was building up in Ireland. The
post-war economic boom had yielded to a slump in late 1920. Having climbed
from 101 points in 1914 to a peak of 288 points in 1920, the agricultural price
index fell steadily to 160 points in 1924. As the recession spread to manu-
facturing, the value of exports tumbled from £204.8m in 1920 to £129.6m in
1921. By December 1921, out of 439,193 insured workers, 25.8 per cent were
unemployed, with a further 4.2 per cent on short time.[2] Since 15 April 1921,
'Black Friday', when the 'triple alliance' of miners, railwaymen and transport
workers collapsed, wages had been falling rapidly in Britain. It was hoped that
a similar pattern would obtain in Ireland, with the railwaymen providing the
initial sacrificial victims. Instead, exploiting the prevailing lawlessness, workers
offered a dogged, often violent, resistance, and the wage-cutting offensive
staggered on in phases, each related to assertions of state power, with trade
unions succumbing section by section, until December 1923, when Labour's
syndicalist spirit expired in the farmyards of County Waterford and the 'red
flag times' were over.

Roddy Connolly clung to the view that the CPI was too small to influence
labour militancy, and devoted himself to effecting an alliance with republicans.
His position on the Anglo-Irish treaty swung wildly, from quietly savouring
the windfall of recruiting disappointed republicans, to execrating it for leaving
Ireland within the empire, to envisaging the CPI working within in to desta-
bilise the British empire. But like a flag flapping about a pole, he had an
anchor point: communists could best offset their marginality through the
republican movement, and the split over the treaty would place the IRA under

1 Quoted in Degras, *The Communist International, Vol. 1*, p. 138.
2 O'Connor, *Syndicalism in Ireland*, p. 98.

the control of die-hards with a pragmatic social outlook, the type of nation-alists most susceptible to Wolfe Tone's dictum: 'if the men of property will not help us they must fall; we will free ourselves with the aid of the large and respectable class of the community – the men of no property'.[3] This was indeed the traditional separatist fallback position, resorted to from the United Irishmen to the Provisionals, and the communists did come close to clinching a deal with the IRA. That they failed was not due exclusively to a lack of interest on the republican side.

WAR! WHAT FOR?

Republicans first heard of the substance of the Anglo-Irish treaty from Willie Gallacher. Acting on a tip from 'a thoroughly trustworthy source', Gallacher took the morning boat train from Euston on 6 December to warn that the Irish negotiators had caved in to British demands. The news was a bombshell to the CPGB, which had assumed the peace talks would break down on the issue of allegiance to the crown and that Sinn Féin would split prior to any agreement.[4] It had also been developing links with republicans. During the truce Cathal Brugha, Minister of Defence, and Desmond Fitzgerald, Director of Propaganda, had had several meetings with Tom Johnson and William O'Brien on operations in Britain and enlisting assistance from British workers in the event of renewed hostilities. O'Brien introduced Brugha to Gallacher and CPGB chairman Arthur MacManus, if only to dispel some naïve expec-tations. Landing in Dublin on 6 December, Gallacher was taken by Johnson to see Brugha, Liam Mellows, Director of Purchases, and Rory O'Connor, Director of Engineering. Arguing that the bourgeoisie would back the London compromise, he pressed them to arrest the returning signatories and rally the masses to the republic; he had in his pocket a programme they might put to the people. Mellows and O'Connor were enthusiastic. Johnson, typi-cally, counselled caution. Brugha demurred. 'We believe in you Gallacher', he said, 'we know that we can trust you, but we don't believe in your Communism and we don't want it in Ireland.' 'Well', said Gallacher, 'you'll find Collins and Griffith won't hesitate when they feel strong enough.'[5]

3   Editorial, *Workers' Republic*, 28 Jan. 1922. Tone, founder of the United Irishmen in 1791, made the celebrated comment in 1796.

4   *Workers' Republic*, 17 Dec. 1921.

5   On Gallacher's intervention see O'Brien, *Forth the Banners Go*, p. 158; Gaughan, *Thomas Johnson*, pp. 191–2; Greaves, *Liam Mellows*, pp. 268–9. The Gallacher–Brugha exchange is from the *Workers' Voice*, 21 May 1932. Gallacher wrote various versions of it but they all amounted to the same thing.

The *Workers' Republic* went to press on 6 December with an editorial saying 'War! What for? . . . If it is Peace we certainly are elated'.[6] Connolly had been coy about his prognoses on the peace talks in Ireland, perhaps the better to feign a tone of shocked betrayal when the time came. On 17 December a suitably outraged *Workers' Republic* published a manifesto predicting 'civil war and social hell . . . if [the treaty] is accepted'. The issue was the empire, the rationale was Trotsky's thesis on the approaching Anglo-American conflict.

THE EMPIRE IS ROCKING! It is being broken and crushed in India, destroyed in Egypt, and will soon be torn asunder by proletarian uprising in England itself. Above all, the hostile attitude of America theatens to seal its doom. Faced with the greatest crisis in its history it foregoes its claim to rule unchallenged in Ireland, thereby effects a compromise with the weaker spirits among the republicans, and immensely strengthens its position in the coming inevitable conflict with America.

The editorial declared: 'the people and fighters of Ireland must stand resolutely for de Valera and Brugha – and this despite however reactionary either may be as regards the workers' aims'. The treaty was an embarrassing result for the CPGB and its Irish expert, T. A. Jackson, and Connolly could not resist saying 'I told you so'.[7] Jackson wrote with mixed feelings on the treaty before the CPGB came in line with the CPI on 31 December.[8]

So convinced was Connolly of anti-treatyism as the hinge of strategy, that the CPI ignored Comintern policy for the next 12 months. On 18 December the ECCI directed that in view of the reverses experienced by the European working class, affiliates should pursue united fronts with reformists. In April 1922 representatives of the Second, Third, and 'two and a half' Internationals met in Berlin to consider conditions for common action.[9] While the discussions failed, the Comintern remained pessimistic about the prospects for revolution and continued to endorse united front tactics. The enormous controversy generated among communists by the 18 December directive bypassed Ireland. The *Workers' Republic* responded serenely on 4 February, with an ingenuous respect that reads like choice satire:

After the advanced meeting of the [ECCI] it may be expected that a whole, co-ordinated fight of all the workers' organisations, of all the different parties of the

6   *Workers' Republic*, 10 Dec. 1921.
7   *Workers' Republic*, 17 Dec. 1921.
8   *Communist*, 31 Dec. 1921.
9   McDermott and Agnew, *The Comintern*, pp. 33, 229.

workers, the Communists, the Socialists, the Labourites, the various half and half groups will be in full swing, will be already on the road to success.

In Ireland, it went on, Labour's neutrality on the treaty, above all, rendered the united front option impossible.[10] 'We see the class fight mingled in a fight of Republicanism against Free Statism . . . To say that the field is clear for the Irish proletariat to fight solely against capitalism, as the Labour Party says is to announce a laughable criminal absurdity.' The CPI did try in vain to affiliate to the ILPTUC, but the better to prosecute its case rather than collaborate with the leadership.[11]

THE WOBBLY REPUBLIC

Communists did not entirely neglect social unrest, and became involved briefly with the unemployed, and with evicted tenants prior to the Civil War. Normally the CPI would hold public meetings each Sunday morning and evening in Dublin city. Occasional forays were made into adjacent rural areas like Finglas and Glasnevin during the farm strikes that hit the county in the spring. Favourite speakers' topics were the capitalist offensive, the release of Jim Larkin, famine relief, and, of course, the treaty. A section of WIR or Mezhrabpom had been formed in November, as a result of a letter from Willi Münzenberg, and regular appeals were issued to alleviate famine in Russia. The brainchild of Münzenberg, Moscow's public relations 'wunderkind', Mezhrabpom was the first Comintern front. The CPI called a trade union conference on aid for Russia in January, but its efforts to broaden support beyond the meagre resources of the party met no success. The ITGWU – and employers – donated through separate channels.[12] The *Workers' Republic* also publicised the anti-semitic pogroms of Ukrainian nationalists and initiatives of Dublin Jews in aid of the Ukrainian Jews' Relief Fund.[13]

The CPI's unhappy connection with the unemployed began on 9 January with a public meeting at which an unemployed committee was formed, chaired by Liam O'Flaherty. O'Flaherty had been converted to socialism while serving with the Irish Guards on the western front. After being invalided out of the British army he set off tramping about the Mediterannean and the Americas,

10 *Voice of Labour*, 17 Dec. 1921, 14 Jan., 18 Mar. 1922, urged neutrality.
11 RGASPI, Report of the CPI to the ECCI, Oct. 1921 to Oct. 1922, 495/89/16–56/139.
12 RGASPI, Report of the CPI to the ECCI, Oct. 1921 to Oct. 1922, 495/89/16–62; *Workers' Republic*, 18–25 Mar. 1922.
13 O'Riordan, 'Connolly socialism and the Jewish worker', pp. 127–8.

joining the Wobblies in Canada and the Communist Party in New York. He returned to settle in Ireland in December 1921, and was soon a familiar figure haranging crowds outside Liberty Hall, or sitting for hours each day in a shabby coat and muffler at Nelson's Pillar selling the *Workers' Republic*, his pitch a gathering point of kindred spirits.[14] Two other CPI comrades were on the committee, Jim Phelan and Séan McIntyre. Phelan, a tall, powerfully built man from the Liberties of Dublin, had taken to life as a tramp at the age of 11, and been a sometime member of the Citizen Army and the IRA. McIntyre had 'fled' to New York in 1915, been recommended by Larkin to a German agent for propaganda and sabotage work in Vladivostok in October 1917, and was later gaoled as a Wobbly.[15] All three were typical Wobblies in outlook, temperament and lifestyle. A fourth associate was a British army captain named Montgomery. The unemployed movement enjoyed some success. These were the only weeks when the *Workers' Republic* paid its way. When the Lord Mayor refused to make a hall available to the unemployed, the quartet resorted to direct action. On 18 January, with Montgomery wearing his uniform, kit and revolver, they led the unemployed to seize the Rotunda concert rooms in central Dublin, hoist a red flag, and proclaim the Irish Soviet Workers' Republic. Their manifesto was O'Flaherty's first publication. One could say that Phelan was impressed. 'Its language has not, I think, been approached since the days of the American War of Independence and the first French Revolution . . . No single document of the Second World War came anywhere near it for sheer literary power.'[16] However, the crowds massing outside the Rotunda did not come to applaud. And the CPI privately deprecated the soviet as a 'childish stunt'. After four days, with one instance of shooting from the Rotunda, the CPI and IRA negotiated an evacuation, persuading O'Flaherty that employers had equipped the mob for an armed assault.

Phelan, McIntyre and O'Flaherty fled to Cork, and the unemployed movement collapsed in a crossfire of accusations. A party investigation was held into alleged misappropriation of funds by O'Flaherty and McIntyre immediately prior to leaving the Rotunda. It upheld charges that a small sum had gone astray. Phelan drifted on to Liverpool. McIntyre stayed in Cork, and was later involved with one of the soviets declared by Tipperary creamery

14   Peter Costello, *Liam O'Flaherty's Ireland* (Dublin, 1996), pp. 29–41; Michael McInerney, 'O'Flaherty in politics', *The Irish Times*, 27 Aug. 1976.

15   Jim Phelan, *The Name's Phelan: The First Part of the Autobiography of Jim Phelan* (Belfast, 1993); *Manchester Guardian*, 12 June 1923; Emmet Larkin, *James Larkin*, pp. 217–18. I am obliged to Barry McLoughlin and D. R. O'Connor Lysaght for details on McIntyre.

16   Phelan, *The Name's Phelan*, p. 275.

workers that spring.[17] O'Flaherty returned to the party in Dublin. He took the penman's revenge in *The Informer*. Set in 1923–4, the plot featured Gypo Nolan, on the run from 'the Revolutionary Organisation' as it teetered on the brink of becoming a power in the land in a manner approximate to one of Connolly's fantasies in 1922. The organisation's commandant, Dan Gallagher, was invested with many of the vices attributed to Connolly by his critics, and the novel included a fictional report from a Comintern agent which suggests how a frustrated minority in the CPI might have seen Comintern policy and the Irish proletariat:

> For the moment it would be a tactical blunder to expel Comrade Gallagher from the International. At the same time there can be no doubt that the Irish section has deviated entirely from the principles of revolutionary Communism as laid down in the laws of the International. Comrade Gallagher rules the national Organization purely and simply as a dictator. There is a semblance of an Executive Committee but only in name. The tactics are guided by whatever whim is uppermost in Comrade Gallagher's mind at the moment. Contrary to the orders issued from Headquarters, the Organization is purely military and has made any hardly any attempt to come into the open as a legal political party. This is perhaps not entirely due to Comrade Gallagher's fault. There are local causes, arising out of the recent struggle for national independence, which has left the working class in the grip of a romantic love of conspiracy, a strong religious and bourgeois-nationalist outlook on life and a hatred of constitutional methods. This makes it difficult for the moment to check Comrade Gallagher's hold.[18]

The 'railway crisis' did not trigger the domino effect anticipated by employers, and February produced another false dawn of 'decisive conflict'.[19] In late January the first of about 80 workplace occupations that year took place at Mallow, where the Quartertown flour mills were seized. Demands for wage cuts also led to a spate of soviets in May, when the extensive networks of creameries and factories belonging to the Cleeve combine were occupied. Other soviets were declared by timber millers and gasworkers. These months,

17   Paddy Bergin, 'Liam O'Flaherty', *Labour History News* 6 (1990), pp. 6–7; *Workers' Republic*, 28 Jan. 1922; RGASPI, Report of the CPI to the ECCI, Oct. 1921 to Oct. 1922, 495/89/16–40/145; Liam O'Flaherty, *Shame The Devil* (London, 1934), p. 22; Phelan, *The Name's Phelan*, p. 275.

18   Liam O'Flaherty, *The Informer* (London, 1949), pp. 75–6.

19   Government decontrol of the railways on 14 Aug. 1921 was followed by demands for wage cuts. Arbitration pre-empted a national official strike, but intermittent unofficial action occurred until the crisis was resolved in Feb. On the railway crisis and the soviets see O'Connor, *Syndicalism in Ireland*, pp. 102–4.

when state forces were weak and the fledgling provisional government was willing to restrain employers, were Labour's best chance of escaping the catastrophe that befell it in 1923. Although the CPI had members in Mallow, and the Cleeve soviets were led by ITGWU officials behind the Revolutionary SPI in 1919, Connolly confined his interest in industrial unrest to comment in the *Workers' Republic*. Whatever influence the tiny CPI might exert on a few soviets was small beer compared with the prize of shaping the republican revolution.

OUR ONLY HOPE

The abiding problem was how to influence the anti-treatyites, and the prospects were going from bad to worse. On 7 January Dáil Éireann ratified the treaty by 64–57 votes. Republicans withdrew from the Dáil, and the provisional government was formed on 14 January. Still, republicans ignored an offer of six of the eight pages of the *Workers' Republic*, appeals for offensive action, and advice to devise a social programme.[20] Connolly was reduced to amusing himself by inducing a new slant on policy through an imagined Socratic dialogue with a republican. The 'policy' amounted to a daft pipedream in which spontaneous direct action would lead to workers' councils, and a soviet government which would accept the treaty but realise a 'Bolshevik republic' working to destablise the empire from within.[21]

Labour edged ever closer to a pro-treaty position. On 18 February the CPI made a futile attempt to co-ordinate 'revolutionary' delegates to the ILPTUC special conference on the next Dáil elections. Three days later the conference voted 115–82 against abstaining from the elections, and the closeness of the vote left the CPI a little rueful at having left its intervention so late. Only one comrade, Walter Carpenter Sr, was present at the conference.[22] Implicitly the decision swung the nominally neutral Labour Party behind the treaty settlement. After the IRA ratcheted up the tension by seizing the Four Courts for a GHQ, the ILPTUC gave further proof of its preference for political stability by convening a general strike against militarism on 24 April, its fourth and final such stoppage since 1918. This time, employers co-operated heartily with what was seen as an anti-IRA gesture.[23] The CPI organised three counter demonstrations against the 'great lockout'.[24] The Labour Party would back a

20 Milotte, *Communism in Modern Ireland*, pp. 55–7.
21 *Workers' Republic*, 28 Jan. to 25 Feb. 1922.
22 RGASPI, Report of the CPI to the ECCI, Oct. 1921 to Oct. 1922, 495/89/16–74. *Workers' Republic*, 1 Apr. 1922.
23 Mitchell, *Labour in Irish Politics*, pp. 153–7.
24 RGASPI, Report of the CPI to the ECCI, Oct. 1921 to Oct. 1922, 495/89/16–62.

number of peace initiatives over the coming months, but would refuse under any circumstances to undermine the Free State.[25] Ever adept at giving radical reasons for conservative decisions, Johnson privately cited the failure of Dáil Éireann to implement the Democratic Programme declining, no doubt, to explain that labour had never pressed for the implementation of the Democratic Programme for fear of being caught up in the revolution. In fact, the Republic had tried to develop the fishing industry on a co-operative basis, created a Department of Labour, and shown benign neutrality to trade union direct action. If that was little enough, it was more than Johnson would ever wring out of Cumann na nGaedheal.[26]

Foreseeing the possibility of civil war with the ratification of the treaty, O'Brien had enquired of the IRA on 10 January if working-class volunteers would be willing to join a 'Workers' Army'.[27] The idea was also put to the Citizen Army. Ostensibly a Labour controlled army would protect workers from either side in the event of war. The Citizen Army had replaced commandant James O'Neill with John Hanratty in January, and it responded positively. The liaison was proceeding, with an army convention held by mid April and units formed, until the strike against militarism exposed the Labour leadership's sentiments. Most of the Citizen Army followed Hanratty in recoiling from O'Brien's embrace. Hanratty then promised Ernie O'Malley that if the Four Courts was attacked, his troops would rally to the IRA.[28] The CPI took cold comfort from Hanratty's line; he had consistently stymied attempts at communist infiltration. Reluctantly the party decided to form its own 'Red Guard'.[29] A few revolvers were acquired and O'Flaherty provided basic training. Connolly knew it was a feeble gesture; the IRA, he wrote, was 'Our only hope'.[30]

The broader military picture was more encouraging. While the provisional government was enlisting an army in Dublin, British troops were evacuating barracks all over the 26 counties and local IRA units were taking their place. On 26–27 March 220 delegates representing some 80 per cent of IRA volunteers convened in defiance of a proclamation, effectively withdrew their allegiance

---

25   Though the Free State did not come into being until 6 Dec. 1922, the term was already in use to describe the provisional regime and its army.

26   Johnson made the point in a meeting with the Four Courts command in April. Greaves, *Liam Mellows*, p. 364; Gaughan, *Thomas Johnson*, p. 200. On the fishing industry see NA, Dáil Éireann papers, DE 2/27, DE 2/52, DE 2/111, DE 2/333–4.

27   UCDA, Ernie O'Malley papers, letter from William O'Brien, 10 Jan. 1922, P17a/161.

28   Fox, *The History of the Irish Citizen Army*, pp. 216–18; Mitchell, *Labour in Irish Politics*, pp. 163–4.

29   *Workers' Republic*, 18–25 Mar. 1922; RGASPI, Report of the CPI to the ECCI, Oct. 1921 to Oct. 1922, 495/89/16–64/79.

30   Milotte, *Communism in Modern Ireland*, p. 59; *Workers' Republic*, 1 Apr. 1922.

from the provisional government, and elected an executive. 'Do we take it that we are going to have a military dictatorship, then?', Rory O'Connor was asked. 'You can take it that way if you like', was his reply.[31] On 12 April Connolly told Moscow: 'it is becoming more apparent that the [IRA] controls the entire situation, that the 80,000 armed [IRA] men are the real dominant factor', adding that some members of IRA executive were calling themelves 'social republicans' and that the 'IRA in large numbers are drifting towards us'. Through leading the IRA the CPI had the possibility of 'jumping from 200 to 20,000 members in the course of the next six months'.[32] This was certainly making a mountain out of a molehill. The IRA's roll call exceeded 100,000, but it is doubtful if its field strength reached a twentieth of that number.[33] The IRA executive contained one CPI member, Peadar O'Donnell, who failed to persuade even his sympathetic colleagues to confer with the party, as they were reluctant to be identified with the 'reds'.[34] The IRA did promulgate an agrarian programme on 1 May, instructing local commandants to seize specified land and property for distribution to the people. The manifesto was largely the work of an agrarian radical, P. J. Ruttledge, with the support of Ernie O'Malley and Thomas Derrig. It was never applied or championed by anti-treatyite politicians.[35] Still, it seemed to the CPI that events were moving in the right direction. 'Civil War necessary' read the headline in the *Workers' Republic* on 6 May.

On 10 May 1922 eight members of the Anglo-American colonial group of the ECCI convened in the Hotel Lux to prepare the groundwork for the Comintern's first major public pronouncement on Ireland. Two thought the treaty would liquidate the national struggle, pointing to the strike against militarism on 24 April. The others disagreed, and approved a lengthy review which recommended unconditional backing for republicans as independence was a pre-requisite of a workers' republic, most workers supported independence, and the Irish struggle weakened the British empire. The review nonetheless ended in a conclusion diametrically opposed to Connolly's: that the national struggle precluded 'a big Communist movement in Ireland for some

31 Dorothy Macardle, *The Irish Republic* (London, 1968), pp. 614–18.

32 RGASPI, Report to the Comintern on the Irish party, R. Connolly, Berlin, 12 Apr. 1922, 5/3/581–9/17.

33 The IRA had a paper strength of 112,650 in July 1921, and enlistment increased after the truce. Florence O'Donoghue, *No Other Law: The Story of Liam Lynch and the Irish Republican Army, 1916–23* (Dublin, 1954), p. 334. However, it is estimated that only 3,000 to 5,000 volunteers saw front line service during the War of Independence, with another 50,000 involved in some secondary way. Mitchell, *Revolutionary Government*, p. 275.

34 RGASPI, Borodin to the ECCI, Interview with delegates from the Irish party, 15 July 1922, 495/89/13–6/23; McLay to the ECCI, 31 Aug. 1922, 495/89/12–39/46.

35 Greaves, *Liam Mellows*, pp. 313–14.

time'.[36] Evidently satisfied with the Colonial Group's analysis, the ECCI laboured to tap the wellsprings of Irish patriotism. Two papers were drafted. A message 'To the workers and peasants of Ireland' deplored the Collins–de Valera pact as a betrayal. The pact, concluded on 20 May, provided for a common Sinn Féin panel of candidates in the forthcoming election, and a coalition government afterwards. Under pressure from London, Michael Collins repudiated it two days before the poll. The second paper, an 'Appeal to the Irish workers', heaped ethnic flattery atop the conventional jargon: 'The glorious traditions of the Celtic genius are now handed over to the care of the Irish working class . . . WORKERS OF IRELAND! The Emerald Isle of the poets can only smile again in the bloom of freedom under the Red Flag of Labour. It can only be truly emancipated by the workers organised into a class conscious party of the proletariat.'[37] The eventual manifesto, addressed to the workers of Britain and Ireland, was mercifully more prosaic:

> It is only the young Communist Party of Ireland which has the courage and the determination to point to the right path and to say: 'It is only after the yoke of the English imperialists has been shaken off that the struggle against the Irish exploiters will have any chance of success!'. . .
> The attitude of the proletarian majority of the Irish Republican Army is a proof that the Irish Communist Party, notwithstanding its short existence, is on the right path and represents the will of the Irish working class.38

The CPI had already condemned the Collins–de Valera pact, and urged workers to give first preference votes to republicans and second preferences to the Labour Party in the June elections.[39] Its only other intervention in the elections was to hold opposition meetings in the constituencies 'of some of the most reactionary candidates'.[40]

By contrast with the Comintern, Narkomindel seemed ready to accord de facto recognition to the Free State. Johnson, whose discreet canvassing for the treaty infuriated republicans, had been quick to cultivate a liaison with the provisional government, and through W. P. Coates, a former ITGWU organiser and secretary of the British 'Hands Off Russia committee', arranged an interview with Leonid Krassin, Soviet trade attaché in London. On 2 February,

36 RGASPI, Anglo-American Colonial Group of the ECCI, minutes, 10 May 1922, 495/72/2–85/95.
37 RGASPI, to the workers and peasants of Ireland, 495/89/104–102/105; appeal to the Irish workers, 495/89/1–21/24.
38 *Workers' Republic*, 1 July 1922.
39 *Workers' Republic*, 17 June 1922.
40 RGASPI, Report of the CPI to the ECCI, Oct. 1921 to Oct. 1922, 495/89/16–62.

Johnson and a provisional government official met Krassin to discuss the establishment of Russo-Irish economic links. While nothing came of the meeting, Krassin said his government 'would welcome . . . close political and commercial relations with the new Irish government', and would be prepared to offer the Irish concessions for the cultivation of timber, wheat or flax in Russia. He also asked if the provisional government would be represented at the forthcoming international conference in Genoa and suggested that the Soviet and Irish delegates hold talks prior to the conference.[41]

WHAT THE HELL DO THEY WANT A REPUBLIC FOR?

The general election on 16 June returned 36 anti-treaty and 58 pro-treaty Sinn Féiners. Labour was elated: just one of its 18 candidates failed, narrowly, to be elected. Seventeen Farmers and independents, all of them pro-treaty, made up the remainder of the third Dáil. *Pravda* described the outcome as a 'victory for British imperialism'.[42] There was a consolation for the CPI: Paddy Gaffney, Labour TD for Carlow, refused to take the oath of allegiance and joined the party.[43] Johnson became leader of the parliamentary Labour group, and Cathal O'Shannon deputy leader. Clinging to some residual republicanism, O'Shannon cited the Collins–de Valera pact to quibble with claims that the election had delivered a mandate for the treaty. But Johnson set the tone for Labour historically in trusting the treaty would retire the national question and clear the decks for 'bread and butter' politics. Johnson's immediate hopes of using Dáil Éireann to prevent war were crushed by the provisional government. The third Dáil was prorogued five times and did not convene until mid September.[44]

At 3.30 a.m. on 28 June, under intense British pressure, the provisional government issued a summary ultimatum to IRA to evacuate the Four Courts. Shelling commenced at 4.15 a.m. The garrison surrendered on 30 June, and the IRA redisposed itself in various city centre hotels. Already the much-desired Civil War was going badly for the CPI. The Citizen Army had joined the IRA's Dublin brigade, demolishing faint hopes that it might take

41 NA, DT, S482; Gaughan, *Thomas Johnson*, pp. 195–6.

42 *Pravda*, 28 June 1922, quoted in White, 'Soviet Russia and the Irish revolution', p. 54.

43 In Jan. 1923 Gaffney was elected to the CPI executive. Milotte, *Communism in Modern Ireland*, p. 66; Mitchell, *Labour in Irish Politics*, p. 177.

44 Bill Kissane, 'Civil society under strain: intermediary organizations and the Irish Civil War', *Irish Political Studies* 15 (2000), p. 5.

common action with the communists.[45] With the fall of the Four Courts, the most promising social republicans, O'Donnell and Mellows, were interned. Both had speculated, as the first salvos whistled in, on what James Connolly would have made of events. Spotting two workers on the quays, seemingly indifferent to the unfolding conflict, O'Donnell had an epiphany: 'My God, Mellows, I'm in the wrong war'.[46] The CPI's 'Red Guard' joined the IRA on 1 July. Amounting to a dozen or so, it could have little impact. After eight days of fighting, the Free State army controlled the capital, some communists were in prison, and the IRA had begun its ignominious retreat. Roddy Connolly hurried to London to arrange for the printing of the *Workers' Republic* through the CPGB; it was found impossible to retain an Irish printer willing to flout the strict Civil War censorship.[47] Relations with the CPGB had continued to deteriorate, aggravated by the party's contact with republicans and Labour Party leaders independently of the CPI, and the *Communist*'s publication of O'Flaherty's criticism of the CPI.[48] On 8 July the *Communist* heartily endorsed CPI policy in a front page editorial, though it had its doubts about an IRA victory: 'Collins . . . knows that whatever befalls, the British power is at his back and that it far outweighs the Republicans'.

On 15 July Connolly and George McLay, the CPI treasurer, were introduced to Mikhail Markovich Borodin, already a legend in Bolshevik circles for his intellectual brilliance and savoir faire. It was characteristic of Borodin's exotic, larger than life aura that his Mancunian secretary, J. T. Murphy, remembered him as 'tall, well-built, black-haired, swarthy-complexioned', whereas the police later described him as '5 foot 10 inches, dark brown hair, grey eyes, fresh complexion'. Born in western Russia, Borodin had lived in America from 1907 to 1918, and had been working for the Comintern in Britain since March under the pseudonym George Brown.[49] In a long and frank debriefing, Connolly and McLay assured him that the IRA would sustain a guerilla war, compelling a British intervention that would destroy the Free State. Borodin gave them a lesson in Marxist materialism:

---

45   One hundred and forty-three members of the Citizen Army fought with the IRA in the Civil War. The Army also gave its stock of 3,000 rounds of .303 ammunition to the IRA. Fox, *The History of the Irish Citizen Army*, pp. 216–23.

46   Hegarty, *Peadar O'Donnell*, pp. 108–9.

47   RGASPI, Report of the CPI to the ECCI, Oct. 1921 to Oct. 1922, 495/89/16–45/46.

48   RGASPI, Report to the Comintern on the Irish party, R. Connolly, Berlin, 12 Apr. 1922, 5/3/581–9/17; Report of the CPI to the ECCI, Oct. 1921 to Oct. 1922, 495/89/16–45/54.

49   J. T. Murphy, *New Horizons* (London, 1941), pp. 88–9; PROL, Memorandum from W. Haldane Porter, Home Office, 22 May 1923, Michael Markovich Borodin, Oct. 1918 to Dec. 1938, KV 2/571; Dan N. Jacobs, *Borodin: Stalin's Man in China* (Cambridge, Mass, 1981), passim.

It is my firm opinion that they will crush the Republicans . . . It is really laughable to fight the Free State on a sentimental plea. They want a Republic. What the hell do they want a Republic for? . . . There are two military sections fighting – one is very strong and the other is very weak. One say Ireland should be fighting for prosperity. The other one is absolutely void of interest in any [such] matters.

Despite pleas that it would probably be a waste of time, Borodin insisted that, if only for propaganda purposes, they present a social programme to the republicans.[50] Together they drafted a document intended to give republicans a popular appeal. The manifesto demanded state ownership of heavy industry, transport and the banks; land redistribution; an eight-hour working day; joint councils of workers, trade unions and the state to regulate working conditions; municipalisation of public services; rationing of housing and abolition of rents; maintenance for the unemployed at trade union rates; and universal arming of workers.[51] A version appeared in the *Workers' Republic* on 29 July, and the paper adjusted its editorial line to concede that people saw little material advantage in opposing the Free State and emphasising the need for republicans to 'attract the masses'.

As the Free State army had fanned out from Dublin, Munster was soon the only province extensively under IRA control. On 26 July Connolly and Seán McLoughlin hastened to Fermoy, in the heart of the fraying 'Munster Republic'. Here in the Old Barracks, Chief of Staff Liam Lynch commanded shadow divisions from his Field GHQ with a self-belief and sense of reality reminiscent of Adolf Hitler in April 1945. At this stage even O'Malley, now Acting Assistant Chief of Staff and director of northern and eastern commands, was unclear as to IRA policy. Only a day earlier Lynch had written to O'Malley, stating the disastrously defensive, legalistic strategy he would cling to: the IRA would wait for Dáil Éireann to act as the government of the republic, and allow no other government to function; the war would be won by guerrilla tactics. Meanwhile, republicans would hold their areas.[52] There was some rationale to the stance in the opening days, when many civic bodies, led by Labour, contended that the Free State aggression could have no legitimacy without a convention of Dáil Éireann.[53] But on 12 July the provisional government made its resolve crystal clear, again proroguing the Dáil and appointing a war council. By all accounts Lynch's insistence on his theses

50 RGASPI, Borodin to the ECCI, interview with delegates from the Irish party, 15 July 1922, 495/89/13–6/23.
51 RGASPI, Report of the CPI to the ECCI, Oct. 1921 to Oct. 1922, 495/89/16–40/145.
52 UCDA, Malley papers, Lynch to Acting Assistant Chief of Staff, 25 July 1922, P17/a/60.
53 Kissane, 'Civil society under strain', pp. 1–23.

brought his interview with Connolly to a sterile conclusion.[54] However, the minutes of Lynch's staff meeting next day are more ambiguous.

> Wrote Lord Mayor Cork re meeting of Dáil. Lord Mayor to come to FGHQ [Field GHQ] this evening 27/7/22. De Valera also written for Republican Party to be asked to form Government. Executive to arrange relationship as between Government and Army. Connolly, President of Communist Party of Ireland, had interview with c/s yesterday 26/7/22. He suggested forming a government which would have a democratic policy, in this way Labour could be got behind Republicans. Can get any amount of arms etc if they can be got into the Country.[55]

The staff meeting on 1 August noted: 'D/O [Director of Operations] to meet a few labour men viz (Lynch–Connolly) take steps to get Labour Propaganda Dept working'.[56]

Over the next few weeks there were a series of intriguing developments. McLoughlin rejoined the IRA as a commandant and was leading a flying column in Tipperary on his eventual capture.[57] Connolly reported in London, and whatever he brought back from Fermoy was weighty enough for Borodin to refer it for a decision in Moscow.[58] Probably in mid August Borodin sent J. T. Murphy and Arthur MacManus to interview republican and communist activists in Dublin. On a mission similar to that of Connolly and McLoughlin at Fermoy, they met 'two of the Chiefs of Staff of the IRA' in a Dublin suburb and signed a joint document for submission to their respective executives.[59] The British had a narrow escape on the return journey. Fortuitously, they both looked clerical – Murphy being 'short, slight and spectacled, with a thin ascetic face like a priest's', and the small-framed MacManus having been a seminarian.[60] Murphy recalled:

54   Milotte, *Communism in Modern Ireland*, pp. 59–61; Greaves, *Liam Mellows*, p. 359.

55   UCDA, O'Malley papers, report of staff meeting, Field GHQ, 27 July 1922, P17a/15.

56   UCDA, O'Malley papers, report of staff meeting, 1 Aug. 1922, P17a/16. Lynch is possibly Eamonn Lynch, an ITGWU official, originally from Cork, who had been interned during the War of Independence. A note to O'Malley on 19 Aug. read: 'Met Eamonn Lynch ITGWU and will try to arrange meeting with you'. UCDA, O'Malley papers, P17a/61.

57   *Irish Independent*, 20 Aug. 1966. I am obliged to Charlie McGuire for this reference.

58   RGASPI, Report of the CPI to the ECCI, Oct. 1921 to Oct. 1922, 495/89/16–72.

59   Murphy, *New Horizons*, pp. 184–6. Murphy uncertainly recalls one of the IRA chiefs as Michael Mallin and says he kept insisting he was a soldier and not a politician. Mallin was a Citizen Army officer, executed in May 1916. A confusion with Ernie O'Malley is a strong possibility. Murphy does not name the other man.

60   Joseph Freeman, *An American Testament: A Narrative of Rebels and Romantics* (London, 1938), pp. 482–3.

I had a copy of the document in my coat pocket, and we boarded a tram. Hardly had it got on the move than it was held up by a contingent of Free State soldiers, who began a search of every passenger. We were sitting on the outside of the car and continued talking as the officer and his men approached. He heard me speaking to MacManus, and recognising that we were visitors said to us: 'It's all right, gentlemen. Don't be alarmed. We are searching for armed Republicans'. What a nice capture he missed! We parted company after getting off the tramcar to go to our respective hotels. MacManus had hardly left me, however, when he was arrested, taken into the hotel where he was staying, stripped and thoroughly searched by Free State soldiers. Fortunately once more, I had the document.[61]

Murphy briefed Moscow that a programme close to that of the CPI had received an 'excellent' reception in republican quarters. If endorsed by the IRA executive, a political department was to be formed, leading to the creation of a new republican party. Opposition from de Valera was anticipated, but as long as the Civil War lasted, Murphy expected de Valera to remain subordinate to the IRA executive. The report then offered a sensational assessment: 'If by every possible means military, economic, political help can be rendered the IRA ... the future of the Republican forces is one with ours.' Murphy worried nonetheless about backsliding in his absence, doubted the ability of the CPI 'in spite of the favourable conditions under which it operates', and advised the Comintern to start a new party.[62]

Connolly was understandably chuffed by the turn of events. Borodin was an important man. In 1923 he was appointed Comintern emissary to China and Soviet legate to Sun Yat-sen, and engineered in the Kuomintang the kind of Communist–nationalist alliance he had had in mind for Ireland. The serious-minded Murphy was influential in the CPGB and respected in Moscow. The 22 August 1922 found Connolly in Berlin ordering the Comintern to provide him with immediate air transport to Moscow. He was definite about the IRA's commitment, less so about the communists.

> All the arrangements are made on the Republican side as far as communications, having a captain for the ship etc. We have to get a ship, reconstruct it so as to carry arms, & get a crew, & buy the arms. The republicans are sending a man, who is already in London, with 10.000 pounds, as preliminary expenses. As well, their Executive guarantees /I have the guarantee in writing/ to pay to us half the cost of any shipment of arms as soon as same is landed in Ireland, & the remainder as soon afterwards as is possible. Borodin suggests that the Executive Comintern contribute half the expenses in every case ...

61   Murphy, *New Horizons*, p. 186.
62   RGASPI, untitled report, undated [1922], 495/89/13–83/84.

For details etc it is necessary I go to Moscow as there does not seem to be
anyone here capable or willing to tackle this big proposition.[63]

Connolly did get to Moscow, but at this point the paper trail peters out.[64] The
CPI or CPGB revealed no inkling of moves afoot other than an editorial in
the *Workers' Republic* on 2 September calling for a republican social programme,
and a more exceptional and pointed article in the *Communist* on 16 September,
which implied that a moment of truth approached: 'To De Valera the lesson
should be by now clear – Either with the proletariat against the Free State
Bourgeoisie or with the Free State and its bourgeoisie against the proletariat.'
It could not have improved the Comintern's ardour for intervention in Ireland
that Fermoy, the last town under IRA control, had been abandoned on 11
August, or that Borodin was arrested in Glasgow on 22 August and sentenced
to six months in jail for illegally entering Britain.[65] Murphy acted in Borodin's
place, and continued to collect material on Ireland with Jack Leckie, who had
tried to raise a red guard in Scotland and was keen on CPGB collaboration
with the IRA. Leckie subsequently carried another proposed republican programme to Ireland.[66] In December Murphy was told that his correspondence
on Ireland had 'for some reason or other' never arrived in Moscow, though
two fragments of one lengthy memorandum survive in the archives, suggesting
that the Comintern did wish to say yea or nay to material aid to the IRA.[67]
    What of republican sources? Republicans were awakening to the importance
of labour in August, but O'Malley's lack of experience of the movement and
tart diplomacy won him no favours. On 3 August his adjutant wrote to
William O'Brien, as secretary of the Labour Party, condemning Labour's co-
operation with the Free State and warning that trade unionists who repaired
communications or transported troops or munitions would be treated as
combatants.[68] The ILPTUC annual conference on 7 August deplored the
threat, O'Shannon declaring 'A plague on both your houses'.[69] The Free State
of course was safely inoculated by Labour's acceptance of the status quo.
O'Donnell responded bitterly to 'The Johnstonian [*sic*] Imperial Labour

63 RGASPI, Connolly to Luise, 22 Aug. 1922, 495/89/12–36. Luise, an official of the KPD acted as a
liaison between the CPI and Moscow.
64 RGASPI, ECCI to CPI, 19 Sept. 1922, saying 'Comrade RC is here representing your party',
495/89/12–53.
65 PROL, Memorandum from W. Haldane Porter, Home Office, 22 May 1923, file of Borodin, KV
2/571.
66 Greaves, *Liam Mellows*, p. 269. I am obliged to Alan Campbell for information on Leckie.
67 RGASPI, Murphy to the Comintern, 12 Dec. 1922, 495/89/11–15.
68 NLI, William O Brien, TÓD [Tomás Ó Deirg] to O'Brien, 3 Aug. 1922, 13957.
69 Greaves, *Liam Mellows*, p. 360.

Party', demanding Johnson's deportation. 'It is England's devilish luck that the Labour Party is led by Johnson just when Labour is faced with tremendous opportunities'.[70] O'Malley persisted with hamfisted efforts:

> I have endeavoured to have ships hit up leaving Dublin but so far I have failed. The Labour people may be inclined to move if I inform them that the mere fact of their assisting the military by running trains will necessitate our destroying the railway facilities ... My previous letter to them has been misunderstood.[71]

While there is no direct evidence of a response to the discussion with Murphy and MacManus, on 8 August O'Malley's adjutant asked Sighle Humphreys, Director of Publicity, Cumann na mBan, to make contact with Nora Connolly and Paddy Gaffney. He also enquired after the cost of producing a weekly paper similar to the *Workers' Republic*.[72] O'Malley himself wrote to Humphreys on 12 August, dismissing his rebuff from the ILPTUC: 'the Labour outlook was to be expected as such. Can you ... put me in touch with official Labour ... I am not in touch with ICA [Irish Citizen Army] or Roddy Connolly's crowd ... It is important that we should utilise such resources as the ICA and the Communist Party'.[73] On 18 August O'Malley asked Mellows for his views on the political and military way forward. It was known that Mellows had cultivated a radical discussion group in Mountjoy, including O'Donnell, Joe McKelvey, Séamus Breslin, a former ITGWU official, Walter Carpenter Jr, Bill Gannon, Éamonn Martin and Dick Barrett. And Lile O'Donel, who smuggled communications into the gaol, had joined the CPI.[74] Mellows immediately recommended the sale of the SS *City of Dortmund* to release £10,000 for the purchase of arms. Days later, in consultation with O'Donnell, he drafted two detailed memoranda advising the formation of a republican civil government with a manifesto based that in the *Workers' Republic* on 29 July and the Democratic Programme.[75] Coincidentally,

70 Military Archives, Captured documents, letter from Peadar O'Donnell, 12 Aug. 1922, Lot 128 a/1118.
71 Ernie O'Malley papers, O'Malley to Lynch, 24 Aug. 1922, P17/a/55.
72 Military Archives, Captured documents, Adjutant Northern and Eastern Command to D/Publicity, Cumann na mBan, 8 Aug. 1922, Lot 128 a/1118.
73 UCDA, Sighle Humphreys papers, Acting Assistant Chief of Staff to Humphreys, 12 Aug. 1922, P106/1964. I am obliged to Brian Hanley for this reference.
74 Lile and Peadar O'Donnell were married in 1924. Ó Drisceoil, *Peadar O'Donnell*, pp. 27–8, 36; Greaves, *Liam Mellows*, p. 362.
75 Greaves, *Liam Mellows*, pp. 362–9; English, *Radicals and the Republic*, p. 53. The 'Dortmund' had been purchased, nominally by International Shippers, Ltd, in early 1922 and was used by the IRA to smuggle munitions from Germany. Robert Briscoe, *For the Life of Me* (London, 1958), p. 105.

editorial staff on *An Phoblacht*, currently being produced in Glasgow, wrote to O'Malley on 15 August, urging republicans to exploit the national postal strike and to ally with the CPI.[76] O'Malley needed no convincing on either score. He had no faith in victory through guerilla methods. On 3 September he informed Lynch of Mellows's proposals, adding: 'The need for a Democratic Republican Constitution is felt and I believe it would get the workers'.[77] O'Malley expanded on the theme on 24 September:

> We consider it imperative that some sort of a Government, whether a Provisional or Republican Government or a Military one, should be inaugurated at once. It is essential to fight the illegality of the Provisional Government, for this purpose a legal committee is necessary. It is necessary to tackle the food question, Transport, Land and Civil Administration. It is indeed time to turn our attention to a constructive policy. I could not obtain Republican Land Scheme. The adjutant is working on the Democratic Programme and he is also organising a legal committee.

Saying his adjutant was preparing a resume of all democratic statements uttered in the Dáil, O'Malley unwittingly fingered the labour case for and against an alliance with republicans: 'Many have never been implemented and never will be by the Southern Parliament'.[78]

Similarly in relation to gunrunning, there is a coincidence of republican and communist sources, but the link remains tantalisingly incomplete. Bob Briscoe had received £10,000 from IRA GHQ in May to arrange from Germany the biggest republican arms importation to date.[79] A deposit of about one sixth of the total cost had been lodged when the Four Courts was attacked. The balance of the money then being unobtainable by GHQ, money drafts were drawn in IRA held Cork in July. By now, portions of the munitions had been moved to the port of shipment and arrangements made for the purchase and clearance of a vessel. Though the banks prevented the Cork drafts from being cashed, the IRA despatched Briscoe and another agent to Germany in late August to complete the 'big deal'. The operation was terminated in September when it became evident that the deal was off, and Briscoe was directed to the USA.[80]

76   UCD, O'Malley papers, letter to O'Malley, 15 Sept. 1922, P17a/159.

77   Military Archives, Captured documents, O'Malley to O/C 1st Southern Division, 9 Sept. 1922, Lot 3; UCDA, O'Malley papers, O'Malley to Lynch, 3 Sept. 1922, P17/a/56.

78   UCDA, O'Malley papers, O'Malley to Lynch, 24 Sept. 1922, P17a/57.

79   Greaves, *Liam Mellows*, p. 314.

80   UCDA, O'Malley papers, GHQ purchases dept, extract from statement made in Aug. 1924, P17a/155; Briscoe, *For the Life of Me*, pp. 183–4; Greaves, *Liam Mellows*, p. 374.

If Lynch, or his staff, had been ambiguous about political options in July, the generalissimo had reverted to his fixed and doomed vision by September. On 12 September he told O'Malley that the time 'had not yet arrived' for the adoption of a republican democratic programme. 'I fear his ideals prevent him from seeing the sane [*sic*] military outlook as others at times', was his rejoinder to Mellows's notes.[81] Insisting – against all sanity – that the military situation was improving, his immediate concern was with resisting demands from de Valera to convene the IRA executive, which had not met since 15 July, knowing that 'Dev' wanted a truce. On 13 September de Valera gave the IRA three options: accept sole responsibility for the struggle, pass the authority to the anti-treaty Dáil, or agree to a compromise between the two. Faced with the loss of political support, the executive assembled on 16–17 October and called on de Valera to form a government.[82] The agenda was confined to military and administrative matters, and questions of 'democratic politics' were excluded.[83] It hardly mattered that Mellows was made Minister for Defence in de Valera's phantom cabinet. The objective now was to salvage an honourable peace from the jaws of defeat.

The provisional government's interception and publication on 21 September of Mellows's 'Notes from Mountjoy' gave fresh hope to the CPI. Though the government derided Mellows's eleventh-hour conversion, saying he was merely pretending to espouse communism so that the IRA could use the workers as 'political cannon fodder', the CPI delighted in the publicity.[84] 'Republican Leaders Adopt Our Programme' declared the *Workers' Republic*. Mellows rejected the claim as 'silly', and the paper did admit that 'he has not yet grasped the full significance' of its doctrine of complete reliance on the working class, but was 'on the right road'.[85] Privately the party was more qualified, telling Moscow it had won three prominent converts – Mellows, O'Donnell and McKelvey – who would build a mass base for social repub-licanism, and counselled the IRA against peace talks with the provisional government. Mellows continued to write on social questions, anticipating an escape from prison.[86] As late as 18 November the CPI was predicting

81 UCDA, O'Malley papers, Lynch to O'Malley, 12 Sept. 1922, P17a/62; Lynch to O'Malley, 19 Sept. 1922, P17a/63.

82 O'Donoghue, *No Other Law*, p. 270; Tim Pat Coogan, *De Valera: Long Fellow, Long Shadow* (London, 1993), pp. 338–9.

83 UCDA, O'Malley papers, adjutant general to O'Malley, 5 Oct. 1922, P17a/64; Greaves, *Liam Mellows*, pp. 379–80.

84 Greaves, *Liam Mellows*, p. 375.

85 *Workers' Republic*, 30 Sept. 1922.

86 Greaves, *Liam Mellows*, pp. 383–4.

the imminent collapse of the Free State under the weight of its military expenditure.[87] Instead, Mellows and McKelvey, with Dick Barrett and Rory O'Connor, were to fall before a Free State firing squad on 8 December in reprisal for the assassination of Seán Hales, TD.

The IRA's search for weapons continued, in Germany and from the Russians.[88] In January 1923 the Free State's Bureau Irlandais in Geneva notified Dublin that the irregulars were looking for guns and a loan of £10,000 from the Soviets, and that Kathleen O'Brennan, a socialist journalist, had arrived in Lausanne with despatches from de Valera to Chicherin and was seen frequently with Chicherin. The Minister for External Affairs promptly directed an agent to Switzerland, who recommended the deployment of Free State secret police to monitor contact between the irregulars and Bolsheviks in Switzerland and Paris, where the Markievicz Club was said to be closely connected with the city's communists. In February the Russian government denied a statement by President Cosgrave that it had knowledge of requests for arms for the IRA, but a political collusion between republicans and Moscow persisted. On 30 March, L. H. Kerney, the Republic's envoy in Paris, added his voice to western appeals to Chicherin for clemency for Monsignor John Cieplak, titular bishop of Accride and a prisoner under sentence of death. Ostensibly a protest, Kerney's telegram was distinctly respectful and made 'in spite of the hypocritical intervention of the British government, which is responsible for the assassination in cold blood of political prisoners in Ireland'. Next day the Russian government took the unusual step of making some acknowledgement of the Republic by including this quote in its response to the British, adding sardonically: 'If similar acts which have taken place under British rule in India and Egypt are taken into consideration, it is hardly possible to regard an appeal, in the name of humanity and sacredness of life, from the British Government as very convincing.' Cieplak was executed. In Civil War republicanism's last appeal to Soviet Russia, Kerney again wired Chicherin in November about the treatment of republican prisoners in Ireland. The Soviet press published the cable without comment.[89]

None of this diplomacy affected the CPI. The Comintern had altered course, and taken the party in its wake. But what was intended to revitalise Irish communism would throw the CPI into its final agonies.

87   RGASPI, Report of the CPI to the ECCI, Oct. 1921 to Oct. 1922, 495/89/16–40/145; *Workers' Republic*, 28 Oct. to 18 Nov. 1922.

88   For Lynch's efforts to obtain guns and a submarine in Germany see Eunan O'Halpin, *Defending Ireland: The Irish State and its Enemies Since 1922* (Oxford, 1999), pp. 28–9; Murphy, *John Chartres*, pp. 142–3.

89   NA, DT, reports from the Bureau Irlandais, Geneva and memoranda to the Minister for External
Affairs, S3147; note on Klishko, assistant official agent of USSR government in Britain, S2108;
O'Brennan had worked with the Pankhursts in England and the James Larkin Defense Committee in
the USA. Though not a member of the communist party, in the mid 1920s, as Elisabeth O'Bern, she
became head of the English department of the Comintern's translation bureau in Moscow, 'a devoted
friend and bitter critic of the new regime'. See RGASPI, personal file, 495/198/1651, and Freeman, *An
American Testament*, pp. 433–4, 444–5, who remembered her in Moscow as unmarried, in her mid-40s,
with greying, bobbed hair, and a thin lined face. I am obliged to Irina Novichenko and Jim Monaghan
for these references. Kathleen's sister, Lily, was a member of Cumann na mBan, typist to Arthur
Griffith in Jan. 1922, and attached to republican headquarters, Suffolk Street, Dublin in autumn 1922,
when she was taken prisoner. UCDA, Lily O'Brennan papers, P13.

FOUR

A FISTFUL OF MARXISTS

THE DEMISE OF THE CPI, 1922-4

The CPI has gone out of existence. A fistful of Marxists, a collection of Sodality
(Sacred Heart) badges, two or three 'great I'd like to be' worms, such was
its composition. Yet it performed a wonderful amount of real work ...
Irish People (Chicago), April 1924.

—

After a year of quasi-insubordination, the fourth world congress of the
Comintern, held in Petrograd and Moscow in November and December 1922,
brought the CPI under ECCI control through the supervision of the CPGB.
In 1923 the prominence of Scots like George McLay, Arthur MacManus, Bob
Stewart and Tom Bell in Irish affairs, and the number of speakers from
Glasgow at its regular propaganda meetings in Beresford Place, would cause
Dublin wags to joke about 'the Communist Party of Scotland'.[1] The changes
and the party's professed determination to be orthodox and disciplined did
little to rectify its endemic troubles. Following a brief recovery, organisational
problems increased, and the national question became even more divisive. Jim
Larkin's return to Ireland placed the future of the party in grave doubt. The
ECCI and the CPGB regarded Big Jim as a much more attractive proposition
to lead Irish communism. For tapping Ireland's global potential, for the struggle
against imperialism and for involving the Irish diaspora in communism, his
powerful and internationally known personality appeared to be an exceptional
asset. Larkin made it clear that if he were to assume that role Moscow would
have to deal exclusively with him. But while the Soviets and the British were
preparing to double cross the CPI, Larkin had his own secret agenda.

A FEW DOLLARS MORE

The CPI sent two deputies, Roddy Connolly and George McLay, to the
fourth world congress. Connolly had recently married, and his bride, Jessica
Maidment, who had been active in the socialist movement in England,

1   UCDA, Seán MacEntee papers, Notes on communism in Saorstát Éireann, P67/523(5), p. 9.
MacManus was born in Belfast in 1891 and moved to Glasgow as a child.

accompanied him.[2] The congress ended the communist courtship of the contemporary IRA. Formally, recruitment from the IRA was to remain a priority, and delegates passed a resolution from Connolly condemning Free State repression and greeting 'the struggling Irish national revolutionaries', but it was more significant that the congress approved a shift of emphasis on the colonial question.[3] Parties in the colonies were to adopt 'dual tasks', organising in both national revolution and class struggle. In Ireland, the emphasis was in practice to be on the latter. Nikolai Bukharin told the congress's Irish commission that the republicans would be defeated, and Connolly and McLay were reprimanded for neglecting class politics and not asserting the independence of the party.[4] On 13 December the ECCI presidium instructed the CPI to concentrate on activity among the proletariat and adopt a position of moral support towards republicans. In vain, J. T. Murphy pleaded that moral support would not impress the republicans and make it harder to win members from the IRA.[5] The ECCI also agreed to send 'an energetic letter' to the CPGB 'on its duties in connection with agitation on the Irish question'.[6] The CPI accepted the new dispensation tamely. Connolly knew what many republicans still refused to accept: that they had lost the Civil War and their thinking was hopelessly out of touch with reality. He knew too that his own gamble for a communist triumph through an alliance with republicans was discredited.

Characteristically, Connolly swung from one extreme to the other. In January 1923 he published three articles in the *Workers' Republic* calling on republicans to accept military defeat, launch a new party, take the oath of allegiance, and enter Dáil Éireann; and on prisoners to sign the 'prison promise', undertaking not to resume hostilities against the state. For some, notably Peadar O'Donnell, the political somersault was too much too soon. For critics of Connolly's previous emphasis on the national question, it seemed glib and arrogant. He had already incurred resentment within the party for alleged egotism, sarcasm, refusal to do 'spade work', and affecting the manner of a bourgeois officer on his inscription into the IRA in June.[7] Hastily, the party convened on 20–21 January with the intention of removing him.

It was the CPI's first (and last) annual congress. A convention scheduled for 6–7 August 1922 had had to be postponed, and Connolly's absence from

2   Maidment was a chartered accountant and later worked for Russian Oil Products in Dublin. She died of blood poisoning in 1930. I am obliged to Charlie McGuire for these details.
3   O'Connor Lysaght, *The Communists and the Irish Revolution*, pp. 91–2.
4   RGASPI, McLay to Luise, report on the situation in Ireland, 26 June 1924, 495/89/27–10/14.
5   RGASPI, Resolution of the presidium of the ECCI on the Irish question, 13 Dec. 1922, 495/89/11–6; Murphy to the Comintern, 12 Dec. 1922, 495/89/11–15.
6   RGASPI, ECCI to the CPI, 18 Dec. 1922, 495/89/12–57.
7   RGASPI, White and O'Leary to the ECCI, 26 Feb. 1923, 495/89/22–35/38.

Ireland between July and 5 October on what was euphemistically described
as 'A Republican Mission (undertaken by the advice of the Comintern
Representative)' had necessitated further delays. Twenty-three members
attended; another 14 were serving with the IRA; 12 were in prison; and a
further 15 sent apologies. Connolly's record as president encountered criticism
and complaints that 'the Party had left the path of Communism for that of
Republicanism'. He was not re-elected to the central committee and replaced
by Miss A. B. F. White as editor of the *Workers' Republic*.[8] Connolly also
clashed with McLay over interpretations of point six of the ECCI's nine-
point directive to the party. Essentially, the directive urged the party to concentrate on activity among the proletariat, and develop its organisation. Point
six read: 'The attitude towards the republicans must consist in moral support
of the forces which are struggling against the army of the so-called "Free
State".' At a second congress, to resolve the dispute, on 18 February, Tom Bell
was present to explain the CPGB's view of the directive and help the CPI
draft its resolutions.[9] Concidentally, the CPI received £90 from the Comintern,
via the CPGB. The ECCI directive was adopted with one dissentient.
Connolly promptly resigned from the party, complaining of slanders against
him. Less convincingly, he informed Moscow that he could not work with the
new leadership as it was too republican, and appealed for the Comintern to
reorganise the party.[10] Within weeks he had returned to the fold.

The Comintern intended to conduct a complete review of the situation
in Ireland at the next meeting of its enlarged plenum. Connolly and two
other Irish delegates were to be present. For months past, MacManus and
J. T. Murphy had been collecting economic and political data on Ireland,
and proposed to have it assessed by Mikhail Borodin on his release from prison,
before forwarding it to Moscow. A joint meeting of the central committees of
the CPI and CPGB was also planned.[11] To what extent these preparations
were implemented is unclear. Borodin was immediately deported to Petrograd
on his release on 22 February, leaving the CPI unable to claim from him £150
in expenses which he had guaranteed to Connolly for his trip to Berlin in
August 1922. With mounting debts and no word yet from Moscow on its

8   RGASPI, Report of the first annual congress of the CPI, 20–21 Jan. 1923, 495/89/21–1/5.

9   RGASPI, Resolution of the presidium of the ECCI on the Irish question, 495/38/7–235/236;
White and O'Leary to ECCI, 26 Feb. 1923, 495/89/22–35/38.

10   RGASPI, White and O'Leary to Luise, 18 Feb. 1923, 495/89/22–2; resolution endorsing the
Comintern directive of policy . . . passed by the CPI, 18 Feb. 1923, 495/89/21–11; Connolly to the ECCI,
19 Feb. 1923, 495/89/22–6/11; Connolly to the ECCI, 20 Feb. 1923, 495/89/2–16/17.

11   RGASPI, MacManus to ECCI, 3 Mar. 1923, 495/18/210–43; Anglo-Saxon referent to ECCI,
16 Apr. 1923, 495/18/210–44.

financial allocation for 1923, the party decided it could not afford to send envoys to the ECCI plenum.[12] Taking advantage of Stewart's presence, the ECCI appointed a commission on Ireland on 4 May comprising Stewart, Bukharin and Vasil Kolarov, a member of the ECCI's presidium and secretariat and a future prime minister of Bulgaria.[13] The Profintern subsequently gave consideration to opening an office in Dublin, with a view to launching a campaign for the affiliation of Irish unions. Its British Bureau had an agent reconnoitring Ireland in the autumn.[14]

The CPI proceeded meanwhile to overhaul its organisation. A cycling corps was formed to boost the circulation of the *Workers' Republic*. In the paper itself, Connolly's prolix analyses of republican politics were replaced with lectures on communist theory. The youth group was revived as An Cumann Ceantarach Óg, the Young Workers' Committee, and promised a full-time propagandist and other assistance by the Young Communist League of Great Britain.[15] The committee sustained an active social agenda, and was sanguine enough in June to plan the extension of its sports section into football and hurling clubs.[16] Local party committees were organised in Newry by James Fearon, who had helped Jim Larkin to found the ITGWU, and in Carlow by Paddy Gaffney, as well as in Dublin and Cork. In April it was claimed that membership had trebled since the January congress.[17] The high point of the CPI's recovery was a well-attended Connolly commemoration in Dublin's Mansion House on 5 June.[18] Less rewarding were the CPI's efforts to secure influence within the trade unions. The Irish Garment Makers' Industrial Union, formerly the International Tailors', Machinists', and Pressers', affiliated to the Profintern, but simply as a gesture to its secretary, Walter Carpenter Sr.

12 PROL, Memorandum from W. Haldane Porter, Home Office, 22 May 1923, Michael Markovich Borodin, Oct. 1918 to Dec. 1938, KV 2/571; British special branch report no. 206, 17 May 1923, CAB 24/160.

13 RGASPI, Protokoll no.20, der Sitzung des Präsidium des EKKI, 4 May 1923, 495/2/79. According to RGASPI the files of the Irish commission are not extant.

14 RGASPI, RILU work in Ireland, undated, 534/7/286–9. This document was probably drafted by the British Bureau of the Profintern; Samuel Bradley to Smith, 12 Sept. 1923, 534/4/44–138.

15 The Young Communist League had been founded in Aug. 1922 with Pat Breslin as president. It was soon disrupted by a Free State army raid. RGASPI, Report of the Young Communist League of Ireland, undated, 533/10/1315–1/4; Tasks of Irish Centre in co-operation with YCLGB [Young Communist League of Great Britain], undated, 533/10/1315–7/10; Irish YCL [Young Communist League] course, undated, 533/10/1316–3/4.

16 *Workers' Republic*, 9 June 1923.

17 RGASPI, Report of the special congress of the CPI, 7–8 Apr. 1923, 495/89/25–18/18a; report of the special congress of the CPI, 7–8 Apr. 1923, 495/89/21–20/21.

18 *Workers' Republic*, 9 June 1923.

Significantly, Carpenter told the Profintern as much and informed them that he was the only communist in the union, and that the union would remain affiliated to the ILPTUC. Moscow overlooked these uncomfortable facts for the propaganda value of an Irish affiliate and the benefit of much needed intelligence on Irish labour.[19]

Paradoxically, Bukharin's prediction that the republican movement would be broken by military defeat made the CPI reluctant to reject militarism. On 17 February the *Workers' Republic* deplored talk of peace and urged republicans to 'fight on', pending a political victory. A major shift in policy followed the IRA's ending of hostilities on 24 May. The CPI published a draft programme which projected national independence as an outcome of, not a means towards, a social revolution. Partition would be resolved through common class struggle, while Anglo-Irish conflict would be replaced with a 'Socialist Federation of the Workers' Republics of Ireland and Great Britain'. Industrial struggle would be conducted on the basis of the Comintern's united front policy, and the CPI would 'resolutely attach itself in the strongest manner to the Irish Labour and Trade Union movement'. All possibilities of legal action would be utilised, including Dáil Éireann; 'individual terrorism, isolated acts of sabotage and spasmodic revolts are proved useless methods of achieving success'. The manifesto concluded: 'The disintegration of the present Republican forces should facilitate the Party in winning to Communism the best working class elements from the Republican leadership and ideology.'[20]

RETURN OF THE DRIFTER

When Jim Larkin was released from Sing Sing prison on 17 January 1923, he was already internationally renowned as a communist. Moscow had followed his case with interest. On 13 August 1920, Chicherin suggested to the politburo of the VKP(b) that he be exchanged for prisoners in Russian custody, an offer the Americans declined.[21] When the USA later asked the Soviets to release one captain Kirkpatrick, they agreed on condition that Larkin be freed.[22] In February 1922 Larkin was elected to the Moscow soviet to represent the

19   RGASPI, Carpenter to Lozovsky, 5 Sept. 1922, 534/7/286–3/4; I. P. K. Bekleidung, Berlin to Irish Garment Makers' Industrial Union, 14 May 1923, 534/6/79–12.

20   *Workers' Republic*, 9 June 1923.

21   The Politburo agreed to swap Larkin for prisoners Kennedy or Kolomotyano, provided the Cheka, the Soviet secret police, approved. I am obliged to Barry McLoughlin for this information.

22   NA, Department of Foreign Affairs files, T. A. Smiddy to Desmond Fitzgerald, 15 Jan. 1923, ES Box 28, file 185.

Moscow International Communist Tailoring Factory by a union of tailors, most of them returnees from the USA. It was not a unique gesture – a number of other class war prisoners in America were similarly honoured – but the Moscow soviet made a special plea that Larkin be allowed to take his seat in the council.[23] On 8 May Larkin was released on bail as a result of a writ of reasonable doubt from the New York appeal court. Grigori Zinoviev cabled the Comintern's 'warmest greetings to the undaunted fighter released from the "democratic" prisons'.[24]

Larkin moved closer to Irish republicanism during his temporary freedom. On 5 June he rejected a Labour Party nomination for one of the Dublin constituencies in the forthcoming general election, knowing that Labour's participation would lead it into propping up the Free State:

Decline emphatically. Charge you and all comrades to remember the purpose of the Union – an injury to one, etc. What of Ulster? Damn politics, and politicians, especially carellists [careerists?]. Let them clean up the mess. Ulstermen's Defence Alliance formed here. We want ship. Remember 1913. Send us 20,000 dollars to furnish ship: ours. Volunteer crew of loaders ready. We will get food cargo here. Red hand. Raise fiery cross. Be true to the principle of the dead and living nation. For the sake of the children of Ulster, fail *not*. Publish. – Jim.[25]

The Ulster Defense Alliance and the food ship became a frenetic crusade, and Larkin planned fundraising rallies across the USA. New York communists took a sceptical view of his latest 'pet organisation', and concluded he would never make a permanent home in the radical movement. In August, Larkin's court appeal failed, and on 31 August he was back in custody.[26]

From the time of his arrest, socialists from New York to New Zealand formed groups to campaign for Larkin's release. A few prominent New York Irish Americans and the American Civil Liberties Union at the behest of the Larkin Defense Committee did the crucial work. The committee had been

---

23   FBI, James Larkin file [no call no.]; UCDA, Desmond Fitzgerald papers, Smiddy to Fitzgerald (?), 26 Jan. 1923, P80/385(11).

24   Larkin, *James Larkin*, pp. 245–6.

25   *The Attempt to Smash*, p. 72; the *Voice of Labour*, 1 Apr. 1922, reported that Larkin was to be nominated for a Dublin city seat, but did not specify the constituency. William O'Brien was elected for South Dublin and Tom Johnson for Dublin County. J. J. O'Farrell failed narrowly in North West Dublin. According to D. R. O'Connor Lysaght, Larkin had been invited to stand for Mid Dublin, the only Dublin constituency Labour did not contest apart from Dublin University. Brian M. Walker, *Parliamentary Election Results in Ireland, 1918–92: Irish Elections to Parliament and Parliamentary Assemblies at Westminster, Belfast, Dublin, Strasbourg* (Dublin, 1992), p. 105.

26   FBI, James Larkin file.

formed originally in Chicago by John Fitzpatrick of the Chicago Federation
of Labor, and worked with the Irish Progressive League and the Irish-
American Labor League, which was more or less the New York Connolly
Club.[27] Tom Foran also maintained a friendly correspondence with the New
York Larkin Defense Committee, whose secretary, T. J. O'Flaherty, an older
brother of Liam, endorsed the ITGWU's hostility to 'the freak release com-
mittee of Dublin'.[28] O'Flaherty later broke with the New York committee.
He and Larkin became bitter enemies over the handling of subscriptions.
Thousands of dollars donated to the release campaign were never accounted
for. Some accused Larkin or his supporters of spending the money on other
causes.[29] Larkin subsequently alleged in Moscow that O'Flaherty and the
American communist party had stolen $50,000 raised for his defence.
Following O'Flaherty's resignation, Jack Carney's wife, Mina, shouldered the
brunt of the work. With the election of Al Smith in November 1922 a window
opened. Smith's victory confirmed that the 'red scare' had abated, and New
York's first Irish-American governor granted a pardon in January.[30]
    Though decided on a future in Ireland, Larkin had something more
ambitious in mind than the drudgery of union work. The Comintern wrote to
him on 3 February, acclaiming his release 'with great joy', and extending an
invitation to visit Soviet Russia 'at your earliest opportunity . . . to discuss a
number of burning questions affecting the international revolutionary movement'.[31] Knowing him to be a maverick, the ECCI took nothing for granted,
and was anxious to hear at first hand of Larkin's views before endorsing him.
As Larkin saw it, here was an opportunity to secure from the Soviets the type
of patronage he had enjoyed from the Germans. A commercial deal with
Moscow would enable him to bankroll freelance political activity. Larkin had
already reactivated the food ship project, and toured New England for the
Ulster Defense Alliance. With Hanna Sheehy Skeffington and Jack Carney
he held meetings in Chicago and raised $1,500 with the help of the local
Connolly Club.[32] His base at 53 Jane Street, New York became the centre of
liaison between communists and republicans in the Irish-American community. It was a troubling development for the Free State representative in

27   Larkin, James Larkin, p. 245; Greaves, The Irish Transport and General Workers' Union, p. 284.
28   Greaves, The Irish Transport and General Workers' Union, p. 316; NLI, O'Brien papers, letters from
New York re Larkin, 15678(1).
29   Ronan Fanning, Michael Kennedy, Dermot Keogh and Eunan O'Halpin (eds), Documents on
Irish Foreign Policy, Vol. II, 1923–1926 (Dublin, 2000), p. 82.
30   O'Connor, James Larkin, pp. 66–9.
31   RGASPI, Comintern to Larkin, 23 Feb. 1923, 495/89/12–1.
32   Irish Worker, 5 Jan. 1924; Irish People (Chicago), Feb. 1924; O'Connor, James Larkin, pp. 67–9.

Washington DC, T. A. Smiddy, who feared that 'Larkin's clique' would open a gun smuggling route for the 'irregulars' and form the buckle of a Bolshevik–IRA network.[33] Larkin said he was going home to fight for a republic, and would work with de Valera, adding 'I condemn certain political activities of the Irish bishops, but I am and will remain a Roman Catholic'.[34] Yet even by his own standards, Larkin was unusually volatile. Within weeks, Smiddy was gleefully telling Dublin that Larkin had split his supporters by denouncing the 'Republican bourgeois' and demanding that de Valera adopt a labour programme.[35]

On 23 March Larkin cabled Tom Foran for £5,000 to buy a steamer. When Foran sought details, a wire on 28 March enquired about money salted away from the 1913 lockout subscriptions, and already spent on expenses arising from the lockout and the purchase of Liberty Hall. While Larkin knew of this cache, the union executive had not told him the sum involved, for fear he would squander it. The cable also claimed: 'have monopoly contract certain Eastern Government, after relief work done', implying that the ship would be a long-term investment. It was not the most propitious time to be demanding money from the union, and Larkin's characteristic secretiveness meant that his business plans were not clear to anyone else. O'Brien in particular resented the self-seeking demands on the union's purse. Despite his capacity for fund-raising – in 1937 he declared to the High Court that he possessed $2,000 on re-entering Ireland – Larkin's total remittances to his union from the USA amounted to a paltry £100. Nor had he done any work for the union. Foran wired a definitive 'no' to the financial requests on 9 April.[36]

Ten days later Larkin was arrested in New York and charged with being an alien anarchist. The Department of Labor and the Federal Bureau of Investigation (FBI) had been trying since 1920 to deport him. Smiddy had warned Dublin that Larkin's return would present 'a grave problem for the Government', but when the British enquired in February if the Free State would object if it issued Larkin with a passport, the cabinet raised no objection; the Criminal Investigation Department had advised that a passport was preferable to deportation, which would prevent him from returning to the USA.[37] Larkin continued to dither as to his plans. He told the detectives who

---

33 Fanning et al., *Documents on Irish Foreign Policy, Vol. II*, pp. 31–4, 80–2; UCDA, Fitzgerald papers, Smiddy to Fitzgerald, 3 Dec. 1922, P80/385(1).

34 FBI, James Larkin file.

35 Fanning et al., *Documents on Irish Foreign Policy, Vol. II*, p. 82.

36 O'Connor, *James Larkin*, p. 68.

37 Fanning et al., *Documents on Irish Foreign Policy, Vol. II*, p. 33; NA, DT, Criminal Investigation Department recommendation, 19 Feb. 1923, S2009.

arrested him that he had no wish to return to Ireland and would like to settle
in Palestine.[38] The day after his arrest he requested the British consul for a
passport for travel to Germany, Austria, and Russia on business matters before
returning to Ireland. The consul offered a passport for the United Kingdom
only.[39] With the passport issue finally resolved, he was deported! On 21 April
he boarded the *Majestic*. Carney shadowed him, below decks, as a stoker.[40]

After disembarking at Southampton, where P. T. Daly and a deputation
from Dublin trades' council briefed him on their disputes with the ITGWU,
Larkin spent three days in London, meeting Willie Gallacher, Arthur
MacManus and Bob Stewart. The three Scots advised him to get a handle on
changes in Ireland before proceeding to Moscow.[41] On 30 April he caught the
Irish mail, and walked down the gangway at Dún Laoghaire in the familiar
long black overcoat and black broad brimmer as if his eight years of exile
hadn't mattered a fingersnap. Addressing a crowd of 4,000 at Liberty Hall, he
dwelt on what would be a major theme of his homecoming speeches: the need
for an immediate, unconditional end to the Civil War.[42] His contacts with
republicans in America had led to misunderstandings. Larkin had deluded
himself into thinking he had acquired a major influence over the anti-treatyites,
and played the peace card as an easy way of courting popularity. Republicans
on the other hand thought Larkin would swing labour behind them, and were
disgusted to hear him calling on the IRA to lay its arms at Mrs Pearse's feet
before the General Post Office.[43]

The one certainty, it seemed, was that there would be trouble in the
ITGWU on Larkin's return. O'Brien and Foran prepared their ground
by calling a special conference of the union on 24–25 April. The delegates
endorsed the executive's refusal to send money to the US to purchase a ship,
and approved amendments to the union rules which restricted the General
Secretary's duties, and locked him within a five-man collective leadership.
With near unanimity, the conference agreed to refer the rules to the branches
for approval and adjourn to await Larkin's arrival.[44] At an executive meeting
on 4 May, Larkin seemed unsure of what course to take. He announced he

38 UCDA, Fitzgerald papers, police department, city of New York, report, P80/385(69/7).

39 FBI, James Larkin file; *Irish Worker*, 5 Jan. 1924; NA, DT, note, 20 Apr. 1924, S2009.

40 Larkin, *James Larkin*, pp. 248–9.

41 Cody, O'Dowd, and Rigney, *The Parliament of Labour*, p. 136; Greaves, *The Irish Transport and General Workers' Union*, p. 317.

42 NLI, O'Brien papers, draft letter on Larkin, 15679 (23).

43 Fanning et al., *Documents on Irish Foreign Policy, Vol. II*, pp. 112–14; UCDA, Moss Twomey papers, Notes on the labour movement, undated [1926?], P69/72 (16).

44 *The Attempt to Smash*, pp. 145–6; Irish Labour History Archive, 'Draft rules for the ITGWU', 1923.

1. Roddy Connolly (centre right) and Éadhmonn MacAlpine (far left)
with Lenin at the second Comintern congress in Petrograd, 1920

2. Nikolai Bukharin with Lenin's sister Maria in the *Pravda* office

3. Grigori Zinoviev (*left*), and Lev Kamenev

BRITISH MISSION,
MOSCOW.
April 20th, 1925.

Sir,

Considerable prominence is being given in the Soviet press to the situation in Ireland, where 750,000 peasants are stated to be suffering from famine.

The "Pravda" of April 14th publishes an article by Jim Larkin illustrated with the figure of a fat and propperous Catholic priest in juxtaposition to starving and miserable women and children. Jim Larkin appeals to the readers of the "Pravda" to supply the assistance, which the Irish Government steadfastly refuses; he is of opinion that " the arrival at Dublin of a Red Relief Ship under the Red Flag would also be of great political importance".

The "Izvestiya" states that the Russian Red Cross has voted a sum of five thousand roubles for the Irish famine-sufferers, to be sent through its representative in Great Britain.

I have etc,
(Sd)R.M.HODGSON.

The Right Honourable,
    Austen Chamberlain, M.P.,
        etc.,   etc.,   etc.

4. Letter copied to the Free State Governor General on 18 May 1925. The British authorities kept the Irish government informed of Irish communist activities overseas and of Soviet interest in Ireland (National Archives)

6. Jack Carney in
Moscow, probably
1925 (RGASPI)

5. J. T. Murphy, from his
autobiography, published in 1941
after his break with the CPGB

7. Jim Larkin,
probably taken
when he visited
Moscow, 1924
(RGASPI)

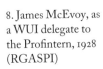

8. James McEvoy, as
a WUI delegate to
the Profintern, 1928
(RGASPI)

The Irish Worker League

READ
"THE IRISH WORKER"
SATURDAY
ONE PENNY

Unity Hall

Dublin

Telephone: Dublin 2686

February 2,1928

NATIONAL
EXECUTIVE
COMMITTEE

All communications
to be addressed to
the Committee, not
to individuals

Dear Comrade:-
At meetings of the E.C. held January 13.and Feb.1.,
you are requested to submit the attached questionnaire to the president of the CI,Comrade B. You are to demand definite answers,to be
set down in writing on the enclosed questionnaire and to be counter-
signed by Comrades B. and P. You are further requested to demand a
fullin sitting of the presidium. The E.C. would be glad if you would
limit your stay at the centre to not more than five days. Calle date
of arrival and also date of departure.
                              On behalf of the I.W.L.
                              Yours fraternally

[signature]
[signature: Seán S. Kelly]   Political Bureau

[signature: Bernard Conway]
[signature: Jack Carney]   Executive Secretary

9. Instructions and credentials for the IWL delegation to Moscow, 1928.
Attached were 18 questions for Bukharin, detailing Larkin's
grievances with the Comintern. Within the star emblem is
'Irish Worker League Worker and Peasant' (RGASPI)

óglaiġ na h-éiReann.
(IRISH REPUBLICAN ARMY)

Dept. **Brig.Adjt.**

Ref. No. **Special,**

Áro-OıꝼıꞬ :

bpıoꞬáıꝺ Áṫa Cliaṫ.

October 9th, 1932.

To: Sean Murray,

Revolutionary Workers' Groups,

206, Pearse Street,

Dublin.

A Chara,

To acknowledge receipt of yours of the 7th inst;
While the objects for which your meeting is called has the
full sympathies of the Brigade Staff, I regret to inform
you that owing to standing orders the Brigade as a Unit,
cannot parade at any meetings,demonstrations,etc, which are
not under the direct control of the Army G.H.Q.
Assuring you of our full co-operation as individuals,and
wishing the purpose for which Sunday's demonstration is
called all success.

Is mise,

Brig.Adjt.

10. Correspondence such as this was sent to Moscow as proof of the Irish commission's activities. Seán Murray has added an explanation beneath the letter. The stationery reflected the IRA's legal status at the time (RGASPI)

11. Jim Prendergast,
Lenin School, 1934–5,
in the uniform of the
International Brigades
(RGASPI)

12. Donal O'Reilly,
Lenin School, 1931–?,
in the uniform of the
International Brigades
(RGASPI)

13. Val Morahan, Lenin School, 1935–7
(RGASPI)

14. Liam McGregor, Lenin School, 1935–7,
killed in action in Spain, 1938 (RGASPI)

15. William Morrison, Lenin
School, 1935–7 (RGASPI)

16. Betty Sinclair, Lenin School,
1934–5, addressing a Communist
Party meeting in the 1960s

17. The Irish delegation at the congress of the Krestintern in Berlin, March 1930. Peadar O'Donnell is at the head of the table, with Bob Stewart to his right.

19. Tommy Watters, CPI general secretary, 1941–2, photographed *c.* 1970

18. Seán Murray, Lenin School, 1927–30, CPI general secretary, 1933–41 (RGASPI)

20. W. H. 'Bill' McCullough, Communist Party general secretary, 1942–6

October 20th, 1932.

Letter to Ireland.

Dear Friends,

Your letter dated September 9th received today. The matter that you especially emphasise at the end of your letter had already been attended to several weeks ago.

We wish to call your attention to several points which arise from your letter:

The proposal to organise a joint training centre with the republicans is very vague. We would like to get detailed information regarding the programme of the proposed training centre, who will control it, and who will be the teachers. It is quite correct to go into such a proposition if this will provide us with an opportunity of carrying on our propaganda, but even then such a joint training centre cannot be considered to be a substitute for our own training centre which undertakes the task of training centres for the CPI.

We are against changing the main slogan by the addition of the word "revolutionary". This change would give an altogether wrong direction to our struggle. To talk about a Revolutionary Workers and Farmers Government means narrowing our main slogan. The government of the Workers' and Farmers' Republic is not limited only to revolutionary workers and farmers, but it is the government of the whole of the workers and small farmers including those who are not revolutionary. If the substitution of the word "government" for "republic" will make our agitation easier and more popular there is no reason why in our agitation we should not use it. But you should consider carefully if it would not be wise to retain the word republic because of the long tradition that the idea of a republic has among the masses in Ireland. The main thing is that the content of the slogan must be made clear: The Workers and Farmers Republic is a synonim for the dictatorship of the proletariat the state form of which shall be the soviets of workers and farmers.

Regarding the proposal to direct the main fire against the British concerns it will be necessary to combat any tendency to let up in the struggle against the Irish capitalists. In concrete instances it should be possible to mobilise the workers against English concerns such as Gallaghers Tobacco factory, but in no case can we drag at the tail of Irish capitalism. In this period when there is going on a development of the movement of the workers and agricultural labourers in defence of their economic interests (especially regarding unemployment) it is necessary to concentrate on the development of this struggle and direct it against the local and national governments. The slogan of "nationalisation without compensation" can be used in an agitational manner to expose the inability of the government and its supporters to undertake any real measures against the English concerns or Irish capitalism. But even from this standpoint the slogan must be linked up with the needs of the workers and small farmers, with the question of which class is to control the industries, to raise the question of which government is going to nationalise the industries either the capitalist government or DeValera or the Workers' and Farmers' Government.

Besides the above points of your letter we beg you to make your letters more elaborate and concrete. You write about the confusion which exists regarding the line to be followed, but do not mention specifically or what points. Regarding the strength of the RWG, trade union work, and especially the plans for the campaign to found the CPI

21. Page one of a letter from the Anglo-American secretariat to the RWG. During the third period, Moscow's supervision was detailed (RGASPI)

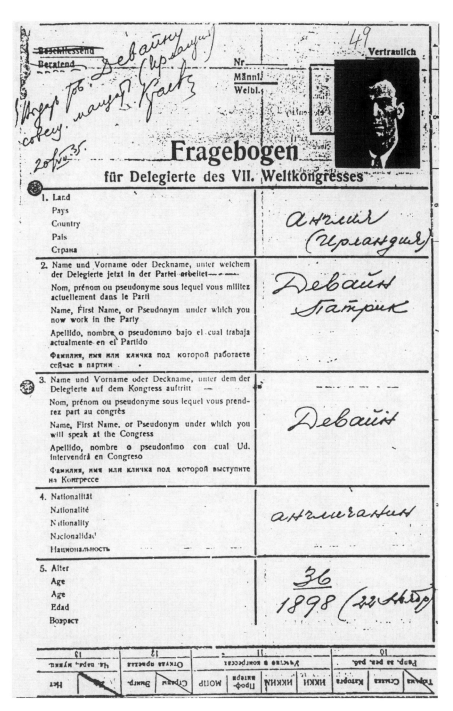

23. International Brigaders, Sam Walters, Francois Mazov, Julius Margolin, Bob Doyle
and Bill Van Felix pay their respects to Big Jim Larkin in Dublin, 1991. After 1932
Larkin wished to forget his communist past and prevented his union from
supporting the Spanish Republic. Despite their private quarrels, it
suited the Communists to applaud him in public (ILHS)

was going to Russia immediately, and that he would resign as General Secretary next day, but instead accepted Foran's idea that he embark on a tour of the branches. At the reconvened ITGWU rules conference, the proposed changes met little resistance from Larkin. Again, he appeared distracted by Russia, saying that 'He had arranged a monopoly of trade between Ireland and Russia, and he would be going to Russia shortly with the permission of the Union, but would not be very long away'. What was to be a two-month tour of the branches began on 20 May.[45] Larkin cut it short after a week and hastened to Dublin. He had seen enough to feel the ITGWU was no longer 'his' any more. For the next year his priorities were decided: Russia would take second place to an attempt to restore 'Larkin's union'.

Larkin made little attempt to offer a coherent critique of union policy. His various allegations of misappropriation of funds, maladministration and contravention of rules transparently amounted to the demand that O'Brien and his allies should be expelled and the union given back to Larkin. The executive was confident of membership backing. The split could not have come at a worse time for the ITGWU. General workers were among the last sectors to avoid wage cuts, and bracing themselves for the bosses's 'big push'. In these circumstances, the executive reckoned, Larkin's antics looked all the more irresponsible and workers would close ranks against him. This indeed proved to be the case in the provinces, where Larkin had few contacts. In Dublin on the other hand, he had a personal relationship with the workers, in contrast to the more bureaucratic style of the executive leaders, and his name was synonymous with militancy at a time when members were beginning to doubt the union's resolve. Certainly, he had the potential to rally the majority of ITGWU members in Dublin to his side.

On 11 June Larkin led a march of about 100 workers through the streets to seize Liberty Hall and the ITGWU offices in Parnell Square. The executive suspended him as General Secretary, and secured an interim injunction to prevent him or his agents interfering with their duties. Larkin quickly handed over the keys of Liberty Hall, hoping perhaps to retain Parnell Square, and carve a bailiwick out of the ITGWU as simply as he had annexed a base in 1918 from the Socialist Party in New York. But the executive persisted, obtaining a mandatory injunction on 18 June. On the following day, the Parnell Square premises was surrendered without resistance.[46]

The revival of the *Irish Worker* on 15 June extended Larkin's offensive to the 'God save the King Labour Party' and its 'English, anti-Irishman' leader, who was born not far from himself in Liverpool. Even by his own fearsome

45   *The Attempt to Smash*, pp. 142–3, 147–8, 260.
46   *Manchester Guardian*, 13–22 June 1923.

standards, Larkin developed an extraordinary hatred of Tom Johnson, and could not pass him in the street without offering abuse.[47] The paper made the cause no clearer. By mid July the public still knew little of the reasons for the ITGWU's internal trouble, and Larkin appeared to be working 'apart and in obscurity'. He had already ruled out contesting the forthcoming general election, expressing disdain for Dáil Éireann, and his most prominent political act that month was to speak at a reception in the Mansion House for Muriel, widow of Terence MacSwiney, just back from the USA, where she had worked hard for his release from prison.[48] The assault on official Labour was complete when Larkinites and republicans aggressively picketed the opening of the ILPTUC annual congress on 6 August. After his supporters had jostled and jeered the delegates, Larkin obstinately contested for the chair of Congress, and was trounced by 147–27 votes.[49] In September Larkin rejected mediation proposals from an ITGWU rank and file committee, and the committee accepted the split as irrevocable.[50]

Larkin had met the CPI's central committee in early May and made 'vague references' to his relations with the Comintern, leaving the committee to ask Moscow for clarity and guidance. Subsequently he ignored the party: 'why take notice of these little wasps?', he told the ITGWU on 14 May.[51] The *Workers' Republic* continued to shower him with encomiums, but the party evidently had its reservations. '[Q]uestions are being constantly asked . . . as to our attitude towards Larkin', it admitted in June. Yet following his split with the ITGWU executive, the CPI offered him 'all support'.[52] Communists needed no reminding of their own disputes with O'Brien. While dismayed by the imbroglio, the Comintern's pursuit of Larkin continued. The ECCI wrote to him on 6 August saying it had hoped to see him earlier and offering a flight to Moscow from Germany.[53] MacManus despaired of Larkin taking an extended break from Ireland and urged the ECCI to have a representative meet him in Holland, France or Germany. 'The task of the reorganisation of the entire Irish movement', he advised, 'should be undertaken almost immediately'.[54] But Larkin was now consumed with the fight against O'Brien and determined to see it through without compromise before addressing his communist project.

47 Gaughan, *Thomas Johnson*, p. 378.
48 *Manchester Guardian*, 2, 16, 28 July 1923.
49 NLI, ILPTUC, *Annual Report* (1923), p. 87; *Manchester Guardian*, 7 Aug. 1923.
50 *The Attempt to Smash*, pp. 160–1.
51 PROL, British special branch report no. 206, 17 May 1923, CAB 24/160; *The Attempt to Smash*, p. 148.
52 *Workers' Republic*, 9–16 June 1923.
53 RGASPI, Comintern presidium to Larkin, 6 Aug. 1923, 495/89/20–5.
54 RGASPI, MacManus to the secretariat, ECCI, 5 Sept. 1923, 495/89/22–65/66.

Larkin thought he could trump O'Brien on the industrial front. The 'big push' had come, and the resistance began on 16 July, when 3,000 dockers struck against a pay cut of 2s. per day. The dispute triggered a wave of similar employer demands, marking the final phase of the wage-cutting offensive. By August, some 20,000 workers were on strike or locked out. Larkin took command of the dock strike in Dublin, leaving the ITGWU executive to supply the strike pay. Since May, he had grasped a blatant weakness in Labour strategy – its stolid refusal to exploit the political instability to force the government to restrain the employers. The cabinet took seriously his threat to disrupt the general election failing a settlement of strikes. On 1 August it agreed to request employers to postpone wage cuts for three months, during which conferences would be convened under government auspices. Once the election was over, there was less pressure on the government. On 26 October, the unions in the dock strike accepted a cabinet proposal that the dockers accept a 1s. per day cut, pending an enquiry into wage rates. On Larkin's advice, Dublin dockers voted 687–433 to fight on. The ITGWU executive dismissed the ballot and withdrew strike pay. Within a week, the Dublin dockers accepted the pay cut, and allied occupations suffered related reductions.[55] On 29 October Larkin made a desperate bid to swap labour's crumbling industrial power for political influence, offering President Cosgrave a guarantee of an end to strikes on government terms in return for the release of the 8,000 or so republicans in prison, hundreds of whom had been on hunger strike since 14 October. Cosgrave sent him a curt rejection.[56] Larkin's next fight would be against the ITGWU, in the law courts.

HANG 'EM HIGH

The CPI's spring advances had not been sustained. The sections in Carlow and Newry had collapsed, and its membership of some 70 in Dublin was deemed to be of poor quality.[57] Although the industrial crisis that autumn deepened rank and file disillusionment with the trade union leadership, the CPI was hopelessly inconsequential to a situation complicated by the split between Larkin and the ITGWU executive. McLay wrote to his Comintern correspondent, Luise, on 22 August:

> We have tried to keep the issues down to a basis of 'the movement first' but here everything is being dealt with from the point of view of individuals. Even Larkin

55 O'Connor, *A Labour History of Ireland*, p. 116; Larkin, *James Larkin*, p. 270.
56 NA, DT, Larkin to Cosgrave and reply, 29 Oct. 1923, S2009.
57 RGASPI, CPI, report to 1 Oct. 1923 from April 1923, from George McLay, 495/89/22–74/76.

is hopeless, as far as building a movement is concerned, and he is at present hopelessly outgeneralled, due to his weakness of wanting to dominate everything, which has played into the hands of the reactionaries. Our own ranks are badly disorganised at the moment also . . .

Communist prisoners' dependants were a heavy drain on financial resources, absorbing what little could be raised by the James Connolly Social Club and propaganda meetings. Pressing Luise to expedite the despatch of the party's £75 quarterly allowance, McLay added: 'I am also writing to the British comrades, but I know it is useless, as they are anything but sympathetic . . . There is a strong move to dissolve the CPI and start a workers' party, but we are determined to defeat that.'[58] In the following month the cash-strapped *Workers' Republic* started a football competition, based on forecasting English soccer results.

Despite the 'turn to class', the general election on 27 August again brought the national question to the fore in the CPI. The party had appealed, naïvely and in vain, to the ECCI for £1,500 to fight the election with Larkinite candidates.[59] Two party members contested: Gaffney, unsuccessfully, in Carlow as an independent labour republican, and Peadar O'Donnell, successfully, in Donegal, as a Sinn Féin nominee.[60] Otherwise the CPI watched from the sidelines, commending a list of minimum, reformist demands to trade unionists, advising votes for Labour and Sinn Féin, and advocating a Labour–republican united front against the Free State.[61] Larkin endorsed four candidates nominated by Dublin trades' council, and a fifth in Tipperary. Their electoral target was the Labour Party more than anything else. O'Brien's campaign was harassed, and Johnson had his meetings heckled by Larkin in person. Sinn Féin polled well, but the election hugely disappointed the left, which paid the price of its fractiousness and irrelevance to the industrial struggle. Expecting to build on an excellent showing in 1922, Labour saw its share of the vote fall from 21.3 per cent to 10.6 per cent. O'Brien's defeat was a particular blow to the prestige of the ITGWU and Dublin Workers' Council. While the Larkinites won a mere 4,500 votes, P. T. Daly's creditable 2,100 votes in Dublin North City revitalised Dublin trades' council as a political force.[62] On 8 September

---

58 RGASPI, McLay to Luise, 22 Aug. 1923, 459/89/22–64.

59 RGASPI, McLay and O'Leary to Bukharin, 1 July 1923, 495/89/22–61/62.

60 O'Donnell was scarcely involved with the CPI at this stage and later dismissed his endorsement by the party as a 'gimmick'. Ó Drisceoil, *Peadar O'Donnell*, p. 34.

61 *Workers' Republic*, 25 Aug. 1923.

62 Michael Gallagher, *Political Parties in the Republic of Ireland* (Manchester, 1985), pp. 158–9; Mitchell, *Labour in Irish Politics*, p. 189; Cody, O'Dowd, and Rigney, *The Parliament of Labour*, p. 137.

the *Irish Worker* announced the launch of Larkin's own political movement, the IWL. Redolent of the Daily Herald Leagues, with which he had worked in Britain during the 1913 lockout, the name echoed his glorious past rather than a Leninist future. The modus operandi of the IWL was as yet unclear, but its implications for the CPI could only be negative.

Nonetheless it seemed as if the CPI was intent on self-destruction without Larkin, and it managed to get mangled by an election in which it was scarcely involved. The central committee had agreed to a request from Sinn Féin in Dublin North City to provide speakers, on condition that they were announced as communists and could address topics of their choice. When Connolly and Walter Carpenter (Jr?) got the Dublin branch to demand unconditional support for republicans instead, the central committee objected. Following protracted disputes, McLay, White and Michael J. McCabe resigned from the five-man central committee on 1 October.[63]

The resignations prompted an ECCI request to the CPGB to investigate, and a damning report from Arthur MacManus, who already believed the party to be too republican and scarcely Leninist. According to MacManus, the CPI had fewer than 50 members. Connolly and three other leading comrades had accepted jobs as Sinn Féin organisers. The Dublin branch was riven by personal squabbles, and 'composed mostly of young boys and girls, practically all of whom are still connected with the Catholic Church and have not the slightest knowledge about the Party'.[64] A recently formed Galway section was made up entirely of young republicans, again without 'the slightest knowledge' of communism. The *Workers' Republic*, a 'poor and shoddy document', sold less than half of its weekly print run of 2,000 copies, and was £200 in debt. Average income from sales amounted to £3 10s. per week, while the paper cost £13 per week. The second part of the report dealt with Larkin. Unprompted, he had 'emphatically' encouraged MacManus to have the CPI dissolved. While the IWL had yet to indicate anything specific of its politics, MacManus believed it intended to recruit 'more or less militant workers not only in Ireland but in Great Britain and America as well', and promised that the CPGB would discuss developments with Larkin at the earliest opportunity. The report recommended the liquidation of the CPI; the politburo of the CPGB endorsed it unanimously.[65]

---

63 RGASPI, CPI, report to 1 Oct. 1923 from Apr. 1923, from George McLay, 495/89/22–74/76.

64 MacManus had considered studying for the priesthood and may have been sensitive about religion, but there were numerous and not unfavourable allusions to Christian theology in the *Workers' Republic* of 1923, which may explain the anti-clerical *Irish People*'s dismissive reference to 'a collection of Sodality badges'.

65 RGASPI, report by MacManus and the Politbureau of the CPGB, 11 Oct. 1923, 495/38/7–236/241.

The intrigue with Larkin continued. He visited London in January 1924, and got the CPGB to circularise branches urging the formation of IWL branches in Britain. A London branch was founded in March, by Eadhmonn MacAlpine.[66] MacManus had laid his cards before the Comintern in February:

> The view of our Central Committee . . . is that instead of nurturing an absolutely ineffective and valueless Party such as existed recently, that a determined effort ought to be made to form a Workers' Party . . . Several protracted conversations have taken place between Larkin and members of our Political Bureau on the matter and at our last meeting Larkin finally expressed himself in complete agreement with first, the need for a Workers' Party . . . and secondly, that this Irish Workers' [sic] League should simply be an instrument used to create such a Workers' Party.[67]

MacManus had not been entirely open with Larkin, and there was a hidden agenda.

> You must not imagine that we, on this side, do not fully understand Larkin and all the difficulties of his strong personality and hasty thinking. We appreciate this to the full, but we considered that his capacity for attracting the masses around him and for stimulating them into action was just the essential thing that was required in Ireland at the moment. We also felt that if, side by side with his activities in this direction a strong, co-ordinated group . . . could be built up around him that by this means an organized revolutionary movement might become a possibility. To effectively establish this, however, takes time, as both the process of following and working closely with Larkin on the one hand and at the same time training and developing the Communist group around him on the other, is a very delicate job.[68]

The CPI had closed ranks sufficiently to offer a dying kick against its impending doom. Connolly returned to the central committee and, with his facile capacity for discounting his own share of responsibility for past failures, wrote a trenchant review of the state of the party. 'In all our eighteen months existence as a Communist Party we hardly made ten new Communists . . . Out of the five on [the old central committee] there was only one who was *nearly* a proletarian.'[69] Seán McLoughlin too was back in harness, following his release from Limerick jail on signing the 'prison promise'. At a branch

66   NA, DJ, Larkin file, JUS 8/676.
67   RGASPI, MacManus to Kuusinen, 2 Feb. 1924, 495/38/7–243/244.
68   RGASPI, MacManus to the Workers' Party of America, 2 Feb. 1924, 495/38/7–245/248.
69   *Workers' Republic*, 27 Oct. 1923.

meeting on 30 October 1923, McLay predicted a big influx of members once the jail gates were opened, and as the Free State detained over 10,000 republicans during the year it was not an unreasonable expectation.[70] However, addressing this possibility reopened old divisions. The *Workers' Republic* denounced Larkin's offer to Cosgrave for the release of political prisoners as a betrayal of workers' interests, provoking a censure motion against the central committee from Connolly. At the same time Paddy Read, who wrote for the *Workers' Republic* under the unlikely byline 'O. U. Rube', attacked the CPI's subordination to 'social republicans'.[71] A reorganisation of the party on 12 November saw Connolly appointed political secretary and a new plan of expansion adopted. Read was expelled on 16 November, for indiscipline.[72] The last issue of the *Workers' Republic* appeared the following day. By the end of the month the republican hunger strike had collapsed, following the death of two prisoners. Clutching at straws, the CPI nonetheless appealed to the ECCI against MacManus's 'exceedingly misleading, inaccurate and insulting report' and the CPGB's resolution in favour of the party's liquidation,

in view of the industrial and political situation, the consolidation of the forces of reaction, the impending crisis in the ranks of Republicanism, the move to the left on the part of large sections of the proletariat, and the improvement in Party organisation and prospects due to the release of our comrades from prison.[73]

The CPI was wound up at a congress on 26 January 1924. Enormous debts and the loss of its hall at 14a Eustace Street were given as the reasons for the dissolution, though it seems likely that the Comintern had a hand in the decision.[74] It says something for the credibility of the little party that Liam O'Flaherty's *The Informer*, published in September 1925, became an instant bestseller and the basis of two films. Some thought the political setting even

70 UCDA, Richard Mulcahy papers, report on CPI meeting, 30 Oct. 1923, P7a/87; MacEntee papers, Notes on communism in Saorstát Éireann, P67/523(5), p. 11; NA, DT, communist activities, 1929–30, SO74A. Mulcahy, as Minister for Defence, received detailed army intelligence reports on the CPI from an informer, agent '101A'. See also O'Halpin, *Defending Ireland*, p. 58;
71 *Workers' Republic*, 3–10 Nov. 1923; NA, DT, memo, Sept. 1931, S5864B.
72 UCDA, Mulcahy papers, report on CPI meeting 16 Nov. 1923, P7a/87.
73 RGASPI, R. Connolly, M. J. McCabe, Seán McLoughlin, and Thomas O'Connor to ECCI, 1 Dec. 1923, 495/89/22–81/82.
74 UCDA, Cowan family papers, Séamus McGowan papers, McGowan, McCabe, McLay, O'Leary to comrade[s?] CPI, 14 Feb. 1924, P34/D/54; RGASPI, Irish draft resolution, undated [1927], 495/3/3–15 refers to 'The CI having dissolved the small CPI . . .'. However 'Ireland', undated [1926], 495/89/104–139, an internal ECCI memo refers to the CPI being 'dissolved by a vote of its own members'. Possibly both were true.

Reds and the Green

more significant than the literature. 'I think if you eliminate Bolshevism and muck-raking from Liam O'Flaherty', wrote Desmond Fitzgerald, 'you have a very unimportant writer'.[75] What the ECCI made of the novel is unknown. It could be forgiven for protesting that by that stage it had read enough Irish fiction. And if the CPI had caused it to think of Ireland as a troublesome outpost, the IWL would reduce it to handwringing perplexity.

75 Quoted in John M. Regan, *The Irish Counter-Revolution, 1921–1936: Treatyite Politics and Settlement* (Dublin, 2001), p. 283.

FIVE

AN INFERNAL TRIANGLE
LARKIN, LONDON AND MOSCOW, 1924-6

Jim Larkin and his most immediate associates can think of nothing else but Jim Larkin.
It is difficult to argue or venture any opinion that does not co-incide with
his own, and yet the man is undoubtedly a leader.

HARRY POLLITT

17 April 1924[1]

—

It might seem strange that anyone should think of making himself rich and famous by leading communism in the Ireland of the 1920s, but this was Jim Larkin's intention. There is evidence that Larkin was not in a healthy frame of mind in the 1920s and early 1930s. The ordeal of the 1913 lockout had turned his egocentrism into egomania, and during his first ten years back in Ireland he was plagued with depression, insecurity, paranoia and jealousy; problems probably aggravated by estrangement and separation from his wife, Elizabeth. Yet within Larkin's self-destructive selfishness, there remained a core of rational self-interest. While his methods were contradictory and self-defeating, his project was not quite so absurd. If the economic climate was no longer favourable for militancy, the defeats of 1921-4 created opportunities to harness the dejected foot soldiers of the trade union and republican movements. Communism had not yet acquired the odium with which it was to be invested by the resurgence of Catholic social power after 1929, and the various splits in the labour movement quickly produced a sizeable constituency for 'red Dublin'.

Larkin always had a cavalier attitude to money – other people's at least – and a history of misappropriation of funds. He would have been familiar with fables of Russian largesse – the American Communist Labor Party had liberal access to Soviet embassy coffers – and he reckoned he could milk the Soviets. He had no wish to turn the IWL into an orthodox communist party, realising that political funding would come with conditions and that the party would be used to discipline him. Trade would be a more lucrative and independent source of income. A Russo-Irish commercial exchange, a Soviet backed co-operative, or ideally a sinecure as Russia's commercial agent in the Free State

---

1   RGASPI, Report on the situation in Ireland, 17 Apr. 1924, 495/100/168–1/3.

would generate the revenue to rid him both of the burden of trade union work and political accountability to Moscow, and let him devote his time to the things he liked: editing a paper, freelance agitation and travel. The snag was that the communists would back Larkin only if he formed a party. After protracted negotiations between the Larkins, the CPGB, and the Comintern, a deal was finally concluded in January 1925. Larkin was to lead a communist movement; in return the British would help him consolidate the Workers' Union of Ireland (WUI), and the Soviets would provide financial support and, according to Larkin, establish a trade link with Ireland. The triangular relationship soon became poisoned with dissension, insubordination and deceit. Not only did Larkin refuse to form a communist party, he went to great lengths to ensure that no one else did either. By 1926 the British were conniving with Larkin's critics in an effort to develop an alternative communist party, and by 1927 Moscow too was plotting to clip his wings.

LARKIN GOES TO RUSSIA

The hearing for the lawsuits affecting the ITGWU opened before the Master of the Rolls in Dublin Castle on 12 February 1924. In *Foran and Others* v. *Larkin*, the ITGWU sought injunctions against Larkin entering union premises or obstructing union officials. In *Larkin* v. *the ITGWU*, the plaintiff contended first that the union's 1918 rules had not been properly adopted by the branches, and therefore the then executive and their subsequent actions were illegal, and secondly that the union had used funds for political purposes, without having a legal political fund.[2] The second contention was based ultimately on the infamously anti-trade union Osborne Judgment, a source of some embarrassment to the communists.[3] Larkin lost the cases on 20 February, and faced legal costs of £1,300.[4] On 14 March he was expelled from the union. Initially, he intended to appeal, and in May his supporters signalled their intention to fight on by occupying Liberty Hall until ejected by the army.[5] However, he had also determined to attend the fifth world congress of the

---

2   *The Attempt to Smash*, pp. 1–2.

3   The Osborne Judgment, given by the House of Lords in 1909, ruled that it was illegal for trade unions to use funds for political purposes. The Trade Union Act (1913) modified the judgment to allow a union to make political contributions, provided its members had voted to create a political fund. Trade union leaders resented the restrictions of the Act. Henry Pelling, *A History of British Trade Unionism* (London, 1974), pp. 130–2.

4   RGASPI, Harry Pollitt, Report on the situation in Ireland, 17 Apr. 1924, 495/100/168–1/3.

5   Larkin, *James Larkin*, pp. 279–80; NA, DJ, Larkin file, JUS 8/676.

Comintern in Moscow in June. In January he had applied for passports for himself and young Jim, his eldest son, to visit Berlin on transport-related business. What that business was, the Larkins declined to specify, and their applications were duly returned. Big Jim nonetheless decided that Russia could no longer be postponed, and dropped the appeal. The government would later query how he managed to travel without a passport.[6]

Whether to impress his hosts in Moscow or in response to internal pressure, Larkin convened the IWL's first conference in April, on Easter Sunday. He had envisaged the League as a campaign force rather than a party, and spoken airily of developing an international network mobilising the Irish diaspora behind struggles in Ireland. To date, only Dublin and London branches had emerged, and the former did little more than occasional fund-raising for striking gas workers and republican prisoners' dependants. Meetings were often cancelled simply because Larkin could not be present. Already CPI veterans were drifting out in disgust. In April the *Irish People* reported that the CPI's 'best elements' were attempting to build the nucleus of a new party in workers' republican clubs and Connolly education clubs.[7] Ever anxious to acquire intelligence on Ireland, the ECCI invited the Irish Republican Workers' Party to send a delegate to the fifth world congress.[8] However, no more was heard of the party. It seemed that the CPI veterans could create structures, but not members, while Larkin was averse to structures, but did have supporters. The IWL had enrolled 500 members on its inauguration, and led a march of 6,000 people to mourn the death of Lenin in January 1924.[9] On his first visit to Ireland in April, Harry Pollitt despaired over the depth of the divisions caused by the Civil War and the ITGWU split, but was impressed with Larkin's popularity. On a trip to Roscrea he found:

> a mass of streamers welcoming Larkin to the town. Over 500 workers paid 7s. each to travel by excursion with Larkin . . . last Sunday he called a meeting in Dubln to demand that all the prisoners be set free. I am assured that it was one of the largest meetings ever seen in the city.[10]

Pollitt reckoned the IWL had a 'tremendous chance' if Larkin would take it seriously. The CPGB concluded that Pollitt's report fully justified its policy

---

6   NA, DJ, Larkin file, JUS 8/676.
7   *Irish People* (Chicago), Apr. 1924, pp. 13, 18.
8   RGASPI, ECCI to CPI, 8 Apr. 1924, 495/89/27–3; ECCI to secretary Irish Republican Workers' Party, formerly Comparty, Ireland, 2 June [1924], 495/89/27–4.
9   Cody, O'Dowd, and Rigney, *The Parliament of Labour*, p. 143.
10 RGASPI, Harry Pollitt, Report on the situation in Ireland, 17 Apr. 1924, 495/100/168–1/3.

on Ireland. On Easter Sunday the IWL adopted a constitution, appointed an executive, and introduced a dues scheme. Larkin became honorary president. P. T. Daly and other officers of Dublin trades' council dominated the executive, which also included Muriel MacSwiney and Jack Dempsey, heavyweight boxing champion of the world. One CPI veteran, Bob Murray, was elected to the executive in June, but soon resigned in protest at the IWL's inactivity.[11] Neither was George McLay convinced: he warned the ECCI that Larkin would never develop a party and was best confined to trade unionism.[12]

The Comintern invited Larkin to its fifth congress 'as a representative of the Irish working class'. He left Dublin on 2 June, travelling by steamer via London and Leningrad.[13] The congress, which opened in the Kremlin on 17 June, was to be a turning point for the movement. The ECCI had been shaken by the failure of a planned communist uprising in Germany in October 1923, and was moving towards acceptance of 'socialism in one country' and Bolshevisation. At national level, Bolshevisation meant the application of the Leninist principles of unity, discipline and democratic centralism. Crucially, Bolsheviks understood their national sections to belong to a world party directed by the ECCI. In the global context, it also meant the subordination of the Comintern to the Soviet party and the interests of the Soviet Union.[14] It was all the same to Larkin, for whom communism was just the old class struggle in new clothes, and the Comintern a crock of gold. He seldom spoke publicly in Moscow, and revealed his parochialism during the debate on the national and colonial questions.

> I mount this tribune with some deference, and only at the request of Comrade Zinoviev, who said the congress was interested in Ireland. I have failed to notice it. The congress seems interested only with those parties which have the biggest membership . . . I appeal to you comrades to turn your eyes to the Irish proletariat. We are not confined to Ireland. We have millions in England, Scotland, the United States, Australia and South Africa. It is the duty of the Communist International to get this great mass, mostly proletarians, interested in the great Communist movement.[15]

It meant nothing to Larkin that the congress modified its line against bourgeois nationalist movements taken at the fourth congress, and approved strategic

---

11   Milotte, *Communism in Modern Ireland*, p. 74.
12   RGASPI, McLay to the ECCI, 26 June 1924, 495/89/27-10/14.
13   RGASPI, ECCI to Larkin, 2 June 1924, 495/89/27-5; NA, DJ, Larkin file, JUS 8/676.
14   McDermott and Agnew, *The Comintern*, pp. 41-68.
15   Donal Nevin, 'Workers of the world', in Nevin, *James Larkin*, p. 336; Milotte, *Communism in Modern Ireland*, pp. 75-6.

alliances between communists and nationalists in the colonies. He would follow his agenda regardless. His other speech at the congress endorsed the CPGB's support for 'united front' tactics with the British Labour Party, and disputed the ECCI's view that the British working class was moving left.[16]

As the Comintern congress closed, the third congress of the Profintern opened. Regarding himself, quite rightly, as an expert on industrial conflict, Larkin played a livelier part in the debates, and again revealed his ideological and temperamental differences with Bolshevism. Emphasising the importance of co-operatives to the trade union movement, he recalled a big lockout in Dublin 'some years ago' and how food ships from the British co-operative society had 'procured the victory of the struggle'.[17] The muddle as to the outcome of the 1913 lockout was not as ingenuous as it seemed. Larkin was privately lobbying for a Soviet-backed co-operative in Dublin.[18] Later he dismissed a paper by Aleksandr Lozovsky, the Profintern secretary, on 'The strategy of strikes', ridiculing the idea that strikes could be ordered along military lines.[19] All in all, he had not found the conferences congenial. 'I do not belong to those kinds of people who make a living by attending congresses', he told Zinoviev afterwards, 'I detest such people'.[20]

More to his taste were the privileges with which the Soviet state hoped to impress distinguished guests. Larkin later claimed to have been made a chief of battalion in the Red Army – an honour conferred on a few westerners – and travelled 11,000 miles around the Soviet Union, visiting Novgorod, the Caucasus and Georgia. Back in Dublin on 25 August, he was obviously chuffed with his treatment. Thousands paraded to Dawson Street, headed by a banner inscribed in Russian: 'Greetings to the Revolutionary Transport Workers of Dublin from the Moscow Transport Workers', and on the obverse, 'Unite in the Soviet Federated Republics'. To those crammed inside the Mansion House, Larkin delivered a eulogy of Russia, saying he had 'an agreement and pledges for the establishment of direct commercial relations with Russia, which was the wealthiest country in the world', and boasting of his election to the ECCI as 'one of the 25 Commissioners to rule and govern the earth'.[21] William O'Brien wondered why the Comintern needed the other

---

16   Milotte, *Communism in Modern Ireland*, p. 76.

17   RGASPI, third Profintern world congress, fourth session, undated [1924], 534/1/31–34/35.

18   RGASPI, Larkin to Zinoviev, undated [1925], 495/89/32–13/26.

19   Larkin, *James Larkin*, pp. 277–8.

20   RGASPI, Larkin to Zinoviev, undated [1925], 495/89/32–13/26.

21   Larkin, *James Larkin*, p. 279; Donal Nevin, 'Workers of the world', p. 337. The banner was presented to Larkin at the Profintern congress. RGASPI, third Profintern world congress, undated [1924], 534/1/42.

24.[22] In fact, Larkin had been appointed as one of 26 candidate members of the ECCI, which contained a further 44 members; on this occasion the presidium had selected the nominees and the slate was unanimously ratified en bloc by the congress. It was still an extraordinary achievement for one who was not even a member of a communist party.[23]

RED DUBLIN

Shortly before Larkin's departure to Russia, a dispute broke out in Alliance and Dublin Gas. On 20 May, the gas workers voted overwhelmingly to invite Larkin to attend a meeting. Strike action was approved by the ITGWU's no. 1 branch, but O'Brien, now ITGWU general secretary, refused strike pay because of Larkin's involvement. Larkin then asked all ITGWU members to pay their subscriptions to the gas workers' dispute committee. One week later, the gas company reached a satisfactory settlement with the workers, not the ITGWU. On 30 May, Jim's brother Peter notified ITGWU members that a Port, Gas, and General Workers' Provisional Committee would receive all union dues until further notice, and on 15 June Peter and young Jim launched the WUI.

Before leaving for Moscow, Big Jim had instructed Peter to stick with the ITGWU. He claimed later that he had hoped to win back the masses through the IWL. For the moment he was financially secure, and had no need of a union.[24] Why the big man was ignored on this occasion is not certain. In a letter to Willie Gallacher, Young Jim implied that it was an operational necessity for Larkinites, that the union would an integral part of the communist movement, and that he had favoured a split for some time.

> We are at last moving forward and everything depends upon our good work. One small omission and everything could be ruined again. This explains our fears in the last week . . . Our newspaper is beginning to establish itself and it is of the utmost importance that there are no interruptions in its publication. The fact that we have called the new union the 'Workers' Union' occurred because of our political line. We now have a 'Workers' Union' just as we will in the future have a 'Workers' Party'.[25]

22   *The Irish Times*, 30–31 Mar. 1956.

23   Jane Degras (ed.), *The Communist International, 1919–1943: Documents, Vol. 2, 1923–1928* (London, 1971), p. 572.

24   RGASPI, Larkin to Zinoviev, undated [1925], 495/89/32–13/26. In 1937 Larkin declared to the High Court that he possessed $2,000 on re-entering Ireland in 1923, on which he lived following his suspension as ITGWU general secretary. NLI, O'Brien papers, 15679(6).

25   RGASPI, Larkin Jr to Willie Gallacher, 16 June 1924, 495/84/27–6/7 [translated from a copy in German].

Peter was at least as headstrong and radical as his brother. Born in Liverpool in 1880, the second youngest of the Larkin children, he had represented Liverpool dockers at the foundation of the British Industrial Syndicalist Education League in 1910, and joined the IWW in the US. In 1916 he was one of 12 Wobblies imprisoned for treason in Australia. Released in 1920, he finally settled in Dublin in 1923. from 1907 he had worked intermittently with Big Jim in Ireland.[26] Possibly Peter did not share his brother's egocentric view of events and was encouraged by the objective basis for a split. If Jim's war on the ITGWU executive was personal, the membership split echoed too the earlier divisions of the European left into communists and social democrats. On paper at least, the ILPTUC had committed itself to revolutionary syndicalist aims during the economic boom from 1917 to 1920. When boom yielded to slump, an inexperienced leadership, intoxicated by four triumphal years, pledged to 'hold the harvest', and resist all wage cuts on a united basis. Instead, Congress soon discarded its syndicalist pretensions, and from 1921 to 1923 trade unions suffered successive defeats in conventional, sectionalist strikes.[27] For Labour to have promised so much and delivered so little generated extensive rank and file disillusionment. And while the ITGWU executive could boast an impressive record of resistance to wage cuts up to the summer of 1923, that claim was in tatters by 1924.

Two thirds of ITGWU's Dublin membership, 16,000 workers, joined the WUI, as did 20 out of 300 branches in the provinces, where Big Jim had never been very active.[28] The WUI immediately appealed for financial aid to the CPGB, who declined to help, citing the Comintern's policy of opposing the creation of parallel unions, and underestimating the length to which Moscow was prepared to go to accommodate its prize recruit.[29] Jim had little choice but to accept the loss of the ITGWU as a *fait accompli*. He became WUI general secretary and Peter was made national organiser.

There was now a significant and defined constituency for communism. Aside from the WUI and the IWL, a further 5,000 workers were affiliated to the 'all red' Dublin trades' council, which sent delegates to conferences of the British Minority Movement – a communist led rank and file fraction which had replaced the British bureau of the Profintern – in 1925, 1926 and 1928.

26   Greaves, *The Irish Transport and General Workers' Union*, pp. 89–90. Nevin, *James Larkin*, pp. 439–44.
27   For unrest between 1917 and 1923 see O'Connor, *Syndicalism in Ireland*, pp. 96–167.
28   Larkin, *James Larkin*, pp. 280–2; Donal Nevin, 'Larkin and the Workers' Union of Ireland', in Nevin, *James Larkin*, pp. 342–3.
29   RGASPI, Larkin Jr to Gallacher, 16 June 1924, and reply, 18 June 1924, 495/89/27–6/9; report on Ireland, undated [1924], 495/89/104–98.

Dundalk trades' council was also sympathetic to the Minority Movement; both trades' councils convened an 'all-Ireland conference of labour' at Easter 1925 to demand action on unemployment.[30] Communists saw too a propitious field of propaganda in the IRA. From 1920 to 1922, the Comintern had looked to the IRA as the trigger of revolution in Ireland. Subsequently it held that communists must fill that role, but it continued to see the republican movement as a potential auxiliary and a promising source of quality recruits. Though shattered as a force, the IRA had 14,541 volunteers in August 1924, the bulk of them bewildered by the Free State's facile Civil War victory, demoralised by Sinn Féin sclerosis and, in ECCI eyes, ripe for the plucking.[31]

CUTTING A DEAL

It took six months to resolve the role of the WUI and IWL as communist organs. With the CPI despatched, Jim had no further use for the British, and resisted any CPGB involvement with Irish affairs. Pollitt had found him unforthcoming as to his plans in April: 'Nothing that we may say or do will influence him', he told London.[32] In the autumn Jim's mood worsened. He was coming under financial pressure and would be declared a bankrupt in the High Court on 21 November for failing to pay costs arising from his litigation against the ITGWU.[33] He had also inherited a baptism of fire as WUI general secretary. From June onwards, inter-union disputes had broken out in building, the fishmarkets, the docks and the cinemas, as the WUI struck against the employment of ITGWU members. On 9 August, the *Irish Worker* had declared: 'The Transport Union card is nothing but a pass to a scab. There is only going to be one labourers' union in Ireland and that will be the Workers' Union, which has earned its place by right of conquest.'[34] Jim's biggest headache was a wage and demarcation dispute at Inchicore, which had extended to 700 WUI members on the railway. When he persuaded the men to return, over 100 were not re-employed. What followed was typical of the controversies that would dog the WUI in the 1920s. Seán McLoughlin, the WUI's no. 2 branch secretary and one of the few CPI veterans still working with the

---

30 Cody, O'Dowd, and Rigney, *The Parliament of Labour*, pp. 140–1; NLI, ILPTUC, *31st Annual Report for 1924–25* (1925), p. 37.

31 Hanley, *The IRA*, p. 11. The figure is based on an IRA estimate.

32 RGASPI, Harry Pollitt, Report on the situation in Ireland, 17 Apr. 1924, 495/100/168–1/3.

33 NA, DT, Election to Dáil Éireann and 'unseating' of James Larkin Sr, an undischarged bankrupt, 1927–8, S5562.

34 Donal Nevin, 'Titan at bay', in Nevin, *James Larkin*, p. 80; Larkin, *James Larkin*, p. 284.

Larkins, protested that Jim had promised financial support to any men who were victimised. Jim ignored the pleas, blamed the debacle on McLoughlin, and accused him of embezzling union funds. Inevitably, McLoughlin's days in Larkin's union were numbered, and he left Ireland finally for England. Jim sent his version of events to the CPGB, while McLoughlin wrote his own account of his disillusionment with the hero of 1913.[35] Privately, Jim disowned the WUI's first flush of militancy, blaming the 'terrible inability' of incompetent functionaries, including Peter, 'super-revolutionaries', and 'careerists' for taking the union to the brink of insolvency. He also claimed that the circulation of the *Irish Worker* had fallen by 50 per cent in his absence.[36]

The ITGWU riposte was uncompromising and relentless. By August, the *Voice of Labour* was carrying stories of physical assaults by the 'OBU [One Big Union] Defence League' on WUI activists.[37] Though confident the Larkins would bankrupt their union, O'Brien was quite happy to help the police and employers accelerate the process. On 29 November a police detective reported that he was having informants enrolled in 'Larkin's mob' 'through the medium of the ITGWU'. That same day the *Voice* proclaimed that in future ITGWU members would take the place of WUI strikers unless they were engaged in a genuine trade dispute. The inter-union war had a serious propaganda dimension too. Both sides distributed abusive handbills, and Larkin sometimes devoted half the *Irish Worker* to the ITGWU.[38] O'Brien probably edited *The Attempt to Smash the Irish Transport and General Workers' Union*, a selection of documents on Jim and the split, and the *Voice* printed what was later published as *Some Pages from Union History: The Facts Concerning Larkin's Departure to America*. On 20 November, at a meeting with Gallacher, Tom Bell, Arthur MacManus and a Comintern emissary from the KPD, Jim refused to engage in realistic discussion and rejected interference from Moscow as well as London. Predicting that Jim would eventually 'turn against us', the KPD referent recommended the cultivation of links with radical republicans.[39]

Once again it was Peter, often described as a primitive, but currently more stable than his brother, who broke the stalemate. Peter joined a commission in Moscow in December, comprising representatives of the Comintern, the Profintern, the CPGB and the Minority Movement. His report to the commission grossly inflated WUI and IWL membership, the former being given

35 NLI, O'Brien papers, Seán McLoughlin, 'How Inchicore was lost', 15670; *The Irish Times*, 16, 25–6 Aug. 1924; *Voice of Labour*, 11 Oct. 1924. I am obliged to Charlie McGuire for these references.
36 RGASPI, Larkin to Zinoviev, undated [1925], 495/89/32–13/26,.
37 *Voice of Labour*, 30 Aug. 1924.
38 NA, DJ, Larkin file, JUS 8/676; Larkin, *James Larkin*, pp. 283–4.
39 RGASPI, Betrifft Bewegung in Irland, 21 Nov. 1924, 495/89/26–1/6.

as 30,650, and the latter as 6,000. It also alleged persistent obstruction from the CPGB, and condemned the ITGWU for collusion with the government and the British unions in Ireland for regular scabbing.[40] Obtaining reliable, or even relevant, information, and addressing endless complaints would be nagging problems for Moscow in its dealings with Dublin. Peter presented too a memorandum proposing a mutual recognition treaty or a trade agreement between Soviet Russia and the Free State.[41]

Three salient bones of contention emerged in discussions on the commission. Firstly, the British favoured a reconciliation of the ITGWU and the WUI, with communists forming a revolutionary fraction in the merged union, a forlorn prospect, even if the ITGWU was not, as Peter insisted, on the verge of collapse. Secondly, the Larkins introduced a new demand, intended to bolster the WUI: the withdrawal of British unions, 'outposts of British imperialism', from Ireland. The CPGB tendered no ideological objections but were apprehensive. The Minority Movement had only been formed in August, and communists were concerned to emphasise that it was 'not out to disrupt the unions, or to encourage any new unions'.[42] Thirdly, the CPGB wanted the IWL to be a broad workers' party, embracing a communist fraction. Other differences related chiefly to the role of British communists in Ireland, and the IWL in Britain. The British also wanted a group of young republicans invited to Russia for political and military training, an idea the Larkins suspected as an attempt to outflank them.[43]

An accord was endorsed by the presidium of the ECCI on 7 January 1925. The WUI was recognised as the Profintern's voice in Ireland, and was to convene a conference, by May at the latest, to formulate statutes, an economic programme, and proposals for united action with other unions and trade unionists. Communists in reformist unions were to build revolutionary fractions. The IWL was to be transformed into a political party after the WUI conference. Irish trade unionism was recognised as independent of Britain. Irish sections were to deal directly with Moscow (i.e. not through Britain), and have a permanent representative there. The Profintern and Comintern

---

40 RGASPI, reports to the German representation, Moscow, 21, 26 November 1924, 495/89/26–1/6; reports from Peter Larkin, 1924, 495/89/26–25/38, 495/89/104–88/101.

41 RGASPI, Memorandum on Ireland, undated [1924], 495/89/103–15.

42 Allen Hutt, *British Trade Unionism: A Short History* (London, 1975), p. 99.

43 RGASPI, John Pepper, 'Der Konflikt der Irish Workers League mit der Communist Party Gross-Britanniens', 27 Dec. 1924, 495/89/26–22/24. Pepper was the pseudonym of József Pogány, a Hungarian with experience of the KPD and the Communist Party of America, and a rising Comintern functionary. In 1926 he became an alternate member of the ECCI secretariat. He was arrested and executed in 1937.

were to have representatives in Ireland. Irish Worker League or WUI activities in Britain were to be co-ordinated with the CPGB or the Minority Movement, and vice versa; and communists in both countries were to fight for the withdrawal of British unions from Ireland. A group of young republicans was, with Jim's approval, to be invited to Moscow. The *Irish Worker* was to be supported, and the *Daily Worker*, organ of the Workers' Party of America, was to cease its attacks on Larkin.[44] The source of this thorn in Jim's side was T. J. O'Flaherty, author of the famous 'As we see it' column, and a critic of Larkin's policy towards the ITGWU. As the column was very popular and O'Flaherty was rarely sober, he managed to defy party and Comintern strictures on what was an indefensible breach of communist protocol. Jim consistently complained about him.[45]

The ECCI resolution said nothing on what was, for Jim, the crucial part of the package. Subsequently he complained to Zinoviev that following his visit to Russia in 1924:

I and my comrades were left to our own devices and the promises made by you, by M., T., and L., apart from the miserable £100 which didn't even cover my costs, were the only comradely gestures received. Your suggestion of a personal link by [sending] a ship or goods or even the very presence of your emblem would have been of immense value.[46]

He also referred to promises 'concerning the founding of a co-operative and the means to do so'. The ECCI did allocate £1,000 to Ireland. But Jim wanted the money immediately, control over the Comintern's Irish budget, and a Soviet trade initiative with the Free State. Instead, the balance of the money – £900 – was lodged with the CPGB for the establishment of a press in Ireland. Comintern officials put nothing in writing concerning trade relations, possibly

44   RGASPI, Protokoll no.18 der Sitzung des Präsidium des EKKI, 7 Jan. 1925, 495/2/37; Resolution on the Irish question of the presidium of the ECCI, 7 Jan. 1925, 495/89/28–22/24; 'The immediate tasks of the Profintern in Ireland', 1925, 534/6/77–20/22; minutes of the Executive Bureau, Profintern, 7 Jan. 1925, 534/3/107–34. In 1920 the Communist Labor Party and a faction of the Communist Party of America had united as the Workers' Party of America, which also served as a legal front for the illegal Communist Party of America. The Workers' Party changed its name to the Workers' (Communist) Party of America in 1925 and to the Communist Party of the USA in 1929.
45   RGASPI, Pepper to ECCI secretariat, 14 Sept. 1925, 495/89/30–6.
46   RGASPI, Larkin to Zinoviev, undated [1925], 495/89/32–13/26. 'M., T., and L.' were probably Dimitri Manuilsky, rapporteur on the national question at the fifth Comintern congress, Mikhail Tomsky, who delivered a report at the third Profintern congress, and Lozovsky. I am obliged to Barry McLoughlin for these details and for translating Larkin's letter from German.

for fear of compromising Narkomindel.[47] It may well have been a wise pre-
caution. Two letters pertaining to Larkin were among 'a mass of documents'
seized by the British police in arrests of CPGB leaders in October 1925; both
were passed on to the Irish authorities.[48]

'OBJECTIVE DIFFICULTIES OF THE SITUATION'

In January 1925, the CPGB seconded Bob Stewart to Ireland to help
implement the plan of action. Stewart stayed with Jim, Peter, their sister Delia
and her husband in Delia's flat in 17 Gardiner's Place. It was a good vantage
point from which to see Jim's lighter side and appreciate his personal problems.
The pair got on exceptionally well – their common horror of drink assisted –
and Stewart did not exaggerate in saying 'I was one of the few men he really
trusted politically'.[49] Already Jim's impatience with Moscow was mounting as
his financial troubles deepened. He made a second visit to Russia in February
for the fifth enlarged plenum of the ECCI, only to discover it was postponed
to March. On returning through London he was informed by A. J. Bennett
that aid depended on progress, for which he blamed the CPGB.[50] In March
he made the first of ever-greater retrenchments of WUI ambitions, offering to
recognise ITGWU cards in divided employments.[51] In April he lost a court

47   RGASPI, Brown to the secretariat, 20 June 1925, 495/89/30–5. Aino Kuusinen, then a Comintern
apparatchik and wife of Otto, secretary of the Comintern, cites the controversy over the 'Zinoviev
letter' in 1924 as a turning point in the International's tetchy relations with Narkomindel. Though the
'letter', instructing the CPGB to engage in illegality and published in the *Daily Mail* before a general
election, was probably a fake, Chicherin was furious and demanded the Comintern cease activities
which might embarrass Narkomindel. Thereafter, certain responsibilities were transferred from the
Comintern. Aino Kuusinen, *Before and After Stalin: A Personal Account of Soviet Russia from the 1920s to
the 1960s* (London, 1974), p. 51.
48   BPP, *Communist Papers: Documents Selected From Those Obtained on the Arrest of the Communist
Leaders on October 14, 21, 1925*, Cmd 2682 (1926), XXIII, 585; UCDA, MacEntee papers, Notes on
communism in Saorstát Éireann, P67/523(5), p. 22.
49   Theresa Moriarty, 'Delia Larkin: relative obscurity', in Nevin, *James Larkin*, p. 437; Robert
Stewart, *Breaking the Fetters; The Memoirs of Bob Stewart* (London, 1967), pp. 149–50.
50   RGASPI, Larkin to Zinoviev, undated [1925], 495/89/32–13/26. The fifth enlarged plenum met
between 21 March and 6 April, its first meeting since July 1924. Bennett, alias D. A. Petrovski, was
born in Russia as Max Goldfarb. Comintern representative to the CPGB, and director of the
propaganda bureau of the ECCI, 1927–9, from 1929 he worked with the Soviet secret police. He and
his wife, the English communist Rose Cohen, disappeared during Stalin's purges. Cohen's death was
a particular embarrassment to the CPGB.
51   Larkin, *James Larkin*, p. 284.

case over two libels in the *Irish Worker*, against Tom Johnson, and Denis Cullen, an official of the Bakers' Union, and was saddled with legal costs of £1,600.[52] On principle he refused to pay the damages to the plaintiffs and was declared bankrupt, again. The paper, a flabby caricature of its pre-war self, ceased production after 9 May. It now made even less sense for Jim to frustrate his benefactors, but strategy was never his forte.

Stewart first set up sections of two Comintern fronts, ICWPA and WIR. Their function would be to channel relief to victims of the near famine conditions along the western seaboard and to prisoners' dependants, and thereby draw republicans to communism. In many parts of the west, dreadful weather in 1924 had led to the total failure of the potato crop and made the saving of turf impossible. On 28 January 1925 the *Irish News* reported that in Eshnadarragh, near the Fermanagh border with Monaghan:

> For the past three weeks hundreds of industrious people have been enduring the pangs of hunger and some of them would have died of sheer starvation were it not for the efforts of a local relief committee and the kindness of some shopkeepers . . . last year both the potato and oat crops were a total failure. The rearing of pigs had to be altogether abandoned owing to the scarcity of feeding stuffs and many farmers were obliged to sell their cattle to buy the necessaries of life.

The *Irish Worker* put the number in distress at 75,000, and, possibly owing to a typographical error, the figure of 750,000 was cited by WIR internationally.[53] In the spring the Free State government started a scheme to supply seed oats and potatoes, but in September the Department of Agriculture estimated that 5,000 families were still unable to provide for themselves.[54] Larkin became president of the Irish section of WIR, Stewart was secretary, and they were joined on the executive by officers of Dublin trades' council, the IWL, and radical republicans like Charlotte Despard, Maud Gonne, Hanna Sheehy Skeffington, and Peadar O'Donnell. The ILPTUC declined a request from international WIR to participate: Johnson objected to 'souperism' and the leadership of 'a man whose life is spent destroying solidarity and disrupting the Irish Trade Union Movement'.[55]

52 *The Irish Reports* (1925), the Law Library, Dublin; Larkin, *James Larkin*, p. 284; Gaughan, *Thomas Johnson*, pp. 272–6.

53 *Irish Worker*, 14 Mar. 1925; NA, DT, L. S. Amery to T. M. Healy, 18 May 1925, S4437.

54 NA, DT, secretary, Department of Agriculture to the President, 23 Sept. 1925, S1693.

55 RGASPI, Constitution d'un Comité Irlandais de secours, undated, 538/2/29–69; NLI, Hanna Sheehy Skeffington papers, notice of committee meeting, 8 Apr. 1925, 24,117; ILPTUC, *31st Annual Report for 1924–25* (1925), p. 37; *Irish Worker*, 7 Mar. 1925.

The WIR central office in Berlin intended the 'Irish action' to be a high profile operation of international significance. Willi Münzenberg demanded a big propaganda effort, with funds raised in Russia, the USA, Canada and Australia, and the famine blamed on both the Free State government and British imperialism.[56] The potential for enlisting the Irish abroad was obvious. There was also a diplomatic dimension. In 1924 elements in the British Trades Union Congress had mooted unity talks between the social democrat dominated International Federation of Trade Unions and the Profintern. A British Congress delegation had visited Russia and co-sponsored an Anglo-Russian joint advisory council on labour unity. Pursuent to its united front tactics, the fifth enlarged plenum of the ECCI attached 'immense importance' to the Anglo-Russian rapprochement, and WIR hoped its aid to their recent colony would impress the British on the value of international fraternity.[57]

In May the British government notified the Free State governor general that 'considerable prominence is being given in the Soviet press to the situation in Ireland'. *Pravda* had published an article by Larkin, illustrated with photos of 'a fat and prosperous' priest and starving women and children, calling for the despatch of a 'Red Relief Ship' to Dublin.[58] Larkin and Mrs Despard addressed a WIR conference in London in April, chaired by George Lansbury, MP, a leader of the British left, at which prominence was given to victims of the recent earthquake in Japan, and famine in Germany and Ireland. Helen Crawfurd, international secretary, announced that £1,017 had been received for Ireland.[59] The bulk of donations had come from Germany and Britain, including 200 gold marks from Berlin, £60 from Saxony, £100 from British WIR, and numerous small donations. The WIR committee in Dublin concentrated its efforts on the worst affected areas, in south west Donegal and Mayo. By 31 May foodstuffs to the value of £725 had been distributed through local committees to some 400 families in these areas.[60]

The Irish operation ran into terminal difficulties over the summer and autumn. As Larkin's suspicion and jealousy got the better of him, he found

56 RGASPI, IAH, Antrage des Genossen Münzenberg in der Sitzung des Zentralkomitees, 21 Feb. 1925, 538/26/26–31.

57 Degras, *The Communist International, Vol. 2*, p. 184; RGASPI, Comité central du Secours Ouvrier International au Comité Anglo-Russe pour l'unite syndicale, 4 Apr. [1924], 538/2/27–33/34.

58 NA, DT, L. S. Amery to T. M. Healy, 18 May 1925, S4437.

59 RGASPI, Secours Ouvrier International, 27 February 1925, 538/2/29–32; La famine en Irlande, 5 Mar. 1925, 538/2/29–33; Conférence du Secours Ouvrier International a Londres, 19 Apr. [1925], 538/2/29–40/42.

60 *Irish Worker*, 14 Feb., 7–14 Mar., 2 May 1925; RGASPI, Constitution d'un Comité irlandais de secours, undated, 538/2/29–69; Internationale Arbeiterhilfe, Bericht über Hilfstaetigkeit, 31 May 1925, 538/2/27–67/74.

fault on all sides. In Ireland, he claimed, 'An intrigue grew . . . my suggestions [and] advice were ignored, [WIR] became a club for persons practicing charity, who wanted to see themselves admired and where persons of a certain political group were given posts'; the British had an 'imperialist attitude'; Berlin did not do enough to condemn his detractors in the Irish labour movement; and in the USA, O'Flaherty was supposed to be embezzling funds. It was particularly galling for Larkin, as he waited impatiently for substantial finance or a sinecure from Moscow, that O'Flaherty, of all people, was 'feathered' with the job of secretary of the American Committee for Irish Assistance by the Workers' Party of America, and that O'Flaherty's friend, J. P. McCarthy, was given a junket to America to report on Ireland.[61] Gallacher travelled to Dublin in July to rescue WIR from collapse. Larkin complained that every promise made to him in Moscow had been broken, and left Gallacher speechless when he said he had read CPGB correspondence on Ireland in the Comintern archives. A grant of £100 from the Profintern temporarily deflated the crisis. But a bigger pitfall lay ahead. George Lansbury's visit to Dublin on 24 July to present WIR with £500 from the Russian Red Cross again inflamed Larkin's suspicion that the British were trying to belittle him. Though Lansbury had championed the 'fiery cross' in 1913 as editor of the *Daily Herald*, Larkin had developed a strong antipathy to him. In fact the CPGB had wanted Larkin to present the cheque; Lansbury, a noted pacifist and humanitarian, was chosen on the insistence of the Russian Red Cross.[62] Neither was Berlin too pleased with events. The whole point of a front was to broaden support, and WIR's policy was to foster trade union unity and united front tactics. In Ireland, however, it was compelled to back the WUI in its quarrel with Congress and the ITGWU.

Vicious inter-union conflict in the autumn delivered the fatal blow to WIR, and marked a turning point for the WUI. In July the Dublin Coal Merchants' Association locked out ITGWU and WUI workers 'until a satisfactory guarantee is obtained that the men employed in the coal yards will work amicably together'. Many employers had long been urging similar action, and in August the Dublin Employers' Federation pledged support to the coal merchants, in a determined attack on Larkinism. On 12 August ITGWU members resumed work 'to end the tyranny of the Larkin family organisation in the coal trade', enabling colliers to be unloaded under police protection.[63] The WUI men replied desperately, launching a mass assault on

61 RGASPI, Larkin to Zinoviev, undated [1925], 495/89/32–13/26; Larkin, Bericht über die Arbeit der IAH in Irland, 21 Sept. 1925, 495/89/32–27/39.

62 Albert Inkpin, general secretary of the CPGB, described Lansbury as 'one of the worst and most subtle enemies of our party'. RGASPI, Inkpin to Bennett, 10 July 1925, 495/100/242–3.

63 Larkin, *James Larkin*, p. 285; *Voice of Labour*, 22 Aug. 1925.

ITGWU dockers at the North Wall on 2 September. In separate incidents, a bomb was thrown into a dock shed housing ITGWU members, and groups of men visited homes of ITGWU workers and intimidated their families.[64] When the ITGWU supplied coal delivery drivers to break the WUI resistance, Larkin threatened sympathetic action wherever deliveries were made, but only the gas workers struck in sympathy, and they were compelled to return next day. Larkin had tried to sustain the struggle by forming the Unity Coal Company and importing coal, mainly from Wales. The first shipment of 250 tons arrived in Dublin on 29 July, and was sold from the ship to WUI members and the needy. Larkin lost money on the venture. By mid September, the merchants were on the point of victory, and the WUI eventually ordered its men back to work.[65] Having inherited a surplus of £472 from the turbulent second half of 1924, the WUI ended 1925 with a deficit of almost £4,800. Fortuitously, employers did not press on to smash the union, content to have checked its militancy. Apart from a gallant gesture of solidarity with British miners in 1926, the WUI's role as a revolutionary union was over. Strike pay plummeted from £9,344 in 1925, to £45 in 1926, and £131 in 1927, rising to an annual average of £1,100 for 1928–30. Working expenses, on the other hand, consumed an increasing proportion of revenue up to 1928, when they amounted to 99 per cent of income. While the WUI enrolled a few thousand 'non-benefit' members, its true strength can be gauged from annual subscriptions – each member being worth about £1 per annum – which fell from £9,212 for the second half of 1924, to £9,026 for 1925, and £5,830 for 1926, a figure not consistently exceeded until 1931.[66]

On 22 August 1925 Larkin and Stewart had cabled Berlin for aid to open WIR food dispensaries for 'children of locked out Dublin dockers'. The central executive approved, unaware of the internecine implications until the ILPTUC issued a circular attacking WIR for backing Larkin's war against the Irish labour movement. Trade unionists on the British WIR executive complained of being placed in an impossible situation. Lansbury threatened to withdraw from WIR, and Mrs Sheehy Skeffington and others resigned. Münzenberg asked the Profintern for advice, saying that WIR's policies in Ireland and Britain were being torn in opposite directions.[67] Larkin sent Moscow a lengthy, unapologetic report, blaming all and sundry in WIR. In a detailed rebuttal, WIR concluded that 'the activities of the Irish committee had therefore the worst possible consequences for the state of affairs within

64 Gaughan, *Thomas Johnson*, pp. 270–1.

65 Larkin, *James Larkin*, pp. 285–6; Gaughan, *Thomas Johnson*, p. 271; Nevin, *James Larkin*, p. 345.

66 For WUI membership and finances see NA, Registry of Friendly Society files, WUI file, 369T A.

67 RGASPI, Münzenberg to the Profintern, undated, 538/2/27–160.

the international organization'.[68] No more was heard of WIR in Ireland, but there were embarrassing consequences. In December 1925 the British Home Secretary misread in the House of Commons a letter to the CPGB – one of the 'mass of documents' seized in police raids – to imply that Larkin wanted WIR money to subvent the WUI. In 1926 a British parliamentary paper actually stated that Larkin had purloined famine relief funds for the WUI.[69] There is no doubt that Larkin put his pride before the victims of the famine, but no evidence that he stole the bread from their mouths.

The Irish section of ICWPA was founded at a conference in Dublin in March. Four hundred members were enrolled, and the executive included representatives of the WUI, IWL and republicans. By December ICWPA had 1,000 members in Dublin and Belfast, and several small groups elsewhere. It reported that there were 97 republicans in prison and ten workers jailed for trade union activities, and ICWPA had provided legal aid for two of the trade unionists and was maintaining the dependants of ten prisoners, donating 10*s*. per week for each person. 'The [international executive] itself sent direct to the Republican Party quite a considerable sum for help'. The Dublin group also sponsored a Lenin commemoration in Banba hall in February 1926, at which Bob Stewart 'spoke finely'. 'Wonderful day', noted Mrs Despard.[70] Two months later the group's involvement with Roddy Connolly's Workers' Party of Ireland (WPI), an attempt to develop an alternative to the IWL, caused ructions between WUI members and others on its executive. 'And in the labour world it's all hideous chaos', the hapless octogenarian chairman, Mrs Despard, confided to her diary: 'splits, suspicions, mutual recriminations everywhere. The great Jim will tolerate nothing of which he is not the boss.' Larkin made a rare appearance at the next meeting to make the point in person and unchivalrously 'denounced certain of the members as antiques'.[71] Thereafter the Dublin group was inactive. 'Things are about as bad as they can be in Dublin', reported an international ICWPA representative in October. Mrs Despard blamed Larkin, saying no one in Ireland, including herself, would work with him. The snag was that ICWPA was nominally based in the WUI's offices. The referent continued, summing up the wider dilemma of the Comintern:

68 RGASPI, Larkin, Bericht über die Arbeit der IAH in Irland, 21 Sept. 1925, 495/89/32–27/39; L. Gibarti, Bemarkungen zum Bericht des Genossen James Larkin über die irische Aktion der IAH, undated, 495/89/32–40/44.

69 British House of Commons debates, 1 Dec. 1925, vol.188, cols 2101–2; BPP, *Communist Papers: Documents Selected From Those Obtained on the Arrest of the Communist Leaders on October 14, 21, 1925*, Cmd 2682 (1926), XXIII, 585.

70 PRONI, Charlotte Despard papers, diary, 4, 7 Feb. 1926, D/2479/1/9.

71 PRONI, Despard papers, diary, 23, 29 April 1926, D/2479/1/9.

What are we to do? Dissolve MOPR and place it in control of another group? This is impossible. That would mean open war with Larkin and we could not as yet stand against him. Also the whole position would have to be in consultation with ECCI as big political issues would arise. So I managed to get agreement amongst several sections that ICWPA in Dublin should and must function later but for the present the position must remain in the air.

The referent also sought the withdrawal of Larkin's mandates to act for ICWPA. The Belfast group remained vibrant, with the affiliation of four Northern Ireland Labour Party branches, the Independent Labour Party, and five trade union branches. Given the fractiousness in Dublin, it wished to affiliate to the British ICWPA. It was persuaded not to make a formal break with Dublin for the moment.[72]

A key aim of the communist fronts in Ireland was to lay the basis for the founding of a party on 24 May 1925. Reflecting the CPGB's preference, it was to be called the Workers' Party of Ireland, and neither the manifesto nor the draft constitution mentioned communism, though the internal structure was as recommended by the ECCI. Party objectives were relatively moderate: an independent republic, state control of the banks, transport and foreign trade, and a series of immediate demands such as an eight hour day, a minimum wage, and work or maintenance for the unemployed.[73] In April Stewart believed that good progress was being made, and the CPGB released £50 from its Irish fund for the preparations. Larkin sat on the preparatory committee, but as the deadline approached, he became increasingly contrary, and 'could not find room' in the *Irish Worker* to publish the manifesto. Then, after going about 'with the manifesto in his pocket for days', and telling Stewart not to worry, he refused to sign it, and declined to attend the launch. Hundreds did attend and 200 applied to join, but Stewart thought it pointless to proceed.[74] Bennett despatched a gentle rebuke, followed by an assurance that £1,000 was available for a press, and that he was willing to negotiate for a Profintern office in Dublin. Larkin refused to receive the letters.[75] In spite of the fiasco he endorsed candidates in the local elections in June, in which his admirers in Nenagh achieved some success.[76]

72 RGASPI, report on ICWPA, Irish section, for Anglo-American secretariat, 15 Nov. 1926, 495/89/36–59/61. See also Carney's comments on ICWPA in RGASPI, Report on Ireland, undated [1926], 495/89/104–18/45.
73 RGASPI, To the Irish working class [Workers' Party of Ireland manifesto, 1925], 495/89/106–34/36; see model statutes for a communist party, drafted by the ECCI orgbureau, Degras, *The Communist International, Vol. 2*, pp. 172–9.
74 Milotte, *Communism in Modern Ireland*, pp. 79–80; Stewart, *Breaking the Fetters*, p. 154.
75 RGASPI, E. H. Brown, Resumee des Briefes von Stewart, 9 June 1925, 495/89/30–9/10.
76 RGASPI, Larkin to Zinoviev, undated [1925], 495/89/32–13/26.

Stewart and Bennett remained sympathetic to Larkin, whose trials – sometimes literally so – were piteous enough. At the time – the penny would drop eventually – Stewart rationalised that the root cause of the sabotage was finance. Swallowing a sense of personal betrayal, he advised E. H. Brown, British representative at the Comintern, that Larkin was holding out for three concessions: £1,000 for the WUI, control over Comintern funds for Ireland and direct communication with Moscow, and a Soviet initiative to open commercial relations with the Free State.[77] In briefs to the ECCI, Brown endorsed the first two demands, significantly omitting any reference to trade, and added that the Comintern might send Larkin a personal letter, deploring O'Flaherty's articles. The alternative, he argued, could well be the collapse of the WUI and the basis for a mass party.[78] An ECCI commission recommended the release of the £900 held in London, with £250 to be used for the WUI and £650 for the party; the appointment of Bennett to negotiate with Larkin and control funding for Ireland with power to increase the Irish budget; and a letter on the gadfly O'Flaherty.[79] The ECCI agreed, with minor amendments, and Zinoviev wrote a personal letter to Larkin expressing sympathy with his 'severe difficulties'; Larkin resented the implication. Of course the seed capital for the party was never sent, and the WUI was still looking for the £250 in 1928.[80]

The arrival of Jack Carney in Moscow in August 1925 as Irish resident representative did nothing to improve Anglo–Soviet–Irish understanding. Nor did it diminish the importance of the British leg of the tripod, as the Comintern continued to consult the British regional or länder secretariat in Moscow in dealing with Ireland. The British even had a hand in Carney's appointment. Having served as Larkin's fidus Achates in 1923, Carney had returned to the America in 1924 to edit *Labour Unity* in San Francisco. He left California in April 1925 at the Comintern's request, but then found himself stranded in New York awaiting further instructions; the ECCI was possibly having second thoughts owing to difficulties with Larkin. Ironically the CPGB urged his expedition to Moscow in the belief that he would be a settling influence on Larkin, and 'very serviceable in pushing for a Workers' Party'.[81]

77 RGASPI, E. H. Brown, Resumee des Briefes von Stewart, 9 June 1925, 495/89/30–9/10.
78 UCDA, MacEntee papers, Notes on communism in Saorstát Éireann, P67/523(5), pp. 22–4; RGASPI, Brown to English section, Comintern, 9 June 1925, 495/89/30–11/13.
79 RGASPI, Brown to Comintern secretariat, 20 June 1925, 495/89/30–5. Of course, £50 from the fund in London had been spent on the intended launch of the Irish party.
80 RGASPI, Larkin to Zinoviev, undated [1925], 495/89/32–13/26; Protokoll nr.70 der Sitzung des Büro des Sekretariats des EKKI, 22 June 1925, 495/20/948; IWL questionnaire, 2 Feb. 1928, 495/89/49–1/3. Larkin also wrote separately to Lozovsky on 13 Mar. 1928 asking him to settle 'this long outstanding financial irritation', 534/7/286–86.
81 RGASPI, Inkpin to Bennett, 10 July 1925, 495/100/242–3; Carney to the ECCI, 20 July 1927, 495/89/42–3.

Carney had acquired a solid reputation from his record in the USA, but where Big Jim was concerned, a ferocious loyalty dissipated all reason, and he was ever ready to cover his hero's failings in a smokescreen of slander, mendacity or aggression. In September he 'shouted wildly' at an ECCI orgbureau inquest on Ireland, attributing the absence of a party to the burden of WUI work, CPGB sabotage, and – to Brown's bemusement – the ECCI breaking its promises of big financial aid. It was agreed that a commission be appointed to consider reports from Ireland, 'examine how far promises to Larkin had been made and not kept by the [Comintern]', and prepare material for future ECCI plena.[82] In October, another inaugural conference of the party was abandoned. As in May, Stewart had made the arrangements, and Larkin did not turn up. Carney pleaded, opaquely, that the problem lay with 'objective difficulties of the situation'.[83]

Aside from the business of organising the party, Stewart had angered Larkin by arranging a republican visit to Russia in June. The delegates were not the young, impressionable radicals that had been envisaged in the January 1925 agreement. The IRA selected the apolitical Seán Russell, a future chief of staff, and Pa Murray, officer commanding Britain – the title amused the Russians. Éamon de Valera asked his adviser, Gerry Boland, to tag along as political chaperone and 'keep them out of mischief'. Formally they went as envoys of de Valera's phantom government and Russell and Murray's aim was to secure arms and arrangements for training in the red air force: Russell thought pilots would be very useful in the event of war and had five volunteers given air training in Chicago in 1932. The delegation returned after a few weeks without concluding any military agreements, their hosts saying that Ireland was too remote to be of interest. Following an interview with Stalin, Murray believed the real obstacle lay with concern about the consequences of Soviet weaponry being captured by the British. Boland – like McCartan before him – suspected too that the Russians were growing nervous about the IRA presence and the possibility of a British protest, a suspicion confirmed by General Walter Krivitsky after he defected to the west in 1937. What was of interest to the Russians was espionage against Britain. A scheme for IRA–Soviet co-operation in this respect was agreed with Russell and approved by Seán Lemass, de Valera's minister for defence. 'Mr X', in Berlin, provided Murray with requests for items such as drawings of aeronautical instruments and gas masks, which were reportedly supplied within weeks. But Russell felt

82 UCDA, MacEntee papers, Notes on communism in Saorstát Éireann, P67/523(5), pp. 24–6; RGASPI, L. Gibarti, Bemarkungen zum Bericht des Genossen James Larkin über die irische Aktion der IAH, undated, 495/89/32–40/44.

83 RGASPI, Recommendations [to the Irish commission], undated [1926], 495/89/28–27/28.

that 'X' wished to use Murray as a Soviet agent rather than deal with the IRA per se, and the liaison faded.[84] It may be this, or a subsequent operation that Krivitsky, who specialised in German affairs, had in mind when he informed British intelligence of a meeting with three IRA officers in Holland about 1927.

> He worked with them purely as intelligence agents and for a time got quite useful information out of them, at the same time experiencing difficulty in evading attempts to interest him in the terrorist activities of their organisation. After a short time the Polit Bureau temporarily forbade any dealings with the Irish in order to avoid possible prejudice to their attempts to obtain credits in London.

When the proscription was lifted, Krivitsky again worked with the IRA, until they presented him with 'definite suggestions for collaboration in a terrorist plan'. He then terminated the contacts, concluding that the risk was too great.[85]

For Larkin, another intractable problem was bubbling over. The Minority Movement had been dismayed by the January 1925 agreement's provision for a campaign for the withdrawal of British unions from Ireland. As secretary of the Movement, Pollitt told Moscow that it would multiply the disruption affecting Irish labour and 'stir up more difficulties' with unions in Britain; nothing would be done pending talks with Larkin.[86] Larkin had attended a Minority Movement conference in London in January and gave it a rapturous report in the *Irish Worker*.[87] Outraged by Pollitt's betrayal, he walked into the Movement's annual conference in August in foul mood. Brushing aside a hearty reception, he showered abuse on those present, including the Dublin delegates, and declared that he would clear the British unions out of Ireland.[88] To his fury, in September the British helped Dublin trades' council to inaugurate an Irish Minority Movement, with backing from 35 trade unions, union branches, and trades' councils.[89] Both sides to the dispute submitted extensive reports to the Profintern. The Minority Movement contended that an attempt to remove the British unions would create disruption and cause massive legal and financial complications; Irish labour's primary problem was division and the way forward was to liquidate of the central schism between

84 O'Halpin, *Defending Ireland*, pp. 72–3; Hanley, *The IRA*, p. 34; see Gerry Boland's recollections of the visit in Michael McInerney, 'Gerry Boland's story', *The Irish Times*, 11 Oct. 1968; Tim Pat Coogan, *The IRA* (London, 1984), pp. 126–7; and PROL, Krivitsky file, KV 2/805.

85 PROL, Krivitsky file, KV 2/805.

86 RGASPI, Pollitt to the Profintern, 5 Feb. 1925, 534/7/26–38/39.

87 *Irish Worker*, 31 Jan. 1925.

88 RGASPI, Pollitt to Lozovsky, 2 Sept. 1925, 534/7/26–154/156.

89 Cody, O'Dowd, and Rigney, *The Parliament of Labour*, pp. 139–47.

the ITGWU and the WUI through a campaign by communist fractions in both unions.[90] Carney might have done better. Even the CPGB acknowledged the necessity of an independent labour and political movement in Ireland. Instead Carney tendered a shoddy presentation, short on facts, long on Larkin's heroic record, and studded with sweeping assaults on the ITGWU, the Labour Party, the British unions, and the Irish Minority Movement.[91] Lozovsky, the most sceptical of the Soviets on Larkin, later dismissed it sarcastically, complaining that it was impossible to get concrete information from the Irish and that 'Comrade Carney speaks as if Ireland had the very worst reactionaries and the very best revolutionaries'.[92]

The ECCI had passed the dispute to a prestigious commission comprising Klara Zetkin, Jules Humbert-Droz, John Pepper, Brown, Allison, Charlie Johnson, and Peter Larkin. Accepting the British case, and noting that a campaign to withdraw British unions from Ireland would encounter hostility in Britain, it proposed that a new autonomous all-Ireland Minority Movement be created, dealing independently with Moscow. The ECCI approved unanimously.[93] Carney's standing in Moscow never recovered. The British länder secretariat got the ECCI to suspend decisions on Irish affairs pending a discussion with Larkin. Carney lost his salary from the Comintern and he went to work for the Profintern, not a comfortable station given the enmity between himself and Lozovsky. The Profintern too sought to bypass him, recommending commissions to examine the Irish disputes with the CPGB and the American party, preparatory to Larkin's presence at its next plenum. When Larkin left his faithful friend twisting in the wind by refusing to communicate with Moscow, Lozovsky suggested he return to Dublin. In a final slight, the Comintern never reimbursed him for £45 expenses incurred in travelling from California to New York en route to Moscow in 1925. 'During the two years that I have acted as Irish representative I have not received any friendship from the CI', he wrote in 1927. 'What I had to tolerate in M [Moscow] is known to those in charge'.[94]

Dublin trades' council duly planned to re-launch the Irish Minority Movement on 14 February 1926, with Jim and Tom Mann, chairman of the

90 RGASPI, report, undated [1925], 495/89/104–153/161.

91 RGASPI, Remarques du Cam. [J. T.] Murphy, undated [1925], 495/89/28–28; Report on Ireland, undated [1925], 495/89/104–162/183.

92 RGASPI, Minutes of the executive bureau, RILU, 28 Jan. 1926, 534/3/150–255/265.

93 RGASPI, Report to ECCI secretariat, 12 Jan. [1926], 495/89/28–31; Irish resolution on trade union work, undated [1926], 495/89/33–2/3.

94 RGASPI, Carney to the secretariat, 17 Mar. 1926, 495/89/36–1; Carney to Lozovsky, 17 Mar. 1926, 495/89/36–2; minutes of the meeting of the executive bureau, RILU, 28 Jan. 1928, 534/2/150; Carney to Comintern, 20 July 1927, 495/89/42–3.

British Minority Movement, as the star speakers. It made no sense for Larkin to oppose the trades' council. It was his only ally in the labour movement, and had granted a loan of £200 to the WUI, which was so short of funds that it had affiliated 1,000 members to the council, with a promise to affiliate the remainder when finances allowed. Nonetheless Larkin pulled out of the meeting at the last minute, saying he had not been given adequate notice. The council then resolved to sever all ties with him.[95]

Larkin's communist project was now reduced to a shambles, and he was, as the Gardai put it, 'unpopular with all parties'. He had alienated his friends in Ireland. The WUI was in decline and impoverished. The IWL was moribund. The British were working behind his back in cultivating alternative allies in Ireland. There was no sign of Russian commercial links with the Free State, and the Comintern was obviously unwilling to release substantial funding before the creation of a party. A man described by the Department of Justice as 'a dangerous revolutionist' in 1924, would generate 'no cause whatsoever for anxiety about his relations with Russia' during the British general strike of 1926.[96] One consolation for Larkin remained: Moscow still believed that if little could be done with him, nothing could be done without him.

95 Cody, O'Dowd, and Rigney, *The Parliament of Labour*, p. 142.
96 NA, DJ, Larkin file, JUS 8/676.

SIX

THE SEARCH FOR A
COUNTERBALANCE, 1926–9

It would be a good thing if we could bring to the front a group of active workers
who could serve as a counterbalance to Larkin. The [Comintern] representative
[in Ireland] should endeavour to single out such a group . . . if it is not done,
the organisation will be at the constant mercy of the caprices of Larkin.

IOSEF FINEBERG

August 1927[1]

—

The quarrels and setbacks of 1925 did not diminish Moscow's interest in
Ireland. Globally, the Comintern was becoming more interventionist and
more concerned with realising its dream of total uniformity among its
affiliates. Bolshevisation, adopted as a slogan at the fifth world congress in
1924, was refined at the fifth enlarged ECCI plenum in 1925. The sixth world
congress in 1928 affirmed that 'The Communist International . . . is the union
of communist parties in various countries into a single world communist party'.
At the sixth plenum in March 1926, 11 regional secretariats were created, one of
which dealt with Britain, the Netherlands, the Dutch East Indies, Australia,
South Africa, India and Ireland.[2] In a further reshuffle, Ireland was brought
under an Anglo-American secretariat which also covered Australia, Britain,
Canada, New Zealand, the Philippines, South Africa and the USA. The
regional secretariats assumed an increasingly important role in the Comintern
apparatus from 1928.[3] Soon after the sixth plenum the inordinate peculiarities
of the Irish question took a new twist. Unaware of his low standing in Moscow,
Roddy Connolly led the first attempt to displace the IWL. Connolly's
initiative never had the slightest prospect of success. The ECCI believed that
the Irish lacked the understanding of Marxism-Leninism to do more than
create another small, fractious sect, and had no wish to revisit the old CPI. It

---

1   RGASPI, Digest of communications received from representative [in] Ireland, undated
[Aug, 1927], 495/89/104–184/189.

2   Degras, *The Communist International, Vol. 2*, pp. 271–2, 456.

3   Huber, 'Structure of the Moscow apparatus of the Comintern and decision-making', p. 44;
Andrew Thorpe, *The British Communist Party and Moscow, 1920–43* (Manchester, 2000), pp. 12–13.

knew too that collusion with Jim Larkin's critics would inflame his notorious jealousy, and if it had lost confidence in Larkin, it regarded his goodwill and that of the WUI as important to the construction of a mass base, which itself was deemed a vital characteristic of a Bolshevik party. Moreover, as Larkin like to remind Moscow, the WUI was one of the few anglophone trade unions in the Profintern.

Radicals in Ireland were bewildered that the Comintern should continue to endorse the moribund IWL, but the WPI affair did cause the ECCI to consider ways of tackling the Larkin problem. Its first response was to send resident representatives to Ireland. Two innovations in international policy also opened avenues of advance. In May 1926 tuition commenced at the International Lenin School in Moscow. Intended to function as a 'cadre-forge', the school was a key element in the goal of Bolshevising communist parties worldwide, and Nikolai Bukharin, who succeeded Grigori Zinoviev as leader of the Comintern in November 1926, was made rector. In 1927 the ECCI decided that Irish students must be enrolled at the school if dependency on Larkin were to be reduced and the basis of a Bolshevik party created. The Comintern's incremental development of ancillary and front organisations offered a second line of advance, and one of particular relevance to relations with republicans. From 1927 onwards the IRA renewed contact with communism in what would become a plethora of radical fronts. Moscow's own interest in the IRA was, of course, not confined to politics, and included espionage. When the counterbalancing policy was applied in a fourth area, the Russian Oil Products operation in Dublin in 1928, it inadvertently destroyed the rationale for Larkin's link with Moscow.

THERE IS STARTED THE IDEA OF A WORKERS' PARTY

With Bob Stewart's return to England and Dublin trades' council's breach with Larkin, Roddy Connolly and his associates despaired of the IWL. The 'idea of a Workers' Party' started with discussions among ICWPA members in February 1926, and Connolly moved quickly to found the James Connolly Workers' Education Club as an embryo.[4] In March the club decided to establish the WPI. The initiative was prompted by the split in Sinn Féin at its árd fheis on 9 March over Éamon de Valera's proposal that absention from Dáil Éireann be a matter of policy rather than principle; when the motion was rejected, de Valera founded Fianna Fáil in May. With or without Larkin – he was invited to join – Connolly determined to have a party in place to pick up

4   PRONI, Despard papers, diary, 28 Feb., 5 Mar. 1926, D/2479/1/9.

the fallout from the latest upheaval in the republican movement.[5] One particularly valuable recruit from Sinn Féin was Charlotte Despard. With her characteristic impetuous generosity, and in one of those not infrequent ironies of socialist history, her dividend – exceptionally large that year – from the Muir Mills at Cawnpore, 'the Manchester of India', was made over to Connolly in monthly instalments for the party. She also hosted a number of WPI aeríochtaí at Roebuck House.[6]

On 3–4 and 7 April, 78 people attended a founding conference, at which the party was named the WPI (Workers' and Working-Farmers' Party). A constitution and programme were discussed, and an interim National Executive Committee elected. The officers were drawn from the three main strands of party support, and included CPI veterans George McLay (political secretary), Connolly (educational organiser), and Walter Carpenter (youth organiser); Dublin trades' council secretary, P. T. Daly (industrial and trade union organiser); and, from the republican strand, Mrs Despard (women's organiser).[7] The conference resolutions advertised the party's roots in ICWPA and hinted at either prior or anticipated collusion with the CPGB.

> That this first Congress of the Workers' Party of Ireland, strongly protests against the imprisonment of members of the working class by the Free State, Northern and British Governments . . . The Congress further compliments the CPGB on its successful working class fighting policy, resulting in the capitalist class imprisoning 12 of its leading officials . . .
>
> That this first Congress of the Workers' Party sends fraternal greetings to the Sunday Worker as the militant expression of the Left Wing elements in the Labour movement in Britain and fully endorses the policy of a United Front and in particular fighting for the formation of an Industrial Alliance to resist and defeat the attack of the bosses on the miners, engineers, railwaymen and other sections of the workers.[8]

Only one other resolution was adopted, pledging to establish cordial relations with revolutionary parties in Britain, the USA, Canada and Australia.[9] The

5 RGASPI, WPI, report of formation and the activities of the party, 1926, 495/89/34–8/9.

6 Andro Linklater, *An Unhusbanded Life: Charlotte Despard, Suffragette, Socialist, and Sinn Féiner* (London, 1980), pp. 232–3; *Irish Hammer and Plough*, 17 July, 21 Aug. 1926; PRONI, Despard papers, diary, 28 Feb., 7, 9 Mar., 9 Apr. 1926, D/2479/1/9.

7 RGASPI, McLay to ECCI, 24 June 1926, 495/89/34–4.

8 RGASPI, WPI report, undated [1926], 495/89/34–10. In Oct. 1925 the British Labour Party annual conference refused to consider the affiliation of the CPGB. Communists then launched a 'national left wing movement' with the *Sunday Worker* as its organ.

9 RGASPI, WPI report, undated [1926], 495/89/34–11.

WPI declared itself to be socialist republican in the James Connolly tradition, and its manifesto was similar to that proposed by the CPI in July 1922 as a social programme for republicans. Land, natural resources, banks, transport and heavy industry would be publicly owned. 'Small scale industry shall remain private property pending its gradual organization on co-operative lines . . . The entire economic life of the country shall be organised and controlled by a National Economic Council in the general interests all Irish workers and toilers.'[10]

Larkin hastened to London, most likely to register a protest with the CPGB, and raised stormy opposition to the new party within ICWPA. When the WPI gave notice of a May Day rally, he employed his usual stratagem of announcing a demonstration of his own. Anxious to make unity a theme of the party, the WPI avoided a clash, and Connolly's son also surrendered 'Connolly day' – 12 May – to Larkin, who rarely uttered a good word about his old subaltern in private. Larkin staged an impressive commemoration at which the unemployed association band concluded the proceedings with the 'Internationale'. The WPI held its Connolly commemoration, and first public meeting, on 9 May. Mrs Despard thought the attendance 'splendid' and 50 new members joined. There followed a burst of intense activity, with over a dozen WPI street meetings in Dublin in May.[11] The British general strike on 3 May in opposition to the miners' lockout was of course a stimulant. The massive stoppage electrified labour, and speculation was rife about what might be asked of Ireland. Dublin trades' council issued a daily stop press *Dublin Labour Bulletin* from 8 May. Larkin had rushed out a cheap, stencilled edition of the *Irish Worker* on 2 May, declaring: 'Workers of Ireland the fight in Britain is your fight'. After the collapse of the general strike on 12 May the rival communist groups gave discrete aid to the British miners, who fought on until December. The WUI blacked British coal imports for 11 weeks, until coal was discharged under guard. It also raised funds for the miners and hosted three Welsh choirs, five Scottish pipe bands, and 'what is called a jazz band'. Larkin would later complain bitterly of the lack of British communist support for his efforts. He was scathing too about the WPI, its bourgeois patrons especially.[12] After a long diplomatic restraint, and some favourable references to his activities, the *Irish Hammer and Plough* rebutted Larkin's 'stupid attacks' in August.[13] The *Hammer and Plough* had appeared on 22 May as the WPI's

10   RGASPI, The Workers' Party: its objects, means, programme, and immediate demands, undated [1926], 539/3/642–10.
11   *Irish Hammer and Plough*, 22 May 1926; PRONI, Despard papers, diary, 12, 18, 23, 29 April, 1, 4, 9 May 1926, D/2479/1/9.
12   RGASPI, Larkin at Profintern session, 21 Dec. 1926, 534/3/173–119/130.
13   *Irish Hammer and Plough*, 22 May, 7 Aug. 1926.

weekly organ: 'plough' was thought to be more modern than 'sickle'. Edited by
Connolly, it was a punchy little four-page newssheet, obviously produced on
a shoestring budget. In October, after Mrs Despard had purchased a printing
press, the paper was replaced with the *Workers' Republic*.[14]

Big meetings of the unemployed in and around O'Connell Street were an
almost weekly occurrence in 1926, with almost one in four insured workers
idle, and thousands exhausting their insurance benefit and becoming dependent
on home assistance provided by local government. Connolly had chaired a
meeting of 1,000 members of the unemployed association at Butchers' Hall in
March. When the Dublin commissioners reduced the weekly home assistance
rate to 7s. 6d. and introduced a work test, the WPI launched the Irish National
Unemployed Movement (INUM) under the leadership of Christy Ferguson.
Captain Jack White, Maud Gonne and Peadar O'Donnell addressed the
inaugural meeting on 26 July. The INUM claimed 230 members. Following a
mass protest against an eviction, it assumed a 'military form'. On 5 September
the INUM held a 'monster meeting' in College Green, at which speakers
included Seán Lemass, Seán MacEntee and Constance Markievicz. The
countess said the only solution to unemployment was to do what had been
done in Russia. The proceedings terminated with a rendition of the 'Red
Flag'.[15] The INUM subsequently organised marches to the Dublin Union,
and compelled the commissioners to abandon the work test, but was unable to
raise the home assistance rate. Mrs Despard sold capital to contribute to
the INUM's own relief fund. Meanwhile internal disputes were affecting the
INUM committee and Ferguson resigned. 'The unemployed have been difficult', noted Mrs Despard in December, 'It seems impossible to organise
them'. The INUM was succeeded in 1927 by the Unemployed Workers' and
Peasants' Association.[16]

Tactically, the WPI embraced the united front, calling for a council of
unions, including the WUI, to fight industrial struggles, and for 'unity among
all progressive parties' against the Free State. As particular emphasis was
placed on gleaning support from republicans, commensurate attention was
devoted to the agrarian question, agricultural labourers, and small farmers.
Members were active in anti-eviction struggles at Delvin, County Westmeath

14   PRONI, Despard papers, diary, 25 Aug., 2, 6, 11 Oct. 1926, D/2479/1/9. Only a few pages survive
of the *Workers' Republic* from Oct. 1926 to Mar. 1927. See RGASPI, 495/89/38–19, 495/89/38–21,
495/89/46–10/10a.
15   *Irish Hammer and Plough*, 31 July, 4–11 Sept. 1926; PRONI, Despard papers, diary, 23 Mar., 26–27
July 1926, D/2479/1/9.
16   *Workers' Republic*, 2nd issue Oct. 1927; PRONI, Despard papers, diary, 26 Sept., 21–22, 25 Oct.,
3–4 Dec. 1926, D/2479/1/9; Linklater, *An Unhusbanded Life*, pp. 233–4.

and Killeshandra, County Cavan, where branches were formed also at Kildallen, Belturbet and Ballyconnell.[17] In mid August Mrs Despard made a brave trip in her puncture-prone motor to spend a week evangelising in Mayo and purchased a one-ton lorry for the fishermen of Portnacloy to transport their catch to the market. Further forays to Mayo to form workers' republican clubs followed in October and November.[18] An internal party report offered a sidelight on the post 1923 mentality of rural militants, who had virtually no experience of socialist parties, but had witnessed the mushroom growth of the ITGWU in agriculture in 1918 and its equally precipitous collapse in 1923.

> The branches in the country are almost entirely made up of agricultural labourers and small farmers. In the country districts the workers are very backward from the working class point of view and it is very difficult to get them to understand the difference between a trade union and a Workers' Political Party.[19]

By the end of 1926 the WPI claimed 200 members, 130 in two branches in Dublin, and the remainer in branches or groups in Cavan, Westmeath, Mayo, Leitrim and Tipperary, together with support groups in London and Glasgow. Some 30 per cent of the Dublin membership were trade unionists, and many others were unemployed. Many provincial members had belonged to republican clubs, and 20 had been in the ITGWU's agricultural section. 'About 90 per cent of the membership is of sound proletarian workers and about 10 per cent of the petty bourgeois radical type.' While regarding its work to date as 'very satisfactory', few comrades had experience of communist politics and progress would be 'very slow'.[20] Mrs Despard was less sanguine: 'the IWP is still upon its feet; but barely. I am not sure of it. We need stronger . . . intelligent men. Are they to be found? . . . our little organ holds its own . . . They do not appeal to the people and they have no real following.'[21]

As a prospective communist party, the future of the WPI depended on the Comintern. McLay had written to the ECCI on 29 April, requesting affiliation.[22] He had earlier notified the CPGB, which kept also Moscow informed.[23] John Pepper was soon seeking Larkin's response. Ominously,

---

17　*Irish Hammer and Plough*, 17 July 1926.

18　Linklater, *An Unhusbanded Life*, pp. 232–3; PRONI, Charlotte Despard papers, diary, 13–20 Aug., 31 Oct., 5 Nov. 1926, D/2479/1/9.

19　RGASPI, report of formation and the activities of the party, 1926, 495/89/34–8/9.

20　Ibid.

21　PRONI, Despard papers, diary, 6, 11 Dec. 1926, D/2479/1/9.

22　RGASPI, McLay to Comintern, 24 June 1926, copy of letter forwarded 29 Apr., 495/89/34–4.

23　RGASPI, McLay to secretary, CPGB, 20 Apr. 1926, 495/89/34–1.

Pepper stated, 'Our information points to the fact that this Party [the WPI] is to be considered a Communist Party', and demanded a 'detailed report on the conditions which hitherto prevented the carrying out of the decisions of the ECCI'.[24] On 12 July Jack Carney sent a long report to the ECCI. This time he was careful to include figures, if not facts, and WUI membership was put at 18,000. The WPI was described as an 'eyesore' of ne'er do wells, backed by the CPGB, whose real interest was in 'Russian gold'. Conceding that he could not explain Larkin's failure to develop a party, Carney pleaded the burden of WUI work, government repression, the failure to send promised assistance, and, absurdly, a strong belief in the WUI that it was best to try to capture control of Sinn Féin before risking the formation of a party.[25]

The ECCI decided to refer the dispute to its seventh enlarged plenum, which met between 22 November and 16 December. Significantly, the WPI was invited to send a delegate, together with 'an exhaustive report on the economic and political situation of Ireland' and 'detailed facts on the entire labour movement'.[26] Clearly the ECCI was hoping to exploit the situation to obtain the intelligence which Larkin had been refusing to supply. The impecunious WPI was unable to afford representation at the plenum but Larkin was sufficiently stirred to attend, though recovering from illness, probably pneumonia: an ECCI transcript described it as 'serious Rumania'.[27] He brought with him two documents, a detailed application for a loan of £4,000 to revive the *Irish Worker*, and a political review depicting Ireland as a destitute hellhole ruled by

> the most fearful combination of corrupt, politically ignorant and blood-soaked tyrants that ever masqueraded as as a government. Mussolini, Horthy, Primo de Rivera have much to learn from our democratic Premier, Cosgrave, who was formerly a bar tender in a low class public-house (drinking den) and his Fidus Achates Kevin O'Higgins, a lawyer. The cabinet, seven in number, are of the same type.

The review ended with a reminder of the importance of the Irish throughout the world and concluded, in the name of the 'Irish Communist Party', that 'they must be Bolshevised'.[28] Larkin's empty rhetoric no longer deceived anyone in Moscow. When he blamed his difficulties on the CPGB's imperialist attitude at the ECCI presidium, the British delegate calmly pointed out that

24   RGASPI, John Pepper to Larkin, 29 May 1926, 495/89/34–2.
25   RGASPI, report on Ireland, undated [1926], 495/89/104–18/45.
26   RGASPI, Pepper to McLay, 14 Oct. 1926, 495/89/34–5.
27   RGASPI, minutes, executive bureau, RILU, 21 Dec. 1926, 534/3/173–113.
28   RGASPI, letter from Larkin and statement, undated [1926], 495/89/110–136/47.

for all its faults, the CPGB existed, and the Irish party did not.[29] At a Profintern commission on relations between Irish and British affiliates, he attacked the British at length for their performance during the miners' lockout, and demanded an end to Minority Movement activity in Ireland. Dismissing the polemic, Aleksandr Lozovsky asked for facts on Irish trade unionism, and the British made it clear that it would be better to move on without Larkin.[30]

Nonetheless the dispute had a favourable outcome for Larkin. The ECCI resolved: 'The CI having dissolved the small CPI, the Executive refuses to sanction its re-establishment in the shape of the "Workers' Party of Ireland"'. In recognition that, contrary to their protestations, the British had been intriguing in Ireland, the resolution continued: 'the CPGB will abstain from establishing a local British Section or a Communist Party'. The WPI was interpreted as a child of 'misunderstandings' between the IWL and CPGB, and Larkin was promised that in future Irish revolutionary organs would deal independently with the Comintern.[31] Carney returned to Dublin and was replaced with Iosef Fineberg. The Comintern also tried to make progress in Ireland through two resident agents: Christian Hilt and Jack Leckie.[32] In mid 1927 it adopted an efficient system wherein Hilt's reports from Dublin were reviewed by Fineberg over a period, making it possible to compile a moving picture of events instead of reacting to snapshots. Fineberg was soon sceptical of Hilt's fairly optimistic despatches, and thought him 'impressed too much by the Irish comrades', adding 'but he appears to be finding them out'.[33] Larkin complained of Fineberg in 1928, and requested that Seán McIntyre,

29 RGASPI, Protokoll Nr. 83 der Sitzsung des Präsidiums des EKKI, 20 Dec. 1926, 495/2/64a–63/101.
30 RGASPI, Session, 21 Dec. 1926, 534/3/173–119/130.
31 RGASPI, Protokoll Nr. 84 der Sitzung des Präsidiums, 7 Jan. 1927, 495/2/70–7/8; Irish draft resolution, undated [1927], 495/3/3–15/17.
32 RGASPI, Carney to ECCI, 20 July 1927, 495/89/42–3; report on the IWL, 22 Feb. 1928, 495/89/50–51/69. Fineberg (1886–1957) was a member of the British Socialist Party before moving to Russia in 1918. He worked at Comintern headquarters, 1919–31. Hilt was born in Bergen, Norway in 1888, and represented the Norwegian party in the Comintern secretariat, 1925–7. He suffered a nervous breakdown in 1929 and was later employed by the VKP(b) as a translator. Leckie had helped Captain Jack White drill a workers' army in Glasgow around 1920 and was a strong advocate of links between the CPGB and the IRA. He worked in the Comintern information department, 1926–7, and acted as secretary of WIR in Britain in 1928. Technically Leckie was not a Comintern representative, but a functionary seconded to the IWL. I am obliged to Alan Campbell for details on Leckie and Barry McLoughlin for details on Hilt.
33 RGASPI, Digest of communications received from representative [in] Ireland, undated [Aug. 1927], 495/89/104–184/189.

Reds and the Green

then living in Odessa, be appointed Irish representative in Moscow to prevent the Irish sections being 'directed, or misdirected' by the Anglo-American secretariat. The ECCI declined to appoint him.[34]

Assuring Larkin of its co-operation, the CPGB urged Connolly to comply with the ECCI decision.[35] The WPI's political bureau agreed unanimously, but its executive approved by a majority of one. At an aggregate meeting on 27 March, Connolly moved that the party be dissolved in the interests of communist discipline. The motion was defeated heavily in favour of an appeal to the ECCI. Connolly and 11 others resigned their party membership, and McLay became chairman of a new executive.[36] The appeal stressed that the IWL was non-existent, and that the WPI was not another CPI. 'Of the members of the WPI not more than one tenth had any connection with the CPI'. It concluded with a despairing offer of compromise.

> Comrade Larkin's egocentric nature will disrupt any attempt at building a Workers' Party. At least half of the members of the WPI are willing to try to work with him but have no hope of success. We think an Order to the WPI section and to Larkin to effect unity is the best way of getting anything done effectively.[37]

The Comintern never replied.[38]

The continuing WPI issued a new edition of the *Workers' Republic* in March with McLay as editor. An ambitious production, it combined political statements, articles on Soviet Russia, and news of the left, republican groups, and trade unions, with letters on working conditions, sports features, and a racing tipster. Party policy remained the same. In the June general election the WPI advised workers to vote against the Free State, for Labour, Sinn Féin or Fianna Fáil 'in order of your choice'. The only mitigation of its united front tactics was to urge the Labour Party to curb 'imperial' Tom Johnson, whose fearful concern for political stability made him nervous of any modification of the Saorstát constitution.[39] Subsequently the IWL was excluded from the united front. Larkin's sole action in the general election campaign had been to hold an eve of poll meeting in central Dublin and deliver a two-hour rant

34 RGASPI, Larkin to Piatnitsky, 13 Mar. 1928, 495/298T/19–6; letter from Larkin, 18 Apr. 1928, 495/89/49/–12/16.
35 RGASPI, CPGB to Larkin, 9 Feb. 1926, 495/89/42–1; CPGB to Connolly, 8 Feb. 1927, 495/89/42–2.
36 RGASPI, statement by the executive, WPI, Apr. 1927, 495/89/46–8.
37 RGASPI, WPI to the ECCI, 30 Mar. 1927, 495/89/46–1.
38 RGASPI, Report on the IWL, 22 Feb. 1928, 495/89/50–51/69.
39 *Workers' Republic*, 21 May, 4, 18 June 1927.

against all and sundry on the left; WPI officials were accused of misappropriating funds during their CPI days and the *Workers' Republic* replied
personally, comparing him to 'an infuriated animal . . . stamping on the
wreckage' he had made. Aside from this, the IWL's hostility to the Labour
Party conflicted with WPI backing for a Labour–Fianna Fáil coalition.[40]
Despite its dwindling resources – breakdowns of its printing machinery
caused the *Workers' Republic* to appear intermittently from mid June – the
WPI continued to organise meetings during and after the general elections.[41]

<h2 style="text-align:center">AT LAST THE IWL</h2>

The ECCI had approved another Irish offensive on 7 June, and some weeks
later Christian Hilt began a three-month residency in Dublin to push for a
party.[42] Fortuitously, a change of regime seemed at hand. In the general
election, Labour had won 22 seats, the still abstentionist Fianna Fáil won 44,
and Cumann na nGaedheal clung precariously to power with 47 seats. Hilt
employed the carrot at first, urging Moscow to consider Larkin's appeal for
Soviet diplomatic relations with the Free State. He would soon resort to the
stick, prompted by the crisis caused by the assassination of Kevin O'Higgins,
Minister for Justice, on 10 July. The WPI deplored the murder, though one of
the assassins, Bill Gannon, was a party recruit from the IRA.[43] The
government responded with a Public Safety Bill, proposing additional powers
for the army and Garda, and to declare vacant the seats of absentionist TDs.
Hilt presented Larkin with a formal ECCI demand for action on 26 July.[44] An
IWL meeting on 29 July agreed to establish a weekly paper and a bookshop,
draft a political programme, and call a labour unity meeting.[45] On 3 August
Larkin called on Éamon de Valera to convene a meeting of groups to oppose
'the tyrannical measures of the government'.[46] When de Valera obliged, only
he and Larkin turned up for the conference, which lasted all of ten minutes.
Fianna Fáil's entry into Dáil Éireann on 12 August precipitated a second
general election in September.

40 *Workers' Republic*, 18 June, first issue Oct. 1927.
41 *Workers' Republic*, 9 July 1927.
42 RGASPI, minutes of sub-committee to consider letter to IWL, 22 Dec. 1927, 495/89/40–13.
43 *Workers' Republic*, [only issue for] Aug. 1927; Hanley, *The IRA*, p. 49.
44 RGASPI, Digest of communications received from representative [in] Ireland, undated [Aug. 1927], 495/89/104–184/189; to the executive committee, IWL, 26 July 1927, 495/89/42–4/7.
45 RGASPI, Report of IWL meeting, 29 July 1927, 495/89/42–18/19.
46 Gaughan, *Thomas Johnson*, p. 302.

The IWL fielded three candidates in the election: Big Jim in North Dublin, young Jim in County Dublin, and John Lawlor, WUI general president, in South Dublin, and urged first preferences for Fianna Fáil in other constituencies. Aside from a demand for the release of political prisoners, their election address outlined a long list of specific, incremental demands, such as 'the repeal of the amending clauses of the Railway Amalgamation Act and the re-employment of all men dismissed under the railway amalgamation scheme'; IWL national policy was stated briefly as the establishment of a workers' republic, and a workers' constitution for all of Ireland.[47] Earning himself a rare commendation in Comintern despatches, Carney mounted a hectic campaign, organising five to ten meetings each night. The IWL's main target was the Labour Party. Labour officials had challenged Big Jim's nomination on the ground that he was an undischarged bankrupt, and both sides swapped merciless abuse during the campaign.[48] Big Jim hounded Tom Johnson's meetings in person, and on one occasion was physically attacked by Johnson's son.[49] His united front tactics towards Fianna Fáil paid a dividend, and he was supported by Fianna Fáil candidates, as well as by Willie Gallacher and Shapurji Saklatvala, MP.[50] The outcome was a fleeting triumph. The League won 12,500 votes (6.5 per cent of the total in Dublin), compared with 9,000 for the Labour candidates in Dublin. Big Jim romped home on the first count with 7,490 votes, the only communist TD ever elected to Dáil Éireann. Icing the cake, young Jim siphoned enough votes from Labour in County Dublin to unseat Johnson. Labour TDs took their revenge in instigating Big Jim's unseating from Dáil Éireann as a bankrupt.[51] The Comintern offered to clear the debts, but as they arose out of the litigation involving the ITGWU and Johnson, Larkin refused, and duly lost his seat.

The ECCI had no more faith in Larkin after the election than before. The outcome merely confirmed its view that conditions had long been favourable for a party, and that Larkin had been the principal obstacle. Fineberg thought his motivation in activating the IWL was purely to come 'into the limelight'. Larkin continued to fudge about developing a party without 'guarantees', and when Hilt assured him of help, Fineberg noted:

47   RGASPI, IWL election address, Sept. 1927, 495/89/47.

48   Séamus Collins, 'The situation in Ireland', *Communist International*, 1 Feb. 1928, pp. 53–6.

49   Gaughan, *Thomas Johnson*, pp. 302, 309, 324–5; Donal Nevin, 'Workers of the world', in Nevin, *James Larkin*, p. 339.

50   RGASPI, Digest of communications from representative in Ireland, undated [Sept. 1927], 495/89/45–40/44.

51   Collins, 'The situation in Ireland', pp. 53–6; NA, DT, Election to Dáil Éireann and 'unseating' of James Larkin Sr as an undischarged bankrupt, 1927–8, S5562.

To this Larkin replied that he had been given many promises before that were not carried out, with the result that he had got into heavy personal debt. Apparently this interview bore an extremely heated character because the representative says that it brought him to the state that he seriously thought of leaving the country.[52]

Carney subsequently tried to put the IWL on some kind of footing. A press appeal for members attracted 200 letters of enquiry.[53] But when Hilt left Ireland in October, Larkin's procrastination again predominated.

PREPARING TO BYPASS LARKIN

Moscow had already begun to bypass Larkin. Fineberg had observed in August that unless cadres could be found to counterbalance him, the party would be 'at the constant mercy of [his] caprices'.[54] The outcome was the despatch of students to the International Lenin School. Whereas none of the 75 places at the school were allocated to Ireland when the ECCI discussed its establishment in March 1926, seven Irish students were enrolled between November 1927 and March 1928, three in October 1930, four in December 1931, three in early 1934, and the last batch of three in October 1935. The total of 21 – one was rejected by the school as too old – almost matched the number from Switzerland.[55] In part the high Irish involvement reflected the weakness of indigenous communist organisation. Larger parties became increasingly doubtful of the value of the tuition, and frequently did not fill their quotas. Moscow wanted more Irish, but its insistence on bachelors, as the school bursaries made little provision for dependants, was a handicap, and at least one prospective student was refused a passport by the Free State government.[56] With well-founded suspicions, Big Jim had been reluctant to delegate anyone other than young Jim, but his favourite son was keen to repair relations between Dublin and Moscow. For the moment, the project worked to Big

52 RGASPI, Digest of communications from representative in Ireland, undated [Sept. 1927], 495/89/45–42.

53 Ibid.

54 RGASPI, Digest of communications received from representative [in] Ireland, undated [Aug. 1927] 495/89/104–189; digest of communications from representative in Ireland, 22 Sept. 1927, 495/89/45–44.

55 RGASPI, sixth ECCI plenum, 8 Mar. 1926, 495/164/500–50/82. Twenty-four Swiss attended the school, and 41 Belgians. José Gotovitch and Mikhail Narinski et al. (eds), *Komintern, L'Histoire et les Hommes: Dictionnaire Biographique de l'Internationale Communiste en France, en Belgique, au Luxembourg, en Suisse et a Moscou (1919–1943)* (Paris, 2001), pp. 595–8.

56 RGASPI, letter to Irish students, 8 Feb. 1930, 495/89/65–6.

Jim's advantage. It removed a few rebels from Dublin and young Jim persuaded the ECCI that the IWL executive would push for the formation of a party.[57] Big Jim hoped the scholar revolutionaries would give him some leverage in Moscow, and was rebuked for political interference with the students by Laszlo Rudas, the school's Hungarian pro-rector.[58]

A second key development was the cultivation of links with the IRA, whose situation was transformed in 1925–6. In November 1925 the IRA declared its independence from Sinn Féin, and acquired a younger, more radical leadership. The formation of Fianna Fáil dealt a body blow to Sinn Féin, bringing the IRA to the fore in the surviving republican movement. The army council appropriated Sinn Féin's *An Phoblacht* and appointed Peadar O'Donnell as editor. The socialist slant given the paper by O'Donnell comple-mented changes in the composition of the IRA. As membership dwindled – to some 5,000 in November 1926 – it assumed a more plebeian hue, especially after the departure of Fianna Fáil supporters from 1927.[59] By October 1926 republicans were preparing anti-poppy day protests under the rubric of the League Against Imperialism.[60] Whether the League was connected with the communist League Against Colonial Oppresssion is unclear, but in February 1927 Frank Ryan and Donal O'Donoghue attended the Congress of Oppressed Nationalities in Brussels at which Willi Münzenberg established a new, more effective, communist front, entitled the League Against Imperialism. That same year the IRA made the gesture of pledging support for Russia in any Anglo-Soviet war.[61] Prior to the tenth anniversary of the Bolshevik revolution, an International Trade Union Relations Committee was formed in Dublin to send a delegation to Moscow for the celebrations. The ten-man visiting party included three WUI members and Mick Fitzpatrick, a veteran of the CPI, assistant secretary of the Irish National Union of Vintners', Grocers', and Allied Trades' Assistants, and a member of ICWPA and the IRA army coun-cil. Fitzpatrick had had some contact with Hilt during the latter's Irish residency. He had further discussions with Comintern leaders in Moscow, and was appointed to the präsidium of the newly established International Friends of Soviet Russia.[62]

57   RGASPI, minutes of sub-committee on IWL, 22 Dec. 1927, 495/89/40–13/14.
58   McLoughlin, 'Proletarian academics or party functionaries?', pp. 63–79.
59   Ó Drisceoil, *Peadar O'Donnell*, pp. 40–44; Hanley, *The IRA*, pp. 11, 114.
60   PRONI, Despard papers, diary, 8, 22 Oct. 1926, D/2479/1/9.
61   RGASPI, Tätigkeitsbericht der Liga gegen koloniale Unterdrückung, Oct. 1926, 542/1/4–26; O'Halpin, *Defending Ireland*, p. 73.
62   NA, DT, memo, Sept. 1931, S5864B; RGASPI, Irish Labour Defence League annual report, 7 July 1929, 539/3/644–2/5; report on the IWL, 22 Feb. 1928, 495/89/50–51/69.

The ECCI meanwhile grappled with the more embarrassing consequences of the election, which its critics on Britain's far left were quick to exploit. Larkin had called on workers to vote IWL and Fianna Fáil, the WPI had endorsed the Labour Party and Fianna Fáil, while the CPGB issued a statement urging votes for the IWL, Labour and Fianna Fáil, for which it was denounced in the *Workers' Republic*.[63] 'More communist trickery . . . This is what they call practical policies!' scoffed the *Socialist Standard*, organ of the Socialist Party of Great Britain. The campaign had also revived the friction between the IWL and the CPGB. Supplements on Ireland during the hustings in the *Sunday Worker* included interviews with Mrs Despard and Maud Gonne of the WPI, and Saklatvala made contacts with the WPI when in Dublin. In fact the WPI was on its last legs, and the *Workers' Republic* folded in December. The Anglo-American secretariat drafted a detailed brief on policy, endorsing the IWL's tactics in the general election, but advising a more critical line towards Fianna Fáil and less blanket hostility to the Congress based labour movement. It also urged the IWL to become active in the provinces and Northern Ireland, and sugared an appeal for co-operation with the CPGB with the suggestion that the withdrawal of British unions from Ireland might be raised in the 'near future'.[64]

To the surprise of the Anglo-American secretariat, the draft was queried by Otto Kuusinen, secretary of and arguably the most important functionary in the Comintern. In an unpredented personal intervention on Ireland, Kuusinen recommended a united front with Sinn Féin and the IRA rather than Fianna Fáil. An ostensible explanation is that Ireland had assumed a greater importance now that an Irish party seemed a possibility and the rise of Fianna Fáil threatened a terminal crisis for the Free State. Another possibility is that as the Comintern was about to replace its united front policy with the tactics of the third period, Kuusinen and Bukharin wanted directives to Ireland to reflect the new thinking. More likely, Kuusinen wished to encourage the liaison re-established with the IRA and which was being pursued by Razvedupr, Red Army intelligence. Kuusinen was 'closely linked' with Razvedupr and every communist party was supposed to have a military intelligence unit subordinate to Razvedupr.[65] 'If the Ogpu [secret police] or Military Intelligence find it necessary to recruit an agent', Walter Krivitsky recalled, 'their first recruiting ground is the Communist party: if that fails they invariably try and seek out an

---

63 *Workers' Republic*, first issue Oct. 1927.

64 RGASPI, ECCI to IWL, undated [Dec. 1927], 495/3/46–207/211; Collins, 'The situation in Ireland', pp. 53–6.

65 Raymond W. Leonard, *Secret Soldiers of the Revolution: Military Intelligence, 1918–1933* (Westport, Ct, 1999), p. 18.

Irishman'.[66] On 17 March 1928 Michael Burke of Cobh, described as a 'prominent irregular', and two companions were arrested in London with a stock of
20 revolvers. A British parliamentary enquiry found that two £10 banknotes
on Burke's possession were originally part of a consignment despatched by the
Bank for Russian Trade in London to a 'Soviet institute' in Berlin. The
enquiry also revealed evidence of substantial Comintern funding of the
CPGB.[67] Sometime afterwards, Scotland Yard exposed Irish contact in
Holland with Ignace Reiss, Razvedupr's agent for Britain, who had taken up
a residency in Amsterdam in 1928. Again, the surveillance of Irish suspects
had wider, more damaging implications for the communists, as Razvedupr
felt compelled to close the Amsterdam centre. While the provenance of the
mysterious Irishmen is not certain, Reiss's wife distinguished them from the
'Irish Communist Party' – of which she had some knowledge – and remembered them as strongly nationalist, 'fascinated by the Soviet operation and
willing to collaborate with anyone against the British [but] of little use'.[68]
Another curious shard of evidence is cited in a Department of Justice report
on communist–IRA links. Allegedly the Comintern wrote to 'the Irish communists' in February 1928 welcoming the establishment of a 'militant section'
and a 'commission for arming the proletariat'. If the letter is genuine, it is
unlikely that it was sent to Larkin or the IWL, and the department's report is
otherwise riddled with factual errors; yet it is possible that the recipients were
the League Against Imperialism, and the date sounds appropriate.[69]

   Meanwhile, Kuusinen's intervention had led to two lengthy debates in the
ECCI's politsecretariat and presidium, the first time since the fourth world
congress in 1922 that detailed consideration was given to the application of
theory to Ireland. The ECCI's sanguine assessment of Ireland reflected
the thinking behind the third period, and its revised directive to the IWL
illustrates its transitional position between united front and third period
theses and the influence of the latter before their formal endorsement by the
ninth plenum in February.

   Against objections from Willie Gallacher and Fineberg, the presidium
concluded that Fianna Fáil's de facto acceptance of the Free State portended

66 PROL, Krivitsky file, KV 2/805.

67 BPP, *Russian Banks and Communist Funds: Report of an Enquiry into Certain Transactions of the Bank for Russian Trade Ltd, and the Moscow Narodny Bank Ltd*, Cmd 3125 (1928), XXII, 275; Jane Degras (ed.), *Calendar of Soviet Documents on Foreign Policy* (London, 1958), pp. 104–5; NA, DT, memo, Sept. 1931, S5864B. See also *Izvestia*, 15 June 1928, and *The Times*, 12 June 1928.

68 Elisabeth K. Poretsky, *Our Own People: A Memoir of 'Ignace Reiss' and His Friends* (London, 1969), pp. 74, 84. Reiss's real name was Ignace Poretsky. He also used the code names 'Ludwig' or 'Ludwik'; see also the *Daily Mail*, 14 May 1930.

69 NA, DT, memo, Sept. 1931, S5864B.

its abandonment of the national revolutionary struggle, and presented a new opportunity for the IWL to lead the fight against imperialism in a united front with Sinn Féin. Vigorous protests from Gallacher that Fianna Fáil was a mass party, whereas Sinn Féin was 'a monument, not a movement', that the IRA left did not speak for the army, and that IRA strength - believed in Moscow to be about 10,000 – had a largely paper value, were overruled. Bukharin stressed that ideological imperatives alone demanded that communists should ally with Sinn Féin, as the more radical party. Lozovsky added enigmatically: 'the [IRA] people were here, we didn't handle them well . . . and we must correct this mistake'. Determinants of IWL policy were to include:

1 British imperialism, the most aggressive leader of the entire imperialist world reaction, is endeavouring to keep its grip on Ireland by all possible means.
2 A very unstable political situation which divulges more and more the concrete political bankruptcy of the ruling Free State party.
3 Serious economic depression accompanied by growing unemployment.
4 Progressive economic ruin of farmers and leaseholders.
5 A re-grouping of class forces and political parties in the struggle for the national independence of Ireland. Important sections of the bourgeoisie have completely and definitely given up the struggle for Irish independence . . .[70]

In the belief that Fianna Fáil 'will perhaps be able to play the role of a more or less loyal opposition to the Free State party and British imperialism, but it cannot certainly play a leading role in the national-revolutionary struggle', the IWL was to offer a united front to Sinn Féin, and – anticipating the third period's united front from below tactic – to the rank and file and local organisations of Fianna Fáil, and to the rank and file of the Labour Party. It was agreed to adopt the directive provisionally, pending a discussion with Larkin.[71]

Larkin's infamous temper was already being provoked by Hilt's successor, Jack Leckie. Leckie's mission was to organise the IWL with a head office separate from the WUI, install Carney as secretary and editor of a weekly paper, liaise with the recent WUI delegation to Russia regarding publicity, scout for suitable candidates for the Lenin School, and meet with Fitzpatrick. The plan was have a party convention by Easter and confine Larkin to propaganda work. A subsidy of £2,000 was to be made available for the party

---

70 RGASPI, Protokoll Nr. 109 der Sitzung des Präsidiums des EKKI, 28 Jan. 1928, 495/2/95–86/187.
71 RGASPI, minutes of the ECCI politsecretariat, 13 Jan. 1928, 495/3/51–43/93; Protokoll Nr.109 der Sitzung des Präsidiums des EKKI, 28 Jan. 1928, 495/2/95–86/187.

paper. Leaving Moscow on Christmas Day, Leckie spent some time at home in Scotland, and landed in Dublin in mid January. It was a fruitless journey. Larkin and Carney fobbed off his naïve requests to see IWL records, which in all likelihood did not exist, and to meet the IWL executive. Leckie's persistence drove Larkin into a towering rage, and he lodged a formal protest with Bukharin about his interference and negotiations with 'terrorists and feudists'. Leckie had indeed been in contact with McLay and Fitzpatrick, and while the WPI was a beaten docket, Larkin scented a threat in Fitzpatrick and was already doing what he could to keep him offstage.[72] The WUI withheld the logbooks of their delegates to the October revolution celebrations in Moscow from the International Trade Union Relations Committee, preventing it from publishing a souvenir of the visit. The delegates did address several meetings in Dublin, and one in Roscrea, to publicise the trip, but Larkin was in no hurry to start a branch of Friends of Soviet Russia. Only when Fitzpatrick advertised his intention to proceed did he convene a meeting in the Tivoli Theatre on 22 January at which, following a lantern slide show, he and Mrs Despard founded Irish Friends of Soviet Russia.[73]

Leckie left Ireland, sadder and wiser, on 1 February. A week or so later, Larkin and Carney arrived in Moscow for the ninth ECCI plenum. Bukharin spent three hours discussing religion with Larkin, in an effort to elucidate his troublesome Irish enigma. Larkin's defence of the Catholic Church, while foregoing the opportunity to attend mass, left the Comintern chief no more enlightened.[74] Bukharin also invited him to speak in the closing stages of the great debate between Trotsky and Stalin on whether the revolution needed to be international or could survive in one country. Larkin, as usual, declined to comment on Russian affairs, and then offered to draft proposals to heal the rift between the two Soviet leaders. Almost alone among the plenum delegates, he saw the dispute as inter-personal. Nonetheless he inclined to Stalin's side of the argument. Delivering a lecture to 2,000 people at the Moscow Soviet on Ireland, trade unions, and the peasantry, he asked the audience to 'hold up the hands of Stalin', perhaps the only analogy ever drawn between Stalin and the biblical Joshua.[75] He seemed keen to please his hosts. At the plenum he endorsed the third period tactic of hostility to social

72 RGASPI, IWL to ECCI, 2 Feb. 1928, 495/89/49–1/10.
73 RGASPI, letter from Fitzpatrick, 31 Mar. 1928, 495/89/52–24/25; report on the IWL, 22 Feb. 1928, 495/89/50–51/69.
74 Letter from Carney in Donal Nevin, 'Larkin and Connolly', in Nevin, *James Larkin*, p. 400.
75 Jack Carney's recollections of Larkin, pp. 1–2. I am obliged to Emmet Larkin for a copy of this private memoir, written by Carney at his request. For further praise of Stalin see the *Irish Worker*, 18 July 1931.

democratic parties, criticising the CPGB's reservations about the application of the line. 'Our comrades of Great Britain', he declared', 'with the help of the Comintern ... are going to carry their Party and the British working class to a social revolution (Applause)'.[76]

Where his immediate interests were concerned, Larkin was as impossible as ever, indulging in personal attacks on the CPGB leaders in the plenum's trade union commission, faulting their record during the miners' lockout, and complaining of the Minority Movement's refusal to campaign for the withdrawal of British unions from Ireland.[77] In the Irish commission he turned his wrath on republicans to discourage Soviet and CPGB contacts with the IRA, presenting a marathon and exceptionally personal diatribe, which en passsant condemned Connolly's alliance with bourgeois nationalists in 1916, and descended to such exhaustive, petty criticism of the British that the normally meticulous Comintern secretaries abridged the minutes.[78] Despite this terrific subjectivity, Larkin largely got his way. The ECCI modified its directive on Ireland to emphasise that the IWL should operate independently with the proviso that it should seek to win over the best elements of Sinn Féin and the IRA, and recommend electoral transfers to Sinn Féin candidates.[79] Larkin's relations with Lozovsky were more brittle, and a seething antipathy between them worsened to the point that they nearly came to blows. He told Lozovsky that the WUI executive wanted to break with the Profintern unless promises of financial help were made good.[80]

On a lighter note Larkin described with unusually gentle sarcasm his difficulties in obtaining films and other cultural propaganda from the leaden Soviet bureaucracy:

After a long and wearisome lecture from Mme Kameneva [cultural relations department] who felt that she had a message to deliver, and a victim to appreciate it, I convinced her that there were some people in Ireland who are really one removed [sic] from the amoeba stage of life ... She gave me an album containing coloured reprints from many of the Russian painters. A very interesting compilation. I was going to take it with me because I have had such interesting experiences in the USSR regarding promises. But Mme Kameneva would insist that she would send it on along with other interesting matter, by mail. Up to this writing, neither

76 Larkin, *James Larkin*, pp. 291–2.
77 RGASPI, Ninth ECCI plenum, fifth sitting, 13 Feb. 1928, 495/167/75.
78 RGASPI, minutes of the Anglo-American secretariat, 20 Feb. 1928, 495/72/34–1/28.
79 RGASPI, The immediate tasks of the IWL, 7 Apr. 1928, 495/3/62–25/29.
80 Larkin, *James Larkin*, p. 297; RGASPI, Statement from Larkin on WUI disaffiliation from the Profintern, undated [1929], 495/89/104–137.

greetings or album, nor other interesting matter has ever reached this land of primitive people.[81]

Before curtailing his visit to fight the by-election for his Dáil seat, Larkin did receive copies of *The Battleship Potemkin* and another film, which were confiscated as 'inflammable' contraband on his arrival in England, but later returned.[82] Carney subsequently made a big issue of the failure to send cultural material to Ireland.[83]

The wrangling continued at the fourth world congress of the Profintern in March. Three of the five-man WUI delegation presented to Bukharin a questionnaire implicitly critical of Leckie and Comintern contacts with the CPGB, the WPI and the IRA, and enquiring whether the ECCI would pay the WUI £247 allegedly allocated to it by the Profintern in 1925. Larkin also wrote separately to Lozovsky, urging him to settle 'this long outstanding financial irritation'.[84] Curiously, Larkin's letter of introduction warned that 'care should be taken as to any conversations' with a fourth delegate, Jack Dempsey: a prescient apprehension, as Dempsey publicly accused Larkin of dishonesty, leading the latter to conclude that Lozovsky was intriguing against him. Dempsey would later denounce Larkin in Dublin for misappropriating union funds.[85] The spat might have had serious consequences, as the Department of Justice enquired of the Garda commissioner if legal action could be taken. The Gardaí replied that Dempsey's allegations were 'substantially correct', but added that Larkin had squandered 'thousands of pounds from Moscow within the past few years', and hinted that action might be counterproductive:

> The international communist press have howled out time and time again about the strategical importance of Ireland – not from the military standpoint, but because it is universally known that Ireland contains within herself a potentially revolutionary people at England's front door, and the CI demands that Ireland should be the 'Afghanistan' in the enemy's own camp (England), and because

81 RGASPI, Report on films, cultural relations, economic and diplomatic penetration, undated [1928], 495/89/104–133/136.

82 Ibid.

83 RGASPI, Carney to Lozovsky, 19 Nov. 1928, 495/89/52–16/17.

84 RGASPI, IWL questionnaire, 2 Feb. 1928, 495/89/49–1/3; Larkin to Lozovsky, 13 Mar. 1928, 534/7/286–86. On Bischoff see also IWL to VKP(b), 6 Feb. 1929, 534/8/113–13/15.

85 UCDA, MacEntee papers, Notes on communism in Saorstát Éireann, P67/523(5), p. 11; RGASPI, statement from Larkin on WUI disaffiliation from the Profintern, undated [1929], 495/89/104–137; Irish Labour History Archives, Cathal O'Shannon papers, COS 93/12/122a(P).

Larkin has failed to create such a situation there are fairly powerful influences at work to oust him.[86]

The fifth WUI delegate was Bischoff, a native of the Ukraine and a crewman on the battleship *Potemkin* in 1905. The congress itself brought further controversy. Carney announced the WUI's disaffiliation because – of all things – the Profintern 'had no power to enforce discipline over its sections'. In a rambling speech, he again referred to the financial burden on the union, and the Minority Movement's flouting of Profintern policy on British unions in Ireland.[87] With promises of help, the breach was healed and the Irish headed home charged with fulfilling the aims of the Red International. Six months later, the Profintern was complaining of having heard nothing from the WUI.[88]

Aside from anything else, Larkin had come to regard the Profintern link as a liability to the WUI. As his confidence in revolutionary trade unionism, and in the WUI itself, drained away, he was easily rattled by stirrings of Catholic anti-communism. The first of what were intended to be annual 'Catholic social weeks' had been organised in April by the Federation of Catholic Young Men's Societies. The theme of the week was Catholic labour and it featured a series of lectures by P. J. S. Serrarens, secretary of the International Federation of Christian Trade Unions. The secretary of the Dublin trade union unity conference, which was sponsoring merger talks between the rival trades' councils, attended and attacked communist trade unionism and the presence of Irish students in the Lenin School, and Serrarens received favourable coverage in the *Irishman*, organ of the Labour Party and Trade Union Congress. Larkin made a mountain, to Moscow, out of the molehill, ignoring the fact that the lectures had generated little interest in labour circles, and the *Irishman* was taken to task by Frank Robbins of the ITGWU for seeming to encourage Catholic trade unionism, a charge it rejected.[89] Indeed Dublin trades' council had gone so far as to present Bill Denn with an inscribed gold watch to celebrate his admission to 'the Lenin university'.[90] Of genuine significance was the amalgamation in November of Dublin trades' council and Dublin Workers' Council, a belated response to the continuing decline of trade unionism in the city. The Profintern repeatedly called on the WUI to take a stand on the unity talks, and, as Moscow feared,

86 NA, DJ, Larkin file, JUS 8/676.
87 RGASPI, Profintern congress, eighth session, 22 Mar. 1928, 534/1/68–19/27.
88 RGASPI, Profintern to WUI, undated [1928], 534/6/79–33.
89 RGASPI, Letter from Larkin, 18 Apr. 1928, 495/89/49–12/16; *Irishman*, 21–28 Apr. 1928.
90 Irish labour History Archives, Dublin trades' council records, 13 Mar. 1928, 19/DTC/1/12.

none of the trades' council's radical policies was carried over into the new body. The demise of the 'all red council' marked the end of its affiliates' association with communism and left the WUI further isolated.[91]

Larkin still wanted to be a communist in politics, even if his illusions about an alliance with Fianna Fáil were dispelled when the party fielded a candidate in the by-election for his Dáil seat in April. He came third in the contest, with 8,232 votes. Hilt returned to Dublin on 27 April to oversee the transformation of the IWL into a party. An issue of the *Irish Worker* appeared on 12 May, with a print run of 5,000 copies. On 13 May, about 30 people from Dublin, Belfast, Limerick, and Tipperary – all picked by Larkin – attended a conference of the IWL at which the ECCI position on Ireland was endorsed, and Carney elected provisional general secretary. Hilt and Larkin then departed for Berlin for a conference of the WEB, which handled Comintern liaison with the west. Carney despatched an ebullient report on IWL activities in August, adding a warning that Comintern contacts with the IRA 'must be stopped'.[92] In reality, nothing had changed; little was done before Hilt arrived and nothing after he left.

OIL AND TROUBLED WATERS

A fresh dispute had arisen in July when Russian Oil Products Ltd (ROP), a London-based division of Soviet Russia's Neftetrest [Oil Trust], opened a depot in Dublin. Larkin had of course made repeated claims since 1924 of promises that the USSR would become commercially active in Ireland. Since July 1927 Hilt had pressed his case, and in November of that year Maxim Litvinov, assistant commissar of Narkomindel, and Anatoli Lunacharsky, commissar of education, had a promising discussion on a trade exchange with the Irish representative in Geneva.[93] In February 1928 Larkin again pushed for Soviet 'diplomatic and economic penetration' of Ireland, arguing that considerable potential existed for trade in grain, oil and timber. The Soviets, he said, agreed to address the question 'without loss of time', though Iveagh

91 Cody, O'Dowd, and Rigney, *The Parliament of Labour*, pp. 148–50; RGASPI, Report to the ECCI from Christian Hilt, 6 June 1928, 495/89/50–39/42; Profintern to WUI, 6 July 1928, 534/6/79–28/31.

92 RGASPI, letter from Larkin, 18 Apr. 1928, 495/89/49–12/16; report to the ECCI from Christian Hilt, 6 June 1928, 495/89/50–39/42; report from Carney, 8 Aug. 1928, 495/89/50–43/50.

93 RGASPI, Memorandum on the establishment of direct relations between the USSR and the Irish Free State, undated [1927 or 1928], 495/89/107–1/5; Ronan Fanning et al. (eds), *Documents on Irish Foreign Policy, Vol. III, 1926–1932* (Dublin, 2002), M. MacWhite to Joseph P. Walshe, 30 Nov. 1927, p. 162.

House's enthusiasm for an exchange casts some doubt on Narkomindel's sense of urgency.[94] Subsequently the WUI's co-operative approached the Soviet timber trust in London, without results. Unfortunately for Larkin his reputation in business was no more reliable than that in politics. In 1927, as in 1925, he had imported 'unity coal', lost money on the venture, and failed to clear his debts with coal merchants in Liverpool.[95]

When ROP became operational in Dublin, Larkin protested to Moscow that the company was employing non-union labour. Bukharin cabled Dublin to say that the work in question was sub-contracted, and that ROP hired union labour only.[96] Larkin then protested that while ROP had approached the Labour Party and was engaging members of the ITGWU and – almost as execrable in his eyes – the British-based Amalgamated Transport and General Workers' Union, it had made no contact with himself and had refused to hire some WUI members. In September he travelled to London to see the manager, and warned ROP's Russian directors that they would end up 'on the Rock Pile in Siberia'. Getting no satisfaction, he wrote to Bukharin and the Profintern, and had Carney infringe protocol by beseeching Irish students at the Lenin School to register a formal objection.[97] Carney also threatened to withdraw the students from Moscow, complained of Bukharin's failure to fulfil his promises, and announced that the Russian banners presented to the WUI would be returned. Doing his best to turn a crisis into a drama, he told Leckie: 'I would rather be a Trotskyite and be wrong than be right among those at the centre . . . Warn other representatives that they must not come here. Our head office is on the third floor, and the drop is none too small.'[98] As a result of a protest from the Irish students, the Anglo-American secretariat raised the matter with the ECCI secretariat, and assured Dublin that an ROP official from London would 'clear up the whole situation'. As for Bukharin's promises, these 'were contingent upon statements you had to send. These have not been forthcoming. Until they are, nothing can be done.'[99]

94 Fanning et al., *Documents on Irish Foreign Policy, Vol. III, 1926–1932*, Memorandum by the Department of External Affairs to Diarmuid O'Hegarty (Dublin) on Irish Free State commercial relations with the USSR, 7 Apr. 1930, pp. 522–4.
95 RGASPI, Report on films, cultural relations, economic and diplomatic penetration, undated [1928], 495/89/104-133/136; O'Connor, *James Larkin*, p. 85.
96 RGASPI, Bukharin to Larkin, 28 July [1928], 495/89/49-17; note, undated [1928], 495/89/52-5.
97 RGASPI, Profintern to Guser, Larkin's statement, 6 Feb. 1929, 495/89/56-1/7; *Irish Worker*, 22 Nov. 1931; Carney to Heimo, 17 Sept. 1928, 495/89/52-6; Carney to Larkin Jr, 6 Nov. 1928, 495/89/52-13/15.
98 RGASPI, Carney to Jack [Leckie], 16 Oct. 1928, 539/3/643-1/6.
99 RGASPI, Anglo-American secretariat to Piatnitsky, 20 Nov. 1928, 495/89/49-11; Anglo-American secretariat to IWL, 1 Dec. 1928, 495/89/49-20.

The Comintern accepted that ROP had made mistakes, but the Soviets were not willing to deepen their dependency on one who had lost their confidence, or pour troubled waters on their oil. Larkin made his last trip to Russia in January 1929 to ensure that his appeal reached the highest authorities.[100] In a weasel-worded letter he pleaded that unless the dispute was resolved in the WUI's favour, membership opinion would compel him to resign from the union executive, and his place might be taken by non-communists.[101] Stalin heard the case on 7 February at a meeting of the VKP(b) politburo. On the proposal of Lozovsky and Grigori Sokolnikov, soon to be Soviet ambassador to Britain, the politburo agreed that the Soviet trade representative in London should review the ROP apparat in Ireland in the light of Larkin's allegations, and that ROP be directed to employ trade union labour only; preference was to be given to the hiring of WUI members, but the union was not to be allowed organise a monopoly of ROP employees and no deals were done with Larkin on the sale of Russian fuel.[102]

For all his earlier indignation, Carney did not see the ROP affair as a breaking point. On 27 January, saluting the Workers' (Communist) Party of America for a donation of literature to the IWL, he looked forward to closer transatlantic co-operation in the struggle. On 19 February, before Larkin returned, he wrote fraternally to Lozovsky seeking Profintern help with propaganda work. It was probably soon after that Larkin severed his official ties with Moscow.[103] In two undated documents, he announced his political retirement from 'active work', and asked the Comintern to support the Irish at the Lenin School, stressing that young Jim was his own man and an earnest Communist. Moscow respected this request. It was more sceptical of the claim that the IWL remained a genuine affiliate under Carney's leadership. Larkin was less reticent in declaring the WUI's irrevocable disaffiliation from the Profintern, blaming the Profintern's lack of financial support for the union, and Lozovsky for intriguing against him with the WUI delegation to Moscow in March 1928. He also stated that the WUI was 'constantly under fire' for its Profintern membership.[104] It is true that attitudes were changing, as the Catholic Church began to awaken to its social power, and people started

100 Nevin, *James Larkin*, contains a photo of Larkin with Transcaucasus delegates to the seventh all-union conference of Mestrans, dated January 1929, but there is no other evidence of a visit.

101 RGASPI, Profintern to Guser, Larkin's statement, 6 Feb. 1929, 495/89/56–1.

102 RGASPI, Protocol no. 63 of the politburo, 7 Feb. 1929, 17/3/725–1/2. I am obliged to Barry McLoughlin for this reference. In 1930 ROP employees were organised by the Irish Union of Distributive Workers' and Clerks, and the ITGWU. *Workers' Voice*, 31 May 1931.

103 RGASPI, Carney to the Party Convention of the Workers' (Communist) Party, 27 Jan. 1929, 515/1/160–1/3; Carney to Lozovsky, 19 Feb. 1929, 534/7/266–93/94.

104 RGASPI, Letters from Larkin, undated [1929], 495/89/49–18, 495/89/104–137.

to frown on association with Russia. It is true also that Larkin realised that Moscow was preparing to bypass him through the IRA left – which he had tried and failed to stop – and through the Irish at the Lenin School, which he could hardly oppose as this group included young Jim. Yet the ROP business had enormous, and secret, significance for him. After all, the Soviets did agree to 'clear up' ROP and give preferential treatment to the WUI. It would be consistent with Larkin's character and aims in his relations with Moscow if the refusal to do a deal with him on the sale of oil was the real breaking point. It amounted to final proof that he was never going to obtain from Russia the money to be financially independent and free of the burden of union work.

The way was now clear for the Comintern to prepare a new Irish initiative, one that would be completely under its direction.

SEVEN

BOLSHEVISING IRISH
COMMUNISM, 1929-31

In our group there are two main tasks: to win new
good elements, and get rid of the bad elements.
DUBLIN COMMUNIST GROUP
January 1931[1]

—

While the theses of the third period had influenced Comintern policy on
Ireland since January 1928, it was not until Jim Larkin's break with Moscow
that the ECCI was able to apply the theses directly and consistently. The
impact of third period thinking on the preparatory work for the formation of
a second CPI is evident in Moscow's sanguine analysis of Irish politics, in the
tactics prescribed, and in the paramount concern that the Irish party be
Bolshevised. Bolshevisation was integral to the third period, which saw the
final subordination of communist parties throughout the world to the
Comintern. The high degree of central control over the Irish section at this
time was not exceptional, but deemed to be an essential tool of a world party.
Of course central control was easier in the Irish case as a new party was being
built from scratch. Recognising the derisory level of Marxist–Leninist consciousness in the country, and the importance of Larkin, the WUI, and
republicans to the creation of a mass base, the ECCI decided to implement its
plan of campaign in two phases. In the first, the class against class line would
be applied to reformist trade unions and Labour parties only, united front
tactics continued with republicans, and a diplomatic silence observed on
Larkin and the WUI. The ECCI still hoped to lure Larkin back to the fold.
At the very least it wanted his neutrality towards a new party and a communist
fraction in the WUI. Once a core group was in being, then class against class
would be applied generally. The idea behind class against class was to dif-
ferentiate revolutionaries from reformists, and push the former into joining
the communists. Throughout the process, emphasis would be placed on the
Bolshevisation of cadres.

1   RGASPI, Abridgement of report of Neptun, 26 Jan. 1931, 495/89/64–2.

The ECCI misread what were to be the two key sources of cadres, the WUI and the IRA. Jack Carney had put WUI membership at 18,000, and if the ECCI knew him to be prone to exaggeration, it is unlikely that it realised that the actual muster was closer to 6,000 by 1929, the union's internal affairs being shrouded in an obfuscation which baffled observers in Dublin no less than Moscow.[2] More importantly, the ECCI mistook the WUI for a conventional, democratic union. Its assumption that in a worst-case scenario of opposition from Larkin it could work with a fraction within the WUI underestimated the lengths that Larkin could go to prevent infiltration of the union. With respect to the IRA, Moscow expected a rapid and radical evolution out of keeping with the organisation's stubborn history. Ultimately, the contradiction in Comintern strategy lay in the fact that its preparations and early successes were based on united front policies, but its eventual intention was to apply the slogans of the third period.

SPINNING THE RED WEB

Larkin's breach with Moscow was not generally known in Dublin before September 1929. He continued to receive Comintern emissaries and, on occasion, upstage his rivals with counter-demonstrations.[3] Nonetheless revolutionary groups and communist fronts became increasingly prominent throughout the year in industrial agitation and in association with republicanism. Two groups set up in 1928 were instrumental in linking both currents: the Trade Union Unity League, founded by Michael Fitzpatrick and IRA colleagues as a rank and file 'underground', and the James Connolly Workers' Club, convened initially to commemorate the October revolution, and soon a haunt of old CPI and WPI stalwarts.[4] The club readopted the educational agenda of the earlier Connolly Workers' Education Club, affiliating to the British Labour Research Department and the British National Council of Labour Colleges, and published two pamphlets, *The James Connolly Song Book* and *An Imperialistic War or Revolution?* Again, Charlotte Despard was a patron.[5] Police reckoned

---

2   Officially, the WUI claimed 15,095 members in 1928, and 16,159 in 1929, but it gave its income for these years as £4,337 and £6,335 respectively, and each member was worth about £1 per annum. NA, Registry of Friendly Societies files, WUI file, 369T.

3   RGASPI, Ben Ainley to the political bureau [CPGB], 25 Aug. 1929, 495/89/59–1/3.

4   RGASPI, letter from Fitzpatrick, 27 Mar. 1928, 495/89/52–24/25; UCDA, Cowan family papers, Séamus McGowan papers, secretary, International Trade Union Relations Committee to the James Connolly Workers' Club, 12 Oct. 1929, P34/D/37(56).

5   UCDA, Cowan family papers, Séamus McGowan papers, secretary, International Trade Union Relations Committee to the James Connolly Workers' Club, 12 October 1929, P34/D/37; NLI, *James Connolly Song Book*, LOp71.

the club to have a membership of 100 adults and 50 children in September 1929.[6] The prompt to action in industry was Larkin's disappointing leadership of a dispute at the Inchicore railway works. Of all sectors in the still contracting trade union movement, transport was worst hit, and it would become a key theatre for communists. Rationalisation of road and rail services in the five years after 1926 led to wage cuts and some 5,000 redundancies. Larkin became chairman of an inter-union council of action at Inchicore. The council's acceptance of redundancies and pay cuts of ten per cent, following a strike in early 1929, generated a fresh resolve to challenge Larkin.[7] Christy Ferguson formed a shopfloor cell in the Inchicore works in May and produced a rank and file paper, the *Steam Hammer*. The paper folded after a two day unofficial sit-in protest against a wage cut in June, and the dismissal of militants. Putting his personal circumstance to good use, Ferguson revived the INUM in July.[8]

An increasingly important strand in the republican–communist matrix was the League Against Imperialism. The League drew 2,000 people to hear British miners' leader A. J. Cook in Dublin in October 1928, and 2,500 to an anti-British Legion rally in November. Peadar O'Donnell and Seán MacBride represented Ireland at the League's second world congress in Frankfurt am Main in July 1929. Éamon de Valera had visited the League's Berlin office in September 1928, and indicated that Fianna Fáil might affiliate 'internationally'; he had reservations about associating Fianna Fáil with anti-American policies, or with communism in Ireland. Fianna Fáil sent 20s. to the Frankfurt congress, and would occasionally endorse its activities in Ireland.[9] In February 1929 O'Donnell and David Fitzgerald proposed to the IRA army convention the adoption of a socialist programme entitled 'Saor Éire'.[10] While the proposal was rejected, there was a growing acceptance within the IRA of the need for a political project to keep the organisation abreast of the times. In April the army council created Comhairle na Poblachta as an umbrella uniting military bodies like the IRA and Cumann na mBan with political elements like Sinn Féin and the second Dáil.[11] The failure of Comhairle na Poblachta strengthened the hand of left republicans.

6   NA, DJ, report, 16 Sept. 1929, JUS 8/686.

7   RGASPI, Ben Ainley to the political bureau, 25 Aug. 1929, 495/89/54–1.

8   Milotte, *Communism in Modern Ireland*, pp. 101–2.

9   United States National Archives, Washington DC, State Department document file, report from Great Britain, 26 Feb. 1929, 841D.00B/5. I am obliged to Eunan O'Halpin for this reference. RGASPI, *Informations-und Pressedienst, Zweiter antiimperialistisher Weltkongresse*, 20–31 July 1929, 542/1/96–28/29; NA, DJ, Anti-imperialists (1928–1933), JUS 8/682.

10 Ó Drisceoil, *Peadar O'Donnell*, p. 52.

11 Cronin, *Frank Ryan*, p. 33.

In April 1929 Roddy Connolly outlined to the Connolly Club a scheme for
a Workers' Defence Corps, the intention being that it should first work with
the IRA and then absorb it.[12] While a number of republican and communist
auxiliary groups already existed, this was the start of what would become a
tangled web of inter-woven revolutionary organisations. On 7 July the three
main strands of proto-communism – leftists in Dublin and Belfast and republicans – gelled to convene the first national conference of the Irish Labour
Defence League, which was to be the new name for the Irish section of
ICWPA. Mrs Despard and ICWPA head office subvented the conference.
Delegates represented the Dublin and Belfast branches, the Women Prisoners'
Defence League, the Republican Political Prisoners' Committee, the IRA,
the Connolly Workers' Club, and five trade union branches and three branches
of the Northern Ireland Labour Party (NILP). The Labour Defence League
claimed the affiliation of 700 trade unionists in Dublin and 3,000 in Belfast,
and an individual membership of over 120 in October. The substantial IRA
input included members of the army council, and at least eight of the 15-member
executive were republicans. At its first meeting the executive ratified a proposal to form a Workers' Defence Corps, with the IRA supplying the nucleus.[13]
On 21 August, with five strikes running in the city, including action by
tramwaymen and busmen, the Labour Defence League issued a campaign
bulletin, *Dublin Strike News*. That week the Connolly Workers' Club drew a
sizeable crowd – 700 according to the Gardai, over 2,000 according to a CPGB
speaker – to an anti-war meeting, the proceedings terminating with a rendition
of the Red Flag by the club choir. The CPGB man was highly impressed.[14]
'August 1929', *Dublin Strike News* declared, 'may well be a historic month
witness[ing] the resurgence of Irish labour'. And there was truth in the claim.
Having fallen from 229,000 in 1920 to 92,000 in 1929, membership affiliated
to the ITUC began to recover, reaching a peak of 173,000 in 1941.[15]

12 NA, DT, report, 7 May 1929, S3581–6.
13 RGASPI, Irish Labour Defence League annual report, 7 July 1929, and report of 1st annual
conference, 29 July 1929, 539/3/644–2/5; Irish Labour Defence League, report from 7 July to 30 Sept.
1929, 539/3/644–7/9; letter to the Irish Labour Defence League, 3 Jan. 1931, 539/3/645–1; NA, DT,
Department of Justice report, 19 July 1929, S5074A; Mary M. Banta, 'The red scare in the Irish Free
State, 1929–37' (MA, UCD, 1982), p. 11.
14 NA, DJ, report, 20 Aug. 1929, JUS 8/686; RGASPI, Ben Ainley to the political bureau, 25 Aug.
1929, 495/89/54–1/3.
15 Donal Nevin (ed.), *Trade Union Century* (Dublin, 1994), p. 433. The last issue of *Dublin Strike
News* appeared on 3 Sept.

THE COMINTERN'S INITIATIVE

None of the revolutionaries in Ireland had Moscow's approval or trust in the business of party formation. Establishing a communist party was not simply a matter of convening a meeting in Dublin and adopting a programme. The ECCI needed to be confident that the party would be Bolshevised. In particular, it was concerned about the delicate question of relations with Larkin. The response to Larkin's disengagement illustrates something of how the Comintern apparatus functioned. The first step in the process was the nomination of a commission on 8 June 1929 by the ECCI's standing commission.[16] The appointment of commissions, in effect committees, to deal with problems of all sorts was usual. Convened on an ad hoc basis, their size and membership depended on the gravity of the agenda, but those on Ireland usually included at least one British comrade – for want of a trusted Irish expert – and one Russian – the monitoring of Comintern decision making by members of the VKP(b) being typical of the third period. Irish students at the Lenin School were consulted as required. In this instance, the commission was appointed within the Anglo-American secretariat and consisted of J. R. Campbell, a Scot, B. A. Vassiliev, a former Comintern representative in Britain, and A. J. Bennett. The commission heard a report from Tom Bell, now with the Profintern, and on 24 July the Anglo-American secretariat recommended support for the publication of a paper in Ireland 'provided our control and lead [*sic*] of the weekly are safeguarded', sending comrades to Ireland immediately, the adoption of the slogan 'united free workers and peasants Irish republic', and the development of an Irish party.[17] On 26 July the politsecretariat endorsed the proposals with minor amendments.[18]

When the general chistka or purge of Bukharinites and other 'right-wing' elements from communist parties reached the Lenin School in September, it provided a convenient opportunity to cleanse the Irish students of Larkinite sympathies. Suspected Larkinites were isolated from the revision of policy on Ireland, and Bell had young Jim removed as the anglophone sector's 'partorg', or party organiser, a prestigious post which entailed responsibility for the politics and academic progress of students. An English comrade, Harry Wicks, replaced him. Objections from Larkin Jr, Pat Breslin, Seán Murray and Charlie Ashmore about their 'progressive and intentional exclusion . . . from discussions on Irish questions', led to an official investigation into the accusations. Chaired by the African-American Henry Hall, it found in favour of the Irish, but Larkin was not reinstated as partorg.[19]

16   RGASPI, Protokoll nr. 46 der Sitzung der Standizen Kommission des EKKI, 8 June 1929, 495/7/-.

17   RGASPI, A. J. Bennett to the political secretariat, ECCI, 24 July 1929, 495/3/151–96.

18   RGASPI, Protokoll nr.45 der Sitzung des Politsekr. des EKKI, 26 July 1929, 495/3/-.

19   McLoughlin, 'Proletarian academics or party functionaries?', p. 68.

The chistka procedure was itself gruelling. Wicks recalled:

> Each of us was 'cleansed' in turn. For each, we would all gather in the main
> auditorium. The chistka went on and on, from morning till night, for weeks. All
> school work was suspended. Each of us had to stand alone, up on the platform in
> front of a row of Red Army colonels and generals and other high dignitaries; our
> Cleansing Commission which was under the jurisdiction of the Central Committee
> of the party. And they or anyone in the school could ask you questions about your
> social origins, your biography, your politics – about anything which might smell or
> be made smelly. You did at least have the right to reply in your own language. But
> as soon as any gap was found in your biography, the questions would come surging
> through that gap. Everyone had to be cleansed, from [Klavdiya] Kirsanova [acting
> rector] down, including of course every student. When the discussion on each
> person had been closed, there was no vote. But the chistka commission would
> immediately make its decision, which would be communicated to the party nucleus
> bureau in the school.[20]

Coupled with the chistka was the new device of public 'self-criticism'. The
Irish were not alone in detesting the practice, and the strain is evident in
young Jim's confession to charges of opposing theses on the IWL and WUI:

> It is correct that it was difficult to extricate myself from Larkin's influence, but the
> school has helped me in this. I hope that it will always be possible for me, as a
> party-member, to reach the correct point of view in all questions and that we will
> only have to take Larkin's influence into account in as much as he shares our views.[21]

He was also prevailed on to advise his father of moves ahead and ask him to
keep silent.[22]

A commission assembled in Ireland in September and October, comprising Bell, the senior appointee as ECCI 'instructor', Bob Stewart, seconded
from the CPGB, and Dan Buckley, a student released from the Lenin School
from a republican background in Cork, who was to operate in his native
heath.[23] Their brief was to develop a preparatory commission on the formation of a party initially. Policy was to be guided by class against class, but

---

20   Harry Wicks, *Keeping My Head: The Memoirs of a British Bolshevik* (London, 1992), p. 92.

21   Barry McLoughlin, 'Proletarian academics or party functionaries?', pp. 63–79.

22   RGASPI, Arthur [?] to Frank [?], 17 Nov. 1929, 495/89/54–53. 'Frank' is likely to have been Tom
Bell.

23   RGASPI, Preliminary report on the present situation and on our Irish policy, 26 Oct. 1929,
495/89/54–19/25.

republicans and the WUI were to be exempted from the line pending
instructions; no contact was to be made with Larkin, and no criticism directed
against him.[24] Discretion was the first casualty of the campaign. George
McLay heard of the policy from J. R. Campbell in London and advised the
Connolly Club, which was preparing to transform itself into a party 'adhering
to the programme' of the Comintern.[25]

The Comintern could now enjoy regular contact with Ireland for the first
time. Its standard post was a monthly courier service, run by the OMS.
Travellers to Moscow from Ireland or Britain would be used when possible,
and express couriers were not unknown. The normal route for despatches was
directly through the WEB, but whenever the Irish came under CPGB
dominance, communications would be more likely to go first to London. The
replacement of the Berlin corridor with Stockholm after Hitler came to
power, made the CPGB more central to Dublin–Moscow communications.
So too did the establishment of secret radio links between the Comintern and
its leading affiliates in late 1933 and early 1934, as messages for Ireland were
wired to London. The OMS also distributed money to foreign sections and
agents, and it was probably not the fault of its legendary couriers that the Irish
secretariat grew accustomed to receiving payments in arrears.[26] The cost of the
Irish operation, in 1929–30 especially when two or three full-time organisers
were maintained and a high proportion of supporters were unemployed, far
exceeded domestic income. Funding was not a problem initially, when
Herbert S. 'Roddy' Ward, a wealthy English revolutionary and brother-in-
law of the future British Home Secretary, Sir Samuel Hoare, bankrolled the
INUM and propaganda. Thanks largely to Ward, Bell was able to produce
200 posters and 25,000 leaflets for INUM rallies on 6 March 1930, open a
bookshop later that month; and publish the weekly *Workers' Voice* in April
with a print run of 3,000 copies, at a cost of £18 per issue.[27] One of Ward's
imaginative ventures was to hire Dublin cinemas for the screening of Soviet
films.[28] Ward's breach with Irish communists in November 1930 left them in
dire financial straits. The *Workers' Voice* was trimmed in size, Stewart raised a

24 RGASPI, Tom Bell to Bell, 27 Oct. 1929, 495/89/54–34); Tom Bell to the politsecretariat, and
Anglo-American secretariat, ECCI, 26 Nov. 1929, 495/89/64–64; Joint report on the WUI, S. Murray
and J. Larkin Jr, 2 Aug. 1930, 495/89/63–19/27.

25 UCDA, Cowan family papers, Séamus McGowan papers, McLay to the secretary, James
Connolly Workers' Club, Sept. 1929, P34/D/34(24).

26 RGASPI, Stewart to Robin [Page Arnot?], 25 May 1931, 495/89/65–48/51. Arnot was CPGB
representative in Moscow, from Nov. 1930 to Nov. 1931.

27 RGASPI, Report of the CI Commission in Ireland to the Anglo-American secretariat, ECCI,
and WEB, 17 Mar. 1930, 495/89/62–1/4.

28 Milotte, *Communism in Modern Ireland*, p. 97; *Workers' Voice*, 26 July, 20 Sept. 1930.

loan of £150 in England, and help was received from the Labour Defence League.[29] The politsecretariat cushioned the blow with a grant of £76 per quarter, but Stewart pleaded in May 1931 that the Irish secretariat needed £22 15s. per week minimum, of this sum the paper cost £14 and earned £5. Though the politsecretariat responded quickly with a vote of 4,000 roubles (about £385) to the *Workers' Voice* for the year, the paper was suspended in June, and did not reappear until money had been raised in the USA and Britain.[30] The Labour Defence League too received a yearly subvention from ICWPA up to 1931, while Mrs Despard was a generous sponsor of the League and Friends of Soviet Russia.[31]

Once a despatch from Ireland reached Moscow, procedure became cumbersome. Reports normally went in the first instance to the Anglo-American secretariat, which insisted on receipt of all minutes of leading committee meetings, instructions to groups, and all publications, together with regular progress reports.[32] Up to six copies of documents, including translations into German or Russian, might be typed for the relevant Comintern departments, so that a report could take over a month to reach the politsecretariat. The Anglo-American secretariat vetted material from Ireland, kept itself informed of Irish affairs through other channels, such as newspapers, the CPGB and visitors, and offered regular criticisms of misinterpretation of doctrine or misapplication of tactics. Policy decisions were determined by the politsecretariat, normally on the advice of the Anglo-American secretariat or a commission. Letters to Dublin from the Anglo-American secretariat, or directives from the politsecretariat, did not restrict themselves to generalities. Treating politics as if it were an exact science, they offered precise instructions on slogans, programmes, tactics, timing, and tone of statements. In contrast with its more sympathetic treatment of the first CPI, the Comintern made little allowance for the difficulties besetting its Irish section. Communications tendered terse congratulation on progress, and extensively berated the recipients on their failings. Instructions were often counsels of perfection, or couched in an ambivalence which vindicated the Comintern whatever the outcome. One letter, for example, advised: 'The work of winning over the workers, agricultural labourers and poor farmers who are still republican adherents requires the

29 RGASPI, General election report, Feb. 1932, 495/4/205–15.

30 RGASPI, Stewart to Robin [Page Arnot?], 25 May 1931, 495/89/65–48/51; Protokoll nr. 145 der Sitzung der Politischen Kommission des Pol. Sekr. EKKI, 3 June 1931, 495/4/112–7; Report from Ireland, 20 Aug. 1931, 495/89/64–58/62.

31 RGASPI, letter to the Irish Labour Defence League, 3 Jan. 1931, 539/3/645–1); Linklater, *An Unhusbanded Life*, pp. 238–9.

32 RGASPI, Anglo-American secretariat to secretariat, Ireland, 23 Feb. 1930, 495/89/61–1.

greatest patience in overcoming their prejudices, but at the same time an audacity in action which will gain their respect.'[33] While its analysis was grounded on good factual intelligence, the Comintern clung to a hopelessly exaggerated concept of the level of ideological articulation in Ireland, and attached inordinate significance to the use of a phrase or to minor modifications of a slogan. Following Moscow's recommendations on handling republicans and Larkin, in particular, must have been especially tortuous. If policy application led to setbacks, the blame was invariably pinned on tactical mismanagement or doctrinal misunderstanding in Dublin. The principle of democratic centralism made it virtually impossible for the Irish to change policy without going to Moscow.

The Irish leadership endured the regime stoically. For communists, discipline was not merely an essential tool of a world party, but a proud mark of their worthiness to elite status as the vanguard of the revolution, and a virtue not given to all. Throughout the phase of party building, emphasis was placed on weeding out 'bad elements'. By 1931 Bell, Buckley, Ward and Ferguson had been so characterised, and Larkin Jr was censured obliquely for not making good use of his seat on Dublin corporation.[34] Whether the technique of public 'self-criticism', which Irish students at the Lenin School had found distasteful, was employed in Ireland is unclear. One Russian draft report urged its introduction to combat internal dissent, but there is incomplete evidence that the commendation was deleted from the final version.[35] Comintern policy was observed, though some of its demands were impossible or over ambitious, others – priority for the defence of the Soviet Union, open avowal of communism, or opposition to 'religious prejudices' against communism – could not acquire their intended importance in Ireland, and others – notably the application of class against class to the IRA and WUI in 1931 – were prosecuted with a suspicious lack of vigour.[36] Aside from occasional pleas for aid, the Irish secretariat made only one formal protest to the Comintern. Larkin's uncharacteristic silence about the web being spun about him kept the communists guessing. He had told Moscow that he wished to retire from politic, a claim echoed by young Jim.[37] But Bell had no faith in Moscow's

33 RGASPI, To the secretariat, Ireland, 26 Feb. 1931, 495/89/65–23.

34 RGASPI, Abridgement of report of Neptun, 26 Jan. 1931, 495/89/64–2/3; report from secretariat, 31 Jan. 1931, 495/89/65–1/4; to the secretariat, Ireland, 26 Feb. 1931, 495/89/65–20.

35 RGASPI, Material for the report on the siuation and theses of the RWG, 11 Feb. 1931, 495/14/334–1; to the secretariat, Ireland, 26 Feb. 1931, 495/89/65–19/23.

36 RGASPI, Draft resolution on Ireland for meeting of Anglo-American secretariat, 20 Apr. 1930, 495/89/61–2/9; Instructions on Ireland, 16 Apr. 1931, 495/89/59–7/11; letter to Ireland, 23 Sept. 1932, 495/20/251–89/98.

37 RGASPI, Arthur [?] to Frank [?], 17 Nov. 1929, 495/89/54–53.

benign scenario and warned that Larkin had promised to 'settle their hash'.[38] On discovering in December 1929 that the Profintern had invited Larkin to its next plenum, he, Stewart and Buckley promptly complained to the ECCI that 'when we started this work we understood that the policy of the Comintern was to work independently of Larkin', and demanded a clarification of Moscow's position.[39]

On 26 October 1929 Bell sent the politsecretariat a dismissive report on existing radical groups. The WUI, he wrote, had become a reformist union, and Larkin's 'outrageous conduct' made it impossible to use the IWL as a basis for a party. The IRA left was 'terribly confused' on social questions and had lost 'practically all proletarian elements'. Other leftist organisations in Dublin – the Connolly Club, the Labour Defence League, the Trade Union Unity League, and the League Against Imperialism – amounted to no more than 50 activists, had no influence on the masses, and were 'in the grip of the most paralysing sectarianism'. He proposed instead to forge the nucleus of a party from ex-IRA men and 'good elements' in the INUM, the unemployed being otherwise regarded as serviceable for street protests but too undisciplined and curmudgeonly for party work. To widen his trade union contacts, Bell had revived the International Trade Union Relations Committee, to which 12 unions in Dublin had affiliated.[40] Communists were heartened by the decision of Dublin trades' council to proceed with contributing to a trade union delegation to the Soviet Union for the October revolution celebrations, despite last minute complaints, led by the ITGWU. In reality the sudden nervousness was another indication that labour's hitherto relaxed attitude towards association with the first workers' state was fading; and the delegates disappointed their hosts in Moscow, who reckoned that only one of the eight would be of use to the party. Indeed only Tommy Geehan did join the party, but others, notably Helena Molony, would be of ancillary service.[41] On 5 December Bell advised the politsecretariat that a centre and a newspaper could be expected within two months. He urged the return of five named students from the Lenin School. However Kirsanova opposed the release of her students before

38 RGASPI, Tom Bell to Bell, ??? 27 Oct. 1929, 495/89/64–63.

39 RGASPI, Bell, Buckley and Stewart to the ECCI, 5 Dec. 1929, 495/89/54–76.

40 RGASPI, Preliminary report on the present situation and on our Irish policy, 26 Oct. 1929, 495/89/54–19/25; Arthur [?] to Frank [?], 17 Nov. 1929, 495/89/54–53/63a.

41 Cody, O'Dowd, and Rigney, *The Parliament of Labour*, p. 160; RGASPI, Arthur [?] to Frank [?], 17 Nov. 1929, 495/89/54–53/63a. The remaining delegates were Robert Tynan, P. T. Daly (Dublin trades' council); Miss N. K. Price (Dublin); William McMullan, H. S. Ward (Belfast); Terry Waldron (Bray trades' council); Ned Tucker (National Society of Brushmakers); and Paddy Holohan (Irish National Union of Woodworkers). *Irish Workers' Voice*, 7 Jan. 1933.

completion of their courses and the first Irish cohort did not return home until the summer of 1930.[42]

In January 1930 the Workers' Research Bureau was opened at Bachelor's Walk, Dublin as a base of operations. Roddy Ward, who had worked in the British Labour Research Department, became its director and secretary.[43] Irish Friends of Soviet Russia was revived in February with a committee comprised mainly of republicans. 'About 250' attended its inaugural congress in Banba Hall in April, and 'about a hundred signed up as members'.[44] After difficulties in obtaining passports, an eight person delegation, including Mrs Despard, Hanna Sheehy Skeffington, assistant editor of *An Phoblacht*, David Fitzgerald, Seán Dowling, who had led the Revolutionary SPI in 1919, Sighle Dowling, president of the Women Workers' Union, Jack O'Neill, George Gilmore and Harry Kernoff, visited Russia in August. Over the next year the Friends organised regular public meetings to present glowing accounts of the Soviet system – sometimes literally in magic lantern shows – and protested against hostile coverage of Russia in the *Irish Independent*.[45] *An Phoblacht* gave them more comprehensive publicity than the *Workers' Voice*. Seven delegates, representing a range of occupations, were invited to the 1931 May Day celebrations in Moscow by the Central Trade Union Council of the Soviet Union, but the government refused to issue passports for the purpose, and only Rosamond Jacob and Mrs M. K. Connery, who were already in possession of passports, succeeding in attending.[46]

In areas more proximate to party building, varying levels of support were enlisted in four distinct theatres: Northern Ireland, the unemployed, small farmers and the IRA. Since 1920 an unaffiliated communist circle had existed in Belfast, some in sporadic contact with the CPGB, others with the WPI and ICWPA. With objections from anglo-centric comrades who formed their own 'Vanguard' group, the Belfast communists agreed to join the proposed Irish Revolutionary Workers' Party, and to these were added recruits in the NILP. By March the Irish secretariat reckoned it had 30 members in Belfast and five in Coleraine.[47] Within weeks it had lost substantial support after it

42 RGASPI, Bell to politsecretariat, ECCI, 5 Dec. 1929, 495/89/54–75; Arthur [?] to Frank [?], 17 Nov. 1929, 495/89/54–53/63a; McLoughlin, 'Proletarian academics or party functionaries?', p. 67.

43 NA, DT, Crime Special Branch report to the secretary, Department of Justice, 5 May 1930, S5074B.

44 *An Phoblacht*, 12 Apr. 1930; *Workers' Voice*, 12 Apr. 1930.

45 *Workers' Voice*, 23 Aug., 13, 27 Sept. 1930; *Irish Democrat*, Feb. 1949; *An Phoblacht*, 7 Mar., 16 May 1931; Margaret Ward, *Hanna Sheehy Skeffington: A Life* (Cork, 1997), pp. 294–6; *Irish Workers' Voice*, 7 Jan. 1933.

46 *An Phoblacht*, 27 June, 18 July 1931.

47 RGASPI, Report of the CI commission in Ireland to the Anglo-American secretariat, ECCI, and WEB, 17 Mar. 1930, 495/89/62–1/4.

confronted the NILP with a programme of demands at the party's annual conference: when the communists' proposals were defeated, most of their NILP associates opted to stay in the party rather than follow the injunction to leave. No collaboration between communists and republicans developed in Belfast, and the former focused chiefly on the unemployed and the shipyards. They had some success in selling the *Workers' Voice* or the CPGB's *Daily Worker*, mobilising the unemployed, and organising outdoor meetings – a May Day rally attracted 3,000 people. Three communist candidates won 1,183 votes in the Poor Law Guardian elections in Belfast in June.[48]

With Ward's financial assistance considerable headway was made among the unemployed. The Dublin INUM had enrolled over 300 members;[49] and on 6 March, designated by the Comintern as an international day of protest against unemployment, INUM rallies attracted an estimated 4,000 in Dublin, 5,000 in Belfast, and 400 in Coleraine, where an unemployed association was set up. Bell reckoned the turnout would have been much higher but for arrests of leaders in Dublin and inadequate preparations in Belfast. His one unqualified disappointment was the absence of any response in Cork, where one of Ferguson's meetings in February had been disrupted by protesters shouting about religious persecution in Russia.[50] There had also been a backlash in Derry. The local unemployed movement had affiliated to the INUM, but disowned 'socialism or Bolshevism' following a visit from Ferguson in January.[51]

The most important work was done with Peadar O'Donnell. O'Donnell's campaign against the payment of land annuities, begun in 1926, had been revived in 1928 with the launch of the Anti-Tribute League. From January 1930 Stewart and O'Donnell worked to transform the League into a section of the European Peasants' Congress, itself an attempt to revitalise the Krestintern, or Peasants' International. O'Donnell travelled to Berlin to see the organising committee of the forthcoming European Peasants' congress, and met local committees of the Anti-Tribute League, who agreed to form an Irish Working Farmers' Committee. The committee's office at 6 Upper O'Connell Street, Dublin was the venue for a series of discussions in March at which O'Donnell and Stewart persuaded IRA volunteers to join a Preparatory Committee for the Formation of a Workers' Revolutionary Party. O'Donnell and other

48 RGASPI, Short history of the RWG in Northern Ireland, 21 May 1932, 495/89/80–15/23; *Workers' Voice*, 7–14 June 1930.
49 NA, DT, report on revolutionary organisations, 4 Apr. 1930, S5864A.
50 RGASPI, Report of the CI commission in Ireland to the Anglo-American secretariat, ECCI, and WEB, 17 Mar. 1930, 495/89/62–1/4.
51 Máirtín Ó Catháin, '"Struggle or starve": Derry unemployed workers' movements, 1926–35', *Saothar* 28 (2004), pp. 49–60.

republicans joined Bell, Stewart and Ferguson on the executive of the preparatory committeee. In a report to Moscow, Bell implied that IRA approval
went well beyond a few sympathisers, and claimed to have had 'an official
conference with representatives of the Army Council'. The new Dublin
communist group had 75 members, of whom 30 were active in the IRA. Bell
was not impressed with their calibre.

> The ideology of these workers is very hard to explain. Only a few of them have any
> conception of Communist theory and practice. The great majority of them are
> former soldiers of the Irish Republican Army, and many of them are still members
> of that organisation . . . Characteristically there are strong putschist tendencies
> among them . . . Our greatest weakness is that we have very little material from
> which to build up strong local leaderships because of the absolute lack of any
> previous experience in political work.[52]

The recruits had no objections to a programme of appropriation of the means
of production, land to working farmers, and an all-Ireland workers' republic;
but Bell and Stewart noted resistance to naming the proposed party 'communist', for fear that it would alienate Catholics and mainstream labour.[53]

On 23 March 43 delegates from committees in the midlands and west
assembled in Galway for the inaugural congress of the Irish Working Farmers'
Committee and endorse the programme of the European Peasants' Congress.
The committee's manifesto demanded a workers' and small farmers' republic,
abolition of land rents and annuities, the freeing of land and fisheries for the
use of working farmers and fishermen, opposition to recruitment into the
British military, resistance to forced sales of cattle and land, and struggle
against the suppression of local councils and the appointment of managers.
The Galway conference also sent fraternal greetings to the Preparatory
Committee for the Formation of a Workers' Revolutionary Party, which was
depicted as its urban counterpart. O'Donnell then led a delegation to the
Peasants' Congress, which opened, under his presidency, in Berlin on 27 March.
He was also elected to the permanent committee of the congress.[54]

The appearance of the weekly *Workers' Voice* on 5 April, with Bell as editor,

---

52 RGASPI, Report of the CI commission in Ireland to the Anglo-American secretariat, ECCI,
and WEB, 17 Mar. 1930, 495/89/62–1/4.

53 Ó Drisceoil, *Peadar O'Donnell*, pp. 59–60; RGASPI, Report of the CI commission in Ireland to
the Anglo-American secretariat, ECCI, and WEB, 17 Mar. 1930, 495/89/62–1/4; NA, DT, report on
Workers' Revolutionary Party, 5 Apr. 1930, S5074B; DJ, Workers' Revolutionary Party, 1930–33, JUS
8/691.

54 Ó Drisceoil, *Peadar O'Donnell*, pp. 58–60; *Workers' Voice*, 5 Apr. 1930.

provided what was regarded as an indispensable medium to agitation in a fifth theatre, trade unionism. Here the line was straightforward class against class. Bell applied it robustly in merciless attacks on labour leaders and, contrary to instructions, threw the odd swipe at the WUI.[55] He did not have long to wait before recording the first backlash. Dublin trades' council debarred the INUM from using the Trades Hall following the movement's disruption of a Labour Party rally in the Mansion House.[56] The *Voice* devoted particular attention to transport, and the communists' main industrial initiative was to back 600 busmen who struck the Irish Omnibus Company in May against a wage cut and for union recognition. The communists gained some influence with an unofficial strike committee in Dublin, and throughout the country IRA volunteers and activists of the Working Farmers' Committee organised attacks on scab buses. The struggle ended, largely in defeat, in July and it brought the communists no recruits.[57]

EXTENDING CLASS AGAINST CLASS

In the summer of 1930 the ECCI resolved to advance the process of Bolshevisation by extending class against class to republicans. It was a rash move against a constituency on which the Irish secretariat was heavily dependent. In addition to supplying the core of the Dublin communist group, republicans dominated all of the communist fronts, and had proved useful in INUM demonstrations, the bus strike, and providing sympathetic coverage in *An Phoblacht*, which claimed to sell 8,000 copies per week.[58] Moreover, republicans assumed that the united front approach would continue. O'Donnell welcomed the assaults on the 'Imperial Labour Party', not grasping their ideological provenance.[59] More generally, republicans gave no indication of readiness to embrace communism tout court. Indeed the *Workers' Voice* had criticised the platform at the inaugural congress of Friends of Soviet Russia for distinguishing between the Friends and communism.[60] Moscow knew too of other difficulties. In Cork, 'the bottom [had] fallen out of the barrow more than once'.[61] Internal rifts had paralysed the Labour Defence League. Garda

55 *Workers' Voice*, 5 Apr., 24 May, 1930.
56 *Workers' Voice*, 12–26 Apr. 1930.
57 Milotte, *Communism in Modern Ireland*, pp. 102–3.
58 Hanley, *The IRA*, p. 53.
59 Ó Drisceoil, *Peadar O'Donnell*, p. 61.
60 *Workers' Voice*, 12 Apr. 1930.
61 RGASPI, report of Bob Stewart, 12 Mar. 1930, 495/89/63–2/3.

raids and arrests were increasing and having a disruptive effect on agitation, and clerical opposition was mounting.[62] However Moscow saw Bolshevisation as a prerequisite of party formation and an answer to the problems facing the Irish secretariat.

Following reports from Bell and Stewart in March, a 2,700-word resolution, dated 17 April, covering the economic, agrarian, and political situation in Ireland, was drafted for a meeting of the Anglo-American secretariat on 20 April. It argued that the moment was right for the launch of a party. Acknowledging the challenges posed by the confusion of ideas and fear of clerical and reformist labour hostility, the paper advised that these could best be tackled through doctrinal clarity, the application of class against class to the IRA and Larkin, and forthright opposition to religious and other prejudices against communism.[63] The draft was annotated by the Anglo-American secretariat, and subjected to further revision by the ECCI. In June and July the ECCI dictated several drafts of a 2,000-word letter to comrades in Ireland. The letter sanctioned the harder line towards republicans. It declared the formation of a party 'a pressing necessity', but, evidently sceptical of the ideological preparedness of Irish workers, required the prior completion of five specific preparations: the establishment of nuclei in factories and mass organisations; increased circulation of the *Workers' Voice*; a propaganda campaign; a discussion on a party in the *Voice*; and the creation of cadre education circles. The proposed programme of the Dublin communist group was criticised for its neglect of the peasant question, and the slogan 'a workers' republic' was to be replaced with 'a workers' and peasants' republic'. The ECCI's most important revision was to demand continued diplomacy towards Larkin. The WUI remained, in ECCI parlance, 'the open revolt of the militant proletariat in Dublin against the treachery of the Labour Party and trade union leaders'. Whether Moscow really believed this, despite intelligence from Dublin to the contrary, is doubtful. The ECCI was anxious to get a WUI delegation to the forthcoming fifth Profintern congress, for prestige purposes, and to plant the seeds of a communist fraction within the union. Larkin Jr carried the instructions home personally when he and Seán Murray returned from the Lenin School in July 1930.[64] Their arrival had a wider significance. Though both had been characterised as 'Larkinites' in the school in 1929, they were deemed to have purged themselves of Big Jim's influence, were highly

62 *Workers' Voice*, 12 Apr. 1930; NA, DT, Crime Special Branch report to the secretary, Department of the President, 28 Oct. 1930, S5074B.
63 RGASPI, Draft resolution on Ireland for meeting of Anglo-American secretariat, 20 Apr. 1930, 495/89/61–2/9.
64 UCDA, MacEntee papers, Notes on communism in Saorstát Éireann, pp. 34–8, P67/523(5).

appraised by their tutors, and seen as the basis of an Irish party leadership. From July 1930 Murray would be employed as a full-time organiser.[65] Evidently forewarned of the policy change, the *Workers' Voice* of 21 June 1930 announced that the Preparatory Committee for the Formation of a Workers' Revolutionary Party would now be known as the Revolutionary Workers' Party. The same issue initiated a debate on strategy with a series of articles on the merits of a broad anti-imperialist alliance versus class against class. There was an Orwellian touch to the kite-flying. The opening sally, by 'Celt', commending what was more or less existing policy, was savaged by the *Voice* on 28 June:

> It is inconsistent as much as it is absurd to expose the corruption and treacherous character of the leadership of Cumann na nGaedheal, Fianna Fáil, or the 'Labour' Party [while] at the same time failing to adequately expose the cant, nonsense and 'up in the clouds' politics of the 'left-wing' republican leadership.

Evidently not privy to the innermost secrets, O'Donnell thought that the article must have been unapproved, and attacked its 'unfathomable stupidity' in *An Phoblacht*.[66] Bell offered a half-hearted apology, saying that the article was merely a contribution to a debate. But the outcome of the debate was already fixed. The final contribution, by Seán Murray, stated:

> The Irish bourgeoisie are no longer 'oppressed' by British imperialism, but are ruling Ireland, North and South, in alliance with British capitalism . . . the old slogans (correct in their time) of 'Ireland against England', 'Independence', 'Republic', must now be replaced by the slogan of 'class against class', 'Workers' and Peasants' Republic', etc.[67]

O'Donnell resigned from the party. His offer to withdraw the resignation if he were appointed national organiser for six months was opposed by Ward and Ferguson.[68] The ECCI was alarmed at the loss of O'Donnell. On 20 August it informed Bell of reports from Larkin Jr, Murray and Bill Joss, another Glaswegian with a watching brief on Ireland, of accumulating difficulties with the IRA. He was asked to comment immediately.[69]

65 RGASPI, Autobiography, Seán Murray, 11 Aug. 1932, 495/218/1–61/62; PROL, Robert Stewart, KV2/1180.

66 Ó Drisceoil, *Peadar O'Donnell*, p. 62.

67 *Workers' Voice*, 12–19 July 1930.

68 RGASPI, Material about Ireland (from the Irish brigade in the Lenin School), 21 May 1932, 495/89/80–1/18.

69 RGASPI, To the delegation in Ireland, 20 Aug. 1930, 495/89/61–23.

Larkin Sr too disappointed the Comintern. Jack Carney still made the odd
gesture of solidarity with the communists, but Big Jim's faith in revolution
was fading. The communists had dutifully avoided him until Murray and
young Jim arranged an audience in July. In an 'extremely difficult' interview,
they found him 'very embittered', especially over the ROP affair, and hurt that
Stewart, with whom he had been friendly, had not been in touch. Tentatively,
Murray and young Jim concluded that an accord was possible if he were
handled with sensitivity. Meanwhile the WUI remained off limits for communists, a situation all the more frustrating as it was rapidly becoming
embedded in reformism, and had recently recruited 400 busmen and 700 rail
workers, who would have provided an ideal point of entry into the heart of
industrial militancy.[70] One Irish delegate, Nixie Boran, attended the Profintern
congress in August, slipping out of Ireland on a cement ship when denied a
passport. Representing communist miners in the Castlecomer coalfield,
Boran spent three months in Russia, visiting mines in the Donetz region and
collective farms in Samara. He would be a valuable recruit, but for the
moment he was less than Moscow had expected.[71]

An ECCI pronouncement followed in September. Typically, it began by
affirming that the line on Ireland was correct. The problem lay with the
application, which had neglected the national question, and failed to differen-
tiate between the WUI and unions 'where the bureaucracy is now completely
social-fascist'. Bell was rebuked for 'political mistakes and [a] generally
sectarian attitude'. Larkin Jr, Murray, and Bill Denn, another graduate of the
Lenin School, were to comprise the new leadership, assisted by Stewart.
There was also to be an investigation of ROP.[72] Bell's removal created trouble
in Belfast, where it was seen as symptomatic of the 'pandering to a clerically-
dominated, fascist-in-embryo Republican Party through its leader Peadar
O'Donnell and the Peasants' Movement'. By the end of the year all but four
comrades had split to form their own group. The dissidents appealed to the
Comintern, which told them to follow the Dublin secretariat.[73] The ECCI
had made policy towards Larkin and republicans no clearer. The ROP dispute
was never resolved, and Big Jim's temper would hardly have been improved by

70 RGASPI, Joint report on WUI, S. Murray and J. Larkin Jr, 2 Aug. 1930, 495/89/63–19/27.
71 *Workers' Voice*, 29 Nov. 1930; Anne Brennan and William Nolan, 'Nixie Boran and the colliery
community of north Kilkenny', in William Nolan and Kevin Whelan (eds), *Kilkenny: History and
Society* (Dublin, 1990), pp. 574–5; information from Anne Boran.
72 RGASPI, Draft resolution on Ireland, 1 Sept. 1930, 495/89/61–19/22.
73 RGASPI, M. McLarnon, Belfast communist group to the secretariat, IRWP, 12 Jan. 1930 [recte
1931], 495/89/63–1; statement to the ECCI [1931], 495/89/66–17/24; Belfast group to Anglo-American
secretariat, 3 Dec. 1931 [recte 1930], 495/89/65–9/11; to the Anglo-American secretariat, 1 Apr. 1931,
495/89/65–37/39; Ireland [undated], 495/89/67–56/59.

the sight of his nemesis in the ITGWU, William O'Brien, being dined by ROP managers and Soviet diplomats at a banquet in the Gresham Hotel on 25 September. O'Brien assured his hosts that labour had no objection to foreign capital.[74] The *Workers' Voice* tactfully ignored the occasion.

The elections for the new Dublin municipal council exposed confusion in the Revolutionary Workers' Party, and tension between Bell and his editorial board. On 27 September the *Workers' Voice* urged readers to vote for the IWL candidates, who 'are standing on a platform of struggle against the renegade reformist Labourites'. The communists fielded two candidates and were given some grounds for optimism. Out of a total poll of almost 70,000, Esther McGregor, a tenants' leader, received a disappointing 129 votes, but young Jim Larkin won 967 votes and was elected. His name was an obvious bonus. The IWL, which still represented itself as communist, marginally outpolled the Labour Party, winning 5,940 first preferences, though of its 12 candidates only Big Jim was returned.[75] In October Larkin revived the *Irish Worker* and prepared to make the IWL more active. On 4 October the *Workers' Voice* declared that the IWL 'had no programme other than that of its leader, Jim Larkin, senr, who posed as "The Friend of the Poor"'. The next issue contained an apology from the editorial board, explaining that the remark was not in conformity with the party's united front policy towards the IWL. But Bell could not restrain his antipathy to Larkin. At an IWL 'open forum' on unemployment in the Mansion House on 23 November, Big Jim denounced the campaign to strangle the *Workers' Voice*, which was being hounded from printer to printer by Catholic pressure groups. Shortly afterwards, Larkin's Camac Press began producing the paper, an arrangement which lasted until February 1931. Incredibly, the *Voice* lambasted a chunk of Larkin's Mansion House speech, calling for tariffs, as 'tripe'.[76]

The Revolutionary Workers' Party's position on republicans was more obscure than contradictory, and again suggested friction between Bell and his colleagues. Aside from the odd remark about the sterility of its politics, the *Workers' Voice* barely acknowledged the republican movement after the debacle in June and July. On 24 September over 1,200 attended a League Against Imperialism meeting on India, addressed inter alia by Krishne Deonarini and young Jim Larkin. Though Frank Ryan ended the proceedings with three cheers for India and the Revolutionary Workers' Party and a rendition of the Red Flag, the *Voice* denigrated the non-communist speeches and stressed that the communists alone had spoken 'the real truth'. A short account of a League

74 *The Irish Times*, 26 Sept. 1930.
75 *The Irish Times*, 29 Sept. to 2 Oct. 1930; *Workers' Voice*, 27 Sept. to 11 Oct. 1930.
76 *Irish Worker*, 29 Nov. 1930; *Workers' Voice*, 29 Nov. 1930.

anti-poppy day protest, with a platform described by Seán MacBride as a republican 'who's who', concluded: 'A number of other speakers addressed the meeting, including E. de Valera, P. O'Donnell, M. Fitzpatrick and Jack O'Neill'.[77] Bell was clearly at variance with senior colleagues. On 18 October *An Phoblacht*, then edited by Ryan, had initiated a debate on strategy, saying: 'We here affirm that we stand for the freedom of all Ireland, the overthrow of the Capitalist-Imperialist system, the handing back to the dispossessed people of all the resources of Ireland'. In November the paper published a proposed Saor Éire constitution, drafted by IRA Chief of Staff Moss Twomey under the pseudonym Manus Ó Ruairc. Writing in the *Workers' Voice* Seán Murray welcomed the debate and urged that it be supported.[78] Publicly at least, the communists said little further on the development.

BOLSHEVISATION

The Bolshevisation of Irish communism was finally completed between November 1930 and January 1931, and it is possible that Neptun, an official in the WEB, oversaw the transition in person.[79] The initiative began with the adoption of what was deemed an essential characteristic of Bolshevised organisation, the substitution of territorial branches with factory cells in order to 'proletarianise' the membership.[80] In November the Dublin section was divided into four groups, covering the Inchicore and railwaymen, Broadstone, the docks and factories, and Guinness's and Jacob's.[81] A new name, RWG, was adopted. Coevally, internal tensions led to the resignation of Ward, and the RWG took the opportunity to remove 'lumpenproletarian elements' who, it argued, had joined the INUM in the expectation of largesse from Ward and junkets to Russia. A conference of the Dublin membership in January confirmed a purge of the INUM. Corruption in the INUM and the conduct of Ferguson and Bell were blamed for the sluggish performance since 1929. Ferguson came under fire on all sides, for sharing Bell's hostility to republicans, for using Ward's money to to surround himself with lumpen elements who

77 Ó Drisceoil, *Peadar O'Donnell*, p. 63; *Workers' Voice*, 4 Oct., 15 Nov. 1930; NA, DJ, Anti-imperialists (1928–33), JUS 8/682.

78 *Workers' Voice*, 25 Oct. 1930.

79 RGASPI, Abridgement of report of Neptun, 26 Jan. 1931. It is not clear if Neptun (alias Robert) visited Ireland, though he wrote as if he were part of the Dublin leadership. Neptun had previous experience of instructing the Dutch party for the WEB. See Rees and Andrew Thorpe, *International Communism and the Communist International*, p. 139.

80 McDermott and Agnew, *The Comintern*, p. 65.

81 *Workers' Voice*, 8 Nov. 1930.

drove away 'good elements', and for a brief, unhappy experience in the Lenin School in October. Within days of his arrival with two Belfast comrades, Tommy Geehan and Tommy Watters, he concocted an unsavoury excuse to secure a speedy repatriation. The truth of his misery, panic attacks induced by a sense of imprisonment, was hardly more palatable to his comrades, who suspected shock brought on by Soviet conditions. Though offered a job with the CPGB, he was labelled a 'declassed astute opportunist' and expelled from the RWG. Bell was recommended for expulsion for his 'opportunist sectarianism' and 'bad conduct' (his alcoholism had drawn repeated comment). 'Even [!] the comrade from Coleraine raised the question of his being drunk at the very first Conference held to launch the *Workers' Voice.*'[82] Bell had already been recalled to Russia and, unfortunately for the Irish, would continue to admonish their national sympathies in his work for the Anglo-American secretariat and the Lenin School. He died in Moscow in 1940. In March the RWG told Moscow that 'the situation has improved, especially in regard to the social composition of the membership . . . We can definitely say that we have now got in Dublin the basis for a party'.[83] The RWG also employed the Bolshevik tactic of creating fractions, which were seen as useful for differentiating revolutionaries from reformists in non-communist organisations. In June the Dublin group had nine members in the IRA, seven in the proposed Saor Éire, and two in Fianna Fáil. Total membership in Dublin stood at 88.[84]

The January conference formally ended the ambiguity towards the IRA and WUI, endorsing class against class unreservedly. Capitalism and British imperialism continued to be seen as the interwoven enemy, and the objective remained the unification of 'the working class, peasantry, and discontented bourgeoisie' in a mass movement, but the 'the conference emphasised the necessity of tirelessly exposing the character of petty-bourgeois nationalism in the leadership of the Irish Republican Army and its tactics and policy, which would inevitably lead to the defeat of the revolutionary struggles of the Irish workers', and 'saw the necessity of carrying on the clearest revolutionary criticism of the "centrist" policy of the [WUI] leadership, which threatened to

---

82 RGASPI, Letter to students in the Lenin School, Feb. 1930, 495/98/65–6; Case of F, undated [1930], 495/8965–7/8; Bob Stewart to the politcommission, 18 Oct. 1930, 495/4/63–204; C. N. Ferguson to the RWG, 7 Nov. 1930, 495/89/63–36/37; Lambert [pseudonym of Donal O'Reilly], Material about Ireland (from the Irish brigade in the Lenin School), 21 May 1932, 495/89/80–1/18; RWG, notice to members re Dublin conference, 10–11 Jan. 1931, 495/89/67–12/13; conference of the RWG in Dublin, 10–11 Jan. 1931, 495/89/104–190/91; Ireland, report from secretariat, 31 Jan. 1931, 495/89/65–1/4.

83 RGASPI, Report from Ireland, Mar. 1931, 495/89/67–51/55.

84 RGASPI, Report of Dublin organisation, June 1931, 495/89/67–60/62.

transform this organisation of revolutionary workers into a "left" screen for the Labor [sic] Party and the reactionary trade union officialdom'.[85] The only united fronts with republicans or Larkinites would be united fronts from below, and there was to be a stronger focus on industrial conflict and on Belfast. In a further affirmation of third period ideology, which depicted social democratic parties as 'social fascist' and the greatest obstacle to revolution, the conference resolved that Fianna Fáil was 'the most dangerous enemy of the Irish toilers'.[86] In practice, criticism of the IRA and WUI in the *Workers' Voice* was sparing, compared with the vitriol poured regularly on Fianna Fáil, the Labour Party and trade union leaders. What is remarkable is not that Moscow's demands for a more assiduous critique received a perfunctory response, but that at a time when the IRA was moving left and borrowing ideas and techniques from communism, the RWG complied with a policy that isolated them from IRA dominated Comintern fronts, intensified their marginality, and conflicted with the visceral sympathies of most of their members.[87] Here was a classic example of the contradiction of Bolshevisation, and the dilemma of many contemporary communist parties: choosing between 'Bolshevik universalism and national specificity'.[88]

It is not difficult to understand why the Irish chose Bolshevism without protest. The shambolic record of previous communist groups discredited dissent from Moscow. The RWG had been created by the Comintern and was led, in January 1931, by three graduates of the Lenin School. Communism in Ireland owed everything to the Comintern. It provided the myth, the model of organisation, the cadres, and, to a degree, the finance which made the struggle possible. The size of the Irish movement was in itself a force for dependency. Internationally, it was usually the case that the smaller the party the greater the level of Moscow-centrism. Bolshevisation undoubtedly brought disadvantages: chiefly a self-defeating sectarianism during the third period, and programmatic discontinuity as the line changed repeatedly from 1932. But it also gave the far left an unprecedented discipline, which enabled the RWG to embark on the most heroic phase of Irish communism in a climate incomparably less favourable than that enjoyed by its predecessors in the 1920s.

85   RGASPI, Conference of the RWG in Dublin, 10–11 Jan. 1931, 495/89/104–190/91.
86   RGASPI, Resolutions on the political situation in Ireland, 7 Feb. 1931, 495/89/67–14/16a.
87   RGASPI, To the secretariat, Ireland, 26 Feb. 1931, 495/89/65–19/23.
88   McDermott and Agnew, *The Comintern*, p. 65.

EIGHT

BETWEEN THE HAMMER
AND THE ANVIL, 1931-3

*Well Seán I have been through the mill since last we met. On Sunday Jim Larkin and
Comrade Joss came here. I asked them to my place for tea. My people refused to prepare
tea saying they were antichrist and what not. It hurt me to the bone ...*
Letter to Seán Murray from a comrade in Kilkenny[1]

—

Now that Bolshevised cadre groups were in place, it was expected that the
RWG would march briskly towards the creation of a party, and the party
would lead the people to socialism. For the ECCI, the party was not simply a
ratchet in organisational growth, it was essential to the completion of the
Bolshevisation process, without which the correct leadership could not be
offered to the masses. The implications were understood in Ireland, and not
all comrades were happy about it. The RWG followed a pure third period line
in 1931, concentrating on industrial struggle, and confronting the 'social
fascists' of reformist labour. The national question was ignored, even as
republicans were incubating Saor Éire. The approach reaped some ephemeral
gains in Northern Ireland, but brought no rewards in the Free State. After the
Fianna Fáil election triumph in 1932 and the onset of the economic war, the
ECCI agreed that a greater emphasis be placed on anti-imperialism, provided
the class against class line was maintained in other respects. Membership of
the RWG rose significantly over the coming months, but when the party was
eventually founded, support was on the wane.

Conditions had seemed favourable. Many thought the great depression
that followed the Wall Street crash of 1929 had sounded the death knell of
capitalism. The 'social fascists' were in disarray, with the Labour Party in
decline, the NILP marginalised by Stormont's abolition of proportional
representation, and the British Labour Party, the NILP's role model, rocked
by Prime Minister Ramsay MacDonald's defection. The IRA was overhauling
its strategy under communist influence, and the accession of Fianna Fáil to
power shifted the political centre to the left. So why did the communists fail
to gain anything more than a tenuous toehold during these years of crisis? An

---

1   RGASPI, letter from Patrick O'Farrell, undated [1932], 495/89/83–94/99.

RWG review in 1932 identified four main obstacles: state repression, labour reformism, the 'virtual' collapse of Larkinism, and the Catholic Church.[2] Essentially, the communists were caught between the anvil of an impermeable trade union movement, and the hammers of church and state. The Papal campaign against religious persecution in Soviet Russia in 1930, and the revival of Catholic social action in *Quadragesimo Anno* in May 1931, were followed by a combined assault from the government and the bishops in the red scare of 1931. When the RWG recovered a year later, Catholics instigated a more intense campaign of reaction. The communists might have sheltered from the church in the trade unions, or consolidated outside the unions had it not been for the church. Moscow had anticipated the hammers, but not the anvil. Buffeted on all sides, it was as much as the communists could do to survive.

INDUSTRIAL UNREST

Efforts at direct engagement on the shop floor usually followed a pattern of intervention with marginalised sectors, opposition from trade union officials, and retreat for want of support, organisation or finance. A partial exception to the pattern was the formation of the Irish Mines, Quarries, and Allied Workers' Union at Castlecomer in December 1930. In a revision of policy, the fifth Profintern congress in August had approved the creation of parallel red unions, and on Nixie Boran's return from Russia he led 30 miners out of the ITGWU. Boran made it clear that his aim was to organise all miners, quarry-men, and roadworkers in a Profintern affiliate, committed to class against class. A second branch was formed at Ballyragget in February with 13 members. In the teeth of clerical opposition the red union made slow progress, but Boran had a strong personal following and was elected a checkweighman.[3]

The biggest struggle of the period for communists was the Dublin building strike. With fractions in the WUI, the ITGWU, and the Irish National Union of Woodworkers, the RWG had some hope of influencing events. Two leading members of the Woodworkers, Charlie Ashmore and Bill Denn, were graduates of the Lenin School, and the union had concluded a solidarity pact with the Forest and Woodworkers' Union of the Soviet Union.[4] In

2   NLI, Donal O'Reilly papers, resolution, uncatalogued, ACC.5891.
3   Brennan and Nolan, 'Nixie Boran and the colliery community of north Kilkenny', pp. 574–7. Checkweighmen were paid by the colliers to ensure that the tonnages allocated to them by the company were accurate.
4   RGASPI, Dublin building trade dispute, RS [Bob Stewart] and SM [Seán Murray] to Robin [Page Arnot?], 17 Mar. 1931, 495/89/69–2; an den Nationalen Holzarbeiterverband Irlands, 495/89/69–4/6.

December 1930 RWG militants created a rank and file group to encourage opposition to a proposed wage cut.[5] After 12 January, when 3,000 workers struck officially, the rank and file group pressed for an extension of the dispute. Three hundred workers attended a conference convened by the group on 18 February.[6] However, when the strike ended in April, with acceptance of a modified pay cut, the RWG had lost as much as they had gained. Union leaders had refused to accept any communist influence over strike policy. The National Union of Woodworkers had severed its connection with the Soviet Forest and Woodworkers' Union on receiving no help from Russia other than literature.[7] Relations with Big Jim Larkin had worsened. In one instance he walked off a platform at College Green rather than speak with communists, and the *Workers' Voice* denounced his leadership as 'bankrupt'.[8] While welcoming the symbolic extension of the class against class line, the querulous Comintern criticised the attack for being 'sudden and unprepared'. The RWG's rank and file group soldiered on, issuing an edition of the *Building Worker* in May.[9]

In line with the turn to class, the *Workers' Voice* published weekly letters – ostensibly from shop floor workers to add Bolshevist authenticism – on conditions in various employments, especially linen mills. One exposé evoked a response in the Dublin mill of the Greenmount and Boyne Linen Company, at Harold's Cross. On 16 February the company posted notice of a ten per cent wage cut. The 230 employees promptly struck for a 20 per cent wage increase.[10] Without a trade union they faced a daunting challenge. The communist presence on the strike committee led to their isolation by the labour movement and attempts to link the dispute with a similar strike in Lurgan were countered by union officials.[11] On 18 March employers tried to reopen the mill with the backing of 16 employees and police escorts. The Labour Defence League helped to mobilise mass pickets on a daily basis.[12] The RWG persuaded the workforce to join the WUI, for want of something better, and in late April Larkin Sr addressed several mass meetings. Larkin's brief rapprochement

5   *Workers' Voice*, 6, 20 Dec. 1930, 10 Jan. 1931.

6   *Workers' Voice*, 21 Feb. 1931.

7   RGASPI, Troy before the Anglo-American secretariat, 10 June 1932, 495/72/188–186.

8   RGASPI, Report from Ireland, 22 Mar. 1931, 495/89/67–54; CPI, *Communist Party of Ireland*, p. 30; *Workers' Voice*, 31 Jan. 1931.

9   RGASPI, Instructions on Ireland, 16 Apr. 1931, 495/89/59–7/11; *The Building Worker*, May 1931, 495/89/69–7.

10   *Workers' Voice*, 21 Feb. 1931.

11   RGASPI, Material about Ireland (From the Irish brigade in the Lenin School), 21 May 1932, 495/89/80–15/18.

12   *Workers' Voice*, 28 Mar. 1931.

with the RWG extended to that year's May Day celebrations, when the WUI band led the communist parade in Dublin, and 400 people turned up to hear young Jim and Bill Rust, CPGB.[13] The defeat of the Greenmount strike in mid May was not unmitigated. The workers were promised their jobs back, and 200 remained members of the WUI.[14]

The Belfast group had first attempted shop floor organisation in July 1930 when it liaised with employees in the Jennymount linen mill who were facing a wage cut. It proved impossible to establish a communist committee in the mill. The group issued a bulletin on behalf of workers, but trade union intervention secured a withdrawal of both the pay cut and the communist influence. After the split in late 1930, Bob Stewart moved to Belfast to rebuild the group. Stewart recalled that he worked 'closely' with republicans, and thought their politics 'quite progressive', though he admitted to a partiality to anyone wearing a pioneer pin. His return to his native Dundee to fight the general election in October would be big loss.[15] In July 1931 Tom Mann spent five days in the city spearheading a recruitment drive; 200 were enrolled, half of whom were lost within six weeks. With the collapse of the British Labour government on 23 August – over proposals to cut unemployment benefit – and Ramsay MacDonald's decision to form a coalition government with the Liberals and Conservatives, another opportunity unfolded. Campaigns on unemployment made progress in Belfast and led to the creation of groups in Ballymena and Ballymoney. From August, the RWG claimed, trade union and factory work 'vastly improved'. Rank and file committees were formed in the shipyards, in three of the city's biggest linen mills, and on the railway. A seamen's branch of the Minority Movement recruited 40 members. September marked a peak of activity. Arrests of communists increased, and the Ulster Protestant League led violent opposition to communist street meetings. The League had recently been formed to 'safeguard the employment of Protestants', a recurring theme with Unionist MPs during the depression, and published the monthly *Ulster Protestant*.[16] In May 1932 membership of the Belfast RWG stood at a modest 50 and was declining. About 500 copies weekly of the *Workers' Voice* were being sold in the city, and 15 quire of the *Daily Worker*, the latter mainly at the shipyards. Dublin noted that some preferred the CPGB paper, especially after the *Voice* reappeared with an anti-imperialist emphasis in April, and suspected a lack of conviction in the new line in Belfast.[17]

13 NA, DJ, Workers' Revolutionary Party, JUS 8/691.

14 RGASPI, [RWG] secretariat, 22 Mar. 1931, 495/89/65–40/42; *Workers' Voice*, 2 May to 27 June 1931.

15 Stewart, *Breaking the Fetters*, pp. 180–2.

16 Andrew Boyd, *Holy War in Belfast* (Belfast, 1987), pp. 205–18.

17 RGASPI, Short history of RWG in Northern Ireland, undated [May 1932], 495/89/80–15/18; S. Murray, Ireland, group organisation, 8 June 1932, 495/89/78–30/41; Murray before the Anglo-American secretariat, 10 June 1932, 495/72/188–161; Milotte, *Communism in Modern Ireland*, pp. 126–8.

If the industrial agitation did not trigger a mass rank and file movement, the RWG believed that Bolshevisation had been a turning point and remained committed to class against class throughout the year. On 7 June 1931 Bill Rust spoke on the eleventh ECCI plenum, which had called for a more intense application of third period theses.[18] Rust's aim in Dublin was also to press for the formation of a party. The *Workers' Voice* had been running a debate on the topic, and on 27 June it reported that 'plans were now taking practical shape', adding 'The central question . . . is the building up of a Workers' Press. Without the WORKERS' VOICE the organisation of the Communist Party is impossible.' It was the last issue of the *Voice* that summer. It reappeared on 5 September, after its war chest of £58 was augmented with a further £35, half of which came from the USA. For some months in late 1931 the Comintern boosted its subvention to £12 per week, before reducing it to £8 in 1932.[19] The new series was certainly better produced and claimed its circulation was 500 copies higher than in June.[20]

The autumn saw Seán Murray emerge as the guiding figure of the RWG. Since Tom Bell's demotion in September 1930, the RWG had been directed by a secretariat consisting of Murray, Larkin Jr, and Bill Denn, with Bob Stewart as adviser. By mid 1931 Denn was becoming distracted by trade union work, and Stewart had moved to Belfast. Murray, Larkin Jr, Jim Hale and Joe Troy comprised the secretariat in 1932. Larkin was retained because of his name. There were growing complaints of him failing to make best use of his corporation seat and allowing himself to be constrained by his father: 'unless he is rooted out of the Larkin family concern his effectiveness for the party is going to be very poor', noted one RWG report.[21] Hale, with Loftus Johnston, Christy Clarke and Donal O'Reilly had left for the Lenin School in December 1931 and served as a liaison in Moscow. Troy remained a central figure in Dublin, but Murray, with the advantage of being a full-time party worker and some standing as a theorist, would dominate the RWG and CPI until the aftermath of the Republican Congress conference in Rathmines in 1934, and survive in more circumscribed circumstances as general secretary until 1941. Born in 1898 in Cushendall, Murray had left school aged 11 to work on the family farm. He joined Sinn Féin in 1917 and the 2nd Brigade, 3rd Northern Division, IRA in 1919, attaining the rank of battalion O/C. After ten months' internment, he attended the IRA convention in March 1922, where he met

18   *Workers' Voice*, 13 June 1931.

19   RGASPI, 'Workers' Voice defence fund', Aug. 1931, 495/89/64–62; General election, Feb. 1932, 495/4/205–15/16.

20   *Workers' Voice*, 19 Sept. 1931.

21   RGASPI, Report re national meeting of RWG, 5–6 Nov. 1932, 495/89/82–14/18.

Peadar O'Donnell who would become his closest friend and confidant. He first associated with communism in Glasgow. Moving to London, he was secretary of the London IWL and joined the CPGB, who recommended him to the Lenin School. Murray attributed his initial interest in socialism to reading James Connolly and remained at heart a socialist republican, 'a great Fenian', in O'Donnell's estimation.[22] However, unlike his predecessors, Roddy Connolly and Big Jim Larkin, he would prove to be a diligent servant of Moscow. His courage and abilities would be tested severely in what were to be the best of times and the worst of times for Irish communism during the Comintern era.

ROSE TINTS AND RED SCARE

The Catholic Church's relatively restrained attitude to communism altered profoundly in 1930. Some change was to be expected. More pressing problems distracted the hierarchy between 1917 and 1923, and under Big Jim Larkin's aegis communism had seemed nebulous. It certainly was more covert, and less obviously connected with Russia. The church may also have been wary of confronting Larkin, mindful of the moral defeat it had suffered during the 1913 lockout, or fearful of alienating his bedrock of support in the tenements of Dublin. When a mild challenge to communism was mounted in 1928, it took the form of mooting the alternative of Christian trade unionism. Even though the IWL continued to call itself communist after 1929, and the revived *Irish Worker* included articles in praise of Russia, Larkin escaped heavy clerical censure. The British agitators who surfaced in Dublin in 1929–30 with an inexplicable supply of funds and forthright pro-Soviet propaganda were an easier target. The *Irish Catholic* immediately denounced the *Workers' Voice* as a 'pestilential sheet' and declared: 'No measure could be too drastic or too summary for the immediate stamping out of the plague that threatens to affect Irish life'. In July the Catholic Truth Society compelled the Longford Printing and Publishing Company to cease handling the *Voice*. After a stopgap sojourn with the Progressive Printing Works, owned by what the Gardaí described as an apolitical English couple, a 12-month contract was signed with the City and County Press, Dún Laoghaire. It was not long before the *Voice* lost its third printer under pressure from the *Catholic Mind*.[23] The Irish Catholic offensive echoed Papal policy, and Pius XI's increasing preoccupation with Russia.

22 Emmet O'Connor, 'Seán Murray', in Keith Gildart, David Howell, and Neville Kirk (eds), *Dictionary of Labour Biography, Vol. XI* (London, 2003), pp. 200–5.
23 Milotte, *Communism in Modern Ireland*, pp. 103–4; NA, DJ, file on *Irish Workers' Voice*, JUS 8/692.

With the exception of a campaign against Catholics between 1921 and 1923, non-Orthodox religious communities in Russia had enjoyed toleration until shortly before the 1930s, when a policy of Russification of the Soviet peoples also entailed the end of tolerance. Pope Pius formally condemned the repression in 1930. Months earlier, Joseph Cardinal MacRory, who had received the red hat in 1929, had issued a similar statement. But there was also a domestic concern which gave Irish Catholic anti-communism a totalitarian character of its own. From 1925 the bishops had again begun to prioritise problems of social morals in response to the new temptations surrounding the dance hall and the cinema. The centenary celebrations of Catholic emancipation graphically demonstrated the potential of clerical power in independent Ireland, and, in episcopal eyes, an embarrassing contrast between popular piety and the social immorality. The revival of communism thus collided with an expansion of the imperium of the church, and was seen as an affront to clerical authority.

Underestimating its grip on the masses, the ECCI's Irish experts made little allowance for the anticipated hostility from the Catholic Church. A resolution drafted by the Anglo-American secretariat concluded: 'the confused ideologies prevailing among the radical republican and labour groups, make it essential to combat all inclinations to capitulate to religious and other prejudices'.[24] The *Workers' Voice* qualified this line somewhat by combining criticism of clerical attitudes in Ireland with frequent articles on religious freedom in Russia. For some fellow travellers, the paper was still too blunt. Helena Molony expressed her reservations to Moscow, saying that the Friends of Soviet Russia were more effective in addressing clerical hostility as they were led by 'people familiar and sympathetic with the National and religious psychology of the Irish people'. The approach of the *Workers' Voice*, she thought, 'leaves much to be desired'.[25] Under the editorial direction of Seán Murray, the *Voice* tried to be less dogmatic on religion, and Murray evidently raised the question in Moscow in 1932. He was informed that the RWG must not flinch:

> Every case of the clergy openly aiding the capitalists and imperialists against the workers and small farmers must be utilised to expose the class basis and role of religion and the church . . . As regards accepting members into the RWG who are imbued with religious prejudices no barriers should be raised, but it should be made clear that loyalty to the Communist Party, and Party discipline, comes first . . . and that they cannot as Communists use the Party platform to propagate religious

24　RGASPI, Draft resolution on Ireland for meeting of Anglo-American secretariat, 20 Apr. 1930, 495/89/61–2/9.

25　RGASPI, letter from Helena Molony, Aug. 1930, 534/7/286–98/99.

beliefs. The Party must carry on a systematic educational campaign to overcome religious prejudices.[26]

Regardless, Murray softened the line further in 1933. 'There is no mention of religion in the [manifesto] and this is not done for tactical reasons, but as a question of principle', he told the foundation congress of the second CPI. 'Religion is not a fundamental question and it is on the economic issues that we must lead the fight.'[27]

Aside from articles on Soviet toleration of religion, the *Workers' Voice* regularly included features on Russian culture, housing, and the progress of its massive industrialisation project, the first five-year plan, complete with photos of Lenin, Stalin and happy workers like the 'Jolly Russian farm girl driving her tractor'. Conveying the awesome magnitude of the Soviet endeavour, one heading ran: 'Shannon scheme surpassed, High power plant in USSR'.[28] That the five-year plan entailed a major reduction in living standards, and forced collectivisation of agriculture leading to peasant revolts and famine was of course ignored. So what did Irish communists really know of Russia? Jack Carney, Larkin, and students of the Lenin School were in a better position to be informed than others, and it would seem that a combination of Soviet secrecy, mistrust of anti-Soviet propaganda, and defensiveness about 'the first workers' state' obscured the grim realities of famine, poverty and terror. Carney included a rare reference to conditions in Russia in a letter to young Jim Larkin: 'Attacks on the USSR, playing up alleged famine stories, but no word from our crowd [the Comintern] to give us facts to counteract this lying propaganda.'[29] Even the anti-communist *Irishman* ridiculed reports of peasant rebellion in Russia.[30] Big Jim, despite his grievances with Moscow and abandonment of communism in 1932, remained a lifelong champion of the Soviet Union and Stalin's leadership. A savage editorial in the *Irish Worker* gloating over the dismissal of two directors of ROP and their anticipated despatch to 'the Rock Pile in Siberia' suggests some knowledge of the dark side of Stalinism. Yet his reservations about the regime extended only to private criticisms of shoddy workmanship, the arrogance of officialdom, and a corrosion of idealism.[31] Nor did graduates of the Lenin School return with their faith

---

26   RGASPI, letter to Ireland, 23 Sept. 1932, 495/20/251–89/98.

27   RGASPI, Report of the CPI congress, June 1933, 495/89/88–18.

28   *Workers' Voice*, 23 Apr. 1932.

29   RGASPI, Carney to Larkin Jr, 6 Nov. 1928, 495/89/52–13/15.

30   *Irishman*, 8 Dec. 1928.

31   *Irish Worker*, 22 Nov. 1930; John de Courcy Ireland, 'As I remember Big Jim', in Nevin, *James Larkin*, p. 448.

impaired, and though the school discouraged contacts with Russians or foreigners in Russia, up to the early 1930s students undertaking the *praktikum* were free to travel without supervision. Seán Murray, young Jim and Harry Wicks had completed their *praktika* in the summer of 1929 in Daghestan, and were shocked by the primitive conditions and the status of women in the predominantly Muslim region. 'Our desire to be loyal to party concepts was stretched', according to Wicks, 'Young Jim Larkin simply could not stop talking about it'. Later they holidayed in the Ukraine and Leningrad, where Wicks was shaken to see the acute housing shortage being alleviated by the construction of slums, and find that his hosts had not enough food to join him in a meal.[32] While Wicks turned Trotskyist soon after returning to England, the cause was the party line rather than Soviet life. Internationally, few of those who broke with the Comintern cited conditions in Russia as a reason.

Murray had a very personal experience of the system in trying to secure a passport for his Soviet wife. It was a difficult but not impossible request, and at least two British graduates of the Lenin School brought home Russian wives.[33] Both Murrays were members of the VKP(b) and accepted the discipline that went with it.

> Their [VKP(b)] advice is that it would not be correct for her to register as my wife etc without first having the permission of the party leading organs. That this will be allright there is no suggestion [*sic*] my wife, quite correctly, refuses to do anything without the full consent of the party. I agree with this.[34]

For whatever reason, Mrs Murray did not leave Russia, and the marriage was not known of in Ireland.

Progressives were understandably sceptical of anti-Soviet propaganda, which emanated chiefly from the Catholic Church and lay Catholic press, the *Irish Independent*, and British populist newspapers. *An Phoblacht* featured a series of items in February 1930, including an open letter from Peadar O'Donnell to Cardinal MacRory, denying the existence of religious persecution in Russia. It also gave extensive coverage to eyewitness accounts of Russia by Friends of Soviet Russia delegations. In May 1931 Dublin trades' council unanimously condemned the refusal to issue passports for Russia, and the 'alarming rumours which have been circulated with regard to conditions in

---

32 McLoughlin, 'Delegated to the "new world"', pp. 37–9; Wicks, *Keeping My Head*, pp. 109–14.

33 John McIlroy, Barry McLoughlin, Alan Campbell, and John Halstead, 'Forging the faithful: the British at the International Lenin School', *Labour History Review* 68, 1 (Apr. 2003), p. 117.

34 RGASPI, Murray to Mingulin [undated], 495/14/335–21/23. I. G. Mingulin was a leading functionary in the Anglo-American secretariat.

the USSR, of which no proof has been given'.[35] Perhaps less understandably, fellow travellers were easily deceived by showcases of achievement in the land which invented 'Potemkinisation'. Helena Molony reckoned the Soviet regime had more popular support than the Free State.[36] Following their visit to Leningrad, Moscow and Baku in 1930, the Friends of Soviet Russia – like so many other contemporary tourists – returned wide-eyed with excitement. The genuine advances of women in Soviet public life had made a particular impression. 'The greatest experiment in the world was in progress in Russia', Hanna Sheehy Skeffington told a meeting in Dublin, 'the workers [were] taking over control of affairs themselves. The workers' reaction to factories and machines was comprehensive, and enthusiasm had a solid basis . . . The position of women was such that feminism was not needed.' Charlotte Despard, a veteran campaigner on penal reform, had visited Soviet prisons, and was pleased to report: 'there were no locked doors in the prisons, the prisoners managing their own affairs'.[37] On their tour of Leningrad, Moscow and Kiev in May 1931, Rosamond Jacob and M. K. Connery found the prison system impressive in its 'wisdom and humanity'. They were equally struck by the freedom and equality of women and

> felt the wonderful force of mass enthusiasm among [the people], and the self-sacrifice and determination with which they are pushing forward the Five Year plan to success . . . We saw the great importance attached to the agricultural worker in the USSR, where the greatest pains are taken to bring factories, schools and town institutes of every sort into close touch with the villages.[38]

The image of Russia as a land of full employment, striding to prosperity at a time when the capitalist west was plunging deeper into economic depression, was a factor particularly in the success of the INUM, and the RWG complained of 'The integrity of comrades [being] tampered with by promises of rewards, trips to USSR'.[39] As W. T. Cosgrave told the Catholic bishops: 'conditions are unusually favourable to the spread of conspiracy such as the present. There is the example and encouragement of Russia.'[40]

Saor Éire was a salient example of the widening appeal of communism: a rare case in Irish history of communism as opportunism. An IRA army

---

35   *An Phoblacht*, 6 June 1931.
36   *An Phoblacht*, 1 Feb. 1930.
37   *Workers' Voice*, 25 Oct. 1930.
38   *An Phoblacht*, 18 July 1931.
39   RGASPI, Ireland, report from secretariat, 31 Jan. 1931, 495/89/65–1/4.
40   NA, DT, memo, Sept. 1931, S5864B.

convention in April 1931 backed a proposal to build a political movement on the basis of IRA battalions and O'Donnell's working farmer committees. The 'state of feeling generally was so favourable', wrote Moss Twomey, that 'It was the conviction of the Army Council, that the Revolutionary movement, to be successful should command a backing among the people'.[41] In response to objections to 'class hatreds and other doctrines foreign to the national aspirations of the Irish people', Twomey declared:

> If it is Communism to undo the Conquest . . . to destroy landlordism in its many forms and restore their heritage to the dispossessed; to enable those who produce wealth to obtain the fullest advantage of that wealth . . . to end robbery and exploitation by a privileged minority; then Tone, Emmet, Mitchel, Lalor, Connolly, Pearse, and Mellows were Communists, and the Irish Republican Army is a Communist organisation.[42]

If this was not communism as the Comintern knew it, the distinctions were too subtle for most people in Ireland.

The capture of Saor Éire papers on Seán MacBride in Kerry in July provided the cabinet with what it purported to be significant evidence of IRA communism. In reality the debate on Saor Éire was a matter of public record, for readers of *An Phoblacht* at any rate, and the government had long been aware of links between republicans and communists. Through exchanges of information with the British, interception of mail, seizure of documents in raids, and highly placed informers, the state intelligence services had a fairly accurate picture of the membership and direction of revolutionary organisations, without mastering the nuances of their politics or tactics. While the chief concern lay with the IRA, all communist related groups were monitored and, where possible, infiltrated. In one instance the special branch asked Scotland Yard to have banknotes used by Herbert Ward traced in London.[43] The Gardaí knew of links with the Comintern, but still found it hard to credit its influence. 'The number of these revolutionary organisations . . . is bewildering and each week so to speak gives birth to new ones', noted a report in 1930. 'The Communist Internationale may be prompting these activities but one gets the impression that they are simply the manifestations of the professional agitator without whom the Communist Internationale would be powerless.'[44] As with republicans, the communists were subjected to continual

41 UCDA, Twomey papers, army council to Clan na Gael, 7 May 1932, P69/185 (298–302).

42 *An Phoblacht*, 16 May 1931.

43 NA, DT, David Neligan [head, special branch] to the secretary, Department of Justice, 5 May 1930, S5074B.

44 NA, DT, Report on revolutionary organisations, 4 Apr. 1930, S5864A.

raids and arrests, so much so in early 1930 that Bell reckoned the government had resolved to smash the movement at birth. Prospective visitors to Russia were frequently denied passports by the Department of Justice, which affirmed that the issue of a passport was dependent on the applicant's 'known character and views'.[45]

There were two differences to the situation in 1931. First, the government purported to be disturbed by an increase in IRA military activity, for which there was inconclusive evidence. In the first six months of 1931 the IRA had killed an informer, a Garda superintendent, and a witness in a prosecution led by the superintendent. The cabinet feared a new IRA policy of shooting senior Garda officers, and it did not believe that an increase in the strength of the special branch or Gardaí would contain the threat.[46] The Department of Justice put IRA membership at 4,800, a little less than the 1926 figure, but there were indications of a surge in recruitment in 1931, and area reports from Garda sergeants complained of losing control of the country.[47] Ten thousand people defied a ban on the Wolfe Tone commemoration in June, leaving police and troops in steel helmets and armoured cars to look on helplessly.[48] Secondly, it seemed that revolutionism was moving into a more effective mode. According to the government: 'The active membership of communistic organisations as such is comparatively small, but the acceptance of Communistic doctrines by other organisations is alarmingly rapid.' Military Intelligence echoed the point:

> The interesting feature of the whole matter from the writer's point of view is the success with which the Communist Section are permeating the other groups with their theories and ideas. In '23, '24, and '25, a small Communist party existed . . . the party was barely able to hold together and exist. Now four years later it would seem to have been fairly successful in getting all extreme sections (in Dublin at least) to more or less adopt its views. The position would seem to be that a gradual change is taking place in the ideas and objectives of the extreme organisations. Formerly they were purely 'National'[:] in the future they will be both 'Revolutionary' (Communist) and National.[49]

45   RGASPI, Report of the CI commission in Ireland to the Anglo-American secretariat, ECCI and WEB, 17 Mar. 1930, 495/89/62–1/4; *An Phoblacht*, 16 May 1931.

46   O'Halpin, *Defending Ireland*, pp. 68, 78.

47   NA, DT, memo, Sept. 1931, S5864B; Hanley, *The IRA*, pp. 80–1.

48   Ó Drisceoil, *Peadar O'Donnell*, pp. 65–6; *An Phoblacht*, 27 June 1931.

49   NA, DT, memo, Sept. 1931, S5864B; UCDA, Dan Bryan papers, report, undated [1929], P71/6(1–7).

MacBride's Saor Éire papers, by Department of Justice reckoning, marked 'the definite union' of the IRA and communism, and an alliance in which the former would provide the military muscle and 'in return the Communists supply to the Irish Republican Army as a potential recruit every man who, whether from poverty or principle or mere love of agitation, is anxious to see the system of private property and private enterprise destroyed in this state'. Nor was this gross misreading of events confined to the authorities. It seemed to many less biased observers, like Tom Johnson, that 'the IRA appears to have been captured by the communist wing'.[50]

In fact, the Comintern feared Saor Éire. At his desk in Moscow, Bell reflected the prevailing line in describing it as 'an attempt on the part of the petty bourgeois leaders to steer the rising tide of unrest among the masses into channels where they can control it, and prevent the formation of a Communist Party'.[51] The RWG fraction within it aimed to persuade the IRA left to join the communists, not form a rival party. Seán Murray assured Moscow: 'We opposed its formation in conversations and in meetings with republican comrades. We urged a wider base among the rank and file of workers and peasants and an appeal to the Orange workers.' Less convincingly, he claimed the RWG had little choice but to go along with the project to avoid alienating republican revolutionaries.[52] Murray was consulted on the Saor Éire programme and its founding convention in Dublin on 26–27 September included 150 delegates from the RWG, the Irish Working Farmers' Committee, the IRA and Cumann na mBan. The constitution adopted pledged Saor Éire to the overthrow of British imperialism and Irish capitalism, to bring wealth under the control of workers and working farmers, and to restore Gaelic culture. Fraternal greetings were sent to Soviet Russia. In a race against the anticipated coercive legislation, Murray and Shapurji Saklatvala joined Peadar O'Donnell in a series of meetings to organise local branches.[53]

It is doubtful if the Comintern line, had the cabinet been aware of it, would have made any difference to government policy. The Garda commissioner, Eoin O'Duffy, had favoured 'comprehensive' legislation since mid 1929 at least and did not seem bothered about the facts.[54] Garda reportage on

50   NA, DT, memo, Sept. 1931, S5864B; Dermot Keogh, 'Hogan, communism, and the challenge of contemporary history', in Donnchadh Ó Corráin (ed.), *James Hogan: Revolutionary, Historian, and Political Scientist* (Cork, 2001), pp. 62–3.

51   RGASPI, Material for Anglo-American secretariat, meeting 6 Nov. 1931, The situation in Ireland, referent T. Bell, 495/89/64–72/76.

52   RGASPI, Murray before the Anglo-American secretariat, 10 June 1932, 495/72/188–140/175.

53   CPI, *Communist Party of Ireland*, p. 48; Ó Drisceoil, *Peadar O'Donnell*, pp. 67–8; Banta, 'The red scare in the Irish Free State', p. 38.

54   Regan, *The Irish Counter-Revolution*, p. 288.

communist groups had declined from late 1930: instead of the RWG, the government would ban the Workers' Revolutionary Party, the title discontinued in November 1930. Primarily the government feared the IRA, and the republican version of communism. But communism was also an essential pretext. Cosgrave had earlier failed to secure a condemnation of republicanism from the Catholic hierarchy. Playing the red card he tried again, and sent Cardinal MacRory secret documents as evidence that 'We are confronted with a completely new situation. Doctrines are being taught and practised which were never before countenanced amongst us and I feel that the influence of the Church alone will be able to prevail in the struggle against them.' Similarly, a communist taint would legitimate the suppression of an overt political movement which might have led republicans away from military conspiracy. 'Nothing in the [Public Safety] Bill forbids the advocacy of political beliefs', Cosgrave told Dáil Éireann, adding 'The advocacy in this state of Communistic doctrines by those same men [Saor Éire] or their close allies who are also members of a secret illegal armed association . . . cannot be tolerated and they have I submit put themselves beyond the pale of constitutional activities.'[55] The red scare also teed up Cumann na nGaedheal's contention in the 1932 general election that the IRA would play Lenin to de Valera's Kerensky.

Dáil Éireann enacted the Public Safety bill on 17 October. Next day, a pastoral letter read at Sunday masses deplored 'the growing evidence of a campaign of Revolution and Communism', and declared Saor Éire and the IRA 'sinful and irreligious'. On 20 October the government reintroduced military courts to try political offences and proscribed Saor Éire, the IRA, Fianna Éireann, Cumann na mBan, the Labour Defence League, Friends of Soviet Russia, the Irish Working Farmers' Committee, the Workers' Research Bureau, the Anti-Tribute League, the Women Prisoners' Defence League, the Workers' Defence Corps and the Workers' Revolutionary Party. Interestingly, the IWL was not named, though O'Duffy had considered including the WUI.[56] When thousands attended a League Against Imperialism protest against poppy day in Dublin, it too was banned.[57] Hundreds of arrests, proscriptions of meetings, and the suspension of *An Phoblacht* – after four successive issues were banned – reduced republican activity to subsistence level.[58] It was a similar story with the RWG. Even lorry drivers and commercial

55 Quotes from Jonathon Hamill, 'Saor Éire and the IRA: an exercise in deception?', *Saothar*, 20 (1995), p. 63.

56 Milotte, *Communism in Modern Ireland*, pp. 108–11.

57 J. Bowyer Bell, *The Secret Army: A History of the IRA, 1915–1970* (London, 1972), pp. 113–14.

58 See *An Phoblacht*'s stop-gap replacement, *Republican File*, 28 Nov. 1931 to 5 Mar. 1932.

travellers of ROP were stopped and searched. The cabinet agreed that the *Workers' Voice* should be suppressed 'on every possible occasion'. Two issues were confiscated, one was heavily censored, and two more appeared as a cyclostyled bulletin until in December the censorship and production difficulties led the RWG to suspend the paper.[59] Though not formally proscribed, the RWG considered themselves to be de facto illegal.

REVISING CLASS AGAINST CLASS

The Anglo-American secretariat insisted that the RWG contest the forthcoming general election in all possible constituencies under the slogan 'For an independent workers' and farmers' republic'; young Jim Larkin was to be nominated in North Dublin and WUI branches drawn into a united front.[60] Not for the first time, Big Jim had other ideas and fought North Dublin himself – as a communist on the old IWL platform of enmity towards the Labour Party and support for Fianna Fáil – compelling the RWG to switch young Jim to the less propitious South Dublin and make a token effort for Joe Troy in North Dublin. On polling day 'a vociferous army of youngsters, plentifully bedecked with red sashes and red jerseys and carrying red flags' paraded through the streets in Big Jim's support, and Shapurji Saklatvala accompanied him on a tour of the polling stations. The RWG mounted a big effort, producing a campaign paper, the *Vanguard*, 60,000 election addresses, and thousands of leaflets for specific groups like the unemployed and republicans. In total they spent £340 on the election, of which £100 came from the CPGB.[61] It was hardly the best use of resources. Young Jim polled 917 votes, and Troy 170. After his own disappointing tally of 3,860 first preferences, Big Jim forsook revolutionism, retiring the IWL, and discontinuing the *Irish Worker* after 12 March.[62] While not actively opposing the communists, he continued to exclude them – and all other dissident voices – from the WUI. In response to criticism of the RWG's failure to develop a united front with the WUI, Troy told Moscow that infiltration of the union was impossible. It had held no annual conference for four years, or branch meetings for over six

---

59 *Workers' Voice*, 7 Nov. 1931; NA, cabinet minutes, 3 Nov. 1931, S4469/17/10; *An Phoblacht*, 21 Nov. 1931.

60 RGASPI, Anglo-American secretariat to Ireland re elections, 7 Jan. 1932, 495/89/75–1.

61 RGASPI, General election, Feb. 1932, 495/4/205–12/14. The RWG's election fund provided £30; where the remainder came from is unclear.

62 O'Connor, *James Larkin*, pp. 96–7; RGASPI, Results of the Irish Free State elections, undated [1932], 495/72/197–14/16.

years, and the only meetings permitted were those dominated by Big Jim, who would ramble on for hours on whatever took his fancy.[63]

Shortly before the election campaign the RWG had published a general resolution on strategy, couched in orthodox third period values, in the ECCI's gazette *International Press Correspondence* or *Inprecorr*.[64] A testy Comintern inquest on the election noted with dismay the RWG's use of nationalist 'phraseology' and slogans like 'Ireland free and united'. 'Connolly takes the place of Lenin as the proletarian leader', it complained, and, most irreverently, 'one manifesto states that "Lenin and the Russian workers have proven the correctness of Connolly's position"'.[65] For once, the Irish would prevail over the Anglo-American secretariat, and effect a sudden and significant change in the line soon after Fianna Fáil took office. The incoming government suspended the Public Safety Act, released political prisoners, and decriminalised the IRA, whose membership more than doubled to 10,000–12,000 over the next 12 months.[66] Moreover, a round of disputes with Britain over constitutional reform, tariffs and the land annuities seemed inevitable. These same events had contrary implications for the IRA army council and the RWG. The former decided that Saor Éire was no longer imperative, had the project shelved, and began to restrain the republican left; the latter concluded that it was time to advertise its anti-imperialism. When the *Workers' Voice* reappeared on 9 April, with the aid of a loan of £28 from Mrs Despard, its tone and presentation was notably more nationalist: the next issue featured a front page portrait of Parnell, of all people.[67] In May, a lengthy article by Gerhart Eisler on 'The Irish Free State and British imperialism' in the *Communist International* confirmed Moscow's imprimatur on the change.

> It would be wrong to take a negative position in regard to the De Valera demands, on the premise that the national grievances divert the class struggle . . . No, the Irish Communists must understand that the national grievances of the broad Irish masses are closely connected with their social demands, and they must stand out as the champions of both their national and social demands.
>
> If the Irish Communists do not take this position, they will remain completely isolated from the Irish working class . . .

63   RGASPI, Troy before the Anglo-American secretariat, 495/72/188–182.

64   NLI, Donal O'Reilly papers, resolution, uncatalogued, ACC.5891. The English language edition of *Inprecorr* was published in London.

65   RGASPI, Results of the Irish Free State elections, undated [1932], 495/72/197–14/16.

66   Hanley, *The IRA*, pp. 14–16;

67   RGASPI, General election, Feb. 1932, 495/4/205–15/16.

Eisler was not an Irish specialist and selected presumably because as a teacher in the Lenin School he would have been in contact with the Irish students.[68]

The thrust of Eisler's article was directed against the *Daily Worker*, which had taken a 'tactically incorrect position' in being too critical of de Valera. And if Moscow was anxious that the CPGB should not bracket itself with the 'British imperialists and Social-fascists' in their 'vituperous campaign' against the Irish people, it was concerned too that the RWG should not become too nationalist. In June Murray and Troy were in Moscow to clarify the revision with the Anglo-American secretariat. The neglect of anti-imperialism was a mistake, Murray argued. The RWG had been 'too sharp' on de Valera in the general election and the *Workers' Voice* had not been sufficiently Irish in character. 'The outstanding fact of the Irish position at the moment', said Murray, 'is that Ireland is again involved in struggle with British imperialism'.[69] Troy dealt with problems of organisation in trade unions, where the RWG had no more than three weak fractions, in the WUI, the National Union of Railwaymen, and the Irish National Union of Woodworkers. He also sought guidance on the problem of British-based unions, which where becoming increasingly unpopular in the Free State but consolidating in the North.[70]

Troy's points received a quick response. The RWG should combat British 'labour imperialism', but 'the struggle for an independent militant Irish trade union movement can only be successful after a struggle in trade union branches and workplaces against reformists'. The 'bankrupt collapse of Larkin to reformism' made organisation in the WUI essential if militancy was not to be further dissipated by the Larkin leadership.[71] Murray's remarks were referred to the ECCI's politcommission, in effect a sub-committee of the polit-secretariat, and it was late September before an ambivalent adjudication was despatched.

The main political weakness of the RWG has been the underestimation of the role and significance of the national struggle . . . This has resulted many times in the past in isolating the RWG because it appeared that the national-liberation struggle was a hindrance in the struggle for socialism, whereas, in reality, it is a

68 Eisler (1887–1968) had worked in the Austrian and German communist movements, later becoming president of the German Democratic Republic's radio and television commission. Curiously he referred to the Irish communists as 'the Irish Workers' League'. His article was reprinted as a pamphlet as 'Historical Reprints no. 18' (Cork Workers' Club, 1976).

69 RGASPI, Murray before the Anglo-American secretariat, 10 June 1932, 495/72/188–140/175; report on the situation in Ireland, 11 June 1932, 495/72/188–138/139.

70 RGASPI, Troy before the Anglo-American secretariat, 10 June 1932, 495/72/188–190.

71 RGASPI, Draft letter to members of the RWG, 5 July 1932, 534/6/79–71/76.

great supplementary revolutionary force . . . Recently this has been overcome to a
great extent as seen in the changed policy of the 'Workers' Voice'.

At the same time the third period characterisation of other groups was
upheld. De Valera's policy was 'national-reformist' towards British imperialism and 'social reactionary' at home. While supporting Fianna Fáil's fight
against Britain, the RWG was to stress that complete independence could be
won only through revolutionary mass agitation, and by maintaining their
independence from the IRA or Sinn Féin. The Saor Éire programme 'covered
[the IRA's] objectives of a bourgeois republic . . . to form a barrier towards the
developing of a mass revolutionary movement. The RWG must work among
the workers in the IRA to win them over.'[72] Murray took as much liberty with
the revision as he could. In September he joined republicans on the executive
of the Boycott British [goods] League, and on 8 October the *Workers' Voice*
became the *Irish Workers' Voice*.[73] The RWG's objective, he told the CPGB,
was to win 'the leadership of the national revolutionary struggle . . . The
Communist Party must be the party of national independence'.[74]

For all its caution about the policy revision, the politcommission does
seem to have been sanguine about the prospects, and granted the RWG
$1,088 for the second half of the year.[75] A directive condemned the *Daily
Worker*'s attacks on de Valera and told the CPGB to save its venom for British
imperialism. A campaign fund was to be opened for Ireland, and customised
appeals made to Irish workers in Britain. A special edition of the *Daily Worker*
was to be printed without birth control advertisements, so that it might legally
enter the Free State. Similarly, the Communist Party of the USA (CPUSA)
was directed 'immediately [to] begin systematic propaganda and agitational
activity among the Irish workers around the issues of the national struggle in
Ireland', develop a network of Irish workers' clubs as 'the main organisational
forms of the CP [communist party] work among the Irish workers in
America', and raise funds for Ireland.[76] In return the ECCI expected a party
of 500–600 members by 1933, with factory nuclei trained to work illegally
under the rules of communist conspiracy.[77]

72 RGASPI, letter to Ireland, 23 Sept. 1932, 495/20/251–89/98.

73 Banta, 'The red scare in the Irish Free State', p. 90; *An Phoblacht*, 24 Sept. 1932.

74 *Daily Worker*, 28 Nov. 1932, quoted in Milotte, *Communism in Modern Ireland*, p. 114.

75 RGASPI, Protokoll (B) Nr.263 der Sitzung des Polit.Kommission des pol. Sekr. EKKIv.27 July
1932, 495/4/205–6.

76 RGASPI, letter to the CPGB on the Irish question, adopted by the pol-commission, 9 Aug. 1932,
495/4/207–168/171; letter to the CPUSA on the Irish situation, accepted by the pol-commission, 9
Aug. 1932, 495/4/207–207/210.

77 RGASPI, Tasks of the RWG in Ireland, 1 Aug. 1932, 495/89/73–75/95.

ZENITH OF THE RED STAR

The second half of 1932 was the high tide of communism in Ireland during the Comintern era. Between June and November the weekly print run of the *Workers' Voice* was increased from 1,750 to 3,000 copies. In June the RWG had under 200 members, including 73 in Dublin, 50 in Belfast, and 16 in Kilkenny, with others in Ballymena, Coleraine, Tyrone, Longford, Offaly, Leitrim, Clare, Mayo, Wexford, Dundalk and Tipperary. Groups had recently been formed in New York and London.[78] The creation of new groups in places like Oola, County Limerick and Cullen, County Tipperary during a recruitment drive in Munster in October signalled the RWG's determination to exploit its closer links with the IRA and become a nationwide force. A Republican Workers' Group, comprising about 30 volunteers, was formed within the Dublin IRA, primarily to influence policy rather than win recruits. Moss Twomey had his agents keep it under surveillance. By November RWG membership had risen to 339, including 120 in Belfast, 40 in Kilkenny, 30 in Cork, 15 in Tipperary, and 12 in Waterford.[79] The growth had a fragile base, being due largely to the accretion of untested nuclei and to spectacular, but very contingent, advances in Belfast and Castlecomer.

Unemployment in Northern Ireland was now in excess of 100,000, and those who had exhausted their insurance benefits were reliant on employment on out door relief schemes run by the Board of Guardians or food parcels from the Guardians. In July the Belfast RWG formed an Out Door Relief Workers' Committee to agitate for better pay and conditions. Similar campaigns by the communist-led National Unemployed Workers' Movement were generating unrest in Britain, and led to riots in Birkenhead on 13 September. On 3 October the 2,000 out door relief workers in Belfast struck. That evening 20,000 marched through the city in their support. Mass meetings culminated in serious disturbances on 11 October when the Royal Ulster Constabulary (RUC) tried to prevent a banned march. Catholics and Protestants united in battles with the RUC, who replied with gunfire, leaving two dead, 15 wounded, and at least 19 suffering other injuries. Heeding the tocsin sounded by Protestant clergy and businessmen, the authorities opened negotiations with Belfast trades' council, which was threatening to call a general strike. On 14 October, the Guardians raised relief rates by 15–150 per cent. The Out Door Relief Workers' Committee hailed a 'glorious victory'.[80] The Belfast example encouraged

78   RGASPI, S. Murray, Ireland, group organisation, 8 June 1932, 495/89/78–30/41.

79   RGASPI, Report re national meeting of RWG, 5–6 Nov. 1932, 495/89/82–14/18; *Irish Workers' Voice*, 22 Oct. 1932; UCDA, Twomey papers, D/Intelligence to Twomey, 21 Dec. 1932, Brigade O/C to Twomey, 9 Jan. 1933, P/69/53(252–254). I am obliged to Brian Hanley for this reference.

80   For a detailed account of the strike see Devlin, *Yes! We Have No Bananas*, pp. 116–36. See also Milotte, *Communism in Modern Ireland*, pp. 128–32.

demonstrations by the INUM in Dublin, which secured an improvement in
the scale of relief. New branches of the INUM were formed in Belfast,
Carrick on Suir, Clonmel, Dublin, Longford and Waterford, and a national
convention held in the Mansion House in December.[81]

As work resumed in Belfast, the Irish Mines, Quarries, and Allied
Workers' Union struck for a wage increase of 3*d.* per ton in the Castlecomer
coalfield. Four hundred miners joined the strike. Work resumed on 28
November when the union reluctantly accepted an increase of 2*d.* per ton
following mediation by TDs. While not a complete victory, the union felt
confident enough to plan the construction of a union hall.[82]

On 3 November, with the help of Peadar O'Donnell and leading republicans, the Workers' College was opened in the home of Mrs Despard in
Eccles Street, Dublin. Murray had suggested in September that the RWG
and IRA might collaborate on a joint education centre and a joint printing
plant. Moscow replied warily, and Murray dropped the idea of formal co-
operation. He was receiving stiff criticism from the Comintern for the
'impermissible line of hiding [the] Communist identity' of the *Workers' Voice*,
a confused attitude to the IRA and de Valera, insufficient attention to the
defence of the Soviet Union, and slow progress on forming a party. Trade
union branches and IRA companies were issued with a prospectus. Two
weekly classes – on Marxist economics and labour history – were organised,
and over 20 students enrolled.[83] Literature was a pressing need. Irish communist publications had been confined to newspapers up to 1931, when the
RWG's Workers' Books published Elinor Burns, *British Imperialism in Ireland:
A Marxist Historical Analysis.* Modern Books, London published another
pamphlet, Ralph Fox, *Marx, Engels, and Lenin on the Irish Revolution* the
following year. Murray raised the matter of literature in Moscow in June 1932.
Some theoretical articles on Ireland appeared in the *Communist International*
and *Inprecorr*, and Moscow sent Brian O'Neill and Larkin Jr guidelines for the
writing of two pamphlets, on the national struggle and peasant movements
respectively. Both were to be completed within six weeks.[84] O'Neill's work
eventually bore fruit in 1933 as *The War for the Land in Ireland* under the

81 *Irish Workers' Voice*, 3 Nov., 10 Dec. 1932.

82 Brennan and Nolan, 'Nixie Boran and the colliery community of north Kilkenny', pp. 577–8;
RGASPI, S. Murray, Ireland, group organisation, 8 June 1932, 495/89/78–30/41; Report re national
meeting of RWG, 5–6 Nov. 1932, 495/89/82–14/18.

83 RGASPI, letter to Ireland, 17 Sept. 1932, 495/89/75–22/25; letter to Ireland, 1 Oct. 1932,
495/89/75–26/28; letter to Ireland, 20 Oct. 1932, 495/89/75–29/29a; Murray to Moscow, 9 Sept. 1932,
495/89/83–42/44; to Anglo-American secretariat, 28 Oct. 1932, 495/89/84–7/11; Ireland, report re
national meeting [5–6 Nov.], 25 Nov. 1932, 495/89/82–19/23.

84 RGASPI, Comintern to O'Neill and Larkin, 15 June 1932, 495/89/75–45.

imprint of the RWG's Sphinx Publications. In January 1933 Sphinx published Murray's pamphlet *The Irish Case for Communism*, setting out the draft manifesto of the CPI, and issued Peadar O'Donnell, *For or Against the Ranchers?*, and Joe Troy, S. I. Gusev, and Harry Pollitt, *The Next Step in Ireland, Britain, and America*; it also offered a 'catalogue of revolutionary literature' by Connolly, Marx, Engels, Lenin, socialist novelists, Bolshevik historians, and anti-fascists, together with 30 or so pamphlets on the Soviet Union.[85]

Meanwhile Murray intended to build a party substantially on republicans. While anti-imperialism might be problematic in the North, the bulk of Belfast members were unemployed, and not regarded as dependable. In their third constituency, workers on the shop floor or in trade unions, the communists were scarcely organised. Following a national conference on 5–6 November 1932, where Murray and Bill Joss briefed delegates on the work of the CPGB, the need for an Irish party, the Comintern, and 'the question of "dictation" from Moscow, the XII plenum, its estimate of the present period etc'. Murray told Moscow that 'most of the delegates were very good types who still lack experience but give great promise. The majority of them were members also of the IRA.' Their own concerns related mainly to how they should respond to the religious question, the Unemployed (Able-Bodied) Men's Association – sponsored by the Catholic Church to combat the INUM – and the issue of IRA membership. The conference agreed to prepare for the formation of a party by February; 'the prospects', Murray thought, 'are very good'.[86] Joss was present too to advise on the creation of a youth section, with the assistance of a British Young Communist League instructor. Twenty-five had agreed to join.[87] Subsequently a series of articles in the *Workers' Voice* on the need for a party addressed unease – which Murray played down – about coming out explicitly as 'communist' and Moscow led. In January the Anglo-American secretariat drafted a directive acknowledging that the radicalisation of the masses under the 'national reformist and social reactionary' Fianna Fáil government was finding expression in the IRA, and commending the RWG to 'win the best elements of the IRA' for the building of a party through united front from below tactics, while guarding carefully against the resurrection of Saor Éire.[88] The RWG reported that its influence 'has been strengthening to a very considerable extent within the ranks of the IRA over the past six months'.[89]

85 RGASPI, A catalogue of revolutionary literature, undated [1933?], 495/89/106–1/7.

86 RGASPI, Circulation of Workers' Voice, 25 Aug. 1932, 495/89/84–3/5; Murray to Moscow, 9 Sept. 1932, 495/89/83–42/44; Report re national meeting of RWG, 5–6 Nov. 1932, 495/89/82–14/18.

87 RGASPI, Report on the situation in Belfast and the steps taken to develop Communist youth organisation, 4 Nov. 1932, 533/10/1317–29.

88 RGASPI, Tactics of the RWG towards the IRA, draft, 1 Jan. 1933, 495/89/86–15/21.

89 RGASPI, The general election in Ireland, undated [1933], 495/89/90–23/30.

The immature state of the strategy was exposed when de Valera called a snap election on 3 January 1933. Hoping to use the hustings as a springboard for the foundation of a party, the RWG made plans for a united campaign with republicans, but proposals to field independent radical candidates came to nothing. Larkin Jr agreed reluctantly to be nominated in Dublin South after Murray refused to stand, but the RWG failed to raise the £100 deposit in time. Problems arose too with its election manifesto. Knowing Murray's proximity to republicanism, the CPGB was alarmed by the IRA's unprecedented decision to support Fianna Fáil in the election, and called him before its colonial committee. The Irish secretariat then deleted from the manifesto a sentence 'regarding voting against the imperialist candidates through Fianna Fáil . . . owing to doubts as to its correctness'. The CPGB nonetheless had the manifesto withdrawn, arguing that de Valera was the 'main enemy'. The RWG put its case to Moscow, insisting that British imperialism was the 'main enemy', and that by 'developing a powerful mass movement against the imperialist agents' it could unmask the vacillations of Fianna Fáil.[90] For the moment the Comintern was more concerned with getting the long-awaited party up and running. Advising on the founding congress, it recommended a special appeal for support and fraternal delegates to the IRA, with the usual caveats about not being 'sucked into the swamp of the IRA'.[91]

Some of the reasons why Murray liked working with the disciplined, focused men of the IRA, and why the communists suffered chronic under-achievement on the industrial front, are illustrated in the fortunes of the Belfast RWG after the out door relief strike. Recriminations soon overshadowed the 'glorious victory'. From the left, the settlement was criticised for not including an extension of relief to single men. From the right, Harry Midgley and the NILP accused the communists of dastardly exploitation of the unemployed, while Belfast trades' council launched a moderate unemployed movement. Tommy Geehan, leader of the Belfast INUM and the out door relief strike, remained popular, polling over 1,000 votes in Belfast's Court ward in the municipal elections in January, but his relations with the RWG became increasingly strained, especially during the major dispute of these years, the 1933 rail strike.[92]

The National Union of Railwaymen had conceded a four per cent pay cut in 1931 and was dismayed to find the railway companies seeking a further ten per cent reduction 12 months later. When the companies refused to meet the

90 Ibid.
91 RGASPI, letter to the RWG re constituent congress of the Irish Communist Party (draft), 28 Mar. 1933, 495/89/86–40; letter from Comintern, undated [Apr? 1933], 495/14/338–38/44.
92 *Irish Workers' Voice*, 21 Jan. 1933.

union half way, the London-based executive reluctantly sanctioned a strike on the Northern systems for 30 January; a government subsidy enabled the Free State railways to defer wage cuts for three months. Of 3,478 members called out, 2,765 responded, along with 1,037 non-unionists. Strikebreaking by busmen, railway clerks and others provoked a violent response. A train was derailed, killing two scabs, and the mainly Protestant strikers were not embarrassed when the IRA – feeling that it had missed an opportunity in the out door relief strike – started to bomb transport installations. The communists gained some support for their attempts to involve the INUM and dockers in the struggle, while the British Minority Movement deployed William Cowe, a Scottish agent of their railway vigilance movement, urged sympathetic action in Britain, and raised £7,000 for the strike fund. Yet in seemingly favourable terrain, the RWG's sole contact among the strikers remained William Crozier, who chaired an unofficial 'central strike committee' in Belfast. Even after the union executive ended the strike on 6 April by unilaterally accepting a five per cent pay cut and the retention of scabs while 700 union members were laid off, the RWG made little out of the widespread rank and file discontent.[93] Cowe brought some 20 militants together in a vigilance committee in Belfast, which petered out after a few weeks; his expectation of a 'strong' vigilance movement in Dublin came to nothing. Once more the communists emerged from industrial conflict with a few sympathisers and nothing concrete.[94]

Publicly, the RWG blamed union officials for frustrating their militancy. Privately, there were internal recriminations about the lack of commitment in Dublin and Belfast. Cowe submitted an extraordinary assessment of the Belfast group.

[T]he position of the groups here in Belfast . . . is very bad. The political level of the comrades here is very low . . .

For instance, for some considerable time the only regular activity which our comrades in Belfast have taken on has been Socials and Dances. At those events our Party members become, along with non-Party elements the worse of drink and the Socials just develop into drunken rabbles. From the Local Organiser downwards such a state of affairs has existed with most of the men comrades and also with some some irresponsible women who are members of the Party. Such

---

93 Milotte, *Communism in Modern Ireland*, pp. 138–40; RGASPI, Minority Movement report, undated [1933], 534/7/53–34/40.
94 RGASPI, Report on Irish rail strike, 23 Mar. 1933, 495/89/91–8/9; report, 1 May 1933, 495/89/91–14/16; Report on rails, 15 May 1933 [W. Cowe?], 495/89/91–20/22; Industrial report from Ireland, 26 July 1933, 495/89/90–21.

things are talked about by the workers in general . . . since the October struggle of
Out Door Relief Workers the party membership has heavily dropped, no organised party activity is carried on in the Irish Unemployed Workers' Movement and
an antagonism exists between the IUWM and the Party . . . not one hands turn
was lifted by the Party members in the recent vital economic struggle – the Irish
Rail Strike . . . to tackle the job of reorganising the local in Belfast . . . some
comrade from the Centre should be placed in charge here for at least three
months.[95]

A review of the Belfast organisation in June noted internal divisions and
'several' attempts by the Dublin secretariat to 'straighten out' relations with
the INUM. Geehan was transferred to other duties, and changes effected in
the party leadership.[96]

REACTION

The communist advance in the autumn of 1932 had provoked a severe riposte,
North and south. It was over the next year that Unionist Party leaders made
their most notorious appeals for sectarian solidarity, evidently to effect as
membership of the Orange Order increased during the slump. Encouraged by
Unionist MPs, the Ulster Protestant League redoubled its efforts where the
October unrest had been most intense. Immediately after the riots the Youth
Evangelistic Campaign brought 20 preachers to Belfast for a three-week
mission against communism. Subsequently the Unionist Party and Protestant
churches organised distress schemes. The Catholic Church in the North had
little to say in public, but discreet clerical pressure would alter the composition
of the Belfast CPI by June 1933, causing Dublin to note: 'the best progress is
now made in the non-nationalist section'.[97] The church was not so circumspect in the Free State.

Within weeks of the RWG's national conference in November 1932, the
Workers' Voice was being put to bed in Glasgow for want of an amenable
printer in Ireland, and Murray was filing letters from around the country on
intensifying Catholic opposition. The Kinvara man who wrote to terminate
contact because the priests had him under pressure is unlikely to have been

95 RGASPI, General position of the RWG, Belfast, W. Cowe, undated [1933], 495/89/91–17/19. See
also RGASPI, Irish report, undated [July 1933], 534/7/65–26/27.

96 RGASPI, Report from Ireland, undated [July 1933], 495/89/91–23.

97 Milotte, *Communism in Modern Ireland*, pp. 137–8; Devlin, *Yes! We Have No Bananas*, pp. 138–40;
RGASPI, Report from Ireland, undated [July 1933], 495/89/91–23.

unique in Galway. The Cork group imploded under rhetorical and physical assaults from the bishop, clergy and confraternity. The incongruously named Bishop Collier of Ossory led a crusade against the Mines, Quarries, and Allied Workers' Union until parishioners in the union's heartland agreed to condemn communism and form a branch of the ITGWU. Membership of the RWG in Kilkenny withered to four or five. One described a visit from his parish priest.

> He started with trying to make me give up the idea of forming RWG. When all [?] failed he said, If I brought a Doctor of Divinity to you he would convince me I was wrong. I said in reply that may be a Doctor of communism would show him where he was wrong. Any way the[y] brought pressure to bear on my people and I had to leave home . . .[98]

In Leitrim, where Jim Gralton led an RWG section, Gralton's Pearse–Connolly Hall was burnt to the ground, and Gralton himself would be deported to the USA in 1933 at the instigation of his parish priest. Longford and Waterford also reported 'hounding and persecution'.[99] Between 19 November and 4 February the Catholic weekly, the *Standard*, replaced its regular front-page assaults on international communism with a series by 'our special representative' on domestic communist and fellow-travelling organisations. As the by-line implied, the *Standard* had a spy in the RWG. For the *Standard*, the issue was not the threat to the church. 'Special representative' could not forbear repeatedly to sneer at the failure of the RWG to make headway, and the *Standard* would later report Nazi confrontations with the German Catholic hierarchy more in sorrow than in anger. Anti-communism had become a principle of faith and loyalty.

Fanned by lenten pastorals and lenten missions, anti-communism reached a crescendo in late March. It would be only the first of several attempts to crush communism in Dublin over the next four years, and these evidently had some degree of co-ordination. The RWG had predicted an attack on its new headquarters, James Connolly House, 64 Great Strand Street, on 11 March, and the *Workers' Voice* later claimed the assailants were 'directed' by Blueshirts.[100]

98 RGASPI, letter from Patrick O'Farrell, undated [1932], 495/89/83–94/99.

99 RGASPI, letter to M. O'Connor, Kinvara, 6 Dec. 1932, 495/89/83–76; letter from T. McGee re RWG, Cork, 30 Nov. 1932, 495/89/83–64/68; report from Ireland, undated [July 1933], 495/89/90–13/18; Brennan and Nolan, 'Nixie Boran and the colliery community of north Kilkenny', pp. 580–81; Luke Gibbons, 'Labour and local history', p. 91; Banta, 'The red scare in the Irish Free State', p. 114; *Irish Workers' Voice*, 18 Feb. 1933.

100 Banta, 'The red scare in the Irish Free State', p. 138; *Irish Workers' Voice*, 1 Apr. 1933.

More consistently behind the clashes over the next few years was the Catholic
Young Men's Society, abetted on occasion by elements from Dublin's street
gangs, the 'animal gangs'. St Patrick's Anti-Communism League had been
founded on 16 March by Patrick Glennon, and it is doubtful if Glennon, an
80-year-old former butler at the Catholic University School, was more than a
figurehead. Later at least, he would have the support of members of the
Catholic Young Men's Society.[101] On Sunday 26 March, communist meetings
in central Dublin were broken up. Next evening several hundred demanded
entry to Connolly House, and proceeded to smash windows until dispersed by
the Guards. On Tuesday, Connolly House was besieged again, and the mob
went on to attack the Workers' College, the INUM office in North Great
George's Street, and the WUI hall in Marlborough Street. On Wednesday
thousands made a third assault on Connolly House, broke into the building,
despite revolver shots, and left it gutted by fire. The Workers' College also was
stoned. Thursday, the final night of disturbances, saw another attack on the
Workers' College. After being held back by the Guards, the crowd moved on
to sing hymns outside the offices of the INUM and the WUI.[102]

The repression continued in the streets during the coming weeks. The
Catholic Young Men's Society staged a public bonfire of communist papers
and advised newsagents against stocking the *Workers' Voice*. St Patrick's Anti-
Communism League led a parade of 1,000 people in Dublin in April, and
another of some 3,000 in June. They were 'prepared to lose their lives rather
than it [communism] should make any headway in Dublin', said Mr O'Looney
of the Catholic Young Men's Association, and there would be a branch of the
league in every parish. June and July saw several attempts to break up communist meetings in central Dublin.[103] Determined the prevent the formation
of a party, the *Standard* commissioned another series on communism in April,
expressing the hope that it would be driven out by 'true Catholic action and
state action if necessary' and not 'mob violence'. To earn his salt, 'special
representative' overreached himself with increasingly far-fetched alarms about
the 'sensational growth' of a 500-strong red army, and was chuffed to find the
Blueshirt and the British *Daily Express* equally impressed with his creative
writing. Unmasked by the CPI, he signed a smug confession in September.[104]
Nor was the sensationalism limited to the populist press. The London *Times*
of 12 May printed a despatch from its Riga correspondent announcing that the

101 NA, DJ, Garda reports, 8 Apr., 14 June 1933, JUS 8/711.

102 Banta, 'The red scare in the Irish Free State', pp. 135, 263, fn. 54; Gibbons, 'Labour and local
history', p. 91; Michael Farrell, 'Anti-communist frenzy', *The Irish Times*, 28 Mar. 1983.

103 *Standard*, 8 Apr., 1–22 July 1933.

104 *Standard*, 29 July to 2 Sept. 1933; *Irish Workers' Voice*, 21 Oct. 1933.

ECCI had decided to create an Irish communist party whose immediate tasks were to include anti-religious agitation and the overthrow of the government.

'Everyone now agrees', the CPI conceded, 'that they fell down on the open mass work after the attack on Connolly house'. In fact all work was dropped for a few weeks. Only two issues of the *Irish Workers' Voice*, padded with illustrations and generic articles, appeared between 1 April and 17 June. Some Dublin comrades went underground and were doubtful about resuming legality, as working openly was called. Murray took to carrying a gun, and kept on the move, after several strangers called to his lodgings. 'Special representative' was sure the party would not appear for months. Nor was there any stomach for challenging the church. T. A. Jackson's report on the rioting in *Daily Worker* was not appreciated: 'the Anti-Religious touch is inevitable with him and the comrades here don't think it the best way to tackle the question'.[105] Indeed a one-page *Workers' Bulletin* issued on 23 April blamed 'rascally capitalist propagandists' for using religion to divide workers. Murray sent a long statement to the CPGB arguing for the futility of any confrontation with religion in Ireland, and against the formation of a body with the name 'communist', a word which had now assumed an extraordinary taboo. Murray later alleged that Frank Aiken, Minister for Defence and an old colleague in the Northern IRA, offered him a position in the civil service if he would renounce the CPI. A visit from the CPGB's Bob McIlhone, a Scot and cohort of Murray's in the Lenin School, and a formal recommendation to the Comintern for immediate action helped to stiffen the RWG's resolve. Trade unions and the Dublin brigade, IRA were invited to join a 'united front' and Bob Stewart canvassed senior IRA officers. The response was discouraging, but a 100-strong 'defence force' was created with the aid of IRA volunteers and members of the defunct Citizen Army. The comrades could still not be persuaded to hold an open party convention.[106]

The founding congress of the second CPI finally convened on the weekend of 3–4 June at 5 Leinster Street, Dublin in a room rented from the Franciscans in the guise of 'the Dublin Total Abstinence Association' with a card outside the door saying 'Temperance meeting'. Remarkably, no suspicions were aroused, and the only breach of security was a leaked report of the proceedings in the *Irish Press* the following Wednesday. Forty-five delegates

---

105 RGASPI, Report from Dublin, undated [April 1933?], 495/89/91–59/61; report on the CPI congress, undated [June 1933], 495/89/90–39/40; PROL, Seán Murray, KV2/1185.

106 RGASPI, *Workers' Bulletin*, 23 Apr. 1933, 495/89/91–41; report, undated [July 1933], 495/89/90–13/18; Ireland, recommendation made by Bob McIlhone, undated [May 1933], 495/89/90–12; report on the CPI congress, undated [June 1933], 495/89/90–39/40; *Standard*, 20 May 1933; PROL, Seán Murray, KV2/1185.

were present, representing 250 members, together with Nora Connolly and Mrs Despard. Apart from the CPGB, the WUI alone sent a fraternal delegate, Jack Carney, who 'came and delivered his usual attack upon the party'. Nonetheless, nothing could dim a defiant sense of achievement. The 'vanguard of the Irish toiling masses', reported the *Workers' Voice*, 'have hurled down their class gauntlet . . . In every delegate there seemed to be a realisation that he or she was participating in an event destined to be historic.' 'We meet to bring into being', said young Jim Larkin, 'the General Staff of the whole struggle of the Irish workers and working farmers'.[107]

Grim defiance and subterfuge was a far cry from the heady days of October 1932 and raising the red flag from the barricades of Belfast to the crossroads of Oola. Were the communists, as is often alleged, paying the price of subordination to Moscow and the sectarianism of the third period? There is substantial evidence that the covert hostility to Saor Éire, and overt hostility towards the NILP were self-defeating. On the other hand, the class against class line probably made little difference in industrial struggle. Quite apart from the prevailing climate, trade unions had their own reasons for opposing communist infiltration. Moreover, the decisive blow to the RWG came from the reaction of religious groups in 1932–3. In that sense the link with Moscow was a severe handicap, and yet it was also the life-support machine of Marxism in Ireland.

107 RGASPI, Report on the CPI congress, undated [June 1933], 495/89/90–39/40; *Irish Press*, 7 June 1933; *Irish Workers' Voice*, 17 June 1933.

NINE

BACK TO THE FRONTS, 1933–6

Does the Irish working class require its own class party . . . Is a
Communist Party necessary in Ireland or something else?
SÉUMAS MACKEE
'The CPI in the present situation', December 1933[1]

—

What form of party became a nagging question for communists and socialist republicans in this period of repeated revision and realignment. Even if MacKee's questions were intended as a rhetorical harangue, they betrayed a very unbolshevik doubt, born of a failure to exploit political change. The anticommunist climate had soon quenched any optimism that the launch of the CPI would rally the cause. Up to the summer of 1934, the chief concern was simply to keep the party going. Initially there was some softening of third-period thinking, and appeals to reformists and republicans for united fronts. But, as was usual in phases of weakness, the CPI became more dependent on Moscow, and up to the thirteenth plenum of the ECCI in December 1933, the Comintern was still trying to stiffen the line. Coevally with the thirteenth plenum, the Irish were whipped in, upbraided for united frontism, and directed to build united fronts from below, primarily against fascism.

Within months, the world communist movement would embrace a historic u-turn, and support united fronts. Traditionally, the turn has been interpreted as a reflex of Soviet foreign policy. Recent research has argued that pressure from western European parties – notably the French – on the Comintern, and from Georgi Dimitrov, appointed the last secretary of the Comintern in 1934, were also influential.[2] In this light the Irish case is particularly interesting as the shift in Ireland was unquestionably precipitated by the Republican Congress. While it has been alleged that Seán Murray encouraged Peadar O'Donnell in the Congress idea, the Comintern archives suggest that the CPI did not want a split in the IRA, and its loyalty to the united front from below line made it uncomfortable about the Congress up to August 1934.[3] The Comintern itself

1   RGASPI, Séumas MacKee [pseudonym of Brian O'Neill], The CPI in the present situation, 28 Dec. 1933, 495/89/87–30/41.
2   McDermott and Agnew, *The Comintern*, pp. 120–30.
3   Ó Drisceoil, *Peadar O'Donnell*, p. 88.

was divided on the new departure, and even when the Irish turn was approved, the Anglo American secretariat remained chary and nervous enough to spell out to the Irish exactly what it meant, and did not mean, by united front. The controversy, and the CPI's contribution to debacle of the Republican Congress, would undermine Murray's leadership.

By contrast, the Irish were passive participants in the next change, though active in discussions in Moscow on how it would be applied in Ireland. The popular front, which extended the approved list of communist allies to bourgeois anti-fascists, was endorsed by the ECCI in January 1935 and ratified at the seventh world congress of the Comintern in July and August. The CPI had no difficulty with the theoretical revision, seeing it as a clarification of the united front strategy and an opportunity to tidy up the confused legacy of 1934.

THE SPIRIT OF ILLEGALITY

The CPI's founding congress elected Seán Murray as its general secretary and adopted 'Ireland's Path to Freedom' as its manifesto. An extended version of Murray's *The Irish Case for Communism*, the manifesto envisaged the fight for communism growing out of the national struggle. 'In the past', Murray told the congress, 'our weakness was that we did not see clearly that it was necessary to change the class leadership of the national struggle'.[4] Speeches from the floor reported on local struggles, alluded to the importance of the occasion, or appealed for more attention to specific issues, such as selling the paper or trade union work. No one opposed Murray's line.[5] In any case it would prove impossible to apply until 1934, when the CPI would be presented with a rather different set of circumstances.

The urgent task was to combat 'voluntary illegality', or the inclination of members not to go public in the prevailing climate. Dismissing their pleas that 'it would simply be torn to pieces by the mob', comrades were pressed to attend a Connolly commemoration in the Mansion House on 4 June, where Murray spoke along with Nora and Roddy Connolly, Hanna Sheehy Skeffington, and Rosamond Jacob. Before the proceedings Peadar O'Donnell and Charlie Gilmore marched 50 IRA men through the streets to act as stewards. Stewards were on hand again to 'squash' disruption when the CPI launched its municipal elections campaign with a rally in central Dublin. Young Jim Larkin and Murray stood for the party, while comrade Esther McGregor was nominated by the Dublin Muncipal Tenants' Association.

4   *Irish Workers' Voice*, 17 June 1933.
5   RGASPI, Speeches at CPI founding congress, 4–5 June 1933, 495/89/88–14/30.

Murray polled 75 votes, Mrs McGregor 186, and young Jim, the CPI's only
local councillor, received 338 votes and lost his seat. Big Jim too was unseated.
By these standards a Belfast candidate did exceptionally well in polling 1,200
votes in the Poor Law Guardians elections.[6]

A post-election stocktaking painted an optimistic picture of the party for
Moscow's eyes, though difficulties in the provinces were acknowledged. Belfast
was commended for its 'wide mass basis of working class support'. Dublin
received a glowing assessment:

> Membership growing weekly, composition improving. New members largely
> being recruited from IRA . . . membership at present 115, trade union membership
> approximately fifty; IRA members number 41; other organisations where members
> work actively are the Unemployed and Municipal Tenants' Movement. Have now
> regular fraction work being carried on in IRA; have now the basis for carrying on
> real fraction work in many trade unions . . .

The review put IRA strength at 11,000 and, most unusually, included an
estimate of its armament.

> Possibly one third the total strength could be armed with the Lee-Enfield rifle,
> while Colt and Webley .45 revolvers cold be found for another third. A handful of
> Lewis and Thompson guns are also possessed. The men are at different stages of
> training; possibly 75 per cent could use rifles, while there are cadres skilled in
> other weapons.[7]

British intelligence had reports of renewed contact between the IRA,
Razvedupr, and the Comintern at this time, though political developments in
Ireland cast doubt on these claims.[8]

The formation of the CPI – or publicity surrounding it at least – had
triggered the final breach with the IRA army council. For months past the
IRA had been trying to neutralise communist sympathisers in its ranks; they
were after all in cahoots with a movement committed to the subversion of the
army. In February the army council had withdrawn speakers from a public
meeting against Jim Gralton's deportation. At the general army convention
on 17–19 March, a proposal to exclude communists was rejected by 29–26

6   *Irish Press*, 5 June 1933; *The Irish Times*, 29 June 1933; RGASPI, Report from Ireland, undated [July
1933], 495/89/90–13/18; report on the CPI congress, undated [June 1933], 495/89/90–39/40.
7   RGASPI, Report from Ireland, undated [July 1933], 495/89/90–13/18; report, Ireland, undated
[July 1933], 495/89/91–23.
8   I am obliged to Eunan O'Halpin for this information.

votes, with the Dublin brigade's four battalions evenly split, but a motion to revive Saor Éire was defeated, and another that volunteers require the approval of headquarters for political activities was passed. Divisions were evident too on the March riots. Charlie Gilmore's claim that his armed defence of Connolly House had IRA authorisation was repudiated, to the barely concealed disgust of *An Phoblacht*, which denounced the riots as 'Hitlerism'. In June, following a statement from the Bishop of Galway, the IRA believed it would be the next victim of the red scare. When the *Daily Express* reported that 20 per cent of those who attended the founding congress of the CPI were IRA volunteers, the army council decided to send a blunt message to its opponents and its fellow travellers, and affirmed a standing order preventing members from belonging to the CPI and condemned communism for its 'denial of God and active hostility to religion'.[9] Sloughing off the red liability did not, as the IRA saw it, mean a shift to the right. If anything, *An Phoblacht* devoted more attention to the social question over the next year, and in January 1934 the IRA published a *Constitution and Governmental Programme for the Republic of Ireland*, its most comprehensive and radical manifesto since the Civil War. But *An Phoblacht*'s appeal was to trade unions and the Labour Party, and the manifesto received a derisive review in the *Workers' Voice* under the heading 'News from nowhere'.[10]

From an organisation which had braved red scares since 1930, the 'retreat from Moscow' was a cruel blow for the CPI, and the reason cited a gratuitous gift to the most mindless of its enemies. Anticipating the expulsion of communists, the CPI hoped the IRA left would fight for change from within but, aware of their seething frustration, forecast a split. Moss Twomey's efforts to rein in *An Phoblacht* had already precipitated the resignation of editors Frank Ryan and Hanna Sheehy Skeffington; there was talk of a new paper in association with the CPI, but the project was aborted for want of funds.[11] Aside from the funding problem, it would have been impossible for a Comintern affiliate during the third period to collaborate in such a project or to encourage the formation of a rival political party.

Over the next six months the CPI battled to hold its own. Party work outside Dublin and Belfast was impossible. And as the party contracted, weekly circulation of the *Workers' Voice* dropped to about 850 copies, income dwindled, issues became intermittent, the number of its correspondents fell, and informative news coverage gave way to generic copy.[12] Production too was

9   *An Phoblacht*, 1–8 April, 10–17 June 1933.
10 *Irish Workers' Voice*, 17 Feb. 1934.
11 RGASPI, Report from Ireland, undated [July 1933], 495/89/90–13/18; report, Ireland, undated [July 1933], 495/89/91–23.
12 RGASPI, Report on CPI organisation, undated [Jan. 1934], 495/89/99–50/53.

difficult. Since the attack on Connolly House in March the CPI had been compelled to print the *Voice* on a small, antiquated machine with a limited supply of worn out type. Thanks to a friendly printer the secretariat issued an impressive range of leaflets on strikes, trade unions, the unemployed, tenants, the deportation of Jim Gralton, and fascism in Ireland and Germany, but lacked the capacity to direct effective engagement. In fact the leafleting was intended to compensate for the difficulty of holding street meetings. Even this outlet was soon closed when the Dublin Typographical Provident Society enforced an embargo on CPI business while the party was using non-union labour to produce the *Workers' Voice*.[13]

The CPGB was scathing about the inaction, but the failing was not confined to the CPI. When 2,000 Irish seafarers struck on 27 June against a working agreement accepted by the British National Union of Seamen, the Minority Movement prepared to campaign for sympathetic action in Britain. However, an agent sent to Dublin withdrew, saying his presence would assist only the employers. 'There was always an element', he later recalled, 'that would yell out "we don't want any communism here"'.[14] The strike ended in victory after 17 days, and an Irish union – the Seamen's and Port Workers' – replaced the discredited National Union of Seamen. The rail and seamen's strikes caused the Minority Movement to reverse the policy it had doggedly defended against Big Jim Larkin in the 1920s. Convinced that 'events of great importance are taking place in Ireland, where the struggle is rapidly intensifying', it requested the Profintern to endorse 'the development of [an] All-Ireland trade union movement, of industrial unions based on the class struggle, and trade union democracy'.[15] The CPI had arrived at a similar conclusion and was already attacking the 'labour imperialist trade union leaders' of the British-based transport unions in Ireland. The Comintern doubted the wisdom of this tactic in Northern Ireland, but did not question it in principle.[16]

Whereas the south presented communists with an intolerant society and a liberal regime, the reverse applied in Northern Ireland. The Belfast CPI registered some progress in forming a branch of Friends of Soviet Russia, with 70 members, and developing the INUM, with 500.[17] From October the

13 RGASPI, CPI, position re printing of Irish Workers' Voice etc, 8 Feb. 1934, 495/89/99–2/3.

14 Pat Murphy, a Cardiff-Irishman, quoted in Stradling, *The Irish in the Spanish Civil War*, p. 133.

15 RGASPI, Points from discussion of Irish seamen's strike at MM [British Minority Movement] secretariat, 6 July 1933, 534/7/53–26; report, Ireland, undated [1933], 534/7/53–42/43; *An Phoblacht*, 15–22 July 1933.

16 RGASPI, The Communist Party and the mass struggles of workers, 22 July 1933, 495/89/89–4/5; Tasks of the CPI, draft, 26 Nov. 1933, 495/89/86–44/50; *Irish Workers' Voice*, 5 Aug. 1933.

17 RGASPI, CPI, politburo, minutes, 10 Mar. 1934, 495/89/99–13/37.

Stormont government took a more severe stance. A march of 70 unemployed workers which left Dublin on 6 October to mark the anniversary of the out door relief strike was stopped at the border. The shooting of an RUC man by the IRA on 8 October caused Stormont to ban all demonstrations. Murray was hauled from a platform by two detectives on 15 October and served with an exclusion order from the six counties. On 17 October, the RUC raided and wrecked the party's offices in east Belfast. When Murray returned to Belfast the following week he was sentenced to one month's hard labour. Until 1941 he was unable to enter Northern Ireland openly, though he slipped back to Cushendall occasionally to see his family. Three of the Belfast CPI leadership – Arthur Griffin, James Kater, and Val Morahan, INUM organiser – were also jailed for related offences. The party appealed – in vain – to Belfast trades' council and the NILP to join a campaign for free speech and the release of political prisoners.[18]

By 1934 the CPI was teetering on the brink of extinction outside Dublin and Belfast. Multiples of members existed in Derry, Leitrim, Longford, Limerick, Kilkenny and Waterford, but were unable to undertake group activity in the face of clerical hostility. In Cork it was claimed that a local organisation of 70 members, 90 per cent of whom were in the IRA, was reduced to two by IRA hostility. In Belfast the roll call had fallen to 60, and in Dublin to 75, of whom little more than 20 were active.[19] The party cited an all-pervasive 'spirit of illegality' as one of the two main causes of its backwardness; the other being the 'retreat, sabotage and hesitation of the Reformist and Republican petty bourgeoisie'.[20] The CPI nonetheless retained an affinity with republicans. When sufficient funds were not forthcoming to contest the Stormont elections in November, it endorsed an IRA candidate instead: as his opponent in Belfast Central was the Nationalist Party leader Joe Devlin, the decision was not too controversial.[21] In December the *Workers' Voice* hailed a 'united front' of trade unions, Fianna Fáil cumainn, and sports clubs in Tralee who demanded a local general strike for the release of 12 republicans arrested for attacking a Blueshirt demonstration. It also commissioned a pamphlet on republicanism by George Gilmore.[22]

18 *Irish Workers' Voice*, 9–16 Dec. 1933, 6 Jan. 1934; Milotte, *Communism in Modern Ireland*, pp. 146–7.

19 RGASPI, Report on CPI organisation, undated [Jan. 1934], 495/89/99–50/53; politburo, CPI, 10 Mar. 1934, 495/89/99–13/23.

20 RGASPI, CPI, resolution, central committee meeting, 10–11 Mar. 1934, 495/89/99–5/12.

21 RGASPI, To the workers of Belfast, Belfast district committee, CPI, 495/89/91–35; *Irish Workers' Voice*, 2 Dec. 1933.

22 *Irish Workers' Voice*, 9–16 Dec. 1933; RGASPI, Position re printing of Irish Workers' Voice etc, 8 Feb. 1934, 495/89/99–2/3.

UNITED FRONT FROM BELOW

The CPI's record came in for sharp criticism from Moscow in a character-istically carping progress report, though the fault-finding did not require an exhaustive analysis.

> It was to be expected that after the formation of the Party the ideological and organisational weaknesses which characterised the RWG would be overcome, or at least serious efforts should be made to overcome them. However, judging from the material to hand, this has not been so.
>
> The main task confronting the CPI is to overcome the lack of clarity in its ideology which is seen in the Workers' Voice and the leaflets and circulars issued by the Secretariat . . .
>
> Since the party Congress very little has been done to popularise the manifesto adopted by the Congress. Besides some speeches delivered at the Congress (in which the erroneous conception is put forward that the CPI is 'a 20th century Society of United Irishmen') the Workers' Voice has printed only one article on the manifesto. Unfortunately since the Congress the Workers' Voice has appeared irregularly, and in its contents appears more as a Left republican journal rather than the organ of the CPI . . .

While this was accurate comment, if harsh, the Comintern also ignored inconvenient facts to interpret policy failure as a failure of application. Thus the report found that 'the chief weakness in [the CPI's trade union work] was that emphasis was not placed on the necessity of building a trade union opposition to the bureaucracy', although the Irish had pursued this line. The nub of the problem for the Comintern's ideologists was the absence of anything distinctly reflective of the third period about the CPI. Even worse, the party had shown a tendency towards united frontism in the use of deviationist slogans like 'Unite against fascism'.[23] The thirteenth ECCI plenum in December affirmed the correctness of class against class and the responsibility of the social fascists for the Nazi regime in Germany. Insisting that with the des-truction of the social democrats, the KPD would triumph, the plenum charged affiliates with opposing war against Russia, preventing the establishment of fascist dictatorships, and applying the united front from below.[24] A position paper on the CPI in December, stressed the need to 'put in the forefront the organising of the united front from below', and though this was to be done in

---

23 RGASPI, Tasks of the CPI, draft, 26 Nov. 1933, 495/89/86–44/50.
24 Jane Degras (ed.), *The Communist International, 1919–1943: Documents, Vol. 3, 1929–1943*, pp. 285–96.

the factories, trade unions, and among the unemployed, the paper dealt mainly with the Blueshirts and 'fascisisation', the jargon for bourgeois state repression introduced under the guise of combatting fascism.[25] Further pressure came from Harry Pollitt, CPGB general secretary from 1929 to 1939, who briefed the CPI on the plenum on 30 December. The ECCI had acceded to the request of the Anglo-American secretariat for a CPI delegate to the plenum. Murray's imprisonment may explain the Irish absence.[26] When queried as to CPI inactivity by Pollitt, Murray had blamed public hostility and the bitterness of IRA leaders towards the party. Revive the Labour Defence League, Pollitt suggested, and campaign on political prisoners to recover IRA support.[27]

In January the CPI called for a united front of labour and republican groups against fascism, and reactivated the Labour Defence League. Nonparty people like Roddy Connolly, Hanna Sheehy Skeffington and Jack Carney were pointedly included, and the Dublin branch had an initial membership of 38, including May Murray and George Gilmore, unofficially representing Sinn Féin and the IRA. The branch quickly restyled itself the Labour League Against Fascism, discarding the older name for its association with the CPI.[28] Hitherto the communists had not prioritised the anti-fascism in Ireland, devoting as much attention to the Brownshirts as the Blueshirts, and the rationale was primarily to apply the theses of the thirteenth plenum. The Comintern intervention was nonetheless timely and effective. Though General O'Duffy had been checked in August when the government banned a march on Leinster House, proscribed his National Guard – the Blueshirts' latest cover name – and invoked Cosgrave's Public Safety Act to reintroduce a military tribunal, fascism acquired a deadlier import in September when Cumann na nGaedheal, the National Centre Party, and the Blueshirts merged as Fine Gael under O'Duffy's leadership. The Labour Party then agreed to support the Fianna Fáil government, and a joint Labour–ITUC manifesto on the 'Fascist Danger' appeared in October.[29] At the same time, the IRA formally opposed confrontation with the Blueshirts, on the assumption that that the government could handle the problem, while the labour leadership seemed equally reluctant to take action. Blueshirt clashes with IRA men, and occasionally Labour or Fianna Fáil supporters, escalated and a tense atmosphere prevailed until O'Duffy's breezy predictions of big advances in the

---

25 RGASPI, Séumas MacKee, The CPI in the present situation, 28 Dec. 1933, 495/89/87–30/41.

26 *Irish Workers' Voice*, 6 Jan. 1934; RGASPI, EKKI Beschlüsse Irland, 15 Sept. 1933, 495/4/261.

27 NA, DJ, Irish Labour Defence League, general file (1934), JUS 8/338.

28 *Irish Workers' Voice*, 13–20 Jan. 1934; RGASPI, Report on Labour Defence League, Sept. 1934, 539/3/645–21/24; NA, DJ, Irish Labour Defence League, general file (1934), JUS 8/338.

29 O'Connor, *A Labour History of Ireland*, p. 131.

June 1934 local elections turned to ashes and made the general an embarrassment to Fine Gael. In these circumstances the communists staged a modest recovery, albeit largely under various flags of convenience, such as the INUM, the Labour League Against Fascism, Friends of Soviet Russia, and workers' study circles in Cork and Waterford. The 'spirit of illegality' and the lack of party structures outside Dublin and Belfast remained serious difficulties.

Ironically, the CPI had not wished for the major united front of the period, the Republican Congress, which was gestating within the IRA, as Peadar O'Donnell et al. worked quietly to ensure that his call for a congress of progressives, rejected at the 1933 IRA general army convention, did not meet a similar fate in 1934. The tragi-comedy echoed 1931, when Saor Éire was both inspired by the republican perception of communism and opposed discreetly by the CPI. Once again, especially in the wake of the thirteenth plenum, the IRA left and the CPI were on different wavelengths; and it is possible that Murray's absence in Moscow in January or February 1934 compounded the misunderstanding. When the communists appealed for a united front, they meant a united front from below. Beneath the headline calls for unity in the *Workers' Voice*, the small print usually included unambiguous attacks on the leaders of labour and republican bodies. While communists and IRA militants shared a hatred of the military tribunal, which convicted 102 anti-fascists as well as 349 Blueshirts in 1934, the CPI also held that de Valera's 'fascisisation' entailed a co-ordinated political and economic strategy to create a reactionary 'new social order'.[30] Moreover, the very fragility of the CPI at this point made it more anxious to cling to orthodoxy. A lengthy review of policy by the central committee on 10–11 March concentrated on the theses of the thirteenth plenum and the third period, affirming that

> the class struggle . . . is becoming more and more acute on the economic issues . . . the Irish situation therefore is no exception to the general crisis of world capitalism, which, in the words of the XIII Plenum . . . is approaching closely to the stage of 'a new round of revolutions and wars'.[31]

A few private reservations on Comintern theses related to the economy and Germany, not the IRA. 'I cannot say I am happy with our analysis of the German situation', Murray ventured, 'the German party should have made a more resolute fight against the coming to power of Hitler'. It was not the view of the majority, and the central committee

---

30   Milotte, p. 148; PROL, Seán Murray, KV2/1185; RGASPI, Séumas MacKee, The CPI in the present situation, 28 Dec. 1933, 495/89/87–30/41.

31   *Irish Workers' Voice*, 24 Mar. 1934.

endorse[d] fully the policy of the C.C. [central committee] of the German Party and the ECCI in rejecting the theories of Neumann and Remmele, and particularly their theory that the [KPD] should have called for an armed insurrection as a gesture against the Nazi coup.[32]

In a resolution to the party, the central committee urged a deepening of commitment to the third period and 'a determined struggle against all right opportunist tendencies and practices which represent the main danger to the Party's growth and development of the revolutionary mass struggle against Fascism'.[33] The passing references to republicanism in the discussion dealt with ways of defending communists within the IRA and gave no hint of preparation for the events that would soon convulse the republican movement.

Days later, on 17–18 March, the IRA army convention rejected the call for a republican congress by one vote, with the executive overwhelmingly against the idea. While there was little difference on paper between the right and left, the left regarded the army council's radicalism as window dressing, and its policy on the Blueshirts as 'laying down carpets for the terror to creep forward'.[34] Rather than wait another year, the left assembled at Athlone on 7–8 April, issued a manifesto – the 'Athlone call' – elected an organising bureau, and pitched into a hectic campaign of agitation, preparatory to the launch of a new movement in the autumn. The *Workers' Voice* responded on 14 April:

> The Communist Party will play its utmost part in the building of this united front movement. But it warns against any attempt to form a new political party. A political party is the leadership of a class. There can be only one correct leadership and policy for the working class – the revolutionary Marxism of the Communist International and the Communist Party.

Ostensibly the CPI was concerned simply with the question – as yet an open one – of whether the Congress would continue as a united front or become a political party. In reality it was grappling with the problem of how its united front from below tactic could be reconciled with the republicans' united front. At first it proposed that the Congress build fronts around anti-fascism and immediate issues, ignoring the grand matter of the national question.[35] Its

---

32   RGASPI, politburo and central committee, CPI, 10–11 Mar. 1934, 495/89/99–13/37. Heinz Neumann was ousted from the KPD leadership in 1932; the thirteenth plenum condemned Hermann Remmele as a member of the 'Neumann group', and stripped him of his functions in the Comintern and KPD leadership.

33   RGASPI, CPI, resolution central ccommittee meeting, 10–11 Mar. 1934, 495/89/99–5/12.

34   RGASPI, Peadar O'Donnell to European Peasants' Congress, 14 Aug. 1933, 495/89/94–11.

35   *Irish Workers' Voice*, 9 June 1934.

own anti-fascist initiatives were encouraging. Dublin trades' council had backed a call for a general strike against fascism on 1 May, and the Labour League Against Fascism May Day parade, headed by the Republican Brass Band, drew a crowd of 500 according to the Garda, and 4,000 according to the CPI. At another rally in July, the CPI estimated the attendance at 2,000.[36] The party later confessed:

> Unfortunately, the Party, until very recently, failed to see the anti-imperialist character of the proposed Congress and attempted to oppose the Republican anti-imperialist slogans by anti-fascism slogans. The Party also devoted much of its time to fighting against the Republican proposals to form an anti-imperialist party at the Congress.[37]

Coincidentally, Murray was abroad again from late March to July, this time in the USA, removing a contact with republicans and one regarded as the resident theorist. Brian O'Neill, alias Aodh MacManus, deputised as party ideologist and may have been less confident about deviation from the perceived orthodoxy. Both the Comintern and the CPGB would later deplore the CPI's negativity towards the Republican Congress, but their apprehension was made plain in a May Day article by Bob McIlhone, now the CPGB's representative in Moscow, in the *Communist International*. Portraying the CPI in a pathetic light, McIlhone urged a deepening of third period theses to rebuild the party: 'The struggle for Communism in Ireland must not be weakened one single instant. To do so would be to capitulate to the national reformist leadership of the Republican movement and to strengthen Fascism.'[38]

Murray's American visit was sponsored by the Irish Workers' Clubs, and aimed to develop the clubs and raise funds for Ireland. The parent club in New York, founded in the spring of 1930, was plagued with internal feuding, and despite the ECCI's injunction in 1932, the CPUSA had failed to create a network of clubs and the *Daily Worker* gave little coverage to Ireland.[39] Murray addressed the eighth national convention of the CPUSA in Cleveland, Ohio in April, and then embarked on a whistlestop tour of the big cities of the east and mid-west. By June the number of Irish Workers' Clubs had multiplied

---

36　Milotte, *Communism in Modern Ireland*, p. 148; *Irish Workers' Voice*, 21 July 1934; NA, DJ, Irish Labour Defence League, general file (1934), JUS 8/338.

37　RGASPI, Irish communist party and the united front, undated [Sept. 1934], 495/89/98–50.

38　*Irish Workers' Voice*, 26 May 1934, partial reprint of R. McIlhone, 'The economic situation in Ireland and tasks of the Communist Party in Ireland', *Communist International*, 1 May.

39　IWV, 12 May 1934; RGASPI, The situation in the New York Irish Workers' Club, 19 Mar. 1933, 515/1/3180–1/3.

from two to 16. The clubs also published Murray's pamphlet *Ireland's Fight for Freedom and the Irish in the USA*. Led by Jim Gralton, the clubs promised $1,000 to the CPI, and the *Daily Worker* appealed for a matching sum. Gralton's instalments were reaching Dublin in July. The party responded more slowly, but at least four CPUSA money orders of $100 each would help to keep the CPI afloat in 1935. The first US aid was spent on the *Irish Workers' Voice* and the *Irish Communist*, a theoretical organ which ran to one issue in August.[40] In another instance of overconfidence, the CPI decided on a campaign to win 400 recruits, with 'shock brigades' – an idea acquired from the CPUSA – targeting manufacture, transport, building, linen and the shipyard.[41] The American tour marked the zenith of Murray's career, and he, or his colleagues, were sufficiently chuffed to indulge a tentative personality cult. "'I expect to see many new faces in the Party ranks on my return" says Comrade Murray. Make [*sic*] one of the new faces to greet the Irish Communist leader', coaxed the *Voice* in a boxed front page feature.[42] 'Seán Murray says' occasionally headed articles in the paper over the next year.

UNITED FRONT: RIGHT ABOUT FACE

On 1 September the *Workers' Voice* fell in line with the Republican Congress bureau's insistence that its focal point would be the republic, and commended an anti-imperialist united front. This 'right-about-face', as a Comintern review described it with no discernable irony, was another example of the ragged retreat of European communist parties from the third period.[43] Since February, when socialists and communists combined on the streets of Paris against a possible fascist coup, the Comintern had allowed a drift from class against class. Who sought and who authorised the change of policy in Ireland? The most likely scenario is that Murray requested ECCI approval on his return from the United States. Certainly, the 'right-about-face' had occurred a little earlier than the Comintern reviewer chose to admit. In February the *Workers' Voice* had reported the French unrest as communist led, adding 'The Socialist (Labour) Party . . . tried to keep the workers tied to the capitalist governments that are moving towards Fascism.'[44] On 18 August the *Voice*

40 *Irish Workers' Voice*, 21 Apr., 23–30 June, 21–28 July 1934; RGASPI, Seán Nolan to CPUSA, 21 Mar., 20 June, 2 July, 27 Sept., 30 Nov. 1935. I am obliged to Tim O'Neill for details on Murray in Ohio.
41 *Irish Workers' Voice*, 18 Aug. 1934.
42 *Irish Workers' Voice*, 30 June 1934.
43 RGASPI, The CPI and the Irish Republican Congress, 19 Jan. 1935, 495/18/1059–1/25.
44 *Irish Workers' Voice*, 17 Feb. 1934.

welcomed an anti-fascist front between the French communist and socialist parties, without pointing out that the front had been formed in June. It is scarcely conceivable that the turn did not have the ECCI's nihil obstat, given its close monitoring of Irish policy. Communication with Moscow had been improved since Harry Pollitt's acquisition of a radio transmitter in February, enabling him to send and receive encrypted wires, which British intelligence did not take long to decypher. Pollitt alone held the code, and though the radio was used for short, important messages only, it enhanced his ability to manage both the CPGB and CPI.[45]

As the Republican Congress prepared for its first conference in Rathmines Town Hall on 29–30 September, the CPGB enquired anxiously about how the CPI would handle this 'most dangerous situation'. Dublin answered belatedly on 18 September. Next day London composed a reply, and it is likely that Willie Gallacher took the letter to Ireland immediately. A day or so later Moscow wired Pollitt with instructions for the CPI. If these were as drafted in a memo of 16 September, the Irish party was to issue a manifesto on the basis of which it was to 'fight for the leadership of the Congress'. While supporting a united front against 'hunger, fascism, and war', it was to 'bring forward the main slogan "Workers' and Farmers' Republic" against the republican slogan of "Irish Republic"'. On 24 September Pollitt radioed Bob McIlhone: 'Gallacher already been IRELAND before receiving your wire. Our comrades were in bad position. We gave directives in general same as what sent by PC [politcommission].'[46] It would not be the last time that Pollitt interpreted the radio messages to suit himself, and in fact there were substantial discrepancies between the CPGB letter and the Moscow memo. Whereas Moscow prescribed a specified slogan and an independent position, the letter complained that, because the CPI's briefing was late and vague on tactics to be applied at Rathmines, 'We cannot work out the details of what our fraction should do at the Congress'. Essentially the letter said: do as you think best, but whatever you do, back a united front and oppose a new political organisation. It is of course possible that the original Moscow memo reached the CPI before 29 September, but Murray was not the man to defy the Comintern. It does seem that Pollitt was the cause of a major blunder by Murray and a calamity for the Republican Congress.

---

45 Andrew Thorpe, *The British Communist Party and Moscow*, p. 210.

46 RGASPI, To the secretariat CPI, 19 Sept. 1934, 495/14/334–24/27; memo to the CPI, 16 Sept. 1934, 495/89/96–46/47; PROL, Government Code and Cypher School decrypts of Comintern messages, 1930–45, HW 17/17. I am obliged to Eunan O'Halpin and Barry McLoughlin for drawing my attention to these decrypts.

Days before the Rathmines hosting, the Congress organising bureau divided on strategy. Michael Price, with the backing of a majority of the bureau, proposed that the conference endorse a new party to achieve a workers' republic. Peadar O'Donnell drafted a minority resolution to continue as a united front, committed simply to 'a republic'. Both sides cried foul. O'Donnell depicted Price's 'weird stunt' as an ambush, though *Republican Congress* had appeared to champion his proposals as early as 16 June, and the communists anticipated them. The Price faction blamed 'Moscow' for bending O'Donnell; Nora Connolly alleged that he turned after an all-night argument with Willie Gallacher, unbeknown to Murray.[47] In reality the villain of the piece was London not Moscow, which was not too embarrassed to amuse bourgeois historians by counterposing 'republic' and 'workers' republic' with 'workers' and farmers' republic'. Murray threw his weight behind O'Donnell, and the communist vote tipped the scales on the day. One hundred and eighty-six delegates were accredited from local Congress groups, the revived Citizen Army, 16 trade union sections and trades' councils, tenant leagues, the Kerry-based Republican Labour Party, and the Socialist Party, formerly the Belfast branch of the British Independent Labour Party; the sizeable communist contingent included representatives of the CPI, the Labour League Against Fascism, the Labour Defence League, the INUM, and fraternal delegates of the New York Irish Workers' Clubs, the League Against Imperialism, the Anti-War League, and the Indian Defence League. The CPI also had members or sympathisers in local Congress groups, notably that in Waterford, which sent eight delegates, all of whom voted for a united front.[48] After a six-hour debate, the united front option was adopted by 99–84 votes.

Murray's tactics alarmed the Anglo-American secretariat: for communists the slogan was always of utmost importance. In a furious directive, it described the situation as one of 'extreme gravity' which threatened 'the liquidation of the CPI inside this united front':

> The CPI delegation in the Congress not only failed to put forward our Communist programatic slogan, but became the tail end of O'Donnell and Co, thus OBJECTIVELY placing ourselves in a position in which we were supporting a policy of REVOLUTIONARY NATIONAL republicanism as AGAINST a so-called PROLETARIAN REPUBLICANISM (here we must emphasise that despite Price, Connolly and Co., and our hatred of their petty bourgeois opportunism, we must recognise that in this Congress they were giving expression to the will of

47 Nora Connolly O'Brien, *We Shall Rise Again* (London, 1981), p. 72.

48 *Republican Congress*, 6 Oct. 1934; UCDA, MacEntee papers, Notes on the Republican Congress movement, P67/527, p. 12; O'Connor, *A Soldier of Liberty*, p. 9.

the great majority of the Irish working class). And by this the CPI created a situation which may lead to a split between the revolutionary republicans and Left trade unionists who OBJECTIVELY represented a great mass of revolutionary opinion among the Irish working class, thus defeating the purpose of the Congress. The Congress presented an ideal situation for the CPI to present its own SLOGAN; 'Irish Workers' and Farmers' Republic' in order to show the LEADING ROLE OF THE COMMUNIST PARTY IN UNITING THE REVOLUTIONARY FORCES, and also to present to the Congress the COMMUNIST PROGRAMME FOR REVOLUTION IN IRELAND. But the CPI, ignoring the telegram directives from the [Anglo-American] Secretariat on this question, failed to maintain its Communist identity in a situation which simply demanded that attitude in order to make the CPI the LEADING FORCE in the Congress.

The CPI was charged with building unity with the Price faction around the correct slogan, circulating a statement of its relation to the Congress, and 'sharply criticising' O'Donnell's position. After a blistering review of party performance, and a long list of very optimistic recommendations – on strengthening its work in Belfast, in the trade unions, and among the unemployed – the secretariat signed off with confidence 'that the Irish comrades shall recognise . . . that we are not making impossible demands'. Higher counsels may not have been so sure, and it is possible that the directive was replaced with a more considerate letter, saying much the same less abrasively.[49]

If so, the velvet glove merely masked a mailed fist that left Murray a casualty of Rathmines. The CPGB's fostering role over the CPI was re-established in November with the secondment of Pat Devine to Ireland as a full-time 'instructor'. A year older than Murray, and a Scotsman, inevitably, Devine had joined the CPGB in 1921, been elected a local councillor, and served in the CPUSA from 1926 to 1932, when he was deported to Britain.[50] The use of London as a channel for Comintern funding of the CPI underpinned the CPGB's status. Moscow would cable Pollitt on his budget each month, and he was obviously a key man for anyone seeking increases or special payments. The money was usually sent monthly via Stockholm in Dutch guilders. In total, the CPI received £164 in 1934, £508 in 1935, and £227 in 1936, including grants for printing and publications. Immediately after the seventh Comintern congress, Murray, Pollitt and I. G. Mingulin of the

49   RGASPI, Directive letter to Ireland, 14 Oct. 1934, 495/89/96–56/64; letter to the CPI Ireland re Republican Congress, 16 Nov. 1934, 495/4/318–8/11.

50   RGASPI, Fragebogen für Delegiete des VII Weltkongresses, 11 July 1935, 494/1/475/5–6a; CPI, *Communist Party of Ireland*, p. 25.

Anglo-American secretariat agreed that £20 per month was the minimum subvention needed to meet the CPI's ordinary expenses. London was still begging Moscow to pay the agreed increase in February 1936.[51] Murray probably held his post as general secretary by default. There was growing criticism of him in Belfast, but the Belfast branch, with 40 members, was virtually an independent operation. Cork's 20 members were inactive. And while there was some acknowledgment of Murray's failings in Dublin, there seemed to be little appetite for leadership among the city's 55 or so members; at least they reacted indifferently to Comintern efforts to have an editorial committee take charge of the *Workers' Voice*.[52] With his willingness to do thankless work and cheery good humour in the face of relentless adversity, Murray remained popular in Dublin, obtaining maximum votes in elections for the district committee in 1937.[53]

Judiciously, the Comintern tolerated a dilatory response to its directives on the Republican Congress. The CPI issued a circular admitting to errors at Rathmines and inviting a response to the Comintern's suggestions, but made no formal correction of errors.[54] A final clarification of Irish policy was drafted in January 1935, ostensibly to elucidate the CPI, but possibly also because the ECCI was still divided on the united front up to December 1934, when Stalin finally endorsed the line. The emphasis and tone of the January document reflected the change, and Stalin's insistence that Moscow should not be blamed for the errors of the third period. Thus the review began by deeming 'a broad united front movement' to be 'imperative', and chided the CPI for its initial reservations about the Republican Congress and 'great waivering in policy' over the summer of 1934. After confirming the Comintern's earlier stance, it concluded in pedagogical style: 'The general principles laid down in the Manifesto for the revolution in Ireland are correct. On this basis the CPI can go forward in its great task of creating a mass Communist Party.'[55]

It was now too late to rescue the earlier unity. Rathmines had led to a series of splits in the Congress, with terrible results. Devine estimated membership of the Dublin group at under 100 in December 1934, and reckoned the Congress to be moribund elsewhere.[56] Those who had defected from the Congress

51 Thorpe, *The British Communist Party*, pp. 210–11; PROL, Government Code and Cypher School decrypts of Comintern messages, 1930–45, HW 17/20, London to Moscow, 6 Feb. 1936.

52 RGASPI, Pat Devine to Bob [McIlhone?], 18 Dec. 1934, 495/14/334–41/47; Irish party press, 2 Nov. 1934, 495/89/98–40/41;

53 RGASPI, Dublin annual general meeting, Feb. 1937, 495/14/339–5/17.

54 RGASPI, CPI circular, 1 Dec. 1934, 495/96–97/102; Pat Devine to Dick [?], 10 May 1935, 495/14/341–7/11.

55 RGASPI, The CPI and the Irish Republican Congress, 19 Jan. 1935, 495/18/1059–1/25.

56 RGASPI, Pat Devine to Bob [McIlhone?], 18 Dec. 1934, 495/14/334–41/47.

blamed the CPI for the debacle, the IRA felt confirmed in its opinion of the communists as wreckers, and there was little hope of a united front with mainstream labour. The Labour Party and the NILP – with a few exceptions – ignored CPI overtures, and the big trade unions kept their distance. Nonetheless the *Workers' Voice* beat out a regular appeal for unity, especially in the increasingly fratricidal trade unions, where the ITGWU was reviving its traditional demand for an Irish based labour movement.

The communists did record some success in orchestrating unrest. Devine was impressed with the possibilities: 'Since the beginning of November mass action has developed at a greater speed than at any time since 1931.'[57] The arrival of the new German ambassador had generated lively street protests. Poppy Day in Dublin had seen over 2,000 bemedalled ex-servicemen parade to a Republican Congress counter-rally to the British Legion ceremonies. On 16 November, after days of unemployed demonstrations, 10,000 attended a meeting in protest at Garda brutality, with speakers from the INUM, the CPI, the Labour League Against Fascism, the IRA, trade unions, and the Republican Congress on the platform.[58] Fifteen trade unions and radical groups were represented at an INUM conference on 1 December.[59] Within months the government raised unemployment benefits by 25 per cent. In Northern Ireland, dole cuts were restored following communist led demonstrations, the INUM opened branches in Newry and Armagh, and a CPI member headed a successful rent strike of 1,500 tenants.[60]

Murray believed that protests of this kind were as much as could be expected. He had suffered enough disappointments with trade unionists to tell Moscow frankly that republicans, not industrial workers, were the CPI's only reliable friends.[61] The Comintern, however, insisted that industrial agitation be the core of the CPI's agenda. Impatient in the wake of Rathmines, the Anglo American secretariat recommended the slogan 'Irish unions for Irish workers', which was modified to a directive to campaign for 'the unification of existing unions' and against all reformist union leaders.[62] The secretariat took a keen interest in the biggest struggle of the period, a strike of over 3,000 Dublin bus and tramwaymen on 2 March 1935. A six-man CPI cell organised a rank and file group which produced over 30 issues of a bulletin, *Unity*, and

57   Ibid.

58   *Republican Congress*, 3, 17–24 Nov. 1934.

59   RGASPI, Pat Devine to Bob [McIlhone?], 18 Dec. 1934, 495/14/334–41/47.

60   Milotte, *Communism in Modern Ireland*, pp. 163–5.

61   RGASPI, Seán Murray before the Anglo-American secretariat, 19 July 1935, 495/14/20–1/27.

62   RGASPI, Directive letter to Ireland, 14 Oct. 1934, 495/89/96–56/64; letter to the CPI Ireland re Republican Congress, 16 Nov. 1934, 495/4/318–8/11.

influenced the strike committee to sustain the dispute to a partially successful
conclusion, in spite of repeated union pressure to compromise. When the
IRA intervened in support of the workers, following the use of army lorries as
public transport, Moscow sent two radio signals to London, urging the CPGB
to mobilise behind the struggle, and the CPI to extend the strike and develop
'joint solidarity' with republican organisations. Sniping at lorries and the
wounding of three Gardaí provoked a vigorous reaction. Before the dispute
ended on 18 May, Connolly House had been raided five times, and there were
numerous arrests of communists and republicans.[63] For all the excitement, it
was a typical strike for the CPI, winning it some sympathy in the heat of the
battle, but nothing permanent.[64]

As another phase of Comintern strategy drew to a close, the CPI had no
more than consolidated a little. Weekly sales of the *Workers' Voice* had risen
from 2,000 to 2,200 since December, though the circulation was concentrated
in Dublin and Belfast, with the latter taking more copies, and the American
subvention remained crucial. Devine congratulated himself that the content
was less nationalist and much improved. Membership stood at about 150.
Nuclei had been established in Castlecomer, Longford, and Cork, but the
nemesis of clerical pressure, rising commensurately with CPI success,
continued to frustrate them. In Dublin too, according to Devine, 'there were
serious capitulatory tendencies shown by our members in the face of [Lenten
religious sermons]. On more than one occasion I had to practically force our
comrades to hold [street] meetings.' The public's fascination with the red
spectre had not abated: Professor James Hogan's 'exposé' of Comintern mani-
pulation of republicans, *Could Ireland Become Communist?*, appeared in February,
and was reprinted in April. More ominously, there were indications that, for
the first time, faith in the Comintern's magisterium was crumbling. Devine
told the CPGB:

> So far as *our Party* is concerned the official position on paper is the same as it was
> at Rathmines for which we criticised them. To all intents and purposes however
> the line of your letter is being put forward at all our meetings and in the Workers'
> Voice. Nevertheless our comrades are still very unclear and hesitate to definitely
> state their opinions when concretely asked to do so. You should prepare for a big
> discussion on this question when next *we meet*.[65]

63 PROL, Government Code and Cypher School decrypts of Comintern messages, 1930–45, HW
17/18, Moscow to London, 5, 9 Apr. 1935; Milotte, *Communism in Modern Ireland*, pp. 159–61.

64 RGASPI, Seán Murray before the Anglo-American secretariat, 19 July 1935, 495/14/20–1/6.

65 Ó Drisceoil, *Peadar O'Donnell*, pp. 91–2; RGASPI, Pat Devine to Bob [McIlhone?], 18 Dec. 1934,
495/14/334–41/47, and 6 Mar. 1935, 341–1/5; Pat Devine to Dick [?], 10 May 1935, 495/14/341–7/11.

No sooner were communists nervously reclaiming the streets of Dublin, than they were losing ground in Belfast. The 12 July came early that year. Even the election agent of Harry Midgley, one of the NILP's most trenchant anti-communists, complained of the impossibility of holding rallies since the start of the royal silver jubilee celebrations in May. Violence erupted on 14 June. Two Protestants were wounded in an exchange of gunfire in Ship Street. At the Custom House steps, Belfast's speakers' corner, Ulster Protestant League orators incited a riot. The mob marched to the York Street interface, attacked Catholic-owned shops, and broke every window in the Socialist Party's Labour Hall. The Ulster Protestant League was also to the fore in smashing five CPI and INUM meetings and wrecking the CPI offices during the month. When shots were fired on Orangemen returning from the field on 12 July, a powderkeg exploded. Who fired the shots is unclear, but it was probably in retaliation for the behaviour of Orange bandsmen. The Order's Imperial Grand Master blamed 'communists and members of the IRA'. Three weeks later there were 11 dead or dying, dozens injured, over 500 Catholic families homeless, and numerous Catholics forced out of their jobs in factories and the shipyards.[66] The violence was the worst Belfast had seen since 1920–2, and unlike similar troubles from 1886 to 1922 there were no political crises to excuse it. For some on the left, that confirmed the lethal lunacy of creating an Orange state. Others faulted the IRA for precipitating the riots – most of the fatalities were Protestants – and the CPI told Moscow in 1937 that its difficulties with Belfast socialists were 'due to the fact that the IRA has the name of being a gang of murderers'.[67]

In these demoralising circumstances, communists would greet the Comintern's next revision with relief.

POPULAR FRONT

The presence of Murray and Devine at the seventh world congress of the Comintern in July and August was the CPI's only input into the formulation of the popular front strategy. Both welcomed what they saw as a consolidation of the united front strategy, and the terms 'united front' or 'people's front' were usually employed by the CPI. The meaning of the line in Ireland still required clarification. Admitting that the CPI 'has to bear a very heavy responsibility'

---

66 Milotte, *Communism in Modern Ireland*, pp. 163–6; Jack Macgougan, 'Letting labour lead: Jack Macgougan and the pursuit of unity, 1913–1958', *Saothar* 14 (1989), p. 114; Boyd, *Holy War in Belfast*, pp. 205–18; Hanley, *The IRA*, pp. 156–7.

67 RGASPI, Meeting on Irish question, 23 May 1937, 495/14/339–27/38.

for the split at Rathmines, and had made 'a very serious error of principle' in endorsing Peadar O'Donnell's slogan and the stages theory, Murray pleaded with the Anglo-American secretariat for a return to the anti-imperialist formula of 1932, on the ground that republicans were indispensable allies:

> the [Republican] Congress movement has enabled us to have a very valuable ally in the struggle against the fascists and against the church, and for the development of a mass movement in Dublin, and its future lies in the development of Congress groups in the countryside and in the rural areas . . . a broad united front of the working class [i.e. industrial workers] has, in my opinion, no possibility, and would be just an ideal.[68]

In August the Irish delegates submitted 'Proposals for the application of the united front in Ireland', intended to end 'the confusion around the fundamental slogan' and take a 'definite' stand for 'complete unity and independence of the country and [a] Workers' and Farmers' Republic'. Organisational unity was the theme. The Republican Congress was to be encouraged to seek readmission to the IRA 'on the basis of full political rights'. Communists were to call for the rehabilitation of the WUI and amalgamations to end trade union multiplicity. And united fronts were to be offered to the Labour Party, the IRA, farmers' associations, and even 'the Republican Communists'. The CPI's class programme was to be based on Irish Trade Union Congress resolutions, and the central aims of the people's front were to be opposition to Irish involvement in British war plans, the removal of coercive legislation, defence of democracy, disbandment of fascist organisations, and national independence.[69]

In a discussion on the Lenin School, Devine raised some complaints common to western parties about the relevance of the tuition, disproportionate criticism of students, and rigid interpretations of party loyalty. Too many graduates, he stated, had left the party after returning home. It was agreed to employ more lecturers from foreign parties, create a separate Irish sector in the school, and draft a special history course for the Irish.[70] Betty Sinclair, Joe Whelan, Jim Prendergast and 'John Snail' (his school pseudonym) had applied for enrolment in early 1934. Bill Gannon had hoped to go, but he

---

68 RGASPI, Seán Murray before the Anglo-American secretariat, 19 July 1935, 495/14/20–1/27.

69 RGASPI, Proposals for the application of the united front in Ireland (by Irish delegation), 26 Aug. 1935, 495/14/335–84/86.

70 Barry McLoughlin, '"The party before anything else": rituals of 'criticism and self-criticism' in the British and Austrian sectors of the International Lenin School, Moscow, 1929–1937', unpublished paper.

had the mixed fortune to be employing a few lorry-drivers, and the CPI decided he was small businessman rather than a proletarian.[71] Sinclair was the only Irishwoman to attend the school, though the Comintern stressed the importance of sending women, and the CPGB sent 27 of its total of 132. 'Snail', born in 1899, was rejected for being above the recently introduced age limit of 35. Whelan and Prendergast were sent down for excessive drinking and keeping late hours. It may not have been coincidental that both had defended their right to personal opinions and, alone in his sector, Prendergast had criticised the summary executions that followed the assassination in December 1934 of Leningrad VKP(b) leader Sergei Kirov. The sector obliged him to sign a dictated apology attributing his various mistakes to 'the alien ideology which I have brought from my country'. The confession concluded: 'It is impermissible that I put forward my personal whims before the desires of the party'.[72] Notwithstanding these blots on Ireland's red escutcheon, and the ECCI's decision in May 1935 that the school should concentrate on cadres from illegal parties, three Irishmen were enrolled in October: Liam McGregor, William Morrison and Val Morahan. They completed their studies in January 1937. As the terror penetrated the school, and 20 members of staff were expelled from the VKP(b), it was decided to suspend courses for legal parties, and recommend western sections to create educational centres in the west. The International Lenin School finally closed in September 1938.[73]

The seventh congress ratified two important changes affecting relations between Comintern and its affiliates. Accepting that popular fronts would need to reflect national political cultures, the ECCI was directed to concentrate on 'the elaboration of the fundamental political and tactical lines of the world labour movement . . . and as a rule to avoid direct intervention in internal organisational matters of communist parties'.[74] To improve internal efficiency, the politsecretariat, the politcommission, and the regional secretariats were replaced with a new secretariat, each of whose ten members took over the brief of one of the regional secretariats. Curiously the countries formerly under the Anglo-American secretariat were allotted to a big, brutal giant of a Frenchman with no love of anglophones, André Marty. Affiliates were to send a permanent representative to Moscow, who would be assigned to one of the

71 Ó Duinnín, *La Niña Bonita Agus An Róisín Dubh*, p. 78.

72 RGASPI, Gordon [pseudonym of Jim Prendergast], statement re breakage of discipline and conspiracy of Graymont, Griffiths, and myself, 14 Feb. 1935, 531/1/171–7/8.

73 McLoughlin, 'Delegated to the "new world"', pp. 37–9; McLoughlin, 'Proletarian academics or party functionaries?', p. 65; McIlroy, McLoughlin, Campbell and Halstead, 'Forging the faithful', pp. 112, 117–18.

74 Degras, *The Communist International, Vol. 3*, p. 354.

ECCI secretariats, an obligation never fulfilled by the CPI. It has been argued that, in practice, the changes were intended to consolidate central control, and they did not mean the end of ECCI intervention in the CPI, only the end of the routine monthly monitoring that had been a feature of the Anglo-American secretariat.[75] The restructuring seemed to herald a fresh start and certainly the congress marked a peak in Dublin–Moscow relations. The relatively large sum of 365 Dutch guilders was allocated to Ireland in September, and it was agreed to raise the party's basic monthly stipend.[76] Doubts about Murray's leadership persisted, but he kept his job and his speech to the congress was published in the *Communist International*.

Back in Ireland, the new policy was being implemented in September by the Labour League Against Fascism and War as it campaigned on the Italian aggression against Abyssinia.[77] It was formally ratified at conferences in October. Essentially, there were to be three theatres of struggle: labour unity for economic and political progress, a people's front against war and fascism, and an anti-imperialist front 'of all oppressed classes (workers, farmers, middle class)', that would unite labour and republicans. The duality of the labour and republican movements was deemed 'a source of great weakness', for which labour leaders were held entirely responsible. The response to the popular front was uniformly enthusiastic. Comrades clearly felt that the more moderate line gave them a better chance of winning support.[78] The theses of the seventh world congress also had a genuine resonance in Ireland, even if they were interpreted more as a call for left-wing solidarity than pan anti-fascism. If Irish fascism was no longer a credible threat, organisational unity had become a popular theme on the far left as it recoiled – not necessarily in the one direction – from the shambolic legacy of Rathmines, the escalation of inter trade union rivalry, and the sectarian disturbances in Belfast. In June the Michael Price faction of the Citizen Army had voted to join the Labour Party or the NILP. Weeks before the CPI deliberations, a republican–labour unity conference had met in Dublin, and *Republican Congress* welcomed rumours of an IRA sponsored political auxiliary.[79] More generally, the Abyssinian crisis was seen as a major step towards a new European war, which de Valera would be dragged into unless the people united in opposition. Europe's wars would dominate the last years of the CPI.

75 Huber, 'Structure of the Moscow apparatus of the Comintern and decision-making', pp. 41–64.

76 PROL, Government Code and Cypher School decrypts of Comintern messages, 1930–45, HW 17/19, Moscow to London, 16 Sept. 1935, HW 17/20, London to Moscow, 27 Jan. 1936.

77 RGASPI, [CPI] against war and fascism since the 7th congress, 2 June 1936, 495/14/341–56/71.

78 UCDA, MacEntee papers, Notes on communism in Saorstát Éireann, P67/523(5), pp. 39–42; RGASPI, Report of the conference of the CPI, 5–6 Oct. 1935, 495/14/337–9/27.

79 Brian Hanley, 'The Citizen Army after 1916', *Saothar* 28 (2004); *Republican Congress*, 28 Sept. 1935.

At the same time, there were severe limits to the application of the popular front strategy. With whom were the fronts to be formed? Abyssinia did not move the masses. Leafleting delegates to the Fianna Fáil árd fheis – 'representative people from all over the country with great respect for one person, Éamon de Valera, and great dissatisfaction with the government' – met a predictable response.[80] Even the bizarre stratagem of a front without communists made little headway. In the People's Anti-Imperialist Front, created with members of Fianna Fáil, Conradh na Gaeilge, the Labour Party and trade unions, the CPI let the Republican Congress act as its proxy. But *Republican Congress* hit terminal problems in December 1935, as its eponymous publishers, and the CPI's only friends in the Free State, continued to atrophy. The People's Anti-Imperialist Front was moribund by the new year.[81] Despite a commendable record of activity from September to January, the CPI had done no more than 'draw in certain liberal minded people'.[82]

Pollitt's visit in January, to speak at a public meeting in Rathmines town hall, left him impressed with the atmosphere in Dublin as it prepared for the twentieth anniversary of Easter Week. The Comintern took seriously his opinion that the occasion was an ideal opportunity to effect labour–republican unity, and commissioned pamphlets from Murray and Brian O'Neill. Murray's *The Irish Revolt: 1916 and After* argued for 'a united labour movement joined to all that is virile in the national cause'. The pamphlets, honeyed words in the *Workers' Voice* for Labour, and calls for trade union unity, had no effect, though Labour was moving left, and in February adopted a radical constitution, committing it to a 'workers' republic'. Comintern analysts regarded the launch of the IRA's political party, Cumann Poblachta na hÉireann, in March as highly significant – partly because Moscow was awakening to the advantages for Russia of one of Cumann Poblachta's major policy objectives, keeping Ireland out of Britain's wars – and suggested extensive measures to assist the CPI and promote labour–republican unity. However Cumann Poblachta abjured alliances, and disappeared within a year.[83]

Beyond the far left, the preconditions of the popular front did not exist. Not only was the political climate not moving left in fear of fascism, it was in some respects moving right, and made more paranoid by popular frontism.

80 *Irish Workers' Voice*, 7–14 Dec. 1935; RGASPI, The national question and the policy of the CPI since the 7th congress CI, 26 May 1936, 495/14/337–168/171.

81 RGASPI, The national question and the policy of the CPI since the 7th congress CI, 26 May 1936, 495/14/337–168/171.

82 RGASPI, [CPI] against war and fascism since the 7th congress, 2 June 1936, 495/14/341–56/71.

83 RGASPI, letter from Pollitt, 12 Jan. 1936, 495/14/220; material on changes in the situation in Ireland and the position of the CPI, 26 Mar. 1936, 495/14/337–115/120.

Apprehensions about what the twentieth anniversary of the Easter Rising might encourage, and Labour's 'workers' republic' constitution, provided timely copy for Lenten pastorals denouncing socialism and radical republicanism. Catholic actionists were on the march again. The Catholic Young Men's Society attempted to disrupt Pollitt's meeting in January. On Easter Sunday it harried the Republican Congress and CPI sections in a parade to Glasnevin. An IRA cycle corps pedalling behind declined to intervene. Next evening some 5,000 gathered at College Green to prevent a CPI rally, at which Willie Gallacher was to speak. After the platform lorry failed to show up, and Peadar O'Donnell famously shinned up a lamp post in a foolhardy bid to address the people, the crowd wrecked the premises of the Republican Congress and tried to do the same to the CPI offices.[84] The suppression of the IRA followed in June, after outrage at two assassinations gave de Valera his chance to act with impunity. *An Phoblacht* closed in July, the third revolutionary paper to fold in six months. Though CPI and Republican Congress members had recently been assaulted by IRA men at Bodenstown, the CPI could take no comfort from the further contraction of anti-establishment forces. Special branch infiltration of the party had already resumed, and it too would be considered for proscription. In any case the 'spirit of illegality' had again taken a grip. The party had been on the defensive since January, and suspended public meetings after Easter. Murray and Jim Larkin Jr withdrew from the Dublin municipal elections in June. Frank Ryan and George Gilmore stood for the Republican Congress with mixed results, Gilmore gleaning a respectable, if inadequate, tally.[85]

Only in Belfast, where the CPI had some sympathisers on the trades' council and in the Socialist Party, which was also a ginger group within the NILP, was some degree of unity with labour realised. The NILP had rejected an offer to field joint 'people's candidates' in general elections, but collaboration at local level allowed Loftus Johnston and Tommy Geehan to contest the municipal and guardians elections in May and June on united front tickets. Johnston finished bottom of the poll in the Court ward with a disappointing 604 votes. Geehan's 1,351 votes in the Clifton ward delighted the party, though he was well adrift of the victorious Unionist.[86]

---

84 RGASPI, [CPI] against war and fascism since the 7th congress, 2 June 1936, 495/14/341–56/71; UCDA, MacEntee papers, Special branch report, 14 Apr. 1936, P67/526(10).

85 RGASPI, [CPI] against war and fascism since the 7th congress, 2 June 1936, 495/14/341–56/71; UCDA, MacEntee papers, Notes on communism in Saorstát Éireann, P67/523(5), pp. 3–5, 20; Cronin, *Frank Ryan*, p. 68.

86 *Irish Workers' Voice*, 16–23 May, 13 June 1936.

The closure of the Republican Congress's Co-op Press, which had printed the *Workers' Voice* since August 1935, completed another frustrating chapter in the history of the young CPI. Pollitt wired Moscow for £100 for a linotype machine, but the last issue of the *Voice* appeared on 13 June. An army losing its colours was scarcely more disgraced than a communist party losing its paper, and Pollitt regarded Murray's inertia in the face of a foreseeable disaster as characteristic. Since January he had told the Comintern repeatedly that the state of the CPI was due entirely to poor leadership, and had discussed the issue openly with comrades in Dublin. If external critics invariably underestimated the problems presented by the Catholic Church and the imperviousness of labour, there were genuine grounds for complaint. The central committee did not meet for over six months after the October 1935 conferences. An initiative to strengthen work within the trade unions had seen the publication of a *Trade Union Information Bulletin*, edited by Larkin Jr, and then fizzled out within weeks. Almost no agitational work was done in the provinces, and Belfast and Dublin continued to drift apart.[87] In July Max Raylock, who had represented the British Anti-War League at the Rathmines conference and was a member of Marty's secretariat, informed Moscow that the position was now critical as personal factors had compelled Devine to return to Britain. Raylock acknowledged that the problem was wider than one man, and he did not exculpate Devine. He also believed that the CPGB could not resolve it. Emphasising Ireland's importance to the anti-imperialist movement, he suggested that an Irish delegation be summoned to Moscow.[88] As Murray faced a bleak future, there was little to indicate that the CPI would soon find its most imperishable cause.

87 PROL, Government Code and Cypher School decrypts of Comintern messages, 1930–45, HW 17/22, London to Moscow, 26 June 1936; RGASPI, Report on situation in Ireland, July 1936, 495/14/337–1/8; UCDA, MacEntee papers, *Trade Union Information Bulletin*, no. 1, Nov. 1936, P67/526(1).
88 RGASPI, M. Raylock, Concerning the CPI, 29 July 1936, 495/14/341–98/101.

TEN

SPAIN, DECLINE AND DISSOLUTION, 1936–43

*It is perhaps considered easier by some to fight fascism in Spain, than work
in the exceptionally difficult conditions in the South of Ireland...*
Comintern memorandum on Ireland for André Marty[1]

—

Contact between Ireland and Moscow diminished after 1935. This was of
course envisaged by the changes in centre–periphery relations approved at the
seventh Comintern congress, but there were other factors which sharpened
the process. The Spanish Civil War preoccupied all communist organs, and
the arbiter of CPI affairs in Moscow, André Marty, was seconded to Spain as
first commissar of the International Brigades. Secondly, the commandatura at
either end of the Dublin–Moscow axis became increasingly inoperative. In
Dublin, leading comrades lapsed or retreated into semi-activity, central committee meetings were held less frequently, and more and more of the burden
of routine work fell on Seán Murray. The Comintern suffered more lethal
internal agonies. In August 1936 Grigori Zinoviev, Lev Kamenev and 14 other
'old Bolsheviks' were tried for subversive activities, allegedly under Trotsky's
direction, in a well-publicised show trial. When they pleaded guilty as charged,
it was clear that no one could be trusted, and no one was safe   from the great
terror which ensued. Within months Stalin decided that the Comintern was
a nest of Trotskyists and spies. Hundreds of functionaries were arrested – 113
ECCI workers in 1937–8 by one estimate – causing panic and demoralisation.
One misfortunate appealed to Stalin: 'many foreigners gather up their belong-
ings every evening in expectation of arrest. Many are half mad and incapable
of working as a result of constant fear.' The Comintern was too an instrument
of the terror as some 400–500 operatives were detailed to help the secret police
screen thousands of members of foreign parties in the Soviet Union. By 1938
the Comintern structures were barely discharging their traditional role.[2] The
thirteenth ECCI plenum in 1933 was the last plenum, the seventh congress the
last congress. Excluding permanent party representatives, the staff of the

1   RGASPI, Memorandum on Ireland, 22 May 1937, 495/89/102–5/9.
2   McDermott and Agnew, *The Comintern*, pp. 120–57.

Marty secretariat dwindled from nine in 1935 to three in 1938.[3] Marty made it plain in 1937 that he was happy for the CPGB to assume the burden of supporting and mentoring the CPI, and London's role in Irish affairs became increasingly pronounced. In 1941 its de facto authority would extend to the very existence of the party.

SPAIN

Seán Murray replaced the *Irish Workers' Voice* on 11 July with the *Worker*, a cyclostyled four-page weekly, edited and largely written by himself. Plans to have it printed were frustrated when the printer reneged on the contract and another could not be found at less than exorbitant prices.[4] One week later, General Franco instigated a revolt against the Madrid government. From 25 July the *Worker* would concentrate on the Spanish Civil War, as it was fought at home and abroad, and become the only anti-Franco paper in Ireland, though the liberal monthly *Ireland To-Day* was sceptical on Franco and the target of clerical censure. The Comintern said nothing on the war until October, but the communist position was clear enough. After the victory of the popular front in elections to the Cortes in February, the Comintern commended the Spanish communist party to forestall reaction by maximising unity against fascism and prioritising democracy before social revolution, a strategy that would be opposed by the anarchists and the Partido Obrero de Unificación Marxista (POUM). While the *Worker* made occasional references to the class basis of the Spanish antagonists, it followed the Spanish and other communist parties in depicting the war as one of democracy against fascism, the defence of bourgeois liberalism being seen as a logical extension of the popular front. As Spain became the measure of all things, the paper judged people by their stand on the war, and even by the terminology they used to describe the forces in conflict. Thus, the popular front charm offensive of the past year was modified to excoriate the 'cowardly' Labour Party and trade union leaders for their silence and, in some cases, open collusion with Francoists.[5] Conversely, any anti-Franco comment, whatever its provenance, was sure of a welcome. Considerable emphasis was placed on rebutting the Catholic view of the war as a crusade for religion, even to the point of alluding to Franco's use of 'heathen Moors'. Like communists everywhere, the *Worker* lionised Catholic critics of Franco. The Comintern had advised the Spanish party to

---

3   Huber, 'Structure of the Moscow apparatus of the Comintern and decision-making', p. 50.
4   *Worker*, 25 July 1936.
5   *Worker*, 26 Sept. 1936, 6 Feb. 1937.

make overtures to the Catholic masses, and it duly condemned 'the provo-
cative burning down of churches and monasteries, since such acts only go to
help counter-revolution'.[6]

Between July 1936 and the summer of 1937, there was no escaping the
Spanish question in Ireland. Inflamed by lurid accounts of anti-clerical atro-
cities, thousands thronged the rallies of the Irish Christian Front, formed
in August by Fine Gael TD Patrick Belton to help Franco and combat
communism. After doing its best to avoid the issue, the Labour Party published a remarkably evasive pamphlet by William Norton, *Cemeteries of Liberty:
Communist and Fascist Dictatorships*, with an introduction by William O'Brien,
general secretary of the ITGWU. Skirting both Spanish and Irish politics,
Norton treated fascism as Nazism, and equated Nazism with Stalinism.[7]
Labour, as Norton would have it, was anti-fascist but not anti-Franco, not
pro-Franco, but definitely anti-communist. Nonetheless, something of a
popular front atmosphere did emerge as Northern labour took an anti-Franco
stance – though dissent or silence were more likely in predominantly Catholic
trade union sectors – and a few writers, intellectuals, and elements of the
embryonic liberal bourgeoisie made common cause with the CPI, the
Republican Congress, the NILP and the Socialist Party who were the only
political forces defending the Spanish government. Irish Friends of the
Spanish Republic launched a fund for medical aid, and Hanna Sheehy
Skeffington convened a Women's Aid Committee which helped Basque
victims of aerial bombing, and later assisted veterans of the International
Brigades.[8] The Earl of Antrim chaired a committee set up by the Socialist
Party to raise funds for an ambulance unit.[9] Branches of the London-based
Left Book Club were formed in Dublin and Belfast, together with study
groups to discuss its monthly offerings. The club was itself a product of the
popular front climate in Britain and the books offered by the club were chosen
by 'fellow travellers'. Both Irish branches also created drama companies, the
New Theatre Group in Dublin and the Theatre Guild in Belfast, and were
instrumental in founding a literary and debating circle in Dublin, the Unity
Club, and the Progressive Publications Society in Belfast.[10] In a similar spirit,

6   E. H. Carr, *The Comintern and the Spanish Civil War* (London, 1984), p. 7; for a critique of the
Worker and Spain see Jackson, 'A rather one sided fight', pp. 79–87.

7   Vincent Geoghegan, 'Cemeteries of liberty: William Norton on communism and fascism',
Saothar 18 (1993), pp. 106–9.

8   Andrée Sheehy Skeffington, *Skeff: A Life of Owen Sheehy Skeffington, 1909–1970* (Dublin, 1991),
pp. 78–85; Ward, *Hanna Sheehy Skeffington*, pp. 321–2.

9   Macgougan, 'Letting Labour lead', p. 114; PRONI, Spanish Medical Aid Relief Committee, 1936,
HA/32/1/558.

10   Klaus, *Strong Words, Brave Deeds*, pp. 28–9; *Irish Democrat*, 18 Dec. 1937.

Leslie Daiken, editor of *Irish Front*, the monthly paper of the London Republican Congress, published *Good-Bye, Twilight*, a collection of 75 poems and ballads by 40 Irish writers, workers, journalists and intellectuals, all 'showing unmistakably out of the experience of the proletariat, that revolutionary poets, playwrights, and novelists are developing an art which reveals more forces in the world than the love of the lecher and the pride of the Narcissist'.[11]

On 27 March 1937 the Progressive Publications Society launched the *Irish Democrat*, with the backing of divers persons, the Republican Congress, the CPI and the Socialist Party, which supplied one third of the seed capital. Other contributions are unknown, but the CPGB provided a grant of £280. Frank Ryan, just back from Spain on convalescence, served as editor until his return to the front in June and printed the paper on the machinery of the old Co-op Press. Murray succeeded him as editor.[12] The eight-page *Democrat* was a big improvement on the *Worker*, with a much wider range of writers and features, but it maintained the *Worker*'s strong focus on Spain, its interpretation of the war, and its use of religion to counter pro-Franco propaganda. The final issue of the *Worker* appeared on 13 March. Murray's promise that it would continue as a monthly was not realised. He found a limited outlet for CPI comment in *Inprecorr*.

In September 1936, the CPI decided to contribute an Irish unit to the International Brigades. One CPI member, Bill Scott, was already with the mainly German Thälmann battalion, XII International Brigade. Bill Gannon, an IRA veteran, was appointed to organise the Irish effort.[13] Soon afterwards the communist investment in republicanism reaped a handsome dividend. In this case the stimulus was more domestic. In August the Carlist Count de Ramirez de Arellano had written to Cardinal MacRory, requesting Irish aid for Spain. The cardinal referred him to Eoin O'Duffy, who offered to enlist an 'Irish brigade' with the help of his latest political group, the National Corporate Party. As the project took shape, the *Irish Independent* claimed that 5,000–6,000 had offered to volunteer. Ultimately about 650 joined O'Duffy in Spain in December. Left-wing republicans felt challenged to respond, the more so as MacRory had publicly described a Republican Congress telegram of solidarity to the Spanish government as 'a scandal' and urged de Valera to suppress the Congress. Their preferred allies were the Basques, a people

11 Leslie H. Daiken (comp), *Good-Bye, Twilight: Songs of the Struggle in Ireland* (London, 1936), xviii.
12 Sheehy Skeffington, *Skeff*, pp. 84–5; Cronin, *Frank Ryan*, p. 104; Macgougan, 'Letting Labour lead', pp. 114, 122; PROL, KV2/1185, Seán Murray (PF 399.199).
13 O'Riordan, *Connolly Column*, pp. 49, 55.

fighting Franco for national independence, with the blessing of their clergy. George Gilmore visited Euskadi to invite Father Ramon LaBorda to speak in Ireland, and on 5 November Ernie O'Malley chaired a meeting of solidarity with the Basques. However, as the Basques needed arms rather than men, republican interest turned to Gannon's recruitment for the International Brigades.[14] On 11 December about 40 volunteers under the command of Frank Ryan steamed out of Westland Row for London, Paris and Spain. One week later a similar number left via Belfast and Rosslare.[15] Over the course of the war the International Brigades received another 50 or so from Ireland – at least 16 in 1937 and eight in 1938 – together with around 100 Irish-born exiles. A further two Irishmen engaged with the anarchist militia, and five joined British medical units in Spain.

Of the approximately 130 International Brigaders who enlisted in Ireland, 34 can be identified as communists and 14 as non-communist republicans. Twenty-five had been in the IRA. The republican contribution was almost certainly higher than these figures suggest, and accounted for the bulk of the initial wave. It is unlikely that more than 10 of the 80 who went out in December 1936 were communists: the Dublin CPI having 12 – out of 75 – members in Spain in February 1937. Subsequently the CPI would provide the plurality of volunteers from Ireland. At least 10 of those who enlisted outside Ireland were members of the London Republican Congress.

Possibly twice as many wanted to go. Socialist Party secretary Jack Macgougan recalled an interest in his party but 'the CP had a monopoly of entry into the International Brigade'. The party identified with the POUM rather than the International Brigades, and selected two of its officials to join the Scotch ambulance unit for which it had raised funds.[16] Uneasy about casualties, Republican Congress leaders sought just enough men to register a credible counterpoint to O'Duffy. Peadar O'Donnell's claim that hundreds had offered to fight but 'he selected only 145' was echoed by Frank Ryan.[17] In Spain, Ryan tried to have repatriated those he deemed to have done a reasonable tour

14   Cronin, *Frank Ryan*, p. 82.

15   Estimates of Irish volunteers in Spain are based on O'Riordan, *Connolly Column*, pp. 162–5; McGarry, *Irish Politics and the Spanish Civil War*, pp. 45–7, 245–8; Cronin, *Frank Ryan*, pp. 78–9; *http://members.lycos.co.uj/spanishcivilwar/*, edited by Kieran Crossey; Marx Memorial Library, London, International Brigade Memorial Archive, boxes 21, 21a, 28, 50, A–12, C, C/2/2, D–7; RGASPI, International Brigades in the Spanish Republican Army, 1936–9, 545/6–, and contemporary newspapers.

16   Macgougan, 'Letting Labour lead', p. 122; PRONI, Spanish Medical Aid Relief Committee, 1936, HA/32/1/558.

17   McInerney, *Peadar O'Donnell*, p. 179; McGarry, *Irish Politics and the Spanish Civil War*, p. 58

of duty. There is also some evidence that the CPI was more selective than communist parties were expected to be. Eoghan Ó Duinnín worried about being turned down by Murray in March 1938. In the event he received a perfunctory examination, related in Ó Duinnín's characteristically comic style:

> Sháigh sé píosa páipéir os comhair mo shúl.
> 'An féidir leat é sin a léamh?'
> 'Go héasca', arsa mise.
> 'Tá tú tofa mar sin. Tá an radharc go maith agat'.
> Ba mhór an faoiseamh dom gur éirigh liom sa dianscrúdú dochtúra seo . . .[18]

Murray rejected the 21-year-old Bob Doyle because of his youth, though Doyle was later approved by the CPGB. And when four New Theatre Group players made a pact to enlist, Murray persuaded two that they would be more useful at home.[19] Spain was a priority issue at the CPI's Dublin district annual general meeting in February 1937, with comrades urged to redouble their efforts in leafleting, postering, raising awareness in trade unions, and collecting funds for the Irish troops. Nothing was said about enlistment, and no one has ever suggested that they were harangued into volunteering by the CPI.[20]

Spain obviously placed a massive strain on CPI resources. But it is doubtful if the party's sinking fortunes can be attributed to the loss of manpower to the International Brigades. Mobilising solidarity with Spain was one of the CPI's few achievements and Ó Duinnín reckoned it brought many despairing comrades back 'from the dead': 'd'éirigh a lán daoine "ó mhairbh" a bhí tar éis éirí tuirseach de mhoilleadóireacht na staire'. Francis Mooney, chairman of the Dublin CPI, said much the same to André Marty, in English of course.[21] Possibly a few joined the CPI just to get to Spain, and the scattering of comrades outside Dublin and Belfast could make no other contribution to the cause. Even in Dublin there was little else to do other than bite on granite. In February 1937 the Dublin section was minuting the failure of its latest campaign to penetrate the trade unions, together with difficulties in organising

18 Translation:
> He shoved a piece of paper in front of my eyes.
> 'Can you read that?'
> 'Easily'. I said.
> 'You're elected so. Your eyesight is good.'
> I was much relieved that I had passed this tough medical examination . . .
> Ó Duinnín, *La Niña Bonita Agus An Róisín Dubh*, p. 11.
19 Klaus, *Strong Words, Brave Deeds*, pp. 19–20; McGarry, *Irish Politics and the Spanish Civil War*, p. 54.
20 RGASPI, Dublin annual general meeting, 27 Feb. 1937, 495/14/339–5/17.
21 Ó Duinnín, *La Niña Bonita Agus An Róisín Dubh*, p. 12.

the unemployed.[22] One negative consequence was the WUI executive's decision to bar officials from speaking on any but a union platform. Larkin Sr may have feared a clerical attack, or seen his chance to extirpate communism from his union, but Jack Carney believed the motive was to force his resignation to reduce the wage bill of the cash strapped WUI. Carney felt passionately about Spain, and it was not unknown for Big Jim to weasel his way round awkward personal decisions. After serving his hero loyally for a quarter of a century, Carney packed his bags for England and journalism. Young Jim ceased to attend party meetings.[23] While he had never fulfilled the promise he had shown in the Lenin School, the loss of his name was a blow to the CPI.

FROM THE POPULAR FRONT TO THE SPANISH DEFENCE

When Francis Mooney arrived in Moscow for May Day with a message for Marty, the Comintern took the opportunity to reassess the popular front formula in Ireland. O'Duffy's brigade had recently withdrawn from the war, pending repatriation, and Moscow was concerned about the consequences. An International Brigades news bulletin attributed O'Duffy's 'desertion' to the inability to 'find fresh troops to fill the gaps caused by the war', evidently unaware that his bandera had suffered more demoralisation than casualties and would be received at home with embarrassment.[24] Despite the ancient and loose usage of the term 'Irish brigade', many assumed O'Duffy's troops to be of brigade strength; even the *Irish Democrat* of 24 April was surprised to learn from the London *Times* that it was actually a battalion of some 640 men. Moscow thought the brigade numbered 2,000, and was impressed that £32,000 had been collected 'from the poverty-stricken people [of Ireland] to help the Spanish fascists'. In fact the Irish hierarchy had raised over £43,000, ostensibly for Spanish Catholics.[25] Augmented by O'Duffy's 'fascist bravos', Comintern analysts expected the Christian Front to mount a serious challenge to de Valera at the next general election and strengthen 'developments toward fascism in Ireland'. As the CPI was ill-equipped to meet the threat, it was argued that the ECCI should apply to the CPI its broad front prescriptions

22   RGASPI, Dublin annual general meeting, 27 Feb. 1937, 495/14/339–5/17.

23   O'Connor, *James Larkin*, p. 100.

24   Marx Memorial Library, London, International Brigade Memorial Archive, box 22, news bulletins and papers of the British battalion, file A: news bulletins of the International Brigades, News Bulletins of the International Brigades, I, Apr. to Dec. 1937, no. 120, 30 Apr. 1937: 'Ireland: the fascists desert their party'.

25   McGarry, *Irish Politics and the Spanish Civil War*, p. 161.

for the Spanish communist party. A paper entitled 'The Irish Free State in relation to the international situation', proposed that the CPI invite into membership 'proved types' such as Owen Sheehy Skeffington, Roddy Connolly and Peadar O'Donnell, and offer 'assistance and advice' to enable Hanna Sheehy Skeffington 'with her immediate circle of associates' to be enrolled. A new popular front should extend its embrace beyond the rank and file of Fianna Fáil, and to this end 'a small group of influential Fianna Fáil people' should be invited to Russia, and cultural and trade relations opened with Ireland.[26] A memo to Marty concluded: 'The main question in our attitude to the elections must be to do everything possible to prevent the victory of the Cosgraveites and Christian Front clerical reaction and fascism, which is the most pressing danger.'[27]

On 23 May Mooney met Marty, Max Raylock, and 'Mehring', pseudonym of R. A. Mirring, an ECCI emissary to the CPGB in 1934 and now the Estonian party's representative to the Comintern.[28] He gave a gloomy review of home affairs. Marty thought the Irish question too complicated for immediate decisions, and suggested Mooney meet Harry Pollitt to arrange the appointment of a commission to prepare for the general election and O'Duffy's return. An Irish delegation should visit Moscow in August for a more substantial discussion. Mooney did not leave completely unarmed. Marty offered the following fortification:

> It is advisable for the Irish party comrades to systematically study Lenin and Stalin, but not, of course all their works. They should study, to begin with, Lenin's 'Left Wing Communism', and Stalin's speech to the Red Army graduates of the Military Academy on *Cadres*. These two things will be sufficient for the time being.[29]

The CPI's election manifesto duly called, not for the replacement of Fianna Fáil, but for 'a vigorous working class and republican opposition' to make Fianna Fáil 'fight'. The party nominated Bill Scott for South Dublin – Big Jim Larkin was standing as an Independent Labour candidate in the more propitious North East Dublin, and it was policy to encourage Larkin to come back into the official labour movement. In addition to serving in Spain, Scott was a bricklayer, and 15,000 building workers had been on strike since 13 April. The CPI achieved no influence over the strike itself, though Frank Mooney was prominent in the amalgamated painters' union, and the *Irish Democrat*

26   RGASPI, Proposals in connection with the CPI, 8 May 1937, 495/89/102–1/4.

27   RGASPI, Memorandum on Ireland, 22 May 1937, 495/89/102–5/9.

28   Thorpe, *The British Communist Party and Moscow*, p. 216.

29   RGASPI, Meeting on the Irish question, 23 May 1937, 495/14/339–27/38.

regularly covered the dispute.[30] Scott soon withdrew in favour of Frank Ryan, who stood as a 'United front against fascism' candidate. On 1 July Ryan polled 875 votes. He had not wished to contest, and was already back in Albacete on 14 June. Fianna Fáil lost eight seats in the election and returned to office with backbench support from the Labour Party. With Fine Gael in mind, the CPI described result as 'a victory for the electorate over reaction'. Polling day saw too the ratification of Bunreacht na hÉireann, of which the CPI was more critical. Radicals of various hues objected to its provisions on private property rights and the role of women, and were disappointed with the failure to declare a republic. Murray went further in *Inprecorr*:

> De Valera and the Catholic Hierarchy are evidently determined to prove to the Northern masses that union with their fellow-countrymen of the South does mean that they wll be placed under the heel of the Vatican. The Protestant masses will never accept this and rightfully so.[31]

The coalition behind the *Irish Democrat* did not survive 1937. Arguably the surprise was that it lasted so long. Disputes on the editorial board were usual, and not confined to Irish politics. The CPI shared the generic communist aversion to Trotskyists: in its only reference to events in Russia, the *Worker* had applauded the trial of 'Trotsky terrorists' in Moscow, and later denounced Trotsky in person.[32] Neither the Socialist Party or the POUM could accurately be described as Trotskyist, but both were seen as such in Dublin and Moscow, and each had their differences with the communists. Certainly, Victor Halley, who, with Jack Macgougan, represented the Socialist Party on the *Irish Democrat* editorial board disliked the communist parties, and as a Shankill Road republican he was not shy of controversy.[33] When fighting erupted in Barcelona on 3–7 May between the POUM, anarchists and anarcho-syndicalists on the one side and the Catalan government and communists on the other, the *Irish Democrat*'s denunciation of the POUM as wreckers and fascists 'in the rear' provoked objections from the Socialist Party.[34] More troublesome were the CPI and Republican Congress efforts to apply an anti-imperialist line. As Mooney had told Marty, relations with the IRA had improved, and the new chief of staff, Tom Barry, was 'very sympathetic and

---

30 *Irish Democrat*, 31 July 1937.

31 Milotte, *Communism in Modern Ireland*, pp. 175–6.

32 *Worker*, 30 Jan., 6 Feb. 1937.

33 RGASPI, J. R. Campbell, The situation in Ireland, 27 Feb. 1939, 495/14/340–10/59; I am obliged to Andrew Boyd for details on Halley.

34 *Irish Democrat*, 8, 22 May 1937; McGarry, *Irish Politics and the Spanish Civil War*, p. 104; CPI, *Communist Party of Ireland*, p. 28.

helpful'.[35] Barry had banned volunteers from going to Spain, but ended the IRA's proscription on CPI membership, and was friendly towards Ryan during his recuperation in Ireland. Ryan printed the six issues of *An Phoblacht* which appeared in the summer of 1937 and penned a few anonymous articles for his old paper. Both Ryan and the CPI complained of having to exclude IRA targeted material from the *Irish Democrat* to accommodate the Socialist Party, whose membership was at once largely Protestant, anti-partition, and averse to the IRA.[36] Struggling with the departure of Ryan, its narrow base, and a significant slackening of popular interest in Spain, the paper pressed on until December. Murray blamed its collapse on mounting debts and 'the growing estrangement' of the Socialist Party: linked factors as the party was relatively rich with a war chest of almost £1,500, ironically the balance of compensation for the burning of its hall on the Crumlin Road by loyalists in the early 1920s. According to Murray the Socialists' 'main objection is that the paper leans too much to Republicanism and they want it to cater for the Protestant workers exclusively', a pejorative view somewhat corroborated by Macgougan who subsequently 'drifted out' of the party because it had 'become hopelessly sectarian'.[37]

Murray advised Moscow of hopeful developments in January 1938, promising new branches and a second CPI congress in May – none having been held since the foundation of the party. In May he published another paper, the *Workers' Republic*, 'a monthly journal of left-wing opinion'. No one was reassured. On 18 May, with Murray and Seán Nolan in attendance, the CPGB's political bureau noted the Irish situation as 'exceptionally serious'. The bureau requested its leading theoretician, Rajani Palme Dutt, to make a personal inspection, and his findings were considered at the CPGB's central committee on 1–2 July. The crux of the discussion hinged around the CPI's attitude to Fianna Fáil, and the Anglo-Irish agreements of April 1938 in particular. The agreements had ended the economic war, settled the land annuities question, and repatriated the treaty ports. In return, de Valera promised that he would not permit Éire to be used as a base of attack against Britain. Murray had denounced the settlement in *Inprecorr* for ignoring partition and tying Ireland to Neville Chamberlain's policy of appeasement.[38] Dutt agreed, saying that it

35   RGASPI, Meeting on the Irish question, 23 May 1937, 495/14/339–27/38.

36   Cronin, *Frank Ryan*, pp. 105–6, 113; RGASPI, Meeting on the Irish question, 23 May 1937, 495/14/339–27/38; see letter from Victor Halley, Socialist Party, dissociating the *Irish Democrat* from the IRA, *Irish Democrat*, 12 June 1937.

37   Macgougan, 'Letting Labour lead', 14, pp. 114, 112; RGASPI, letter from Murray, 14 Jan. 1938, 495/14/340–1/2.

38   *Workers' Republic*, May 1938.

marked the culmination of de Valera's progressive role, and proposing that the CPI publish a pamphlet rejecting the Fianna Fáil claim that 'the Irish are now masters in their own house'. A mass popular front, he argued, could be developed against the de Valera government, through working with the Labour Party and trade unions, focusing on the national question, and countering Catholic opposition. The central committee roundly criticised his proposals. Describing the position in Ireland as 'absolutely catastrophic', Pollitt regretted that the CPI could not be liquidated. Willie Gallacher too, he claimed, favoured liquidation. Murray pleaded for the party's survival, and with his assent, the committee resolved to bring the Irish question before the Comintern, and recommend the CPI in Éire to concentrate its work on Dublin, make a major effort to work with the Labour Party and the unions, and engage sympathetically with opposition from Catholic workers.[39]

Dutt's theses were subjected to a lengthy rejoinder from the CPGB representative to the ECCI, J. R. Campbell. Probably drafted for a Comintern investigation of the CPI, Campbell's brief indicated the degree to which London and Moscow now evaluated the party for its influence on international relations. It also reflected the debate within the CPGB on the popular front, on which Dutt was on the left and uncomfortable with extending the front beyond the left, and Campbell on the right, and for the broadest unity. For Campbell, the CPI's major error had been opposition to Fianna Fáil, a 'progressive, national reformist party of the small capitalists, farmers, and workers' which had resisted pressure to recognise the Franco regime, and steadily eliminated British power over Éire, despite repeated CPI predictions to the contrary. In consequence, the constituent elements of the CPI's popular front – the IRA, left republicans, and the Labour Party – had been marginalised, leaving the Irish party 'an isolated and dwindling sect'. With a sideswipe at the CPGB, Campbell went on:

> As a consequence of the policy of our Party we have not yet seriously raised in Ireland the question of the external Fascist menace to the new won rights of the people of Southern Ireland and the role of Eire (Ireland) as an independent state at the league of nations, and in the Conferenes of the British Dominions . . .
>
> The decline of the Communist Party of Ireland is primarily due to the fact that neither in the theory or practice of that Party, nor in the occasional advice given to it by the Communist Party of Great Britain, is there any sign of an attempt to apply the policy of the 7th World Congress to Ireland . . .

39 RGASPI, Zusammenfassung der Debatte zu dieser Frage auf der ZK-Sitzung der KP Englands am 1 und 2 Juli 1938, 495/20/252–36/49.

The de Valera government has now reached a stage when it will be more difficult to make any advance against the internal forces of reaction. It will be subjected to increasing pressure from the Church, from the Cosgrave party, from the reactionary wing of the capitalist class.

The way forward to forward to a broad front of all the democratic forces in Ireland is for our party to rally all the democratic forces to push the de Valera government to the left . . .[40]

The CPI fell in step in January, announcing its broad support for the Anglo-Irish agreements of 1938 and for Fianna Fáil.[41]

Elaborating on the points above in a review for the Comintern in February 1939, Campbell tackled the leadership issue:

Comrade Murray's devotion to the Party is unquestioned and the difficulties with which he has been faced have not been light ones, but it must be frankly stated that he has shown neither political leadership nor organising ability. There is a lack of confidence in Comrade Murray in Belfast, and in Dublin when the question of his leadership was sharply criticised by a Comrade called Walters [Watters?], there was either no defence, or a half-hearted defence of him by the other comrades.

Campbell favoured the replacing Murray with W. H. McCullough, 'the leading comrade' in Belfast, though he accepted that a Belfastman who 'tends to underestimate the significance of the national question' was not an ideal choice, and 'more important' he thought, McCullough's transfer to Dublin would weaken the CPGB's influence in the National Union of Railwaymen, in which McCullough was secretary of the Belfast number one branch. Campbell recommended that steps be taken to apply the new popular front policy in Ireland, that the CPGB send an instructor to Dublin for a year, that a search be undertaken for a new general secretary, and that if the Irish comrades favoured an investigation to remove Murray, 'it is better that the meeting should take place in Moscow'.[42]

Murray survived for the moment, in diminished circumstances. He was dropped from the Comintern's payroll, on which he had held the nominal post of Irish correspondent of the CPUSA's *Daily Worker*, and ceased to be a full-time party worker.[43] When the *Workers' Republic* folded in August he was

40 RGASPI, The situation in Ireland and the crisis in the Communist Party, 2 Aug. 1938, 495/20/252–22/35; Fragen für die Untersuchung in Irland, 9 Aug. 1939, 495/14/340–3/5.

41 Milotte, *Communism in Modern Ireland*, pp. 177–8.

42 RGASPI, J. R. Campbell, The situation in Ireland, 27 Feb. 1939, 495/14/340–10/59.

43 I am obliged to Andrew Boyd for details on Murray; CPI, *Communist Party of Ireland*, p. 31.

unable to generate enough support to have it replaced with a weekly. Instead, Dublin readers of the British *Daily Worker* formed the Workers' Press League to publish the *Workers' Bulletin*, a duplicated weekly newssheet issued from October 1938 after the CPGB organ was banned in Ireland.[44] Murray had one consolation in the new year. The CPUSA in New York's fifth district requested permission to name its branch after him, 'to express our admiration for your brilliant and courageous leadership'.[45]

NEITHER CHURCHILL NOR HITLER

The Second World War disrupted communications between Ireland and Russia. The archives hold no Comintern position papers on Ireland after 1939. In December 1940 the Comintern noted that its only knowledge of the CPI came from occasional articles by Murray in the New York *Sunday Worker*, statements in *Rundschau über Politik, Wirtschaft & Arbeiterbewegung* and *World News and Views*, both successors to *Inprecorr*, and a telegram from the British *Daily Worker* in June 1940.[46] In a period of repeated modification of the ECCI line, when policy acquired the utmost importance and required cut-glass precision, the CPI became completely reliant for guidance on the CPGB, which continued to receive ECCI instructions by cable or by hand. For the first time, the CPI was truly reduced to an abject mouthpiece of Moscow, and indeed of London. The CPGB had its own reasons for interest in Ireland after September 1939, when partition and neutrality were assets in representing Britain's war aims as imperialist. The CPI's defence of Russia would lead it into repeated u-turns, and create particular difficulties in Belfast. Yet it probably benefited from the fact that, in the Irish context, it was uniquely driven by international events at a time of fascination with the awesome spectacle of Europe at war.

The Dublin branch effected a minor recovery between 1939 and 1941. A relaxation of the anti-communist climate enabled it to resume regular meetings at Mansfield's corner on Abbey Street. Though it abandoned efforts to regain a foothold in the trade union movement, the diminution of working-class membership was partly offset by the recruitment of a few middle-class enthusiasts, a latent consequence of the popular front. In April 1939 the CPI began publication of the four-page *Irish Workers' Weekly*. Once again, Seán Murray was editor. From the second issue it incorporated the *Workers' Bulletin* and it

---

44 *Irish Workers' Weekly*, 21 Dec. 1940.

45 PRONI, Seán Murray papers, CPUSA, New York to Murray, 23 Jan. 1939, D2/62/M/4.

46 RGASPI, Notiz über Irland, 11 Dec. 1940, 495/14/340–6/9.

was later placed under the control of the Workers' Press League, which was open to all readers and aimed to make the *Workers' Weekly* a broad working class organ.[47] The content monitored labour and social unrest with little reference to the CPI. It may have been more than a coincidence that Palme Dutt and Harry Pollitt had adopted a similar approach in 1923 when the CPGB replaced the *Communist* with the similarly titled *Workers' Weekly*.[48]

There was no mistaking the communist provenance of the *Irish Workers' Weekly* in its ardently pro-Soviet coverage of foreign affairs. Initially it urged labour to oppose neutrality against fascism and called for pressure on Britain to speed up its sluggish moves towards an Anglo–French–Soviet pact.[49] 'Nazis can never be our allies', declared the *Workers' Weekly* on 5 August, quoting one of Murray's speeches. On 26 August it welcomed the Molotov–Ribbentrop pact with the headline, 'Soviet Union's policy strengthens peace'. Like kindred parties the CPI was totally unprepared for Stalin's bombshell, and the editorial lamely explained that the pact was not an alliance, simply a non-aggression agreement, and amounted to a defeat for the Axis anti-Comintern pact and Chamberlain's appeasement. On the outbreak of war on 3 September, the CPI, like the CPGB, amended the line to depict the British and French governments as imperialist, while supporting the war itself. The *Workers' Weekly* condemned the Labour Party's silence on the war, saying that if Éire's neutrality made sense, 'the Irish working class cannot be "neutral" on the issues of Fascism versus democracy'.[50] On 16 September it printed a CPI manifesto calling for a people's war against Nazism, adorned with caricatures of a menacing Hitler, a raving Goebbels, and a jolly, transvestite Goering. Unknown to its affiliates, and without consulting their representatives in Moscow, the Comintern secretariat had already bowed to an intervention by Stalin, and adopted a 'short thesis' on 10 September which rejected any distinction between bourgeois democracies and fascist regimes and characterised the war as imperialist. The CPGB adopted the thesis on 3 October, and it was first reflected in the *Workers' Weekly* on 16 October.[51] The CPI's official history makes no reference to the effect of the revised line on Dublin, but, in its only admission of internal party disputes, it says of Belfast: 'As might be expected, there was some confusion among Party members in the North and it took much discussion to convince some members of the correctness of the party's political position.'[52]

47 *Irish Workers' Weekly*, 17 June 1939.

48 Harry Pollitt, *Serving My Time: An Apprenticeship to Politics* (London, 1940), pp. 164–5.

49 *Irish Workers' Weekly*, 22 Apr., 19 Aug. 1939.

50 *Irish Workers' Weekly*, 9 Sept. 1939.

51 Thorpe, *The British Communist Party and Moscow*, pp. 56–60.

52 CPI, *Communist Party of Ireland*, p. 38.

Over the coming months, military developments ratcheted the Comintern's position round the dial to the point where communists were more hostile to the imperialists – the Anglo-French – than the Nazis. After the Red Army's occupation of eastern Poland and the German–Soviet boundary and friendship treaty on 28 September, the Comintern emphasised that the Anglo-French were now the aggressors for refusing to accept Hitler's peace proposals.[53] The Winter War, when the Red Army invaded Finland and Britain and France supplied munitions to Finns and toyed with the idea of military action against Russia, reinforced the process. By 1940 communist parties throughout Europe had gone virtually silent on fascism and were affirming their opposition to Anglo-French war aims. The *Workers' Weekly* echoed each click of the dial. Not even the supreme sacrifice of fallen comrades in Spain was immune from the revision: they were now deemed to have fought against 'Fascist and imperialistic intervention'. In May the *Weekly* deplored de Valera's condemnation of Germany's violation of neutral Belgium, the Netherlands, and Luxembourg as too pro-Allied, adding 'there is no such thing as right or justice in the war waged by the Anglo-French empires against Germany. And vice versa.' On 29 May the CPI adopted the slogan: 'We serve neither Churchill nor Hitler, but Ireland.'[54] It is true that the fall of France exposed a raw nerve as the *Workers' Weekly* blamed 'Munichites' and the 'fascist fifth column' for the 'betrayal' of France. Yet this was also the reflex of the CPGB and the Comintern. Shocked by the French collapse the ECCI persuaded Stalin to allow it issue a declaration on behalf of the French party on 19 June, pledging that 'We, French communists . . . will fight decisively and fiercely against the enslavement of our nation by foreign imperialists.'[55] The statement was published in the *Workers' Weekly* on 29 June. That the *Workers' Weekly* was more than usually critical of fascists over the coming weeks suggests that communists were taking advantage of some slack in the line and not viscerally indifferent as to Churchill or Hitler. But the old war policy was soon restored.

Neutrality and the national question were the key issues for the CPI. Their importance had been underscored by the Soviet daily *Izvestia*.

Though the British Dominions still form part of the British Empire, their peoples are forcefully expressing their opposition to dying for the Bank of England and its war in Europe . . . the refusal of Éire to enter the war and its declaration of neutrality undoubtedly was a defeat for Britain . . . the Irish republicans, united in the

53   McDermott and Agnew, *The Comintern*, p. 200.
54   *Irish Workers' Weekly*, 14 Oct. 1939, 18 May to 1 June 1940.
55   Mcdermott and Agnew, *The Comintern*, p. 201.

Irish Republican Army consider that 'England's difficulties are Ireland's opportunities' for liberation, and in contrast to de Valera demand a determined struggle against England for the immediate unification of Northern Ireland with Éire.[56]

Before 'that pact', as the *Irish Workers' Weekly* occasionally referred to the Molotov–Ribbentrop agreement, implicitly acknowledging its notoriety, the CPI had championed anti-partitionism as a way of pushing southern labour into communion with the more strident anti-fascism of Northern labour. Subsequently it called for a united Ireland as a means of drawing the North out of the war. The CPGB and the Connolly Association, which had evolved out of the London Republican Congress, promoted a 'Hands off Ireland campaign' in opposition to British demands for naval bases in Éire, and Willie Gallacher's pamphlet *Ireland: Can it Remain Neutral?* appeared in 1941. The CPGB also helped to have a collection of James Connolly's writings on the First World War, *A Socialist and War*, published by Lawrence & Wishart. The logical end of this line of thinking was a communist–republican alliance to make another Easter rising. The *Workers' Weekly* certainly suggested that England's difficulty should be Ireland's opportunity. De Valera's 'truce' with Britain on partition was denounced, and some contact developed with the IRA. The authorities replied with occasional seizures of the paper and other publications, the internment of about half a dozen communists, mainly veterans of the Spanish civil war, between 1940 and 1943, and the detention of CPI activists over the weekend of an all-party rally for national defence in June 1940.[57] Yet fundamentally, the CPI was not convinced of the parallels with 1914–16. Murray rebuked the IRA for a statement in August 1940 describing the Third Reich as 'the guardian' of national freedom and saying that if German troops landed in Ireland they would be welcomed as 'friends and liberators'.[58]

In the spring of 1941 the survival of the Dublin CPI seemed assured, and a new leadership was finally appointed. It is likely that Murray had already been replaced as editor of the *Workers' Weekly* by Seán Nolan. Though still much used as a lecturer and speaker at street meetings, he was not mentioned in a history of party newspapers in the *Weekly* in 1940, and on 8 March 1941 the *Weekly* announced baldly that the party's general secretary was Tommy Watters, a compositor from Belfast's Falls Road, currently based in Dublin. There was no acknowledgement of Watters's long-suffering predecessor. If membership remained stubbornly small, the future looked promising. On the one hand,

56 Reprinted in the *Irish Workers' Weekly*, 6 Apr. 1940.
57 CPI, *Communist Party of Ireland*, p. 30.
58 *Irish Workers' Weekly*, 10 Aug. 1940.

the CPI's policy of neutrality and anti-partitionism chimed with public sentiment. On the other, workers were chafing under the burden of wartime social inequality, outraged in particular by the lack of price control, and mobilising against the Wages Standstill Order – which introduced an absolute wage freeze on 7 May 1941 – and the attempt to rationalise trade unions under what would become the Trade Union Act (1941). Meanwhile, the concentration of resources on public meetings and the paper appeared to be an effective economy of force. The *Workers' Weekly* regularly reported improvements in sales – an extra 1,400 copies were claimed on 31 August 1940 – and repeatedly promised an increase in its size. The paper acquired an added value from suppression of the communist press in Britain in January 1941, after which it published CPGB statements on occasion. Above all, communists believed they had a vital role in explaining Stalin's war aims – 'that pact' and the invasions of Poland and Finland having been followed by the Soviet annexations of Bessarabia, Estonia, Latvia and Lithuania – and in keeping Ireland neutral.

The position in the six counties was more ambivalent. A CPI manifesto on 25 November 1939 had demanded Northern Ireland's withdrawal from the war, and in December the Belfast branch launched a campaign to that effect.[59] It also supported the protests for the reprieve of IRA volunteers Peter Barnes and James McCormack, executed in February 1940 for a bombing in Coventry in which neither had been directly involved. While the issue was not controversial in Éire, where the executions were widely deplored, the Belfast campaign led to clashes with the RUC. Stormont suppressed the *Irish Workers' Weekly* in April after it appeared with a facsimile reproduction of the proclamation of Easter week. Its replacement, a Northern paper entitled *Red Hand*, was banned in August for printing an IRA statement. Val Morahan had already been imprisoned for opposition to the war, and Bill McCullough and Betty Sinclair were now gaoled for causing 'disaffection'.[60] The Belfast communists hacked on, campaigning against the extension of conscription to Northern Ireland, and supporting the growing number of strikes, which were illegal under wartime regulations. In the summer of 1941 the branch came under pressure from the CPGB to dissolve. There was considerable resistance as the branch had attracted an appreciable number of intellectuals, notably from the Jewish community; unlike Dublin it had some roots in the trade unions, and it was generally regarded as being of a higher calibre than its southern counterpart. Andrew Boyd remembered it as 'excellent on tactics and propaganda, and well versed in Marxist theory'.[61] The basic problem, for

59 *Irish Workers' Weekly*, 11, 23 Nov., 3 Dec. 1939, 6 Jan. 1940.
60 *Irish Workers' Weekly*, 24 Mar. to 13 Apr., 5–26 Oct., 9 Nov. 1940.
61 I am obliged to Andrew Boyd for his recollections of the Belfast branch in 1940–1.

either London or Moscow, was its stance on the war. All changed on 22 June, the day the *Workers' Weekly* appeared with an article scoffing at capitalist scaremongering about a German invasion of Russia.

NO PARTY, NO PROBLEM

With the German invasion of Russia, Comintern policy on the war and the circumstances of the two Irish branches was reversed. Now the Dublin branch came under the axe. According to the CPI's official history, making common cause with the British ruling class against Irish neutrality was more than it could stomach. At best this is partly true. When the CPI's national committee suggested the liquidation of the branch, a 'great amount of debate' ensued.[62] Young Jim Larkin was consulted, and counselled against dissolution, and his youngest brother, Barney, led the internal opposition.[63] The decisive intervention came from the CPGB. London knew the Comintern wanted unqualified commitment to the war effort – the ECCI had promptly scotched its proposal to back a people's war as distinct from the Churchill cabinet – and it was doubtful about how Moscow's writ would run in neutral Éire. The simple solution was dissolution: a case of, as Stalin might have put it, 'no party, no problem'. On 10 July, the Dublin branch voted 11–9 to 'suspend independent activity and to apply the forces of the branch to working in the Labour and trade union organisations'. 'Literature organisations' were to carry on as before, as did the street meetings at Mansfield's corner, under the auspices of the *Workers' Weekly*.[64]

Winding up the Éire CPI was probably as unnecessary as it was unwise. Dublin communists soon indicated their readiness to back the war. On 6 September the *Workers' Weekly* urged Labour to join a coalition government with Fianna Fáil, and press for an end to Britain's economic sanctions against Éire for its neutrality. The call was followed by a related demand for a 'national labour front'. In October the *Weekly* unveiled a little more of communist policy in attacking Dublin Labour's organ, the *Torch*, for bracketing all the belligerents together: 'Men and nations' right to breathe threatened', ran the headlines, 'Can Irish Labour men be indifferent?' Careful reading of the *Weekly* shows that it believed neutrality ought to have been bartered for economic concessions from Britain and cross-border unity. It was a strong argument, which might have won communists the sympathy of Éire's small

62　CPI, *Communist Party of Ireland*, p. 31.
63　O'Connor, *James Larkin*, p. 107.
64　Milotte, *Communism in Modern Ireland*, p. 191; CPI, *Communist Party of Ireland*, p. 31.

but virtually voiceless pro-war minority. Whether Éire communists were united behind the argument, or whether they would have been permitted to champion it publicly is another question. Following the German invasion, Thomas J. Coyne, controller of censorship, informed the *Weekly* that it would have to be more circumspect about Russia and 'stick to generalities about the capitalist hell and the Communist heaven'. Seán Nolan recalled regular, severe censorship and rewriting of articles, and Coyne queried if Nolan and his colleagues should 'remain at large'.[65] The *Irish Workers' Weekly* made its valedictory appearance on 1 November with an announcement that it was suspending publication for financial reasons. It may be that censorship was the anterior problem, but any implication to that effect would not have been passed by the censor.

Communists in Éire continued, under various cover names, to publish, organise lectures, and convene discussion groups.[66] Their strategy was to work within the Labour Party for a Labour–Fianna Fáil coalition that would take Éire into the war. The rapid growth and radicalisation of Labour after 1940 facilitated entryism, and when young Jim Larkin led the formation of the Dublin Labour Party executive in January 1943, it became dominated by communists. A government informer afterwards alleged that young Jim belonged to the secret hub of communist activity centred on Seán Nolan, though one member of the Nolan group, John de Courcy Ireland, has emphatically denied it. Limited contact with Belfast continued, but the absence of Comintern energy in Éire was evident in the failure of communists to challenge neutrality, despite the fact that it cemented partition and inflicted enormous economic suffering on the working class; it is reasonable to conjecture that the hegemony of de Valera's self-defeating policy would not have intimidated a Bolshevised party. The communists were bounced back to the margins in 1944, when William O'Brien and the ITGWU concocted a red scare in revenge for Big Jim Larkin's admission to the parliamentary Labour Party. An enquiry into communist infiltration led to the expulsion of six members from the party for attending a communist conference in Belfast.[67] Éire communists resurfaced in 1948 as the Irish Workers' League, later the Irish Workers' Party.

In Northern Ireland, the Communist Party's absolute commitment to the war effort, coupled with the phenomenal enthusiasm for all things Soviet throughout the United Kingdom, caused membership to mushroom to 1,000

65   Donal Ó Drisceoil, *Censorship in Ireland, 1939–1945: Neutrality, Politics, and Society* (Cork, 1996), p. 249; CPI, *Communist Party of Ireland*, p. 31.

66   CPI, *Communist Party of Ireland*, p. 31.

67   O'Connor, *James Larkin*, pp. 107–10.

by 1943 and by the end of the war the party had six full-time workers.[68] For a time it continued with an all-Ireland strategy. One of the last documents on Ireland in the Comintern files is a policy statement of June 1942 on how Ireland might play a full part in the war. It concluded with a call for

> an all out war effort, with equality of sacrifice, in the North; and the demand for a coalition government under de Valera in the south, a government that will take over full responsibility in the present serious crisis, we can play our part in the struggle for victory over fascism in 1942.[69]

Ten southern delegates attended a national party conference in Belfast in October, where the agenda covered 'Derry to Cork'.[70] Belfast and Dublin gradually diverged as the Northern party flourished and was drawn by its predominantly Protestant support base into an acceptance of partition. Though membership fell sharply in 1944, and had withered to 172 by 1949, the retention of positions of influence, in the engineering unions especially, and the more tolerant climate in the North, were sufficient to dissuade it from reverting to republicanism.[71] In the 1949 general election, for example, its 'Facts for speakers and canvassers' advised that a socialist Northern Ireland was the safest way to maintain the link with socialist Britain.[72] Policy on partition changed gradually in the 1950s and the Northern and southern parties united as the third CPI in 1970.

Like the CPI in Éire, the Comintern was a casualty of the war. From the outset, contact with affiliates diminished, the ECCI became strictly subordinate to Soviet foreign policy, and the Comintern's intelligence-gathering function was extended in scope and altered in emphasis. Almost half of a four-page review of Ireland in December 1940 was devoted to 'the matter of Irish naval bases', with the analysis based on press and radio reports from London, Germany and the USA.[73] As the Nazis advanced, the Comintern was evacuated from Moscow to the walled city of Ufa in the Urals in October 1941, where it was camouflaged as Scientific Institute no. 205.[74] The invasion rendered its traditional role redundant in that the war defined the line, and the duty of communist parties was obvious. Increasingly, its energies were devoted to

68 Morrissey, 'Betty Sinclair', pp. 126–7.

69 RGASPI, CPI, statement of policy and tasks facing the party, June 1942, 495/74/264–34/36.

70 PRONI, CPI papers, Report of the Irish communist conference, Oct. 1942, D/2702.

71 Milotte, *Communism in Modern Ireland*, p. 122.

72 PRONI, Murray papers, Facts for speakers and canvassers, 1949, D2162/A/16.

73 RGASPI, Notiz über Irland, 11 Dec. 1940, 495/14/340–6/9.

74 Degras, *The Communist International, Vol. 3*, p. 472.

publications, broadcasting to Europe, training cadres to maintain radio contact with sections in occupied countries, and running a cadre school. On 15 May 1943 a statement from the ECCI presidium proposed the dissolution of the International, arguing that the 'deep differences of the historic paths of development of various countries' had been sharpened by the war, and it was no longer feasible to co-ordinate the movement from one centre. Stalin was more candid in telling Reuters that liquidation would expose 'the lie of the Hitlerites to the effect that "Moscow" allegedly intends to intervene in the life of other nations and to "Bolshevise" them', and thereby facilitate unity against the Axis. Comintern functionaries were astonished to read of their fate in *Pravda* on 22 May. Stalin had long been scornful of the notion that the Comintern would effect revolution abroad, and in the 1930s he came to suspect it as a gateway of foreign influence. He had considered dissolution to appease Hitler in 1940 and 1941, but on each occasion the suggestion was overtaken by events.[75] Now in May 1943 the United States government made a request to have the Comintern dissolved. The ECCI presidium met for the last time on 8 June to endorse the unanimous approval of the 31 of its 65 affiliates which had managed to respond. One of the respondents was the CPI. On 10 June the Comintern ceased to exist.[76]

It was not completely the end. Scientific Institute no. 205 survived as an information bureau to keep Soviet leaders abreast of communist and working-class movements abroad.[77] It was joined by Institute no. 99, which worked with German, Italian, Hungarian and Romanian prisoners of war to train cadres for post-war politics; and by Institute no. 100, which took over many of the functions of the Comintern's courier service, the OMS, maintaining radio links and secret contacts with European communist parties.[78] Formally, the successor to the Comintern was the Cominform, the Communist Information Bureau, established in Warsaw in October 1947 to co-ordinate parties throughout Europe. It was dissolved in April 1956 as a gesture to the west and to Marshal Tito's dissident communist regime in Yugoslavia.

Ireland was not to be represented at another international communist conference until November 1957, when Seán Murray, Andy Barr and Seán Nolan attended a world congress of parties in Moscow to mark the fortieth anniversary of the Bolshevik revolution. Further such congresses were held, and Moscow-centrism remained a distinguishing feature of European

---

75   Ibid., p. 199; McDermott and Agnew, *The Comintern*, p. 206.

76   Degras, *The Communist International, Vol. 3*, pp. 476–81; Thorpe, *The British Communist Party and Moscow*, pp. 268–9.

77   Thorpe, *The British Communist Party and Moscow*, p. 210.

78   Degras, *The Communist International, Vol. 3*, p. 476.

communist parties until the 1970s. But there would be no return to the central direction or conformity of the Comintern era, or the dream of a world party building a global revolution under the guidance of a general staff in Moscow.

ELEVEN

CONCLUSION

We overestimated our strength when we created the CI and thought that we would
be able to lead the movement in all countries. This was our mistake . . .

J. STALIN

to the VKP(b) politburo, 21 May 1943[1]

—

Two of the major questions of Comintern history revolve around its relations
with national sections and with Soviet foreign policy, and how the ECCI
came to dominate the former and be dominated by the latter.[2] In assessing
what the Irish case tells us of the Comintern, it should remembered that each
national section was unique and developed its own particular relationship with
Moscow. How representative of ECCI management and policy application
was the Irish experience? In their size, organisational difficulties, and political
context, the Irish sections may have been more characteristic of affiliates on
the colonial fringe than those in Europe. On the other hand, certain factors
made Ireland more intelligible and more mainstream to what was a Eurocentric
ECCI. The Irish spoke English – not as useful as Russian or German, but one
of the Comintern's four lingua franca; they had comparatively good lines of
communication with Russia; they were of relevance to politics in the United
States, Britain, and the British empire; and, with the exception of the dying
months of the last Cumann na nGaedheal government, they could operate
legally – unlike 50 of the 76 communist parties in 1935, for example.

The impact of the Comintern on Irish communist organisation and policy
was fundamental, and largely positive. It is unlikely that a revolutionary party,
outside the republican tradition at least, would have survived for very long
without the Comintern. Before the 1920s, no such party had exceeded the
seven-year stretch of the Irish Socialist Republican Party, which was kept
going by James Connolly and collapsed on his departure to the United States
in 1903. Moscow was vital to the creation of all its Irish sections, and made a
substantial input into the second CPI, training its leading cadres, supplying
agents and finance, and offering a model of party and cadre discipline. One

1   Quoted in McDermott and Agnew, *The Comintern*, p. 209.
2   McDermott and Agnew, *The Comintern*, xx.

236

need only compare the first and second CPIs to appreciate the difference that this made. Almost as significant in sustaining morale was the myth of the Comintern; it was easier to persist in the face of overwhelming odds if one regarded oneself as part of a global vanguard, completing the world revolution in the remaining five sixths of the earth. All Irish communists welcomed the concept and role of the Comintern, with the exception of Jim Larkin, who wanted Soviet trade with the Free State without political interference.

The relationship between Irish communists and the ECCI was not one of equals, but it was voluntary and based on freedom of expression. There is no indication that Irish emissaries to Moscow were subjected to any form of coercion, though things might have been different had they not held a foreign passport or had a country to which they could return. Students at the Lenin School had greater experience of Soviet restrictions, and one who did surrender his passport, Patrick Breslin, died at the hands of the regime, as did so many of those who handled the Irish at one point or other: Bennett, Borodin, Bukharin, Kamenev, Lozovsky, Nuorteva, Pepper, Zinoviev, and probably Krivitsky, Münzenberg and Reiss. Moscow's management of the Irish was, by turns, inadequate, sensitive, strict and lax. The ECCI was still struggling to put in place an effective system of control during the lifetime of the first CPI. It took pains to appease Larkin, making the fullest allowance for his personality problems. Larkin was entirely to blame for the shambles that was the IWL. Reflecting the spirit of Bolshevisation during the third period, the supervision of the Anglo-American secretariat in the early 1930s was fairly harsh in its relentless strictures, though higher organs could be more sympathetic. André Marty was inclined to leave Ireland to the fosterage of the CPGB. The British were tougher taskmasters than the ECCI. Marty's debriefing of Francis Mooney in 1937 was a model of courtesy compared with Seán Murray's humiliation at meetings of the CPGB's politburo and central committee in 1938. While a steady flow of Britons or, more accurately, Scots, did sterling service in Ireland, the British party invariably regarded Irish communists as subordinate to its own interests in Britain, or its agenda on Ireland. The CPGB was never convinced of the merit of an Irish communist party, believing that resources might be better deployed in a broad workers' party, in the Labour Party, or even in Fianna Fáil. It was instrumental in the liquidation of the first CPI, quicker than the ECCI to oppose Larkin, scathing about the performance of the second CPI, and eager to dissolve the Belfast, and later the Dublin, branch in 1941. On two occasions Harry Pollitt seriously damaged Irish relations with the Comintern: in 1925 when, as secretary of the British Minority Movement, he refused to implement the agreement that British communists should campaign for the withdrawal of British trade unions from Ireland; and in 1934, when he misled Murray as to the Comintern's directive on tactics in the Republican Congress's Rathmines conference. Perhaps the CPGB did its worst in pressing for the liquidation of the CPI in Éire in 1941. Neutrality enjoyed a hegemonic popularity, but the CPI might have monopolised the significant and silent minority who doubted the wisdom of playing the quiet mouse among the dogs of war.

In policy making, the ECCI emerges as more anxious to be informed and responsive than dogmatic and dictatorial. Up to 1935, it went to some lengths to keep itself abreast of Irish affairs, and was relatively successful in this respect from 1927. It had already blundered in appointing Larkin as its principal, but it was not the first, or the last, to be deceived by Big Jim's reputation. Its unrealistic expectation of what communists could achieve was due more to the blind faith of ideologists than poor intelligence on Ireland. There was an abiding concern to tailor tactics to Irish conditions, and a reluctance to reach decisions without consultating Irish comrades. The first CPI had a mixed record of compliance with central policy. Roddy Connolly held the Comintern in awe, admiring Lenin as a father figure, but was absolutely convinced in his analysis of post-treaty republicanism. Ignoring the ECCI's directive on united fronts in 1921–2, he pursued his own policy towards the IRA, until brought to heel at the fourth world congress. The CPI then adopted the ECCI's directive to 'turn to class'. When that too failed to arrest its decline, it veered back towards republicanism. From 1929, the ECCI could rely completely on its Bolshevised Irish section. The RWG's silence on Saor Éire was a remarkable demonstration of discipline from comrades who were, for the most part, visceral republicans. Yet Murray was able to secure Moscow's approval of a renewed emphasis on anti-imperialism in 1932. If Comintern theory was not open to question, negotiation on specifics – even at the height of the third period – was possible.

Up to 1935 the Comintern's primary objective in Ireland was not to enforce compliance with a global line, but to make a revolution. From the outset, that led to an intermittent engagement with the IRA. The arguments for an alliance with republicanism were various and overwhelming. Narkomindel regarded British imperialism as its deadliest enemy, the buckle in the belt of capitalist powers encircling the USSR. Any force that might embarrass the British was to be welcomed. Of course, its unwillingness to be associated openly with the IRA placed constraints on ECCI policy, notably in 1922. The Comintern saw Ireland substantially as a colony with an uncompleted national question, a perspective shared by the bulk of Irish comrades, most of whom were typical of communists in colonial countries having background in militant nationalism. The inability of communists to penetrate the southern trade union movement – relations with Northern labour were a trifle more propitious – meant that, as Murray told the Anglo-American secretariat in

1935, the republican nexus was an operational necessity. What the communists wanted from republicans evolved. Following the Anglo-Irish treaty, Roddy Connolly believed that the IRA could make the revolution. At the fourth world congress, the ECCI affirmed the leading role of the party, but continued to regard the IRA as a source of recruits. From 1927 to 1929 the IRA was used as means of outflanking Larkin. The centrality of the party was restored in September 1929, but republicans were still sufficiently important for the ECCI to modify third period tactics for Ireland, and exempt them from class against class. Ultimately, the goal was to subvert and displace the IRA; the last thing the ECCI wanted was a rival republican party, like Saor Éire or the Republican Congress. It may be a measure of the culture of secrecy in the RWG and CPI that republicans failed to recognise these aims until the debacle at Rathmines.

The Comintern's greatest success, and, arguably, its greatest mistakes came in its relations with republicans. That republicans turned repeatedly to communism between 1922 and 1936, despite the debility of indigenous communist organisation, was a remarkable tribute to the myths of the Comintern and the Soviet Union. At the same time, if the standard criticisms that the Comintern divided the left and enforced self-defeating policies on its affiliates have any relevance to Ireland, it is in relation to Saor Éire and the Republican Congress. The class against class line, so often deplored by historians for its counterproductive sectarianism, made little difference to the RWG's prospects of making inroads into the trade unions. But it did discourage the strengthening of links with republicans when the IRA was most susceptible to communism. Murray would acknowledge the errors involved in 1935. After the seventh world congress, the ECCI's Irish policy was simply to apply the line, on the popular front, and later on in the Second World War. It nonetheless took account of factors peculiar to Ireland, such as support for Franco, Anglo-Irish relations and neutrality.

How important was Ireland to the Comintern? No definitive answer is possible without more comparative research on centre–periphery relations. All that can be said with certainty is that the ECCI was most concerned with the bigger European parties, events in Ireland never affected Comintern theory or strategy, the Irish sections were not exceptional in their small membership, and Moscow's interest in any country was not determined by the numerical strength of its communist parties. Undoubtedly the significance of the Irish sections in Moscow was enhanced by the perception of Ireland as an anti-imperialist flashpoint, adjacent to the heart of the British empire, and with a far flung diaspora, which might serve as a bridgehead into the anglophone world, where Marxism was particularly weak. Roddy Connolly was treated with some consideration by Lenin. Larkin appeared to be just the man

to internationalise Irish communism. Yet Moscow still regarded him as a
prize in 1929, when it was clear that he was unlikely to be of more than limited
service in the Free State itself. The most elaborate discussion of Ireland
occurred in early 1928, when policy towards republicans was debated by the
ECCI presidium and politsecretariat; clandestine collaboration between
Razvedupr and the IRA was probably the reason. The ECCI made a substantial investment in rebuilding Irish communism in 1929–30. By 1931 the
financial support from Moscow was diminishing, and the RWG were asking
if their importance in Moscow was also in decline, which the ECCI denied, as
it would. After 1935, Ireland was evaluated chiefly for its relevance to European
affairs. Nonetheless the Comintern's concerns about General O'Duffy and his
Spanish veterans, the repatriation of British naval bases in Éire, and neutrality
in the Second World War, did not stimulate a renewal of its earlier interventionist role, which in any case was not supposed to be the function of the
Comintern during the popular front. Either Marty or his secretariat was content
to leave a fruitless territory to the British. Getting the line right remained
important to the CPI's guardians in London, but aside from the period of the
Molotov–Ribbentrop pact, the CPGB regarded the CPI as expendable.

Prior to the Molotov–Ribbentrop pact, the subordination of the ECCI to
Soviet foreign policy was not obvious in the Irish context. There was a glaring
contrast between Comintern and Narkomindel policy towards Ireland up to
1922, with the latter combining a broad sympathy for republicans with a
determination not to become embroiled in Irish affairs, or take sides on domestic politics. That the ECCI did not subvent an arms ship for the IRA in the
autumn of 1922 may well have been a defining moment in its secret demarcation
disputes with Narkomindel. From 1930 the Irish were enjoined to undertake
campaigns on aspects of Soviet foreign policy, which they largely dismissed as
irrelevant to domestic politics. The popular front signified a new congruity
between Comintern and Soviet policy, but it was not seen primarily as such by
the CPI, and was welcomed instead as a more moderate, and more realistic
strategy. From its inception, the *Irish Workers' Weekly* attached paramount
importance to the security of the USSR, but only after 'that pact' was it evident
to the CPI that the Comintern was no more than Stalin's first line of defence.

Did the communists have any hope of success in Ireland? Their vintage
year was 1932, but their best prospects were in the mid 1920s, when militants
of the defeated labour and republican movements were looking for alternatives.
Once the Catholic Church mobilised against communism in 1930, the window
of opportunity started to close.

Bibliography

A Private papers
B Official records
C Newspapers
D Contemporary books, articles, and pamphlets, and reprints, recollections, and memoirs
E Books, articles, and pamphlets
F Biographies
G Dissertations and websites

A. PRIVATE PAPERS

Dan Bryan papers, UCDA
Charlotte Despard papers, PRONI
Desmond Fitzgerald papers, UCDA
Sighle Humphreys papers, UCDA
Seán MacEntee papers, UCDA
Patrick McCartan papers, NLI
Séamus McGowan papers, Cowan family papers, UCDA
Seán McLoughlin, submission to the Bureau of Military History, NA
Richard Mulcahy papers, UCDA
Seán Murray papers, PRONI
Lily O'Brennan papers, UCDA
William O'Brien papers, NLI
Ernie O'Malley papers, UCDA
Donal O'Reilly papers, NLI
Cathal O'Shannon papers, Irish Labour History Archives
Hanna Sheehy Skeffington papers, NLI
Moss Twomey papers, UCDA

B. PUBLIC RECORDS

RGASPI fondi
  5, secretariat V. I. Lenin
  17, Central committee, Communist Party of the Soviet Union
  489, Second Comintern Congress
  494, Seventh Comintern Congress
  495, ECCI
  515, CPUSA

531, International Lenin School
533, KIM
534, Profintern
538, WIR
539, ICWPA
542, League Against Imperialism
545, International Brigades in the Spanish Republican Army

Irish Labour History Archives
Dublin trades' council records, 1928
ILPTUC, *Annual Report* (1920)
ITGWU, 'Draft rules for the ITGWU' (1923)

Law Library, Dublin
The Irish Reports (1925)

Military Archives
Captured documents, 1922

National Archives
Cabinet minutes, 1931
Dáil Éireann papers
Department of Foreign Affairs papers
Department of Justice papers
Department of the Taoiseach papers
Registry of Friendly Societies files, WUI file, 369T

National Library of Ireland
ILPTUC, *Annual Report* (1923)
ILPTUC, 31st Annual Report for 1924–5 (1925)

Public Record Office of Northern Ireland
Spanish Medical Aid Relief Committee papers, 1936
CPI papers, 1942

British Parliamentary Papers
Intercourse Between Bolshevism and Sinn Féin, Cmd 1326 (1921)
*Communist Papers: Documents Selected From Those Obtained on the Arrest of the Communist
Leaders on October 14, 21, 1925*, Cmd 2682 (1926)
*Russian Banks and Communist Funds: Report of an Enquiry into Certain Transactions of the
Bank for Russian Trade Ltd, and the Moscow Narodny Bank Ltd*, Cmd 3125 (1928)
House of Commons debates, 1 Dec. 1925, vol. 188

Marx Memorial Library, London
International Brigade Memorial Archive

Public Record Office, London
Foreign Office papers
Home Office papers
Government Code and Cypher School decrypts of Comintern messages, 1930–45

Federal Bureau of Investigation, Washington DC
James Larkin file

United States National Archives, Washington DC
State Department document file, report from Great Britain, 1929

C. NEWSPAPERS

An Phoblacht, 1930–3
Building Worker, 1931
Communist, 1920–1
Daily Mail, 1930
Daily Worker, 1932
Irish Democrat, 1937, 1949
Irish Hammer and Plough, 1926
Irish Independent, 1919, 1966
Irish Opinion, 1917–18
Irish People (Chicago), 1924
Irish Press, 1933
The Irish Times, 1919, 1924, 1930, 1933, 1956, 1968, 1974, 1976, 1983
Irish Worker, 1924–5, 1930–1
Irish Workers' Voice, 1932–6
Irish Workers' Weekly, 1939–41
Irishman, 1928.
Manchester Guardian, 1920, 1923
New Ireland, 1919
Republican Congress, 1934–5
Republican File, 1931–2
Socialist, 1919–22
Standard, 1933
The Times, 1928
Voice of Labour, 1918, 1921–2, 1924–5
Watchword of Labour, 1919–20
Worker, 1936–7
Workers' Bulletin, 1933
Workers' Republic, 1921–3, 1926–7, 1938
Workers' Voice, 1930–2

D. CONTEMPORARY BOOKS, ARTICLES AND PAMPHLETS,
AND REPRINTS, RECOLLECTIONS AND MEMOIRS

Barr, Andy, 'An undiminished dream: Andy Barr, communist trade unionist', *Saothar* 16 (1991).
Briscoe, Robert, *For the Life of Me* (London, 1958).
Collins, Séamus, 'The situation in Ireland', *Communist International*, 1 Feb. 1928.
Connolly O'Brien, Nora, *We Shall Rise Again* (London, 1981).
Cork Workers' Club, *Irish Labour and its International Relations in the era of the Second International and the Bolshevik Revolution* (Cork, n.d.).
——, *Sinn Féin and Socialism* (Cork, n.d.).
Daiken, Leslie H. (comp), *Good-Bye, Twilight: Songs of the Struggle in Ireland* (London, 1936).
Darragh, Thomas, 'Revolutionary Ireland and communism', *Communist International*, no. 11–12, June–July 1920.
Dawson, Richard, *Red Terror and Green* (London, 1920).
Deasy, Joe, 'The evolution of an Irish Marxist, 1941–50', *Saothar* 13 (1988).
de Courcy Ireland, John, 'As I remember Big Jim', in Donal Nevin (ed.), *James Larkin: Lion of the Fold* (Dublin, 1998).
Degras, Jane (ed.), *Calendar of Soviet Documents on Foreign Policy* (London, 1958).
—— (ed.), *The Communist International, 1919–1943, Documents, Vol. 1, 1919–1922* (London, 1971).
——, *The Communist International, 1919-1943: Documents, Vol. 2, 1923–1928* (London, 1971).
Eisler, Gerhart, 'The Irish Free State and British imperialism', *Communist International* (May, 1932), reprinted as 'Historical Reprints no.18' (Cork Workers' Club, 1976).
Fanning, Ronan, Michael Kennedy, Dermot Keogh and Eunan O'Halpin, *Documents on Irish Foreign Policy, Vol. II, 1923–1926* (Dublin, 2000).
——, et al. (eds), *Documents on Irish Foreign Policy, vol. III, 1926–1932* (Dublin, 2002).
Fox, R. M., *The History of the Irish Citizen Army* (Dublin, 1944).
Freeman, Joseph, *An American Testament: A Narrative of Rebels and Romantics* (London, 1938).
Gitlow, Benjamin, *The Whole of Their Lives: Communism in America, A Personal History and Intimate Portrayal of its Leaders* (Belmont, Ma., 1965).
Hogan, James, *Could Ireland Become Communist?* (Dublin, 1935).
ILPTUC, *Ireland at Berne: Being the Reports and Memoranda presented to the International Labour and Socialist Conference held at Berne, February 1919* (Dublin, 1919).
ITGWU, *The Attempt to Smash the Irish Transport and General Workers' Union* (Dublin, 1924).
Kuusinen, Aino, *Before and After Stalin: A Personal Account of Soviet Russia from the 1920s to the 1960s* (London, 1974).
Laskey, Heather, 'Roddy Connolly revisits Moscow', *The Irish Times*, 22 Oct. 1974.
MacEoin, Uinseann (ed.), *Survivors: The Story of Ireland's Struggle as Told Through Some of Her Outstanding Living People Recalling Events From the Days of Davitt, Through James Connolly, Brugha, Collins, De Valera, Liam Mellows, and Rory O'Connor to the Present Time* (Dublin, 1980).
Macgougan, Jack, 'Letting labour lead: Jack Macgougan and the pursuit of unity, 1913–1958', *Saothar* 14 (1989).

McCartan, Patrick, *With de Valera in America* (Dublin, 1932).

McEoin, S. P., *Communism and Ireland* (Dublin, 1948).

McIlhone, R., 'The economic situation in Ireland and tasks of the Communist Party in Ireland', *Communist International*, 1 May 1934.

McInerney, Michael, 'Gerry Boland's story', *The Irish Times*, 11 Oct. 1968.

——, 'Roddy Connolly: 60 years of political activity', *The Irish Times*, 27 Aug. 1976.

Monks, Joe, *With the Reds in Andalusia* (London, 1985).

Morrissey, Hazel, *Betty Sinclair: A Woman's Fight for Socialism* (Belfast, 1983).

——, 'Betty Sinclair, A woman's fight for socialism, 1910–80', *Saothar* 9 (1983).

Murphy, J. T. *New Horizons* (London, 1941).

National Labour Party, *Communist Bid to Control Irish Labour* (Dublin, 1944).

O'Brien, William, *Forth the Banners Go: Reminiscences of William O'Brien as told to Edward MacLysaght, D.Litt* (Dublin, 1969).

O'Connor, Peter, *A Soldier of Liberty: Recollections of a Socialist and Anti-Fascist Fighter* (Dublin, 1996).

O'Connor Lysaght, D. R. (ed.), *The Communists and the Irish Revolution: Part One, The Russian Revolutionaries on the Irish National Question, 1899–1924* (Dublin, 1993).

O'Donnell, Peadar, *Salud! An Irishman in Spain* (London, 1937).

Ó Duinnín, Eoghan, *La Nina Bonita agus an Róisín Dubh: Cuimhní Cinn ar Chogadh Cathartha na Spáinne* (Dublin, 1986).

O'Flaherty, Liam, *Shame The Devil* (London, 1934).

——, *The Informer* (London, 1949).

Pathfinder, *The Communist International in Lenin's Time, Volume One: Workers' of the World and Oppressed Peoples Unite! Proceedings and Documents of the Second Congress, 1920* (New York, 1991).

Phelan, Jim, *The Name's Phelan: The First Part of the Autobiography of Jim Phelan* (Belfast, 1993).

Pollitt, Harry, *Serving My Time: An Apprenticeship to Politics* (London, 1940).

Poretsky, Elisabeth K. *Our Own People: A Memoir of 'Ignace Reiss' and His Friends* (London, 1969).

Robbins, Frank, *Under the Starry Plough: Recollections of the Irish Citizen Army* (Dublin, 1977).

Stewart, Robert, *Breaking the Fetters: The Memoirs of Bob Stewart* (London, 1967).

What Happened at Leeds? (London, 1917).

Wicks, Harry, *Keeping My Head: The Memoirs of a British Bolshevik* (London, 1992).

E. LABOUR AND COMMUNIST BIOGRAPHIES

Bergin, Paddy, 'Liam O'Flaherty', *Labour History News* 6 (1990).

Bowler, Stephen, 'Seán Murray, 1898–1961, and the pursuit of Stalinism in one country', *Saothar* 18 (1993).

Brennan, Anne and William Nolan, 'Nixie Boran and the colliery community of north Kilkenny', in William Nolan and Kevin Whelan (eds), *Kilkenny: History and Society* (Dublin, 1990).

Costello, Peter, *Liam O'Flaherty's Ireland* (Dublin, 1996).

Cronin, Seán, *Frank Ryan: The Search for the Republic* (Dublin, 1980).

Feeley, Pat, *The Gralton Affair* (Dublin, 1986).

Gaughan, J. Anthony, *Thomas Johnson, 1872–1963: First Leader of the Labour Party in Dáil Éireann* (Dublin, 1980).

Gibbons, Luke, 'Labour and local history: the case of Jim Gralton, 1886–1945', *Saothar* 14 (1989).

Gotovitch, José and Mikhail Narinski et al. (eds), *Komintern, L'Histoire et les Hommes: Dictionnaire Biographique de l'Internationale Communiste en France, en Belgique, au Luxembourg, en Suisse et a Moscou (1919–1943)* (Paris, 2001).

Greaves, C. Desmond, *The Life and Times of James Connolly* (London, 1961).

——, *Liam Mellows and the Irish Revolution* (London, 1971).

——, *Seán O'Casey: Politics and Art* (London, 1979).

Guckian, Des, *Deported: Jimmy Gralton, 1886–1945* (Carrick-on-Shannon, 1988).

Hegarty, Peter, *Peadar O'Donnell* (Cork, 1999).

Jacobs, Dan N., *Borodin: Stalin's Man in China* (Cambridge, Mass, 1981).

Keogh, Dermot, 'Hogan, communism, and the challenge of contemporary history', in Donnchadh Ó Corráin (ed.), *James Hogan: Revolutionary, Historian, and Political Scientist* (Cork, 2001).

Klaus, H. Gustav (ed.), *Strong Words, Brave Deeds: The Poetry, Life and Times of Thomas O'Brien, Volunteer in the Spanish Civil War* (Dublin, 1994).

Larkin, Emmet, *James Larkin: Irish Labour Leader, 1876–1947* (London, 1965).

Linklater, Andro, *An Unhusbanded Life: Charlotte Despard, Suffragette, Socialist, and Sinn Féiner* (London, 1980).

McInerney, Michael, *Peadar O'Donnell: Irish Social Rebel* (Dublin, 1974).

——, 'O'Flaherty in politics', *The Irish Times*, 27 Aug. 1976.

Moriarty, Theresa, 'Delia Larkin: relative obscurity', in Donal Nevin (ed.), *James Larkin: Lion of the Fold* (Dublin, 1998).

Morrissey, SJ, Thomas J., *A Man Called Hughes: The Life and Times of Séamus Hughes, 1881–1943* (Dublin, 1991).

——, 'William O'Brien, the Socialist Party, and the Church, 1917–21', unpublished paper.

Murphy, Brian P., *John Chartres: Mystery Man of the Treaty* (Dublin, 1995).

Nevin, Donal (ed.), *James Larkin: Lion of the Fold* (Dublin, 1998).

O'Connor, Emmet, 'Labour lives: Cathal O'Shannon', *Saothar* 24 (1999).

——, 'James Larkin in the United States, 1914–1923', *Journal of Contemporary History* 37, 2 (2002).

——, *James Larkin* (Cork, 2002).

——, 'Seán Murray', in Keith Gildart, David Howell, and Neville Kirk (eds), *Dictionary of Labour Biography, Vol. XI* (London, 2003).

O'Connor, Joseph, *Even the Olives are Bleeding: The Life and Times of Charlie Donnelly* (Dublin, 1992).

Ó Drisceoil, Donal, *Peadar O'Donnell* (Cork, 2001).

O'Riordan, Manus, 'Larkin in America: the road to Sing Sing', in Donal Nevin (ed.), *James Larkin: Lion of the Fold* (Dublin, 1998).

Sheehy Skeffington, Andrée, *Skeff: A Life of Owen Sheehy Skeffington, 1909–1970* (Dublin, 1991).

Ward, Margaret, *Hanna Sheehy Skeffington: A Life* (Cork, 1997).

F. OTHER BOOKS, ARTICLES AND PAMPHLETS

Anderson, W. K., *James Connolly and the Irish left* (Dublin, 1994).

Bell, J. Bowyer, *The Secret Army: A History of the IRA, 1915–1970* (London, 1972).

Boyd, Andrew, *Holy War in Belfast* (Belfast, 1987).

Carr, E. H., *The Comintern and the Spanish Civil War* (London, 1984).

Challinor, Raymond, *The Origins of British Bolshevism* (London, 1977).

Cody, Séamus, John O'Dowd and Peter Rigney, *The Parliament of Labour: 100 Years of the Dublin Council of Trade Unions* (Dublin, 1986).

Coogan, Tim Pat, *The IRA* (London, 1984).

——, *De Valera: Long Fellow, Long Shadow* (London, 1993).

CPI, *Communist Party of Ireland: Outline History* (Dublin, 1975).

Cradden, Terry, *Trade Unionism, Socialism, and Partition: The Labour Movement in Northern Ireland, 1939–53* (Belfast, 1993).

Daly, Seán, *Ireland and the First International* (Cork, 1984).

Devlin, Paddy, *Yes We Have No Bananas: Outdoor Relief in Belfast, 1920–39* (Belfast, 1981).

English, Richard, *Radicals and the Republic: Socialist Republicanism in the Irish Free State, 1925–1937* (Oxford, 1994).

Farrell, Brian, *The Founding of Dáil Éireann: Parliament and Nation Building* (Dublin, 1971).

Farrell, Michael, 'Anti-communist frenzy', *The Irish Times*, 28 Mar. 1983.

Gallagher, Michael, *Political Parties in the Republic of Ireland* (Manchester, 1985).

Geoghegan, Vincent, 'Cemeteries of liberty: William Norton on communism and fascism', *Saothar* 18 (1993).

Greaves, C. Desmond, *The Irish Transport and General Workers' Union: The Formative Years, 1909–23* (Dublin, 1982).

Hamill, Jonathon, 'Saor Éire and the IRA: an exercise in deception?', *Saothar* 20 (1995).

Hanley, Brian, *The IRA, 1926–1936* (Dublin, 2002).

——, 'The Citizen Army after 1916', *Saothar* 28 (2004).

Herbert, Michael, *The Wearing of the Green: A Political History of the Irish in Manchester* (London, 2001).

Huber, Peter, 'Structure of the Moscow apparatus of the Comintern and decision-making', in Tim Rees and Andrew Thorpe (eds), *International Communism and the Communist International, 1919–43* (Manchester, 1998).

Hutt, Allen, *British Trade Unionism: A Short History* (London, 1975).

ITGWU, *Fifty Years of Liberty Hall: The Golden Jubilee of the Irish Transport and General Workers' Union, 1909–59* (Dublin, n.d.).

Jackson, Pete, '"A rather one sided fight": the *Worker* and the Spanish Civil War', *Saothar* 23 (1998).

Jackson, T. A., *Ireland Her Own* (London, 1947).

Kendall, Walter, *The Revolutionary Movement in Britain, 1900–21: The Origins of British Communism* (London, 1969).

Kissane, Bill, 'Civil society under strain: intermediary organisations and the Irish Civil War', *Irish Political Studies* 15 (2000).

Laffan, Michael, '"Labour must wait": Ireland's conservative revolution', in Patrick J. Corish (ed.), *Radicals, Rebels, and Establishments* (Belfast, 1985).

Bibliography

248Bibliography
Lee, J. J., *Ireland, 1912–1985: Politics and Society* (Cambridge, 1989).
Leonard, Raymond W., *Secret Soldiers of the Revolution: Military Intelligence, 1918–1933* (Westport, Ct, 1999).
Macardle, Dorothy, *The Irish Republic* (London, 1968).
McDermott, Kevin and Jeremy Agnew, *The Comintern: A History of International Communism from Lenin to Stalin* (London, 1996).
McGarry, Fearghal, *Irish Politics and the Spanish Civil War* (Cork, 1999).
McIlroy, John, Barry McLoughlin, Alan Campbell, and John Halstead, 'Forging the faithful: the British at the International Lenin School', *Labour History Review* 68, 1 (Apr. 2003).
McLoughlin, Barry, 'Proletarian academics or party functionaries? Irish communists at the International Lenin School, Moscow, 1927–37', *Saothar* 22 (1997).
——, 'Delegated to the 'new world': Irish communists at Moscow's International Lenin School, 1927–1937', *History Ireland* (winter, 1999).
——, '"The party before anything else": rituals of "criticism and self-criticism" in the British and Austrian sectors of the International Lenin School, Moscow, 1929–1937', unpublished paper.
—— and Emmet O'Connor, 'Sources on Ireland and the Communist International, 1920–43', *Saothar* 21 (1996).
Milotte, Mike, *Communism in Modern Ireland: The Pursuit of the Workers' Republic Since 1916* (Dublin, 1984).
Mitchell, Arthur, *Labour in Irish Politics, 1890–1930: The Irish Labour Movement in an Age of Revolution* (Dublin, 1974).
——, *Revolutionary Government in Ireland: Dáil Éireann, 1919–22* (Dublin, 1995).
Morely, Vincent, 'Sóisialithe Átha Cliath agus teagasc Daniel De Leon, 1900–1909', *Saothar* 12 (1987).
Morgan, Austen, *Labour and Partition: The Belfast Working Class, 1905–23* (London, 1991).
Morrissey, Hazel, 'The first Communist Party of Ireland, 1921–23', *Irish Socialist Review* (summer, 1983).
Nevin, Donal (ed.), *Trade Union Century* (Dublin, 1994).
Ó Catháin, Máirtín, '"Struggle or starve": Derry unemployed workers' movements, 1926–35', *Saothar* 28 (2004).
Ó Ciosáin, Éamon, *An t-Éireannach, 1934–1937: Nuachtán Sóisialach Gaeltachta* (Dublin, 1993).
O'Connor, Emmet, *Syndicalism in Ireland, 1917–23* (Cork, 1988).
——, *A Labour History of Ireland, 1824–1960* (Dublin, 1992).
——, 'Waterford and IRA gun-running, 1917–22', *Decies: Journal of the Waterford Archaeological & Historical Society* 57 (2001).
O'Connor Lysaght, D. R., 'The Munster soviet creameries', *Saotharlann Staire Éireann* 1 (1981).
O'Donoghue, Florence, *No Other Law: The Story of Liam Lynch and the Irish Republican Army, 1916–23* (Dublin, 1954).
Ó Drisceoil, Donal, *Censorship in Ireland, 1939–1945: Neutrality, Politics, and Society* (Cork, 1996).
O'Halpin, Eunan, *Defending Ireland: The Irish State and its Enemies Since 1922* (Oxford, 1999).
O'Riordan, Manus, 'Connolly socialism and the Jewish worker', *Saothar* 13 (1988).

O'Riordan, Michael, *Connolly Column: The Story of the Irishmen who Fought in the Ranks of the International Brigades in the National Revolutionary War of the Spanish People, 1936–39* (Dublin, 1979).

Patterson, Henry, *The Politics of Illusion: Republicanism and Socialism in Modern Ireland* (London, 1989).

Pelling, Henry, *A History of British Trade Unionism* (London, 1974).

Purdie, Bob, *Politics in the Streets: The Origins of the Civil Rights Movement in Northern Ireland* (Belfast, 1990).

Regan, John M., *The Irish Counter-Revolution, 1921–1936: Treatyite Politics and Settlement* (Dublin, 2001).

Stradling, Robert A., *The Irish in the Spanish Civil War, 1936–1939: Crusades in Conflict* (Manchester, 1999).

Townshend, Charles, 'The Irish railway strike of 1920: industrial action and civil resistance in the struggle for independence', *Irish Historical Studies* XXI, 83 (1979).

Thorpe, Andrew, *The British Communist Party and Moscow, 1920–43* (Manchester, 2000).

Walker, Brian M., *Parliamentary Election Results in Ireland, 1918–92: Irish Elections to Parliament and Parliamentary Assemblies at Westminster, Belfast, Dublin, Strasbourg* (Dublin, 1992).

Ward-Perkins, Sarah (ed.), *Select Guide to Trade Union Records in Dublin: With Details of Unions Operating in Ireland to 1970* (Dublin, 1996).

White, Stephen, 'Soviet Russia and the Irish revolution', *Irish Slavonic Studies* 5 (1984).

——, 'Ireland, Russia, communism, post-communism', *Irish Studies in International Affairs* 8 (1997).

G. DISSERTATIONS AND WEBSITES

Banta, Mary M., 'The red scare in the Irish Free State, 1929–37' (MA, UCD, 1982).

Bowler, Stephen, 'Stalinism in Ireland: the case of Seán Murray' (MSSc, Queen's University, Belfast, 1992). *http://members.lycos.co.uj/spanishcivilwar/*

Index

Easter Rising, 15, 16–17, 32, 51, 211–12, 230
Egypt, 57, 74
Eisler, Gerhart, 176–7
Engels, Friedrich, 181
espionage, 112–13, 117, 129–30
Executive Committee of the Communist
    International (ECCI), 3, 31, 39,
    45–6, 57, 106, 116, 140–1, 144, 149,
    153–6, 236, 238–40
  Amsterdam bureau, 37
  Anglo-American colonial group, 63–4
  apparatus, 7–12
  orgbureau, 8, 112
  plena, 7, 10–11, 78–9, 112, 116, 122, 132,
      165, 181, 189, 195–7, 214
  politcommission, 177–8, 201, 209
  politsecretariat, 12, 130, 137, 144, 147,
      149, 177, 209, 240
  presidium, 7, 51, 77, 79, 98, 130, 234, 240
  secretariat Marty, 214–15
  and the first CPI, 50–1, 76–9, 88–9, 91–2
  and the second CPI, 187, 198–9, 201,
      204, 209–10, 221
  and Larkin, 82, 86, 93, 96–7, 100, 102–4,
      110–12, 114, 117, 121–4, 126–9, 133,
      136, 140–1
  and the RWG, 161, 167, 176, 187
  and Second World War, 227–8, 231, 234

famine (in Ireland), 105–6, 109
famine (in Russia), 58
Farren, Tom, 24
fascisisation, 196–7
fascism, 193, 195–6, 198–201, 208, 210–11,
    215–16, 221–2, 224, 227–8
Fearon, James, 79
Fenians, 6
Ferguson, Christy, 120, 142, 148, 151–2, 155, 158
Ferguson, John, 32
Fermanagh, 105
Fianna Éireann, 33, 48, 174
Fianna Fáil, 117, 128, 136, 155, 159–61, 181–2,
    196, 231–2
  collaboration with communists, 124–6,
      142

communist support for, 129–31, 175–6,
    178, 182, 194, 211, 221–5, 237
finance, first CPI, 44, 78–9, 88–9
  second CPI, 200, 203–4, 210, 213
  Irish Democrat, 217, 223
  IRA, 46, 48
  James Connolly Workers' Education
      Club, 141
  Larkin, 82–3, 93–4, 96, 103, 105–11, 114–5
  RWG, 151, 165, 175–6
  WIR, 106–9
  WPI, 118, 122
Fine Gael, 196–7, 222
Fineberg, Iosef, 41, 116, 123, 126–7, 130
First World War, 2, 13, 16, 51
Fitzgerald, David, 142, 150
Fitzgerald, Desmond, 56, 92
Fitzpatrick, John, 82
Fitzpatrick, Mick, 128, 131–2, 141, 158
Foran, Tom, 17–18, 26–7, 35, 82–5, 94
Fox, Ralph, 180
fractions, 191, 201
France, 41, 86, 189, 200–1
Friends of Soviet Russia, 128, 132, 150, 153,
    167, 169–70, 193, 197
Friends of the Spanish Republic, 216

Gaffney, Paddy, 65, 71, 79, 88
Gallacher, Willie, 33, 52, 56, 84, 98, 101, 107,
    126, 130–1, 201–2, 212, 224, 229
Galway, 89, 152, 184–5, 192
Gannon, Bill, 71, 125, 208, 217
Gardaí, 115, 125, 134–5, 143, 153–4, 166, 171–3,
    186, 199, 205–6
Geehan, Tommy, 149, 159, 182, 184, 212
Geneva, 74, 136
Germany, 10, 21, 30, 40, 46, 48–9, 71–2,
    74, 84, 86, 106, 185, 193, 195, 197,
    228, 233
Gilmore, Charlie, 190, 192
Gilmore, George, 150, 194, 196, 212, 218
Glasgow, 22, 31, 33, 70, 72, 121, 123, 166, 184
Gonne, Maud, 105, 120, 129
Gralton, Jim, 4, 185, 191, 193, 200
Greaves, C. Desmond, 2

Index